D1084002

ARMISTEAD AND HANCOCK

Behind the Gettysburg Legend of Two Friends
at the Turning Point of the Civil War

TOM McMILLAN

STACKPOLE
BOOKS
Guilford, Connecticut

Published by Stackpole Books
An imprint of The Rowman & Littlefield Publishing Group, Inc.
4501 Forbes Blvd., Ste. 200
Lanham, MD 20706
www.rowman.com

Distributed by NATIONAL BOOK NETWORK

British Library Cataloguing in Publication Information available

Library of Congress Cataloging-in-Publication Data

Names: McMillan, Tom, 1956– author.
Title: Armistead and Hancock : behind the Gettysburg legend of two friends
  at the turning point of the Civil War / Tom McMillan.
Other titles: Behind the Gettysburg legend of two friends at the turning
  point of the Civil War
Description: Guilford, Connecticut : Stackpole Books, [2021] | Includes
  bibliographical references and index. | Summary: "Part biography and
  part history, this book clarifies the record regarding the friendship of
  Union general Winfield Hancock and Confederate general Lewis Armistead
  with new information and fresh perspective, reversing misconceptions
  about an amazing story of two friends that has defined the Civil War"—
  Provided by publisher.
Identifiers: LCCN 2021003954 (print) | LCCN 2021003955 (ebook) | ISBN
  9780811769945 (cloth) | ISBN 9780811769952 (epub)
Subjects: LCSH: Gettysburg Campaign, 1863. | Armistead, Lewis A. (Lewis
  Addison), 1817–1863—Friends and associates. | Hancock, Winfield Scott,
  1824–1886—Friends and associates. | Generals—Confederate States of
  America—Friends and associates. | Generals—United States—Friends and
  associates. | United States—History—Civil War, 1861–1865—Biography.
Classification: LCC E475.51 .M36 2021 (print) | LCC E475.51 (ebook) | DDC
  973.7/349—dc23
LC record available at https://lccn.loc.gov/2021003954
LC ebook record available at https://lccn.loc.gov/202100395

CONTENTS

ACKNOWLEDGMENTS

It would be impossible to write about Lewis Armistead without building on the incredible foundation of work done by the general's biographer, the great Gettysburg historian Wayne Motts. In addition to being a Gettysburg Licensed Battlefield Guide and CEO of the National Civil War Museum in Harrisburg, Pennsylvania, Wayne is the country's foremost authority on Armistead and Pickett's Charge. His 2015 book with James A. Hessler, *Pickett's Charge at Gettysburg: A Guide to the Most Famous Attack in American History*, draws part of its Armistead material from the research Wayne did in connection with his 1994 biography, *"Trust in God and Fear Nothing": Gen. Lewis A. Armistead, CSA*. He also has given several talks about Armistead and Hancock for the Gettysburg Foundation, one of which is available on YouTube. Wayne has never stopped looking to uncover tidbits of the Armistead story, creating a pathway for future researchers, and has made huge contributions to our understanding of the Battle of Gettysburg.

There have been many more books written about Winfield Scott Hancock, who, unlike Armistead, lived for more than twenty years after the Civil War and was the Democratic nominee for president of the United States in 1880. The titles are too numerous to mention here, but historians Glenn Tucker, David M. Jordan, D. X. Junkin, A. M. Gambone, and Paul Bretzger (not to mention Hancock's wife, Almira) led the way in building a treasure trove of material about "Hancock the Superb." Some of Hancock's former soldiers, including Francis A. Walker, Henry H. Bingham, and William Mitchell, also wrote in considerable detail about the general, although not always in book form.

I would be remiss if I did not thank the late Michael Shaara, author of the Pulitzer Prize–winning novel *The Killer Angels: A Novel of the Civil War*, and Ron Maxwell, director of the movie *Gettysburg*, which was based on the novel. Their exceptional work generated enormous interest in the Battle of Gettysburg and sparked a huge wave of visitation to Civil War battlefields in the 1990s and 2000s. I have mentioned many times that my first trip to see Maxwell's *Gettysburg* in 1993 reignited my own passion for the history of the battle, and I was honored to attend a twenty-fifth anniversary showing at the Majestic Theater in Gettysburg in 2018. Granted, I quibble with their heavily dramatized presentation of the Armistead–Hancock relationship—one of the reasons for this book—but no one ever did more to bring the battle and the war to a modern audience than those two talented gentlemen. *The Killer Angels* is probably the most impactful book ever written about the battle, and *Gettysburg* made it come alive on screen.

There are so many research outlets that made their materials available, led by the National Archives (much of it digitized at www.fold3.com) and the Library of Congress in Washington, D.C. I owe a special personal thanks to John Heiser at the Gettysburg National Military Park Library and Christopher Barth and his staff at the U.S. Military Academy Library at West Point for their cooperation and assistance.

Several friends took the time to read the manuscript and provide helpful comments, including Colonel Tom Vossler, U.S. Army (retired), a Gettysburg Licensed Battlefield Guide; Jack Carroll, author of *Battle Ready Leadership: Leadership Lessons from Gettysburg for Your Business*; and Doug McGregor, a fellow dedicated battlefield tramper.

My editor at Stackpole Books, Dave Reisch, embraced this project from the start and offered tremendous encouragement and counsel. Patricia Stevenson, Bruce Owens, and Stephanie Otto also made valuable contributions in the publishing process. To everyone at Stackpole, as well as Rowman & Littlefield, thank you.

My agent, Uwe Stender, was a continuing source of support, advice, and encouragement on this, our third book together. Thanks to Uwe and his staff at Triada US Literary Agency.

And there is absolutely no way I could have completed this project without the love, support, and dogged research capabilities of my wife and dearest friend, Colleen, whose impact is felt on every page. Thanks also to Megan, Comrade, Jim, Ethan, Boris, and Natasha for always understanding why our dining room table is hopelessly cluttered with Civil War books. It can finally be cleaned off now—maybe.

Chapter One

Friendship Torn

Brigadier General Lewis Addison Armistead peered out from the edge of a tree line across rolling open farmland just south of Gettysburg, Pennsylvania. It was shortly before the start of Pickett's Charge on July 3, 1863.[1] Shrieking shells from U.S. artillery slammed into tree trunks, and dense blankets of blinding gray smoke covered the field as the former West Point cadet paced anxiously before his Confederate troops, sometimes scrambling up a small rise in terrain to get a better look. But he probably didn't need a field glass to know that the commanding officer of Union soldiers across the ridge was Major General Winfield Scott Hancock, his "old and valued friend" of nineteen years.[2]

The irony was striking. Armistead and Hancock had met in 1844 as young lieutenants with the Sixth U.S. Infantry, posted to the bleak frontier garrison of Fort Towson, Oklahoma, on what was then the country's far southwestern border.[3] Three years later, redeployed to rare foreign combat duty in the Mexican War, they were part of the marauding U.S. force that fought its way across the country and sacked Mexico City, earning brevets for gallantry at the Battle of Churubusco and serving together in the postwar occupation. The 1850s brought more mind-numbing frontier service and a staggering thousand-mile march by the entire Sixth Infantry to the Pacific coast.[4] Their final stops before the Civil War were two tiny dots on the map in southern California—the thinly populated hamlets of Los Angeles (Hancock) and New San Diego (Armistead)—and it was there that they were posted on April 12, 1861, when Southern secessionists fired on Fort Sumter and the country came unhinged.[5]

Lewis Addison Armistead
COURTESY OF GETTYSBURG NATIONAL MILI-
TARY PARK

Winfield Scott Hancock
LIBRARY OF CONGRESS

A unique scene in military history is said to have played out a few months later at the Hancock home in Los Angeles. The staunchly pro-Union officer hosted a get-together for several longtime army friends who were quitting to join the Confederacy, giving them a final chance to clasp hands and share a few stories before going off to fight one another in a catastrophic war. It must have been surreal. The most prominent attendee was General Albert Sidney Johnston, recent ex-commander of the U.S. Army's Department of the Pacific, who abruptly resigned his commission as soon as tempers flared that spring. The "most crushed," however, at least according to Hancock's wife, Almira, "was Major Armistead, who, with tears, which were contagious, streaming down his face, and hands upon Mr. Hancock's shoulders, while looking him steadily in the eye, said, 'Hancock, good-by, you can never know what this has cost me.'"[6]

The decision to resign and break his oath to the United States ripped at every fiber of Armistead's being. The focus of his internal conflict had nothing to do with the issue that caused the war—slavery, which had been part of his life since childhood—and everything to do with his family's deep ties to the U.S. military. Born in North Carolina and raised on a Virginia farm with nineteen slaves, Armistead believed wholeheartedly in southern independence and had owned at least one slave himself. What troubled him was the act of quitting the army and leaving the only friends he'd ever known.[7] Armistead's ancestors had been serving in the American military since his third-great grandfather was named colonel of the local horse militia in Gloucester, Virginia, in 1680. His father, Walker Keith Armistead, was the third man to graduate from West Point and rose to the rank of brigadier general, and his uncle, George Armistead, defended Fort McHenry in the Battle of Baltimore when Francis Scott Key wrote the poem that eventually became "The Star Spangled-Banner." Two other uncles died in the War of 1812.[8] Still, when it came time to render a verdict on his role in the national divide, the twenty-two-year U.S. Army veteran and scion of military royalty aligned himself with his home state and the rebellious South.

Writing about his decision later in 1861, and leaving no doubt about his intentions, Armistead said he "left to fight for my own country and for, and with, my own people—and because they were right, and oppressed."[9] Intentionally or not, his language mimicked that of Virginia's secession ordinance, which used the word "oppression" twice and charged the federal government with "the oppression of the Southern Slaveholding States."[10]

Hancock, by contrast, was Union to the core. The Pennsylvania native was a conservative Democrat who supported the concept of states' rights; yet his singular concern at the time the war broke out was keeping the country intact.[11] Friendly southern soldiers who sought his counsel in the spring of 1861 were told, quite bluntly, "I can give you no advice, as I shall not fight upon the principle of State-rights but for the Union, whole and undivided."[12] Like many northerners at the start of the war, Hancock was focused not on the immediate abolition of slavery but on the forceful continued existence of the *United* States.

It was against this backdrop that the two friends became enemies almost overnight, committed to different sides for different reasons, with different views for the future of the country—and destined to clash two years later on the Civil War's most hallowed battlefield.

Hancock, dashing and resolute, "one of the most soldierly men that ever lived,"[13] was one of the rising stars in the Union by the time the armies reached Gettysburg. His performance as a brigadier general at Williamsburg in May 1862 earned him the sobriquet "Hancock the Superb," and he took command of a division four months later in the midst of battlefield chaos at Antietam. Graduated from West Point, descended from military veterans, possessed of an authoritative presence, and married with two young children, he had a résumé that almost demanded greatness. To the surprise of no one, he became a major general in November 1862, led a division at Fredericksburg and Chancellorsville, and was promoted to command of the Second Corps in June 1863, three weeks before the great battle at Gettysburg.[14]

It was a starkly different story for Armistead, the older man by seven years, whose career had seemingly plateaued by the time of the summer invasion. He was assigned command of a Confederate brigade as far back as April 1862 but advanced no further in rank for more than a year and was never even considered to lead a division, much less a corps. Hardened and bitter in his personal life, he had resigned in disgrace from West Point and then was widowed twice and lost two of his three biological children to disease on the frontier. His brigade saw action in only two pitched battles before 1863 and did little to earn distinction, although Armistead himself was praised repeatedly for verve and personal gallantry.[15] This latest incursion of the North gave him one more chance to uphold his family's military honor.

The account of their friendship and ultimate showdown at Gettysburg, when Armistead's troops attacked Hancock's troops and both men fell wounded, is one of the astonishing personal stories of the Civil War, and yet its details were distorted in the twentieth century by two popular and widely acclaimed works of historic fiction. Michael Shaara's *The Killer Angels: A Novel of the Civil War* won the Pulitzer Prize for fiction in 1975 and turned a dramatized version of the friendship into one of the key themes of the war's most famous battle. The companion movie, *Gettysburg*, a four-hour epic released to theaters almost twenty years later in 1993, raised both men to even greater prominence for a new generation of battlefield visitors. What many readers and viewers did not seem to realize, however, was that the novel and movie took liberties with the historical record to engage a broader audience, tug at heartstrings, and move their stories along. While *The Killer Angels* and *Gettysburg* followed generally accurate outlines of the battle, they created enough scenes with imaginary quotes and drama to smudge the lines between fact and fiction—including with Armistead and Hancock. Some of it was undoubtedly theater at its finest, but it was not pure history.

There is no evidence, for instance, that an emotional Armistead had two misty-eyed conversations with Confederate General James Longstreet on the eve of battle, proclaiming "Win was like a brother to me" or longing to "talk to old Hancock one more time." Nor did Longstreet accede to his request by saying, "When the time comes and he's close, just send a messenger over under a flag of truce and go on over. Ain't nothing to it."[16] There is also no evidence that Hancock waxed poetic about "Lo" Armistead before Pickett's Charge (or even any credible evidence that Armistead's nickname was "Lo"—see the appendix). Armistead died two days after being wounded in the battle, and neither Longstreet nor Hancock mentioned anything of the sort in postwar writings, so the accounts are not based on primary or even secondary sources. The simple explanation is that these conversations never happened.

Civil War scholars and National Park Service rangers have struggled to untangle public perception in the several decades since the movie's release, but few have addressed it as succinctly as Gettysburg Licensed Battlefield Guides Wayne Motts and James Hessler in their 2015 book *Pickett's Charge at Gettysburg: A Guide to the Most Famous Attack in American History*. Calling the popular accounts "heavily fictionalized," they wrote that Armistead and Hancock "were likely aware that they were facing each other on July 3, but there are no contemporary accounts to indicate that the two were emotionally pining for each other during the battle as they do in the popular novel and film."[17]

Former Gettysburg National Military Park ranger and historian D. Scott Hartwig, in his book *A Killer Angels Companion*, adds, "Shaara's story is told so well, his character portrayals are so believable, that the unknowing reader might believe what they are reading *is* history."[18]

One by-product of the movie mania was that a small group of historians lurched to the other extreme and began questioning the depth of the Armistead–Hancock friendship—with a few even wondering, absurdly, whether the two men were friends at all.[19] Could the connection between them have been a figment of Mrs. Hancock's imagination? It is true, in fact, that neither Armistead nor Hancock left behind any letters from the other and that several biographies of Hancock, who ran for president three times and lived until 1886, barely mention Armistead. A deeper dive into available documents and other evidence, however, including testimony from contemporary soldiers, shows that they certainly were friends and had a long personal history dating back to the 1840s. Consider the following:

- Armistead and Hancock served together for sixteen months at small frontier garrisons in the Indian Territory (what is now Oklahoma). Their paths crossed for the first time in October 1844 when Hancock, then twenty years old and fresh out of West Point, was assigned to Fort Towson, where his new friend had been posted for more than a year. The twenty-seven-year-old Armistead likely served as a mentor and sounding board. Both men were transferred to nearby Fort Washita in November 1845 and lived there in the same officers' quarters. Armistead's biographer, Wayne Motts, discovered a rare letter that Armistead wrote from Fort Washita to an army friend in December 1845; Hancock added the P.S. in his own handwriting and also signed his name.[20]

- Armistead and Hancock fought with the same regiment during the Mexican War in 1847–1848. They were cited for gallantry in the Battle of Churubusco and led adjacent platoons during attacks at Molino del Rey.[21] Even more to the point, they were together in the same small company for six months during the postwar occupation of Mexico in 1848; Armistead served as commander of the unit, and Hancock was his lieutenant.[22]

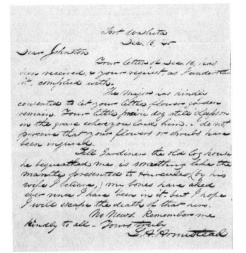
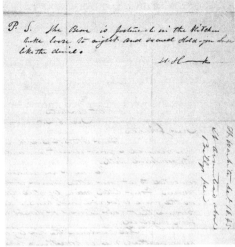

Armistead wrote this letter from Fort Washita in 1845, and Hancock scribbled his signature on the P.S. It is the only document ever found that has both of their signatures.

U.S. MILITARY ACADEMY LIBRARY, WEST POINT, NEW YORK, ABRAHAM ROBINSON JOHNSTON PAPERS, BOX 2

- Anecdotes from fellow soldiers during the occupation period are even more revealing. Henry Heth, who served alongside Hancock in Armistead's company, wrote in his memoirs that he regularly shared meals with his two friends. "Armistead, Hancock and I were messmates," Heth said, "and never was a mess happier than ours." Heth described how he and Hancock often teased the older Armistead.[23] While they were still serving in Mexico, Lieutenant Ralph Kirkham wrote a letter to his wife from Toluca in February 1848 to tell her that "a party of us visited today the highest peak of the mountain which overhangs this city." He identified four members of the group of adventurers as "Lieutenants Hancock, Buckner, Armistead and myself."[24]

- For almost a decade following the war in Mexico, Hancock was frequently posted at Jefferson Barracks near St. Louis—where, at least on occasion, Armistead was also assigned (and where two of his young children, who died at the post, are buried in the barracks cemetery). The two men also traveled to Utah for the

"Mormon Conflict" and were part of the Sixth Infantry's legendary thousand-mile march to the West Coast in the late 1850s. There are no details of their interactions during this period, but it is inconceivable that they didn't connect with one another given the proximity of their assignments.[25]

- Hancock had settled into a new role as the army's quartermaster for Los Angeles in the summer of 1859, while Armistead was sent to protect settlers from attacks by Native Americans in what is now Arizona. One of Hancock's duties was to supply Armistead's troops, and the two men stayed in touch that summer through written correspondence. The July 30, 1859, edition of the *Los Angeles Star* reported that "an express arrived last night from Major Armistead, at Beale's Crossing of the Colorado, to Captain Hancock, Q.M. U.S.A., at present residing here, conveying intelligence" about the Mojave Indians. Two weeks later, on August 13, the *Star* informed its readers that "by the Overland Mail, which arrived yesterday morning, Capt. Hancock, USA, received intelligence from Fort Mohave that the Indians continued their hostility, and that the troops, under Major Armistead, were engaged in pursuing them." The story added that "dispatches have been received by Capt. Hancock from Gen. Clark, and forwarded immediately to Major Armistead."[26]

- Mrs. Hancock's description of her husband's 1861 meeting with several departing Confederates is the basis for much of the Armistead–Hancock legend, and yet it is filled with such extreme emotion and coincidence that some historians question whether it happened at all. It is worth noting, however, that she identified only three attendees by name—Hancock, Armistead, and Albert Sidney Johnston—and all three are known to have been in Los Angeles at the same time on several occasions in the late spring of 1861.[27] Indeed, one of the most relevant parts of her account is a passage rarely cited by historians; she tells of Armistead presenting his U.S. Army major's uniform to Hancock that night, "saying that 'he might sometime need it.'"[28]

- Confirmation of her story comes from a nineteenth-century historian, the Reverend D. X. Junkin, former chaplain of the U.S. Navy, who wrote about the uniform anecdote and identified the source as General Hancock himself. It is significant that Junkin's biography was published seven years *before* Mrs. Hancock's book and was in circulation while Hancock was still alive (meaning the general could have disputed it, which he didn't). According to Junkin, "An interesting incident in connection with General Armistead's defection from the United States Army . . . *is related by General Hancock*. It occurred in Los Angeles early in 1861. . . . On leaving Los Angeles, he presented General Hancock with his major's uniform, saying that the latter 'might sometime need it.'"[29]

- Junkin also was the first to write that Armistead, on the same night, had "placed in [Hancock's] hands for safe-keeping, and to be given to his family if he should fall in battle, certain valuable private papers." With only slight variation, this is the same story Almira Hancock told in her reminiscences seven years later.[30] Mrs. Hancock may have misremembered, and most likely embellished, some of the details of the 1861 get-together, perhaps even confusing the date and guest list, but there can be little doubt that Armistead and Hancock saw each other and talked before going off to war.

- After being wounded at the height of Pickett's Charge, Armistead was encountered by one of Hancock's staff officers as he was carried to the rear. The officer, Henry Bingham, described it in a letter to Hancock after the war: "Observing that his suffering was very great, I said to him, General, I am Captain Bingham of General Hancock's Staff. . . . He then asked me if it was General Winfield Scott Hancock and upon my replying in the affirmative, he informed me that you were an old and valued friend of his."[31]

- It is perhaps indicative of their relationship that Hancock mentioned the name of only one Confederate general in his exhaustive Gettysburg battle report, which filled eleven pages in the army's

Official Records. "When the enemy's line had reached the stone wall," he wrote, "[it was] led by General Armistead."[32]

- Hancock's adjutant, Francis A. Walker, who served with him during the war and later wrote a Hancock biography, addressed the general's prewar friendships in an 1888 paper for the Military Historical Society of Massachusetts: "[Hancock] knew too many of the men who, like his friend Armistead, had reluctantly and painfully broken the main ties of their lives in taking the other side."[33]

- Completing his memoirs in 1897, Henry Heth again referred to the Armistead–Hancock friendship and to Armistead's mortal wounding at Gettysburg. "Those two regimental associates, messmates and devoted friends never met [again] on earth, but I'm sure have met again [in heaven]," he wrote. "I think Armistead was killed by Hancock's troops, and Hancock was wounded by one of Armistead's command. What a commentary on Civil War!"[34]

The two men may not have been "almost brothers," as the novel and movie suggested, or even "best friends" in the modern sense, having been detached from one another for long stretches, but they undoubtedly were good friends, well acquainted over the years, with an uncommon kinship forged through shared military experiences. The personal story that led them to a final bloody confrontation in Pickett's Charge at Gettysburg, where Armistead's men assaulted Hancock's men—portrayed so dramatically in print and on the screen—is one worth reexamining for accuracy and proper context after more than 150 years.

Imagine the morning of July 3, 1863. Two days of vicious fighting had left the armies bloodied and weakened, but both were determined to stay and slug it out—perhaps to make Gettysburg the final battle and determine the fate of the Union. From their strong defensive position on Cemetery Ridge, U.S. troops saw scores of Confederate cannons being repositioned along a wide arc from the Peach Orchard to Seminary Ridge and beyond, all in plain view, the precursor of a calamitous event. But when would it begin?

Winfield Scott Hancock, thirty-nine years old and at the peak of his physical power, was ready for any contingency. He had been a major figure at Gettysburg almost from the start of the battle, taking temporary command of the field on July 1 and heroically plugging holes in the Union line during the prolonged Confederate assault of July 2.[35] Had the Rebels retreated after the second day, he would have gone down in history anyway as the savior of Cemetery Ridge and East Cemetery Hill. But there was much more to come on the third day, and he sensed it, as a sudden and pregnant lull fell over the field.

It was about noon when one of Hancock's division commanders, the iron-willed John Gibbon, called several of the officers together for an opportunistic lunch, having procured "an old and tough rooster" that was cooked into a stew. Hancock, Gibbon, and the commanding general of the army, George G. Meade, sat around on crudely fashioned wooden stools less than a mile from Confederate cannons and enjoyed, at least briefly, one of the oddest feasts in American military history. After finishing their meals, they lit up cigars and leisurely debated what would happen next—until a single thundering shot broke the silence. "Almost instantly," Gibbon wrote, "the whole air above and around us was filled with bursting and screaming projectiles . . . the most infernal pandemonium it has ever been my fortune to look upon."[36]

It was natural for Hancock to fear for the immediate safety of his younger brother, John, who had enlisted in the Forty-Ninth Pennsylvania Infantry at the start of the war and now served as a staff officer in his corps at the division level.[37] But family concerns could not overtake his responsibility to look after the three divisions of his corps and other units that were ducking and hugging the ground nearby. In one of the most inspiring moments of the war, Hancock mounted his horse and rode along the line amid the din, seemingly oblivious to the danger, risking his life to set an example that calmed his anxious men. Staff officer Bingham remembered that the general "started at the right of his line of battle and followed by his Staff, his Corps flag flying in the hands of a brave Irishman of the Sixth New York Cavalry, rode slowly along the terrible crest to the left of his position, while the shot and shell roared and crashed around him, and every moment tore great gaps in the ranks at his side." Bingham called it "a gallant deed of heroic valor."[38]

And yet the fury continued unabated. Even a battle-tested veteran like Hancock was unsure what it meant or what would follow. At one point, he sent a courier to Gibbon to ask for his opinion, but the top subordinate replied, unhelpfully, that "it was the prelude either to a retreat or an assault."[39] A sudden pause in firing only heightened the confusion as a haunting, deadly silence gripped the field. "The artillery fight over, men began to breathe more freely," one Union soldier wrote, "and to ask, What next, I wonder?"[40]

There was much more certainty on the other side of the field, where an infantry attack was planned and ready to go, but family matters also were on the mind of Hancock's old friend, Lewis Armistead. The invading Confederate army included his lone surviving child, Walker Keith (a teenager who had joined his staff as an aide-de-camp), and, possibly, one of his three younger brothers. Captain Bowles Armistead served for four years in a Virginia cavalry unit that came north with the army that summer, but his muster roll record for July 1863 does not state whether he was present or absent at Gettysburg (two other brothers, Walker Jr. and Franck, were in the Confederate service but not at the battle).[41] But Lewis, too, had a far greater responsibility than protecting his bloodlines. His brigade of five Virginia regiments had been serving in Major General George Pickett's division for almost a year and was growing more anxious by the day to test its mettle under fire on enemy soil.

Hell-bent on southern independence and fighting to preserve a way of life that included slavery—a fact that students of the war must never forget—these rebels had eagerly followed Pickett's orders to wade across the Potomac River into northern territory in Maryland on June 24, then surpassed a greater symbolic milestone when they crossed the Pennsylvania border and set up camp in Chambersburg on June 27.[42] For most of the next week, however, they faced an interminable delay. Pickett's division was still charged with guarding supply trains and tearing up the railroad in Chambersburg when the battle at Gettysburg opened four days later on July 1 and did not even begin its twenty-five-mile march to the battlefield until 2:00 a.m. on July 2.[43] Stopping a few miles short of the town to catch their breath and set up camp that evening, they heard the familiarly eerie echoes of gunfire off in the distance. It was a chilling final notice that their services would be needed on the front lines the next day.

The three brigades of approximately five thousand officers and men were placed near a tree line on Seminary Ridge on the morning of July 3, less than a mile from Hancock's weary but waiting troops. The two fearsome armies pawed the turf in nervous anticipation of the clash. "It is appalling, terrific, yet grandly exciting," one man wrote.[44] The artillery duel that Gibbon described as "pandemonium" on the Union side had the same effect here; it sent such tremors through the ranks that the forty-six-year-old Armistead could only advise his jittery soldiers to "lie still boys, there is no safe place here."[45] But it was not long before the combined force of three Confederate divisions under Pickett, J. Johnston Pettigrew, and Isaac Trimble—arranged in two lines of glistening bayonets across a breathtaking mile-wide front—stepped off to begin the fateful infantry assault now known to history as Pickett's Charge.

Armistead's brigade had been placed in a supporting second line, behind that of another old U.S. Army friend, Richard Garnett, to add strength and depth to the Confederate attack. Armistead was one of several commanders who sought to motivate the men with a few appropriate remarks before marching them off into the cauldron. "If I should live for a hundred years," wrote John Lewis, a lieutenant in the Ninth Virginia Regiment, "I shall never forget that moment or the command as given by General Louis [sic] A. Armistead on that day. . . . [He] was possessed of a very loud voice, which could be heard by the whole brigade."[46] Among the historically noteworthy soldiers in Armistead's Rebel ranks were William Aylett, great-grandson of the Revolutionary patriot Patrick Henry, and Robert Tyler Jones, grandson of former U.S. president John Tyler. Jones remembered years later that the general's "stentorian voice rang like a bugle blast in the air." Soon, he said, "every man rose to his feet like clockwork."[47]

After challenging a regimental color-bearer to plant his flag on the enemy's works and urging his troops to "remember your wives, your mothers, your sisters and your sweethearts,"[48] Armistead paused briefly. It was almost as if he wanted to acknowledge the historic irony of the moment. The same U.S. flag he had served with honor for more than two decades, that had once inspired his father and uncles to perform great deeds on American battlefields—and that now was being defended by one of the dearest army friends he'd ever known—was today facing him, defiantly, across the ridge.

Armistead calmly extended his sword as if on dress parade and strode twenty paces in front of his men.

"Right shoulder, shift arms. Forward, march!"[49]

Chapter Two

Armistead at the "Point"

Lewis Addison Armistead was born on February 18, 1817, at the home of his maternal grandparents in New Bern, North Carolina, and there was little doubt that he would one day be a soldier.

Named for two uncles, Lewis and Addison, who died in the War of 1812, he also was the nephew of the hero of Fort McHenry and the son of a rising star in the U.S. Army Corps of Engineers. Earlier ancestors served in the Revolution, including one who survived Valley Forge and another killed in action at the Battle of Brandywine.[1] Making war was the family's preferred career option.

Lewis's father, Walker Keith, held a distinguished place in this clan of military veterans because he was the first to receive formal training in a classroom setting. Walker was one of a handful of promising cadets assigned to the new U.S. Military Academy at West Point, New York, when it opened in 1801 and ranked at the top of the academy's second graduating class in 1803.[2] He entered the service as a second lieutenant in the new Corps of Engineers and advanced steadily over the next fifteen years to first lieutenant, captain, major, lieutenant colonel, and colonel, committed to life as a full-time soldier.[3] In 1814, he married Elizabeth Stanly, the much-sought-after daughter of U.S. Congressman John Stanly and granddaughter of a Revolutionary War financier.[4] Lewis was their first son, born at the Stanly family estate in New Bern while Walker was away on duty in the Chesapeake Bay area.[5]

Lewis's early years were filled with exhilarating stories of military glory, stoking his imagination and narrowing his focus on a well-defined career path. Walker was often off on assignment at posts along the East

Coast—West Point and Baltimore among them—but he purchased a 323-acre farm in Fauquier County, Virginia, in 1818, near the town of Upperville, to provide his family with the stability of a permanent home.[6] It was here, on a sloping hillside plantation called Ben Lomond, that the Armisteads raised nine children born between 1815 and 1838: Lucinda, the oldest, followed by Lewis, Mary, Cornelia, Elizabeth, Virginia, Walker Jr., Franck, and Bowles.[7] (By 1830, according to the U.S. census for Fauquier County, there were also nineteen slaves and two "free colored persons" living there.)[8]

Walker parlayed his stellar performance against the British in the War of 1812 into a series of promotions, moving up to the dual role of colonel and chief engineer of the army in November 1818. For the next two and half years, he oversaw the Engineer Bureau in Washington, D.C., and served as inspector at West Point under the new and powerful superintendent, Sylvanus Thayer. He was reassigned in March 1821 when Congress downsized the army, retaining his rank but becoming colonel of the Third Regiment of Artillery, with headquarters at Fort Washington, about sixty miles from Upperville.[9] The next few years were uneventful because it was a time of relative peace, but he was nonetheless promoted to brigadier general in 1828 for ten years of "faithful service in one grade,"[10] becoming one of the highest-ranking general officers in the country.

Lewis was eleven years old at the time and dreaming of a military career, hopeful of attending West Point when he turned the minimum age of sixteen. His father now had connections in high places in addition to being a distinctive alum. Aware that the "Point" was more demanding academically because of improvements made by Thayer, Walker arranged for Lewis to enroll in the preparatory school at Georgetown College for the 1830–1831 school year, when he was thirteen.[11] One of the young man's most meaningful experiences during his time at Georgetown came when he was baptized by a Jesuit priest who was a member of the school's faculty.[12]

Several years later, in January 1833, Lewis was studying at an unidentified school in Winchester, Virginia, when his father wrote to the secretary of war to "solicit for my son . . . a cadet's warrant" at West Point. The case he made was extreme, even for an excessively doting parent. "His capacity is such as to have the approbation of his gentry and the guardian of the institution," Walker wrote, adding that Lewis was "far advanced in his letters and mathematical studies" and ready to "sustain an examination" for admission. Because his son was so young, and to allay any doubts in Washington as to the seriousness of the request, he signed it "WK Armistead, Brig'r Genl, Commanding 3rd Regt. Artillery."[13]

Walker probably felt guilty about being an absentee father during much of Lewis's childhood. This was not the last time he would use his position near the top of the army's hierarchy to create an opportunity that might otherwise have been unavailable. Later, during his career on the frontier, Lewis would request and receive a disproportionate amount of "leave" from his various posts, possibly because of Walker's rank and legacy.[14] To the surprise of no one, Lewis's application to West Point was fast-tracked toward approval. He soon wrote to the secretary of war to "acknowledge the receipt of my conditional warrant, which I accept," and, whether it was necessary or not, Walker scrawled a note at the bottom of the page that "I hereby approve of the foregoing acceptance of my son."[15]

The West Point of 1833 had a far different look and feel from the primitive school Walker attended thirty-two years earlier.

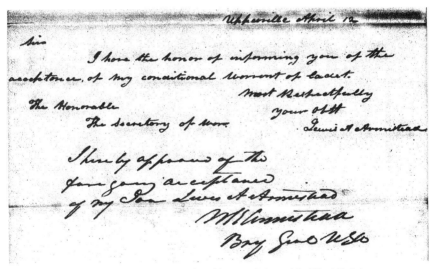

Lewis Armistead's 1833 letter accepting his appointment to West Point
NATIONAL ARCHIVES

New stone buildings, including an academic center and mess hall, dotted the campus and ran along the southeast border of an open field called the "Plain." Cadets were held accountable to classmates and teachers with regular class rankings and revealing, often humiliating demerit tables. Thayer, an 1808 graduate who served as superintendent from 1817 to 1833, established an academic board to oversee the curriculum and created demerit limits for expulsion. He stepped down in the summer of 1833 but was replaced by another alumnus, Rene E. De Russy, a fellow veteran of the War of 1812, who kept the focus firmly on discipline.[16]

One thing that had not changed over the years was the mission of West Point academics—focused far more on engineering than traditional military tactics. President Thomas Jefferson's vision had been for an officer corps well versed in mathematics and related fields of study.[17] A critical analysis of the academy between 1833 and the start of the Civil War determined bluntly that "the men who controlled the institution viewed its mission as being the production of engineers who could also function as soldiers rather than the reverse."[18] Accordingly, students in the fourth (or freshman) class would study only two subjects, math and French, in their first full year on campus.

Math classes started promptly at 8:00 a.m. with recitation for an hour and a half daily, six days a week. The fall term centered on algebra, while the spring term expanded to include plane and solid geometry, plane and spherical trigonometry, mensuration, and analytical geometry. Students often were required to use the blackboard to solve problems and defend their work to the instructor. Afternoon classes in French were designed to "provide cadets with a foundation which would enable them to read scientific and military works in French," involving daily recitations on grammar and translation. Much of this was because Thayer had toured French military schools from 1815 to 1817 and become enamored of the French system, dominated by math and engineering. "In a typical section room," former West Point professor James Morrison wrote in *The Best School*, "some cadets would write sentences and conjugate verbs at the blackboard while others would read aloud from a French text and translate passages into English." Occasionally, the most proficient students would try the more difficult task of translating English into French.[19]

It was into this vortex that first-year cadet Lewis Armistead plunged in the fall of 1833. He couldn't have been more woefully ill prepared. French confused him, mathematics overwhelmed him, and he was quickly outshone by five other future Civil War generals in his class—Braxton Bragg, Jubal Early, Joseph Hooker, John Pemberton, and John Sedgwick.[20] During his first several weeks on campus, he fell ill, missed several days of classes, and was demoted twice to lower sections of math instruction.[21]

The illness was never diagnosed, but it may have been related to stress due to the rigorous challenge of West Point academics. Lewis fell so far behind the other students that he was in danger of flunking out in the first semester of his freshman year—until, as so often happened, his father intervened. Brigadier General Armistead wrote an October 29 letter to the secretary of war, Lewis Cass, explaining that Lewis "had made known to me his recent sickness" and its catastrophic impact on his studies. He asked that his son be given the chance to resign his cadet's appointment with an eye to a brighter future.

"My intention is to place him immediately at one of our best schools," Walker wrote, "which will prepare him with the requisite qualifications for his future success at the Military Academy. May I request, sir, that you will consider him a candidate for reappointment the coming year."[22]

The letter was part of a coordinated effort by the Armistead family because Lewis followed up with his own note to Cass the next day, tactfully dropping his father's name and blaming the illness as the sole reason for his scholastic failings:

> *I have the honour to tender my resignation as a cadet in the United States service, my reason for so doing is explained in my father's letter to you. I would add however, that my sickness has been the only cause of my not progressing, and this at the very commencement of my studies, placed me so far back that I could not regain my standing in the class, all of which I hope you will kindly consider and reappoint me the ensuing year.*[23]

Superintendent De Russy, who knew Walker well—and, more important, knew his rank—took up the cause even before receiving Lewis's letter. Writing to Brigadier General Charles Gratiot, chief engineer of the army, De Russy asked that the overmatched and now "depressed" first-year student be allowed to resign immediately to avoid further academic embarrassment.

"Cadet Armistead would probably have succeeded in his studies had not an illness of several days deprived him of the first and most useful instructions in algebra," the superintendent wrote:

> *This circumstance placed him in a low section and depressed his spirits. In looking over the delinquent reports, I find no other irregularities in Cadet Armistead's conduct than those which would naturally grow out of his present state of mind; I therefore request that he may be permitted to resign at this time, and as it is his wish to prepare himself for the ensuing years, most respectfully recommend him to the favourable notice of the Secretary of War for reappointment in the 4th class of 1834.*[24]

Lewis's resignation was accepted three days later on November 2, 1833. There can be no doubt that his benevolent treatment was the result of his father's influence. No record has been found that he enrolled at another school for the remainder of the academic year, but a new application was submitted to West Point on March 21, 1834, with the special notation that "Genl. Armistead requests a reappointment." Unsurprisingly, Lewis was "found duly qualified by the Academic Board [and] conditionally admitted as a cadet into the Military Academy" at its June meeting, to rank from September 1, as though the first year on campus never happened.[25]

Lewis returned to West Point in the fall of 1834, determined to make a better showing. It stood to reason that his previous experience on campus would give him an edge over the other freshly arrived plebes, and West Point academicians offered a vote of confidence by placing him in the first, or elite, mathematics section.[26] But before he could prove that he belonged back in the classroom, he ran afoul of the school's strict disciplinary standards.

To be fair, West Point's list of more than two hundred regulations often bordered on the absurd. For every understandable rule banning drinking alcohol or cavorting with prostitutes, there was another stating that "no cadet shall read or keep in his room, without permission, any

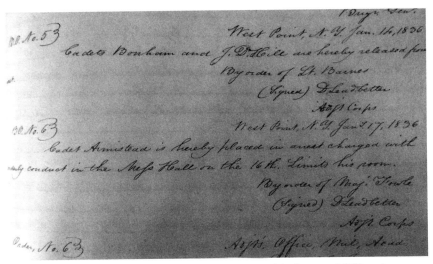

West Point records show that Armistead was arrested in January 1836 and "charged with disorderly conduct in the Mess Hall."

novel, romance or play." Students could receive demerits for playing chess, throwing snowballs, or wearing improperly blackened shoes. Each month, a conduct report was compiled and sent to the secretary of war—the best and worst being highlighted—and any cadet compiling two hundred demerits in one academic year could be thrown out of school. Punishments for lesser violations included extra tours of guard duty, loss of basic privileges, or confinement to "dark" barracks rooms with windows covered by blankets.[27]

Lewis was placed under arrest on November 2 for the grievous act of "going on post without being detailed." In laymen's terms, he had filled in on guard duty for fellow cadet John Watson and answered in Watson's stead during roll call despite not being a member of the "Cadets Guard." The tremors reached all the way to Washington, D.C., where the secretary of war issued Order No. 71, calling for a general court-martial on campus. A five-man board of army officials convened in late November at West Point and heard Armistead plead "not guilty" to two separate charges—one that he answered for Watson and another that he walked his friend's post. Armistead was cleared of the first charge but convicted of the second, considered "conduct subversion of military discipline," and forced to walk four extra tours of Sunday guard duty, one of the academy's lightest punishments.[28]

And yet the whole fiasco was an unnecessary distraction for a borderline student trying to keep up with gifted classmates. On the same day he was arrested in early November, Armistead was demoted to the fifth section of entry-level French.[29] He then was felled at least briefly by the flu epidemic sweeping campus, and his academic prospects seemed dimmer than ever.[30] First-semester test scores from January 1835 show that he placed fiftieth out of sixty-one cadets tested in French and thirty-seventh out of sixty-three in math, ranking in the bottom third of the class overall. It was a talented group of students, to be sure—classmates included the future Confederate general P. G. T. Beauregard—but Armistead's continued lack of achievement raised questions about his general aptitude and fitness for military command.[31]

It got even worse in the spring. Lewis scraped bottom in his June 1835 French test, scoring fifty-second out of fifty-four students and flunking the class (noted coldly on his academic record as "deficient in French"). He wasn't even tested in math, his better subject, because failure in just one class meant a cadet had to repeat the entire year. Complicating matters, he ranked 201st out of 240 cadets at the academy in conduct, seemingly close to being expelled—and, perhaps for good measure, was arrested on July 1, charged with "talking to a citizen within the Post" and sentenced to one extra tour of guard duty.[32]

The 1835–1836 school year would be this third on campus and his third in the freshman class, certainly his final chance. The advantage was that he was taking the same courses for the third time and competing for the most part against younger, less experienced students. It finally paid off. Although still dogged by conduct issues—at one point he earned twenty-two demerits in a month[33]—Armistead's January 1836 scores were marked improvements, placing him twenty-eighth in math, thirty-fourth in French, and thirty-first overall out of fifty-nine cadets, the first time he finished anywhere near the top half of his class. Pushed and probably inspired by future Union generals Henry Halleck and Henry Hunt, he began to have the look and feel of a future army commander.[34]

One incident later that month threatened to derail his career, however. Details are vague and elusive, but USMA Battalion Order No. 6, filed on January 17, asserts that "Cadet Armistead [was] placed in arrest, charged with disorderly conduct in the Mess Hall on the 16th," and promptly confined to his room.[35] Numerous West Point records were destroyed in an 1838 fire, and many other documents have faded or been lost over time, but the strong circumstantial evidence is that Armistead brawled with another cantankerous cadet, the future Confederate general Jubal Early.[36] The most detailed report, albeit secondhand, came in an 1870 book by Major Walter Harrison, a staff officer under General George Pickett. Harrison described it as "a youthful escapade . . . I have been told, the partial cracking of Jubal A. Early's head with a mess-hall plate."[37] An Armistead relative had referred to a cryptic "boyish frolick" in an 1852 letter but offered no additional insight.[38] Early eventually recovered from the lunchroom fracas, even if the plate did not, but neither he nor Armistead spoke about it—or denied the rampant rumors—for the rest of their lives.

Armistead was clearly the aggressor because his West Point career ended at this point, while Early's did not (Early, who entered the academy in the same year as his rival, graduated in 1837).[39] After being held under arrest for two weeks and consulting frantically with his father, Armistead determined that his best option was to resign permanently from West Point. Were he to remain on campus, academy rules would have required a trial, and he was almost certain to be convicted of assaulting Early and either expelled or forced to resign. Stepping away on his own, mortifying as that might be, would enable him to avoid blaring headlines and rehabilitate his reputation back home in Virginia.

Still, there was no guarantee the resignation would be accepted.

Lewis broached the subject with Superintendent De Russy and submitted his official letter on January 29. He was released from arrest that afternoon.[40] The ever-compliant De Russy sent the letter along to General Gratiot in Washington and added his own note of endorsement, reminding the chief engineer of Walker Armistead's legacy with West Point and the army, as if that were necessary:

Armistead's resignation from West Point was accepted several weeks after his arrest for the mess hall incident.

U.S. MILITARY ACADEMY LIBRARY, WEST POINT, NEW YORK

I herewith have the honor to transmit, for the action of the Hon the Secretary of War, Cadet Armistead's Resignation Which I request may be accepted.

Cadet Armistead, through imprudence, had so exposed him lately as to cause his arrest, and had he been tried upon the charges against him, would in all probability have been dismissed [from] the Service: Aware of these facts, he presented his Resignation which on account of his father I hope will be accepted.[41]

The army indeed accepted the resignation on February 2,[42] bringing to an end three tumultuous years in which Lewis struggled, failed, broke rules, fought with another student, faced two court-martial hearings, and, astoundingly, never made it out of the freshman class.

There is a three-year gap in Armistead's life story from 1836 to 1839. Certainly, he went home to Ben Lomond to spend time with his mother and siblings—his youngest brothers, Franck and Bowles, also future Confederate soldiers, were born in 1835 and 1838, respectively[43]—but the only record of his activity was a vague note in his mother's family history that he attended a military school in her home state of North Carolina.[44]

The school was never identified, although it could have been the North Carolina Literary, Scientific, and Military Institution or, more likely, a new academy opened by Colonel Carter Jones at Wilmington in 1836. The Jones school offered part-time instruction in "Infantry and Light Infantry Tactics, together with the Broad Sword Exercises and Cavalry movements . . . [for] Persons wishing to become proficient in Military Science."[45]

(One curious modern account places him back at Georgetown during this time. A website for Georgetown's ROTC program, the "Hoya Battalion," claims that Armistead graduated from Georgetown in the class of 1837 and that he "may even have been the first captain of the College Cadets," but Georgetown academic records do not support this. There is no evidence that he attended Georgetown following his preparatory year as a thirteen-year-old in 1830–1831.[46])

Whatever Armistead did in the three years following his resignation at West Point, his dream was still to serve in the U.S. Army with his father, and they developed a new joint plan to achieve that goal once his final class graduated in 1839. The army by then was mired in a tedious and costly guerilla war with Seminole Indians in Florida and in desperate need of additional officers from the civilian ranks. Lewis's résumé—as a former West Point student, son of a brigadier general, and nephew of a U.S. congressman on his mother's side—made him a prime candidate for such an assignment.

Walker had already served two stints in Florida,[47] and his influence at army headquarters was helpful as always, but the decisive factor may have been the support of Lewis's uncle, Edward Stanly, his mother's brother, a second-term member of the House of Representatives who served on the Committee on Military Affairs. As early as January 10, 1839, Stanly wrote a letter on his nephew's behalf to Secretary of War Joel Poinsett (albeit misspelling Lewis's first name):

My nephew Louis A. Armistead (son of Genl W.K. Armistead of the U.S. Army) is anxious to join the Army and prefers the Dragoon Corps. He is a young man of good moral character, sound constitution—rather athletic, and of good ordinary English education. Will Mr. Poinsett inform me of what steps Mr. Armistead must take to procure an appointment?[48]

Poinsett's response went unrecorded, but the power of the endorsement was clear, even if Lewis was ticketed for the lowest branch of service—the infantry—instead of the mounted dragoons.

Had he graduated with the West Point Class of 1839, along with Henry Halleck and Henry Hunt, he would have been commissioned a second lieutenant on July 1.[49]

As a nongraduate who resigned from the academy to avoid almost certain expulsion, and without even completing his first year of studies, he received his commission on July 10.[50]

He had lost all of nine days in rank.

CHAPTER THREE

Florida and the Frontier

NEWLY MINTED SECOND LIEUTENANT LEWIS ARMISTEAD SIGNED HIS commission papers on July 15, 1839, swearing to "bear true allegiance to the United States of America" and to serve "honestly and faithfully against all enemies and opposers, whatsoever."[1]

Within a week, he was off to the swamps of Florida.

The Second Seminole War had been raging for four years when Lewis reported on August 26 to take his post with Company I of the Sixth Infantry.[2] It was already well on its way to becoming the longest, costliest, most futile contest ever fought against Native Americans.[3] Tasked with uprooting the Seminoles from Florida and moving them west of the Mississippi River, U.S. soldiers were stymied by the clever guerilla tactics of Osceola and other resourceful Seminole chiefs. The army sent its best generals, including the famed Winfield Scott, in 1836 but made shockingly little progress and in some cases was reduced to torching villages.[4]

Conflict between natives and white settlers here dated back to the early 1800s, when Florida was still nominally under Spanish rule. Tensions had increased as escaped slaves from southern plantations poured over the Georgia border to find refuge among the Seminoles, safely beyond the reach of their former masters. General Andrew Jackson introduced organized warfare to the region with a brief reign of terror in 1817–1818, known as the First Seminole War, but Jackson's army was unable to bring the Indians under control.[5] Several years later, however, after Spain formally ceded Florida to the United States, army officials convinced several chiefs to relocate—first to the less desirable land of central Florida and later, by the 1830s, away from their homeland altogether to modern-day Oklahoma.[6]

The Treaty of Payne's Landing, signed in 1832, spelled out the forced migration in coldhearted terms: "The Seminole Indians relinquish to the United States all claim to the lands they at present occupy in the Territory of Florida and agree to emigrate to the country assigned . . . west of the Mississippi River . . . within three (3) years."[7] And yet, instead of packing their belongings and moving passively to the west, many warriors, led by Osceola, chose to stay and fight. As the deadline for removal approached in late 1835, Seminole raiders launched attacks on white settlements, burning houses, taking scalps, and driving terrified residents to the protection of army forts. On December 28, a band of Seminoles and their black allies ambushed U.S. troops under Major Francis Dade near the modern town of Bushnell, killing Dade and all but three of his 108 men. War was on.[8]

Jackson, now in his second term as president, promptly called on General Scott to travel to Florida and forcibly impose the Indian Removal Act. The hero from the War of 1812 devised a textbook battle plan that called for a joint attack with three well-schooled columns of infantry, converging on the unsuspecting Seminoles from different directions. It would have been masterful strategy for a Napoleonic battlefield in Europe. Unfortunately for Scott, the army was unprepared for the hit-and-run tactics of an elusive foe in unfamiliar swampy terrain. The combination of heat, disease, a dearth of supplies, the lack of effective maps, unreliable volunteer troops—and the skill, guile, and pride of the Seminoles—were too much to overcome.[9] Ultimately, Scott's grand plan for victory in Florida was dismantled by guerilla warfare, and he left the theater after several months in May 1836, apparently "with little regret."[10]

Scott was followed by a revolving door of five commanders over the next six years, each facing similar issues as native resistance increased and U.S. morale plummeted. There was a growing sense in Washington that the war might be unwinnable. In addition to fighting noncompliant Seminoles on their own turf, American soldiers faced threats from alligators, panthers, wolves, and swarms of bloodthirsty insects; one outraged trooper described Florida "a howling wilderness, the proper abode of Owls and bats and Snakes."[11] General Thomas Jesup briefly overcame the conditions and sent more than two thousand Indians west of the Mississippi, but he earned the wrath of the American public with deplorable tactics, including the capture of Osceola under a false flag of truce. He was replaced in overall command by the future president of the United States, Zachary Taylor, in 1838.[12]

Lewis Armistead arrived later the next year, at a time when the army was desperate for fresh troops and leadership at all levels.[13] In contrast to many of his war-weary comrades, the new second lieutenant was eager to prove his worth as a soldier and atone for the failure at West Point. He did not have to wait long to test his mettle. On August 29, 1839, just his third day of duty at Fort Andrews, Lewis and Company I had to fight off a lightning assault by forty probing Seminoles.[14] "Almost any small party that ventured too far from its base was open to attack," one historian wrote. "Native Americans attacked a number of regular army units as they gathered wood or escorted supply trains."[15] Having survived his first brush with combat, Lewis was delighted to take up staff roles as acting assistant quartermaster and acting assistant commissary of subsistence, fulfilling those duties for the next nine months until a new commander was assigned to relieve Taylor on May 5, 1840.

His name: Walker K. Armistead.[16]

This latest change in leadership structure brought howls of disapproval from both soldiers and local residents. "General Armistead assumes command . . . to the surprise of all, the mortification of many, and the distrust of not a few," an army captain declared. "What does the grey-bearded and imbecile dotard imagine he can do?"[17]

Another called Walker "puerile,"[18] and one irate citizen wrote to her brother that "Gen. Taylor has left Florida & turned over command to Gen. Armistead, who is no better than a clever old lady, yielding to anybody's opinion & turned from his purpose by every breath."[19]

No one was happier, however, than the new commander's starstruck son. Following a pattern set at West Point, Walker took great care to look after Lewis's well-being and give him chances far beyond his qualifications at the time. General Armistead even arranged for an appointment to a new regiment of dragoons "in favour of my son," although Lewis, curiously, declined it.[20] Instead, he was named as his father's aide-de-camp in May 1840 and moved with him to Fort King (in modern-day Ocala), remaining in that much more tolerable staff role for most of the next twelve months.[21] He would not face the terror of nightly patrols through muck and thickets.

The only disruption in service was a two-month reassignment to train recruits in New York. This occurred while Lewis was recovering from an illness contracted that summer in Florida's swamps. He spent August and September at Fort Columbus in New York Harbor, overseeing new volunteers for the war effort alongside two former West Point classmates and future Civil War generals who were also on recruiting duty, Joseph Hooker and Braxton Bragg.[22] In September, Lewis was assigned to command "Company B of Recruits for General Service" and later that month was on his way to Tampa "with recruits for the 6th Infty." By late October, he was back with his father, "attached to General Armistead's staff, HQ, Army of Florida."[23]

Walker's tenure in command was not as unsuccessful as some in the army had feared, although he could not strike a final, decisive blow to end hostilities.[24] The Seminoles had fewer than one thousand active fighters but remained a surprisingly indomitable foe that year, launching brazen strikes and killing fourteen U.S. soldiers in one month alone (as well as three members of a traveling Shakespearean troupe while stealing many of their costumes to be used for deception in future attacks).[25] Like Jesup and others before him, Walker came to realize that his opponents could never be completely removed from the peninsula.

He agreed to meetings with several chiefs under flags of truce in an attempt to find a resolution, with aide-de-camp Lewis at his side. In a letter to the U.S. secretary of war, Walker wrote,

> They expressed themselves desirous of peace and when told that it was the determination of the Government that they should leave Florida, expressed themselves unwilling to leave a country so well suited to their habits for one of which they know nothing. They begged for time to consider the matter and bring in all their people. I have promised to meet them at Fort King fourteen days from that time.[26]

This was the start of a series of hopeful but ultimately frustrating negotiations between Walker and the Seminoles. During each brief truce, the native warriors would cleverly delay their decision for a while, taking advantage of U.S. hospitality and gathering supplies.[27] Trying his best to end the conflict, Walker obtained government support for a temporary arrangement to allow the Seminoles to live south of a line from Tampa to New Smyrna without harassment. Operations were briefly suspended.[28] Then he even offered to bribe them.

"It is my candid opinion," he wrote,

that the war will not be renewed if the government will give or cede to them the portion of Florida embraced within the line formerly proposed. If such an arrangement could be made, the chiefs might afterwards be bought off.[29]

At various times over the next few months, exhausted bands of Seminoles, weary of this five-year game of cat and mouse, turned themselves in and agreed to move west.[30] By early February, Walker held almost three hundred Indians at Tampa for removal. Sensing increased momentum, he decided to try bribery again, requesting more than $50,000 in government funds for that purpose. Additional chiefs rolled in with their followers in exchange for $5,000 payments, but Walker's policy of halting operations during these periods rankled his subordinate commanders. A core group of obstinate Seminoles still refused to give in, and by May 1841, after a year in command, the general asked to be relieved.[31]

Walker by that time was fifty-eight years old and had served three tours of duty in the Florida swamps, contributing as much as any general to the U.S. war effort.[32] Although criticized for his inconsistent decision making, he had outperformed Scott and done no less than Jesup or Taylor under seemingly impossible conditions in an ill-conceived war. On the day he turned over command to Colonel William Worth, another veteran of the War of 1812, the Seminoles were a seriously degraded force, probably numbering no more than three hundred "fighting men."[33] The end, it seemed, was near.

Walker's departure had an immediate impact on the fortunes of his son, who was sent back to the ranks with Company I of the Sixth Infantry.

It was a dramatic change for Lewis, who had fought only one pitched battle in Florida before moving on to less dangerous staff positions. He was now commanding a company "in the field," trying to hunt the remaining Seminoles.[34] Worth's raiding parties gathered up forty-three more warriors and fought a large battle in the spring, but it was not long before the rising cost in lives and dollars made continuation of the war pointless. The United States called an end to hostilities on August 14, 1842, seven years after the fighting started, with several hundred unconquerable Seminoles still roaming the land. An official peace treaty was never signed (and, in fact, a Third Seminole War would be fought from 1855 to 1858).[35]

Much like his father, Lewis Armistead was not around for the finish in Florida. He received an early dismissal from the war in March 1842, when the Sixth Infantry was assigned to a starkly different environment at Fort Towson in modern-day Oklahoma.[36] There was irony in that the post had been established to protect the Choctaw Nation, which had also moved west against its will.[37]

But Lewis did not report immediately with the others. After three years of uninterrupted duty, he took leave for sixty days and extended it without permission, heading home to Upperville to relax with his family. It was not until August 10 that he arrived at Fort Towson to resume his role as second lieutenant with Company I.[38]

Although there were no alligators, thankfully—or swamps—he found himself at one of the most desolate outposts in the country, about as far from eastern civilization as one could image in the mid-nineteenth century. Fort Towson was located six miles north of the Red River and immediately south of Gates Creek, along the boundary with the Republic of Texas, which was still a sovereign territory and not yet part of the United States. To the west lay a craggy, ill-defined, and soon-to-be-disputed border with Mexico.[39]

Lieutenant Armistead and other officers lived in one-and-a-half-story log structures with limestone foundations on bluffs overlooking Gates Creek. They were charged with protecting a key U.S. transportation route along the Red River and defending the Choctaws from attacks by rival tribes, including the Comanches.[40] It was a bleak, mundane existence interrupted by occasional spasms of hunting, fishing, or Indian terror. Armistead, who also served as assistant acting quartermaster for the post, spent much of the next nineteen years on frontier duty such as this—one of the reasons he sought more than his share of furlough time to escape home to Virginia.

He was granted sixty days of leave on November 15, 1843,[41] but quickly realized it would not be enough for the drastic change of life he had in mind. Sometime on a previous visit home, he had become smitten with Cecilia Lee Love, a twenty-one-year-old descendant of the aristocratic Lee line of Virginia and great-granddaughter of the Revolutionary patriot Richard Henry Lee (and distant cousin of Robert E. Lee).[42] There is no record of how they met, although Armistead biographer Wayne Motts believes the connection may have been made by Cecilia's brother, John, who graduated from West Point in 1841 and was serving nearby in the Indian Territory while Lewis was at Towson.[43] But both families had been prominent in Virginia for centuries, and there were likely many other chances for their paths to cross.

The wedding date was set for February 13 at Lowndes County, Alabama, where Cecilia lived with her sister.[44] The burning question was whether Lewis could remain at home long enough to participate. His original leave expired in mid-January, and a recently granted extension added only thirty days until mid-February—not enough time for him to attend the ceremony and make the six-hundred-mile return trip to Fort Towson. As so often happened in these troubling situations, however, Lewis sought the advice and influence of his father, now serving in an administrative role with the Eighth Military Department at Fort Moultrie, South Carolina.

On January 12, Walker wrote to the adjutant general of the U.S. Army,

My son Lt. Lewis Armistead addressed you a letter on the 1st of the month requesting an extension of his leave of absence for sixty days. The cause for asking for this indulgence was to give him time to fulfill a matrimonial engagement, which will not take place until sometime in the next month. The thirty days now given will not enable him to join his post. Under the circumstances, I now request the indulgence may extend to sixty days, as this

will afford him time to make all his arrangements. His original leave from
General [Zachary] Taylor gave him permission to ask for this time.
    An [order] swiftly granting the indulgence will be conferring a favor
on him as well as myself.[45]

The extension was granted, of course, and Lewis and Cecilia were married before family and friends by her sister's husband, the Reverend William Johnson.[46] It had already been determined that Cecilia would remain in Alabama with the Johnson family while Lewis traveled back to his post at Fort Towson (although no one knew at the time that she became pregnant before he departed).[47] Their time together, as often happened in military marriages of this era, was exceedingly brief.

Lewis's return to the drudgery of frontier army life was brightened on March 30, 1844, when he was promoted to first lieutenant after almost five full years in the service.[48] The embarrassing stain of West Point was finally behind him, replaced by a solid résumé of service in the Second Seminole War and on the far reaches of Indian Territory. He took another brief leave late that summer, perhaps enough time to visit his now very pregnant wife in Alabama, but was back at Towson by mid-October,[49] when he made a personal connection that would last through the remainder of his life and military career.

One of the new arrivals on October 13, 1844, was a twenty-year-old recent graduate from West Point named Winfield Scott Hancock. The two men were part of small gathering of fifteen officers at the post and would have met almost immediately—the twenty-seven-year-old Armistead now second in command of Company I and the fresh-faced Hancock just learning the ropes with Company K.[50] It was the beginning of a long-term friendship that lasted almost twenty years, until Armistead led rebel troops against Hancock and the Union army in the most famous attack of the Civil War. For now, though, in the fall of 1844, they were newfound allies working their way through the military hierarchy and trying to survive the monotony and dangers of the frontier.

Armistead's life had another dramatic change in December when his wife gave birth to their first child, a son, on December 12 at Saint David's Parish in Alabama. They named him Walker Keith in honor of his grandfather.[51] This family tradition of passing first and middle names from one generation to the next had the potential to cause great confusion, however, because one of Lewis's siblings was also named Walker Keith (and went by Walker Jr). It was soon determined that the new arrival would go by W. Keith, or simply "Keith," to distinguish him from the others.[52]

An exasperated Lewis was not able to meet his son and reunite with his wife for another five months, until he was granted leave in May 1845. The normally arduous journey from Oklahoma to Alabama now became one of the most joyous of his life. He returned to his post at Fort Towson by midsummer, continuing as second in command of Company I,[53] then likely obtained another furlough in the fall following news of another, more solemn family event—his father's death on October 13, 1845.[54]

Walker had been battling illness for more than a year and took an unspecified leave of absence from Fort Moultrie in early 1845. On April 1, he wrote the adjutant general to announce, in the quaint military language of the time, "the honor of reporting myself on sick leave." He said he had consulted with "the best medical advisors" and that they had unanimously recommended "my absenting myself from command."[55] He was sixty-two years old and deteriorating rapidly following forty-plus years of service to his country, with one observer noting that his three recent stints in the Florida swamps had unquestionably "undermined his health."[56]

General Armistead spent the last six months of his life at home in Upperville, probably the longest extended period he had lived at the property since buying it in 1818. His brother-in-law, Edward Stanly, the once and future congressman, had the task of informing the military hierarchy of his death, writing separate letters to Adjutant General Roger Jones and Secretary of War William Marcy to provide details and funeral arrangements.

In his letter to General Jones, Stanly wrote,

> *I regret to inform you that your friend & Brother in arms, Brig Genl W.K. Armistead, died suddenly last night at 2 o'clock A.M.*
>
> *Tho' Genl Armistead was my brother in law, yet I must confess great ignorance of his military actions & of doubtless many things that should be*

recorded in his obituary. You have not only an intimate acquaintance with the Man but also of the Officer & I have written to request that you prepare his obituary. Should you do so, you will confer a favor on his family which they will be most happy to acknowledge.[57]

There is no record of a military ceremony at the small Armistead family cemetery at Ben Lomond, and no detailed obituary has ever been

Walker K. Armistead was buried in a small family cemetery on his Ben Lomond property in Fauquier County, Virginia. Today, it is part of privately owned farmland.
COLLEEN MCMILLAN PHOTOS

found. For all his career military achievements, Walker never came close to matching the fame of his brother, George, who had made the heroic two-day stand at the ramparts of Fort McHenry. Years later, after Walker's contemporaries were long gone and after many other memories had faded, it was left to an army historian to briefly eulogize the life of the third-ever graduate from West Point and one of the first brigadier generals in U.S. Army history:

General Armistead was not a brilliant man, but a brave, earnest and faithful soldier. He possessed a very kindly nature; was noted for his generous hospitality; and always conscientiously discharged every duty entrusted to his performance.[58]

Despondent over the death of his father, Lewis reacted the only way he knew—by throwing himself back into his work. In November 1845, he and young Hancock were transferred to Fort Washita, eighty miles west of Towson, forced to test their resilience once more at the outer limits of American-held territory. They were two of only seven officers on duty when they arrived. A history of frontier forts from this period notes that Washita was established four years earlier "by Zachary Taylor . . . in response to the pleas of the Chickasaw Indians for protection from marauding Texans and hostile Indians." It was here in December 1845 that Hancock signed his "P.S." on one of Armistead's letters to a mutual army friend. Lewis otherwise occupied himself by serving as assistant acting quartermaster but grew so tired of such duty—and the constant threats of Indian raids—that he arranged for a twenty-day leave on February 11, 1846.[59] He headed home to Virginia and never returned to Washita.

Lewis traveled to Ben Lomond and was joined there by young Keith and Cecilia, who was pregnant again. The army granted several extensions of leave, enabling them to live together as a family for the first time, and his next move was undetermined until war broke out with Mexico in May 1846. President James Polk called immediately for 50,000 volunteers, and Lewis was assigned to hometown recruiting duty in Upperville, hoping to help meet Virginia's quota.[60] He remained in that role long

Lewis Armistead and Winfield Hancock were part of a small group of U.S. Army officers serving together at Fort Washita in late 1845. On this monthly report from December, Armistead is listed third, Hancock sixth.

NATIONAL ARCHIVES AND ANCESTRY.COM

enough to witness the birth of his second child, a daughter, on June 26, named Flora Lee Love Armistead in honor of her mother's sister.[61]

Much as he enjoyed being home, however, the lure of a foreign conflict and the chance for battlefield glory were too much to overcome for a twenty-nine-year-old career soldier. Anxious to rejoin his unit, Lewis was instead assigned to deliver letters from the War Department to his former regimental commander, Zachary Taylor, now commanding U.S. forces near Monterrey, Mexico. Ben Lomond was located only fifty miles from army headquarters in Washington, D.C., and Armistead's familiarity with Taylor from previous service in Florida and on the frontier made him a logical choice for courier duty. By September 1846, he was off to war once again.[62]

It would not be long before Hancock joined him south of the border.

CHAPTER FOUR

Hancock Comes of Age

BENJAMIN FRANKLIN HANCOCK, A SCHOOLTEACHER AND CHURCH DEA-
con from Montgomery Square, Pennsylvania, had an inherent love of
historic names, so it came as no surprise that when his wife, Elizabeth,
gave birth to twin sons on February 14, 1824, they named one Winfield
Scott, after the preeminent U.S. soldier of the era, and the other Hilary
Baker, after the former mayor of Philadelphia and a delegate to the state's
constitutional convention in 1787.[1]

A third son, born six years later, was named John.[2]

Winfield and Hilary spent their earliest years in Montgomery
Square, near the small town of Lansdale, about twenty miles northwest
of Philadelphia. It was an idyllic rural setting, but Benjamin moved the
family three years later to another nearby village, Norristown in Montgomery County, where he began to read law and openly dreamed of his
young sons becoming attorneys. Hilary, the more studious of the two,
would follow their father's lead and open his own law practice, eventually
moving west and settling in Minnesota. Winfield would not.[3]

The twins were typically inseparable as children, but Winfield's
showmanship and love of military affairs set him apart. It was said that
as a ten-year-old, he led his "company" of junior militia on marches
through the neighborhood streets and was humiliated at one point when
his mother called him home from duty to wash the dishes.[4] "He was
always regarded as a leader among the boys at Norristown," a nineteenth-
century biographer wrote, and when it came time to organize the childhood militia unit, "he was at once selected, by common consent, to hold
the distinguished post of captain."[5] Household discipline aside, Elizabeth

Hancock supported her son's passion by sewing amateur uniforms with mimic army colors and procuring militia equipment, including a small drum and regimental flag. Her grandfather had been a captain under George Washington in the Revolutionary War, and her father, also a veteran of the Revolution, was taken prisoner by the British during the War of 1812.[6] Perhaps the military focus came naturally.

In 1839, when Winfield was fifteen years old, he was selected to read the Declaration of Independence at Norristown's Fourth of July celebration.[7] The pomp and circumstance included "the customary firing of cannon, the ringing of all the bells, the display of the national flag in prominent places, [and] the parade of volunteer soldiers, both adult and juvenile," and Hancock's involvement at such a young age was a nod to his growing reputation.[8] It was about this time that the region's elders began to discuss promoting him as a candidate for the U.S. Military Academy at West Point. A former U.S. congressman, John Sterigere, first broached the subject with Hancock's parents in early 1840 at their home on Airy Street, and an initially reluctant Benjamin (with Elizabeth's ardent support) agreed to approve.[9]

The application process required a letter of recommendation from the district's current congressman, Joseph Fornance, who, like Benjamin, was a member of the county bar and a staunch Democrat. On February 8, 1840, Fornance wrote to the U.S. secretary of war, Joel L. Poinsett, in Washington, D.C.,

> *I have been requested as a personal friend of B.F. Hancock of Norristown, Montgomery County, Pennsylvania to make application for the appointment of his son, Winfield Hancock, as a cadet to the West Point Academy. I am very well acquainted with the young man & believe that he possesses all the necessary qualifications under the rules of the department, but not being able to state specifically his several qualifications, I have requested his father to do so.[10]*

With that, Fornance turned responsibility over to Benjamin, who, despite his reservations, wrote to Poinsett six days later, on Winfield's sixteenth birthday. He had valid reasons for apprehension beyond his fatherly preference for a career in the law. Winfield would be the youngest student at the academy, if accepted, and the smallest in stature at five foot five. Nonetheless, Benjamin made his best case to the secretary, writing, in very lawyerly language,

> *In pursuance of the rules of the War Department on this subject, I herewith send you his qualifications for admission. . . . He arrived at the age of sixteen this month. He is five feet five inches high, well built and has a persevering mind—and is entirely free of any deformity, disease or infirmity, which would render him unfit for the military service, and from any disorder of an infectious or immoral character. He can read and write well and perform with facility and accuracy the various operations of the four ground rules of arithmetic, of reduction of simple and compound proportions and of vulgar and decimal fractions, so that he is well acquainted with all the rules of arithmetic, he has done something at mathematics, and has paid much attention to Natural Philosophy, Chemistry, Algebra, English Grammar, Geography and has been for some time past and is now engaged in learning Latin. . . .*
>
> *I am desirous to have my son admitted and I respectfully solicit for the application a favourable reception if the above shall be found satisfactory.*[11]

Although Winfield was not a natural scholar, he had, in fact, done well at Norristown Academy and a local high school, showing particular aptitude in geology, chemistry, electricity, and art. He built his own electric battery, experimented with nitrous oxide, and entertained fellow students with hilarious caricatures.[12] And yet admission to West Point was not guaranteed. Unlike his future friend Armistead, his father was not a brigadier general and his uncle not a U.S. congressman. Fornance wrote again to Poinsett on March 21, begging for the appointment—he actually used the word "beg"—and asserting that "there can be no objection to Winfield Hancock."[13] Three days later, the application was approved, and Winfield sent an acceptance letter on March 31 in impeccably stylish handwriting:

> *I have the honor to acknowledge the receipt of your communication of the 24th inst. (by the hands of the Honorable J. Fornance) in which you state the President of the United States has this day (24th inst.) conditionally appointed me a cadet in the service of the United States and requesting me*

to inform the War Department of my acceptance or non-acceptance. . . . In reply, I inform you that I accept the appointment and shall cheerfully comply with the rules of the Department relating thereto.

Your Most Obedient Humble Servant,
Win. Scott Hancock[14]

Benjamin added his consent at the bottom of the letter, albeit in less ornate script, noting that Winfield would commit to serve in the U.S. Army for eight years from the time of his admission "unless sooner discharged."[15]

After tying up some loose ends in Norristown and passing the obligatory entrance exam, young Hancock arrived at West Point on July 1, 1840[16]—beginning his army career twenty-three years to the day before the start of the Battle of Gettysburg.

Living away from his parents and twin brother for the first time, Winfield got off to a rocky start in the classroom, placing thirty-second out of fifty-four students during his first year on campus and earning a robust eighty-five demerits.[17] The low academic ranking was particularly galling because the Class of 1844 was one of the most lackluster in West Point history. More than half the members dropped out along the way, and only eight of twenty-five graduates served in the Civil War (five Union, three Confederate).[18] The most distinguished other than Hancock would be Alexander Hays, who led a brigade at Gettysburg; Alfred Pleasanton, commander of Union cavalry at Gettysburg; and Simon Buckner, the Confederate general who later served as governor of Kentucky. The top-ranked graduate, William G. Peck, spurned the army for civilian life and became a professor of mathematics, physics, engineering, and astronomy.[19]

Winfield's problems as a first-year student stemmed mostly from his age and lack of size, leaving him unable to keep up mentally or physically while prone to bursts of immaturity. "I developed late," he said in retrospect, "and at sixteen was too much of a boy, too full of life, to feel the importance of hard study. It would have been better if I had not entered until I was eighteen."[20] Older cadets often used the word "boy" when describing him as a plebe. "He entered at sixteen and looked even younger—a fair-haired, handsome boy," said Don Carlos Buell, who was

Norristown Pennsylvania
March 31 – 1840

Honorable J. R. Poinsett
Secretary of War.

Sir

I have the honor to acknowledge the receipt of your communication of the 24th inst (by the hands of the Honorable J. Fornance) in which you state the President of the United States has this day (24th inst) conditionally appointed me a cadet in the service of the United States &c. and requesting me to inform the War Department of my acceptance or non-acceptance of this Conditional appointment. In reply I inform you that I accept of the appointment and shall cheerfully comply with the rules of the Department relating thereto.

Your Most Obedient & Humble Servant

Win. Scott Hancock

I hereby consent to the above acceptance by my son Win Scott Hancock, and also assent to his signing articles by which he will bind himself to serve the United States eight years from the period he shall be admitted to the Military Academy unless sooner discharged.

March 31 1840

B. F. Hancock

Note that the future General Hancock signed his 1840 West Point acceptance letter as "Win" Scott Hancock.

three years ahead of Hancock at West Point.[21] William B. Franklin, a good friend from the preceding class, said he was "then a small boy scarcely of regulation height, very handsome, and at once became a pet."[22]

But Winfield persevered, overcoming his early challenges to become one of the school's most popular students and, before long, literally growing into a man—gaining seven inches in height to reach six feet by the time he left in 1844.[23] "No one ever outgrew that boyish condition sooner than he did," Franklin said, "and by the time I graduated in 1843, he was as manly a fellow as the Academy ever produced."[24] While catching up in physical stature, Hancock also met and interacted with an astonishing cadre of students during his time on campus, many of whom would go on to become prominent generals in the Civil War. Among those in classes just before or behind him were Ulysses S. Grant, George McClellan, James Longstreet, Thomas (soon to be "Stonewall") Jackson, A. P. Hill, Lafayette McLaws, John Reynolds, Fitz-John Porter, George Sykes, Israel Richardson, Abner Doubleday, Richard Garnett, Cadmus Wilcox, John Gibbon, Ambrose Burnside, and the man who would lead the charge against him in July 1863 at Gettysburg, George Pickett.[25]

Unsurprisingly, one historian called it West Point's "golden era."[26]

Natural competition between these type A personalities led to the occasional school yard scrap to settle differences. At one point during his senior year, Hancock squared off with an unidentified classmate and must have acquitted himself well because Orlando Willcox—a plebe that year and another future Union general—said that his "audacity and pluck on the occasion made him one of the few notables in a class not distinguished by men of character." The most pressing emotion among the spectators was "some alarm lest the authorities find out about it, and spoil the fun."[27] Earlier in his time on campus, however, probably in his second year, Hancock was bullied repeatedly by the much larger William Logan Crittenden and likely would have incurred a vicious beating had classmate Alexander Hays not intervened.

Hays and Hancock entered West Point in the same academic year, but Hays was twenty-one at the time, five years older than Hancock, and had already studied at Allegheny College in Meadville, Pennsylvania, north of Pittsburgh.[28] The strapping son of an Irish immigrant, Hays kept an eye on Hancock at all times, fulfilling the role of a protective older brother, and was aware that he was being treated "very meanly." The simmering feud between Hays and Crittenden led to one of the more spectacular bouts of fisticuffs in West Point history.

They met at a designated spot behind the Kosciuszko Monument and, according to legend, slugged it out for several hours. Witnesses (of whom Hancock certainly was one) said each man suffered fearful damage. One account had both fighters on the ground at the end, although Hays, by virtue of being able to rise to his feet, was declared the winner. But Crittenden "was so badly battered that he had to lie in bed for several days," and, as a result, he never harassed Hancock again.[29]

"When I was a boy I once had a difficulty," Hancock wrote years later, "and Alexander Hays was the first volunteer to assist me and in extracting me from my trouble become involved in aforesaid difficulty himself. I never forgot his generous action on that occasion."[30]

A calmer and more pleasant West Point memory came in the summer of 1843, when the esteemed General Winfield Scott made his annual trip to the New York campus. The purpose of Scott's visit was to assess the potential of the graduating class, but he also sought out several noted underclassmen, including the intriguingly named Winfield Scott Hancock. Scott examined the young man's record and background and was pleased to learn that Hancock was on track to graduate the next year. He had been embarrassed over the years, he said, because a number of his other namesakes "turned out to be great scamps."[31]

This is not to suggest in any way that Hancock excelled academically. He was an average student at best and benefited from the curious fact that his class lost twenty-nine cadets between his first and fourth years—an average of ten a year—which, merely by attrition, improved his class ranking, at least cosmetically. After finishing thirty-second out of fifty-four as a plebe, he was thirty-fifth out of forty-four in this second year, eighteenth out of thirty-four in his third year, and, finally, eighteenth out of twenty-five when he graduated. The only subjects where he ranked in the top ten were drawing, geology, and infantry tactics.[32] A fawning biographer wrote that "during the first two years in the institution, his habits of study appear not to have been so close and assiduous as they became during the last two,"[33] but Hancock's friend and future commander, William F. "Baldy" Smith, conceded years later that "his progress through the course of study was not conspicuous in any way."[34]

The most chilling effect of his low academic standing was that Hancock did not have the chance to select his preferred branch of army service. The top two or three students in each class at West Point automatically entered the corps of engineers, while others would choose (or be assigned to) the topographical engineers, ordnance, artillery, dragoons, and, at the bottom of the list, infantry. Having finished in the lower third of an unimpressive class, Hancock was dispatched to the infantry, entering as a "brevet" second lieutenant because there weren't enough full army commissions at the time to satisfy the entire class.[35]

Hancock graduated on July 1, 1844, and allegedly told General Scott that he wanted to be posted with the regiment "stationed farthest West."[36] Regardless of whether the story is true, he was indeed assigned to Fort Towson on the far southwestern border of the United States—as remote and forlorn a place as then existed in the country.

The nineteenth-century biographer Dr. Junkin wrote that "he sought such service from a desire to see the distant frontier, to roam over the prairies and through its passes and ravines, and to gain personal knowledge of the red men."[37] What Hancock actually thought when he arrived in Oklahoma on October 13, 1844, went unrecorded, but he soon became acquainted with Lewis Armistead, one of a small group of officers at the post. Although Armistead had resigned from West Point because of a "boyish frolic," he had a shared connection with the campus, had served in the army for five years, and was a combat veteran from the Florida swamps—all attributes that made him a natural mentor.

Not much of note happened at Fort Towson during their time there or at nearby Fort Washita, eighty miles away, where both men were transferred in November 1845. The tiny leadership corps at Washita consisted of just six officers, with Armistead serving as acting assistant quartermaster and Hancock as post adjutant.[38] They were together until mid-February 1846, when Armistead wrangled a leave of absence and returned home to Virginia just as war was breaking out with Mexico.[39]

46

After a brief stint on recruiting duty, he was off to the excitement of the front lines.

Hancock remained at Fort Washita, where, having just turned twenty-two years old, he was officially commissioned a second lieutenant and named commander of Company H on June 18.[40] He continued to serve in that capacity until January 1847, when he was attached to the recruiting service at Newport Barracks, Kentucky, despite a stated preference to join the war effort.[41] In March, he led a detachment of sixty recruits to Fort Scott in Missouri but was reassigned to desk duty in Kentucky as soon as the men shipped off to Mexico.[42] Longing for combat and battlefield glory, he was instead relegated to shuffling papers and filling out forms.

Records show that Hancock had aggressively angled to join the Mexican excursion for almost a year. As far back as June 30, 1846, he began a letter-writing campaign to the army's adjutant general to plead his case, at one point consenting to be transferred to another regiment as long as it was connected "to the army in Mexico."[43] But a miscommunication led to a temporary reassignment with a unit of mounted riflemen on the home front, and he was still not headed for the war.

"I did not understand it at the time," Hancock wrote on August 17, 1846, "[because] I wished to be transferred to another regiment *in the field* . . . I should not have accepted the offer."[44]

The army sorted out the mix-up, and Hancock remained in the Sixth Infantry, albeit on recruiting duty, still fuming at having to follow the war through news dispatches. After completing the mission to Fort Scott in the spring of 1847, he wrote to his commanding officer at Newport on May 8, asking to be relieved as a recruiter—in part because his original company had just been assigned to the Mexican combat zone:

> *I have the honor to request that I be ordered with my company ("K"), 6th Inf., which has been ordered to Mexico under Lt. (Thomas) Hendrickson, 1st Lieut. of the company. I am exceedingly anxious to go, as I have not been there, and by waiting I see no chance of getting there at all.*[45]

At about the same time, he wrote to his twin brother at home to express profound displeasure with the army's inertia:

My dear Hilary: I was exceedingly glad on my arrival [back at Newport] to find two long and interesting letters from you. The only thing that grieves me is that I cannot go to Mexico. I made an application to-day to join the army going to the front. Whether the adjutant-general will favor it or not, I do not know, but I think it doubtful. I am actively engaged as assistant superintendent of recruiting service of the western division, and acting as assistant inspector-general; but, though my services are said to useful, I still want to go to Mexico.

Your affectionate brother,
"Winfield"[46]

Hancock waited for more than two weeks, received no response from his commander, and then wrote in a fit of muffled rage to Adjutant General Roger Jones, making what likely was a last-gasp plea: "I have taken the liberty of forwarding for your consideration my written application to accompany Lieut. Hendrickson . . . to Mexico."[47] He sent the letter on May 25. Jones and army headquarters took less than a week to finally relent, ordering him south with a body of recruits and assigning him to rejoin the Sixth Infantry as soon as he arrived in Mexico. Several wistful accounts from the nineteenth century said that Winfield Scott specifically asked for Winfield Scott Hancock to be included, but they remain unproven and are probably apocryphal.

Whatever the reason, Hancock was headed to a battlefield for the first time in his career.

CHAPTER FIVE

Glory in Mexico

THE ANNEXATION OF THE INDEPENDENT REPUBLIC OF TEXAS BY THE United States on the symbolic day of July 4, 1845, brought with it a new wave of expansionist fervor.[1] President James Polk had his eye on acquiring two massive Mexican territories, New Mexico and Alta California, with the goal of extending America's western border from Texas to the Pacific Ocean. His only problem: Mexico wouldn't sell.[2]

Polk authorized a series of cash offers for as much as $30 million on the mistaken notion that Mexican officials would negotiate new borders and willingly part with half of their landmass for cash.[3] America's southern neighbor was already indignant that Texas had been lured into the union of states—calling it "an act of aggression, the most unjust which can be found recorded in the annals of modern history"—and diplomatic relations between the two countries broke off for good when the Mexicans refused to receive Polk's new envoy in December 1845. Responding to the snub, Polk sent Zachary Taylor's army of three thousand men to the banks of the Rio Grande, which the United States considered the dividing line between Texas and Mexico.[4] There is little doubt that he was trying to spark a border war.

The arrival of Taylor's "Army of Occupation" in early March 1846 infuriated the Mexicans, who believed the border was actually 130 miles north at the Nueces River.[5] They saw it as an invasion of their sovereign territory by a land-hungry foreign power. "We were sent to provoke a fight," wrote a young lieutenant in Taylor's army named Ulysses S. Grant, confirming what everyone suspected, "but it was essential that Mexico should commence it."[6] On April 25, 1846, a probing Mexican force on the disputed side of the Rio Grande ambushed two squadrons of dragoons, killing sixteen U.S. soldiers and taking more than forty prisoners. The next day, in a bluntly worded dispatch to army headquarters, Taylor reported that "hostilities may now be considered as commenced."[7]

It took almost two weeks for the letter to make its way from Texas to the White House, but the news was exactly what Polk had wanted. After meeting with Adjutant General Roger Jones and convening a cabinet meeting on Saturday, May 9, he spent two days carefully crafting a war message to Congress that was delivered at noon on Monday, May 11.[8] In it, Polk addressed "the existing state of relations between the United States and Mexico . . . [and] the causes which led to the suspension of diplomatic intercourse between the two countries":[9]

> *Now, after reiterated menaces, Mexico has passed the boundary of the United States, has invaded our territory and shed American blood upon the American soil. She has proclaimed that hostilities have commenced, and that the two nations are now at war.*[10]

Congress officially declared war on May 11, the House passing the resolution by a 173–14 vote (with former president John Quincy Adams among the few dissenters) and the Senate by 40–2. Polk had correctly assessed that "the nation's blood was up."[11] Citizens poured into city centers and town squares to voice their support for the war effort, and tens of thousands of young men took it one step further by volunteering to shoulder arms. One writer thought the spectacle "made the heart of every true American swell with patriotic joy,"[12] and the *Daily Union* newspaper claimed unabashedly that "the whole country is roused to the most earnest and vigorous action."[13]

Lieutenant Lewis Armistead was still home on leave at Ben Lomond when hostilities broke out along the border. He was assigned at once to local recruiting duty at Upperville, where his most challenging task was turning away eager volunteers after the state's required supplement had been met and surpassed. Frustrated by the inactivity—and longing for the kind of battlefield accolades that had eluded him in the Second Seminole War—Lewis pestered his bosses for a return to his regular infantry unit at Fort Washita, where he assumed that the soldiers of Company I of the Sixth U.S. Infantry were preparing to ship off to Mexico. It must have startled him, then, in mid-September 1846, when he was summoned to army headquarters in Washington, D.C., and ordered instead to deliver government war dispatches to General Taylor.[14]

Armistead's daughter, Flora Lee Love, was less than three months old when he departed Ben Lomond for Mexico. He may have been troubled about leaving the family behind—again—but, perhaps in anticipation of a long absence, and having grown up in a slave-owning environment, he had purchased one of his late father's former slaves, a fifty-year-old woman named Maria, to help Cecilia care for the baby and twenty-one-month-old Keith.[15] The government-sanctioned journey to Monterrey took almost a month before Armistead and his small entourage pulled into Taylor's camp on October 11. The next day, Taylor wrote to an army friend at Port Isabel, Texas, that "Lt. Armsted [sic] reached here last night with despatches [sic] from Washington."[16]

Unfortunately for Taylor, the contents of the much-anticipated delivery were hopelessly out of date. The only significant news was that a proposal for peace talks from Secretary of State James Buchanan had been rejected again by the Mexicans, and the only advice was that the war should be "prosecuted with vigor"—hardly insightful to a general at the front. This was no fault of Armistead's, of course, and Taylor did not blame him for bringing little of "any importance," but the old man's mood was uncommonly downcast despite recent successes on the battlefields of Monterrey and Palo Alto. "At any rate," Taylor wrote in the same letter, "I see but little prospect of peace."[17]

Armistead's own disappointment at being assigned as a lowly courier soon gave way to the blood rush of arriving in a war zone. The irony, as he would learn later, is that his regular unit, Company I, never left the United States; had he returned to Fort Washita, he would have missed the conflict altogether. Armistead promptly fell in with the rest of the Sixth Infantry near Monterrey, spending at least part of his time with Company F and awaiting further instructions.[18] They lingered there until a change in command in late November, when the U.S. general in chief,

Winfield Scott, inherited much of Taylor's force with an eye toward seizing the Gulf coast city of Vera Cruz.[19]

Ciudad Veracruz—City of the True Cross—was the country's largest port and an alluring tactical beachhead to land troops for an overland march to Mexico City, some 250 miles away.[20] As far back as early October, Scott had written an operational plan titled "Vera Cruz and Its Castle," describing in detail the ten-thousand-man force required to succeed in such a maneuver.[21] He eventually drew troops from Taylor's preexisting army, including Armistead and the Sixth Infantry, who were serving in a division commanded by General William Worth. But Scott encountered several delays after arriving in the region shortly after Christmas, and his movement on Vera Cruz did not begin in earnest until early March 1847.[22]

He wanted it to be "the largest amphibious invasion yet attempted in history."[23] Scott's plans were again delayed by weather and logistical mishaps, and it was not until 5:30 p.m. on March 9 that the lead elements of Worth's division headed for the shore, disembarking from their surfboats when they reached shallow water and wading cautiously toward the beach.[24] Armistead and the others, including Grant, were startled by the lack of opposition fire. "The Mexicans were very kind to us," Grant wrote, "and threw no obstacles in the way of our landing except an occasional shot from their nearest fort."[25] The American flag was planted on the beach within ten minutes as exultant army bands back on the ships struck up "The Star-Spangled Banner."[26]

Scott soon determined that his best course of action was a siege of the city. A direct assault would come at too steep a price in lives lost at this point of the invasion.[27] It took him almost two weeks to prepare, digging trench lines, mobilizing artillery, and consulting with his young, impressive staff—including future Civil War generals Robert E. Lee, George G. Meade, Joseph E. Johnston, and Armistead's old West Point classmate, P. G. T. Beauregard.[28] When the enemy refused a demand for surrender on March 22, the United States lobbed its first mortar over the city's walls at 4:15 p.m. "From that moment on," wrote Cadmus Wilcox, another future Civil War general, "night and day, the firing continued without intermission."[29]

Over the next four days, a fierce array of U.S. guns hammered away at the city.[30] Armistead and the infantry could only sit and watch through the smoke and haze. According to one assessment, Scott's artillery fired 6,700 shots and shells at the beleaguered Mexican garrison, crumbling buildings and terrifying the populace. The formal capitulation took place on March 27, and "at 11:10 a.m. the American flag rose over the fortifications to a twenty-nine-gun salute by both the Army and the Navy."[31]

Scott's plan to take Vera Cruz had worked brilliantly, with the loss of only thirteen killed and fifty-five wounded, giving him an essential seaside foothold to launch his inland assault on Mexico City.[32]

Little did he know, in the euphoria of the moment, that it would take another six months to get there.

Scott and his staff debated several options for the route to the Mexican capital but settled on the same National Road that Hernan Cortes took to conquer the Aztecs in 1519. He knew there would be necessary stops and no doubt constant harassment from Mexican soldiers and bandits.[33]

He did *not* know there would be so many other obstacles to cause delays, including a shortage of transportation and the temporary downsizing of his army because of expiring short-term volunteer enlistments.[34] But on he went.

Worth's division missed the first minor conflict of the inland invasion, an American victory at the Battle of Cerro Gordo on April 17–18.[35] Armistead and the others formed a reserve force that observed from a safe distance as the Mexicans retreated. After passing Jalapa and Perote's castle, Worth led the way to Puebla, still almost one hundred miles from Mexico City, arriving on May 15 and remaining for almost three months. A frustrated Scott had few options available while he waited for reinforcements to replace departing volunteers. They came in small waves over the summer, but it was not until August 6, when General Franklin Pierce reported with 2,400 additional troops, that he felt confident enough to cut ties with his supply line and begin an all-out drive toward the Mexican capital.[36]

As fate would have it, one of the new arrivals under Pierce was a young second lieutenant from the recruiting service named Winfield Scott Hancock.

Freed from administrative duty by his letter-writing campaign, Hancock had left Newport Barracks with a group of seventy-three recruits on June 21 and traveled via New Orleans to the U.S. beachhead at Vera Cruz.[37] There, he connected with the Twelfth Infantry regiment under Pierce for the treacherous march to Puebla, fighting "several skirmishes" along the route.[38] As previously planned, Hancock rejoined the Sixth Regiment when Pierce's men pulled into Puebla on August 6. There was time only for a brief reunion with Armistead and his other comrades before Scott began the next phase of the campaign.[39]

Worth's division, with Armistead and Hancock, stepped off at "about sunrise" on August 9.[40] It was sometime in the next week that they drew within sight of the soaring towers of Mexico City—maybe twenty-five miles away—and caught their first glimpse of the defending army of General Antonio Lopez de Santa Anna. Scott moved his force of four divisions deliberately toward the capital over the next week and a half with an eye toward reducing Mexican garrisons at the towns of Contreras and Churubusco and the "hacienda of San Antonio." By August 20, he was ready for these preliminary attacks after Robert E. Lee had devised a way to move troops through the edge of a seemingly impassable lava field known as the Pedregal.[41]

One segment of the U.S. Army pushed through Contreras in the morning and punished defenders at San Antonio, causing them to flee in confusion, racing back toward the safety of the capital. Worth's role was to cut off the retreat.[42] Eager for the glory that had so far eluded him in the war, Worth sent Newman Clarke's brigade, with the Fifth, Sixth, and Eighth infantries, storming ahead on the road to Churubusco without conducting a reconnaissance. Armistead, Hancock, and their regiment were second in line as they approached the strongly defended *tete-de-pont*, a fortified bridgehead at the entrance to the town over the Rio Churubusco.[43]

The fighting here was vicious. Much of Clarke's brigade skirted to the right to attack the bridge by flank, but the Sixth was tasked with plowing straight ahead along the main road. As Cadmus Wilcox remembered it, "The Sixth Infantry charged down the causeway as ordered, Lieut. Lewis A. Armistead at the head of the leading platoon."[44] Armistead had fought several times against Indians using guerilla tactics in the Second Seminole War, but this was his first experience facing a well-drilled foreign army in extended face-to-face combat. It made an indelible impression, as Armistead described in detail later:

> We were formed soon after entering the road [facing the tete-de-pont]. I was in command of the second platoon of the Colour Company. The Regiment was then formed in Column of platoons left in front and we advanced at a very rapid gate, a portion of the Enemy having evidently retreated on that road. We advanced in this way until we came to a small bridge near this end of the little village [Churubusco], about 700 yards from the Enemy's work. . . . I saw Captain [William] Hoffman a little in advance on the right of the road, apparently forming some men. He appeared to abandon whatever was his object & came near to where I was & ordered us forward. From the men in front having fallen to the left, my platoon became the leading platoon.[45]

Captain Hoffman credited Armistead with performing "gallantly" at the head of the "front platoon,"[46] but the troops all around him began to waver as relentless Mexican fire took its toll. Santa Anna's men beat back several forays toward the *tete-de-pont*, fighting gallantly in their own right, forcing the Sixth to retreat "butt-end first" on two occasions.[47] It was about this time that Hoffman directed Armistead and a small contingent of other men into the apparent safety of a cornfield to the right of the road. Soon, however, more Mexican musketry would pin them down. "The corn was very thick," Armistead said,

> and it was difficult to keep them together. I advanced to the right & front and after going some 30 yds, I found I had only some 3 or 4 men with me. I laid down and ordered them to lay down, at the edge of the corn, there being an open space beyond. I thought that when the rest of the regiment came on, we would join them, my object being to protect myself & men.[48]

A messenger eventually found Armistead, and his few companions hunched among the cornstalks, ordering them to join company commander William H. T. Walker a short distance ahead. But Walker was in no safer spot than Armistead had been, stranded hopelessly in the corn "with the colours and some 6 to 8 men."[49] The two junior officers held out for maybe ten minutes before determining that their best hope was to fall back about 150 yards in an attempt to find the rest of the regiment. Reforming behind "a small adobe house,"[50] as Armistead remembered it, the Sixth then mustered a determined third attack and, joined by the Fifth and Eighth Regiments, finally captured the bridge and the *tete-de-pont*.[51]

Much is known about Armistead's role at Churubusco because he testified in great detail at court-martial proceedings for a fellow officer later that year. But Hancock was also actively involved in the attack, serving in an adjacent platoon to Armistead and taking temporary command after its leader was injured. He suffered a slight contusion when a musket ball skimmed his knee and yet kept up his advance, writing later to his father about "the theatre of a sanguinary battle."[52]

The victory was a costly one for the Americans, with 133 killed and 865 wounded out of 8,497 engaged, but the day, in retrospect, had been a roaring success, demoralizing the Mexicans and shoving them back inside the walls of the capital.[53]

Armistead's performance under fire had been the greatest of his military career, earning plaudits from three of his superior officers for "leading on gallantly," "leading the charge," and behaving "in the handsomest manner." Major Benjamin Bonneville referred to Armistead and a handful of others when he wrote, "I cannot speak of them too highly to the general commanding on this important and brilliant occasion."[54] The impact was not lost on Generals Scott or Worth, who singled out the former West Point miscreant for "gallant and meritorious conduct at the battles of Contreras and Churubusco" and awarded him a brevet to captain, effective August 20, 1847.[55] More than ten years after resigning from the academy in shame, the son of the late brigadier general and nephew of the hero of Fort McHenry had become a professional soldier worthy of the family name.

Although greatly overshadowed, Hancock also drew praise from senior officers, including Hoffman and Clarke, and won a brevet to first lieutenant in the first pitched battle of his career.[56]

The brief armistice between Scott and Santa Anna in the aftermath of Churubusco was a decision Scott came to regret. He agreed to a cease-fire on August 22 in the hope of a negotiated settlement—"too much blood has already been shed in this unnatural war between the two great republics of this continent," Scott wrote—but he soon realized the Mexicans had duped him, strengthening their fortifications in blatant violation of the truce. On September 6, he sent a terse note to Santa Anna that the hostilities would resume at noon the next day. On September 7, he made good on his promise.[57]

Although still not ready for a grand assault on Mexico City, Scott's short-term target was Molino del Rey (the "King's Mill"), a rambling series of low stone buildings about one thousand yards west of Chapultepec castle. Rumor had it that a foundry there was being used to melt church bells into cannons for a dramatic final stand in defense of the capital. He also learned that large quantities of gunpowder were being stored at Casa Mata nearby.[58] "I resolved, at once, to drive him early the next morning, to seize the powder, and to destroy the foundry," Scott wrote, "leaving the general plan of attack upon the city [to be developed after] full reconnoissances."[59]

Scott did not believe the Molino was heavily defended and therefore assigned just one division—Worth's, which was camped nearby—to mount what he thought would be a relatively routine attack. He couldn't have been more mistaken. Although the Americans took the position within two hours after Worth stepped off on the morning of September 8, they did it while suffering heavy casualties, paying an enormous price for minimal gains in territory—especially after finding no foundry in operation at the site.[60]

Worth arranged for a multipronged attack from all directions, with Clarke's brigade storming Casa Mata on the left.[61] Armistead commanded the lead color company and charged under withering fire to a "bank of earth thrown up out of a ditch which I have since understood was 30 yds. from the Enemy's work."[62] Although pinned down and outnumbered, the men around him engaged in a bloody firefight with desperate Mexican regiments posted behind stone walls and other formidable cover. Armistead said later that he was both emboldened and astonished by the stance of his fellow troops:

The men near me all behaved with remarkable coolness, encouraging and jesting with one another. The fire there was pretty heavy, as heavy as anywhere along the line, I suppose from the fact of the colours generally drawing fire. As an evidence of their coolness, the men would lay down while loading, & when ready to fire would wait for the smoke to clear away or bring down the musket until they could get a good sight. The men around me must have fired from 15 to 18 rounds. . . .

    I will mention another fact to show there was no panic among the men. . . . While retiring, and without any orders that I heard, the men began to rally & form upon the colours while still under the fire of the enemy.[63]

American resilience prevailed in the end, and it was still only mid-morning when Armistead, Hancock, and other stouthearted troops swarmed in victory over the Molino and Casa Mata. But the price for such a strategically hollow victory had been steep. Worth's division suffered 789 casualties out of 3,400 engaged, almost 25 percent, with 116 killed outright.[64] "Sad and melancholy are the events of this day," wrote a lieutenant in the Sixth Regiment. "It was awful!"[65]

Armistead, for his part, won another brevet "for gallant and meritorious" service, this time to the rank of major, for his fearless charge into the teeth of enemy fire.[66] Hancock received no citations for his work but gained more hard-earned combat experience in just his second battle.

Scott took three more days to examine the ground, debating the best route to seize the capital city. It was not until September 11 that he settled on a bold plan to attack Chapultepec, an imposing stone-walled citadel sitting high above the metropolis on its western edge. Many of his top subordinates and engineers, including Lee, had argued for a seemingly less risky assault from the south, but Scott thought Chapultepec was the key position to be taken. Scott ended their decisive war council with one of the most fateful direct orders in American military history: "Gentlemen, we will attack by the western gates."[67]

Chapultepec, home of the Mexican military academy, rose almost menacingly above the valley floor. The soaring height included steep, foreboding hills, "fortified by nature and art," with "nearly precipitous" slopes on three sides[68]—and with a "ten-foot-deep ditch or moat designed to impede the advance of infantry."[69] It might have been impenetrable if well defended. Fortunately for the Americans, Santa Anna could only guess about the direction of their attack and was forced to spread his troops across the city to cover various contingencies. That left a small contingent of 260 troops inside the castle itself and just 600 others defending the walls outside, some of them perched perilously in trees.[70]

Scott's naive hope was that he could reduce the position by artillery fire alone, saving many lives. Accordingly, the American guns opened at 5:00 a.m. on September 12, pounding away at the castle, knocking chunks out of the walls, and partially destroying the roof. But Mexican engineers scrambled to make quick repairs, and the castle defenders, including some "young boys of the College," held their ground.[71] Despite the fury of the U.S. shot and shell, it soon became apparent to Scott that an all-out infantry assault would be required to settle the matter, and he arranged for two divisions to move on Chapultepec the next morning from the relatively gentler slope on the west.

It is here, from a historical perspective, that we should pause to reflect on the astonishing number of Civil War commanders from both sides who served together as Americans at Chapultepec. These included Armistead, Lee, Pickett, Beauregard, Wilcox, Johnston, James Longstreet, Thomas J. Jackson, Edward Johnson, Barnard Bee, and John Magruder from the future Confederacy and Grant, John Reynolds, John Geary, Henry Hunt, Fitz-John Porter, John Sedgwick, Jesse Reno, and Joe Hooker from the Union. Hancock was there but fell ill just before the battle. In a chilling reflection years later, Grant said he considered the Mexico campaign "a conspiracy to acquire territory out of which slave states might be formed for the American Union" and that "the Southern rebellion was largely the outgrowth of the Mexican war."[72]

Scott remained unsure about the strength of his attack plan and wanted two storming parties of 260 men each to lead the way. Armistead, still thirsting for glory in the family tradition—and emboldened by two brevets for gallantry won at previous battles that summer—raised his hand to volunteer. The task for the advance guard was to break through the enemy's defenses while carrying scaling ladders that could be positioned later to hoist troops over the castle's outer walls. It was decidedly dangerous work, considered a "forlorn hope" in the army's terminology of the time, but Scott's ranks overflowed with men such as Armistead who saw the rare chance for promotion and immortality.[73]

Captain Samuel Mackenzie led the storming party and selected Armistead as one of his four company commanders.[74] In this role, the nephew of the hero of Fort McHenry would be at the vanguard one of the most famous military missions in U.S. history, stepping off on September 13, 1847—thirty-three years to the day after the British began their attack on Baltimore harbor. Armistead and his men moved out at about 8:00 a.m., following a two-hour bombardment to soften the Mexican defenses and a preliminary probing mission by Joseph E. Johnston's regiment of Voltigeurs.[75] They passed first over flat, marshy ground and through a grove of cypress trees that one soldier said had been "planted by the kings of Tenochtitlan and Texcoco in the days of their grandeur, power and glory."[76]

"The hill was reported to me to be a continuous slope," McKenzie would recall,

affording no cover from the enemy's fire; and this determined me to place my reliance upon a steady and rapid advance, using the bayonet only. . . . My battalion formed in line of battle at the foot of the hill, with ladders, etc., close in the rear, and moved up in as good order as the ground [now found to be rocky and broken] would permit.[77]

Johnston's men had not pushed the enemy as far as expected, however, and members of the storming party took cover with the Voltigeurs among rocks and depressions in the slope. Bullets flew in torrents. The momentum of the attack was starting to fade, as was, perhaps with it, the outcome of the day, until Armistead and other company commanders rose to lead a second American wave. As Mackenzie reported,

The officers . . . by great exertions got many forward, carrying with them also some of the light troops. The ditch was thus reached, [Lieutenant Armistead being the first to leap into it] through the fire of artillery, musketry, and the hand grenades of the enemy; the ladders were applied, and one of the salients of the work carried. The enemy, overcome and flying from this point, offered afterwards no resistance worthy of being mentioned.[78]

The result of this part of the battle may not have been as swift and neat as Mackenzie remembered, but Armistead's role in a crucial part of the action was unquestioned—and witnessed by many. "The ditch was at length reached," Cadmus Wilcox wrote, "Lieut. Lewis Armistead, Sixth Infantry, being the first to leap into it under artillery and musketry fire."[79] Two of the storming party's other company commanders were cut down by Mexican muskets as they clambered up the ladders and attempted to scale the wall, adding to the frightening list of casualties.[80] But Armistead continued on despite a slight wound of his own and was remembered by P. G. T. Beauregard as one of the first dozen or so U.S. soldiers to set foot inside the castle grounds.[81] Simon B. Buckner, a junior officer from the same regiment, recalled seeing the striking figure of "Lieut. Armistead of the 6th Infantry standing on the angle of the work," trying to exhort others to come forward.[82]

Armistead had a role in planting the regimental colors at Chapultepec,[83] and yet he still had much work to do in the U.S. mop-up effort—a necessary but dangerous task with many Mexican troops still armed and on the run. The Americans used two causeways to approach the capital and subdue the remnants of Santa Anna's much-weakened force.[84] Sporadic fighting continued through the afternoon. Watching in horror as U.S. forces swept over the supposedly impregnable castle walls, the defeated general exclaimed, "I believe if we were to plant our batteries in Hell the damned Yankees would take them from us."[85]

Hancock, though he was too ill to participate, experienced the thrill of victory from his sickbed and beyond, as he described to his twin brother, Hilary, in a letter after the battle:

I shall always be sorry that I was absent. I was laying ill with chills and fever, directly under the fort, at the time the action began. I could not remain under the firing; but, wrapping my blanket about me, I crept to the top of the roof of the nearest house, watched the fight, and had strength enough to cheer with the boys when the Castle fell. The balls whizzed around me, but I kept my post, doing what I could; and I when I learned that the colors I saw hoisted on the conquered walls were those of my own regiment, my heart beat quick at the glorious sight.[86]

The next day was more of a formality as unopposed American troops entered Mexico City proper, hoisting the Star-Spangled Banner in triumph over the National Palace at 7:00 a.m.[87] It was now September 14, thirty-three years to the day—and almost to the moment—that Francis Scott Key had seen that "our flag was still there." This was the first U.S. war fought predominantly on foreign soil and the first since the "Stars and Stripes" had been designated the official banner of the armed forces. One exhausted Pennsylvania teenage soldier wrote in his diary that it was "a proud and gratifying sight to us poor, used-up boys, who have left home and country and everything dear, to witness this sight."[88]

Scott's army "occupied" Mexico for the next nine months while the two sides haggled over a peace treaty.

Reinforcements still poured across the border during this period, including eager young officers from the West Point Class of 1847—one of them a second lieutenant named Henry Heth, who was a distant relative of Armistead's.

Writing long afterward in his memoirs, Heth lamented that "when my class reached Mexico, the war was [essentially] over,"[89] but he still enjoyed the experience of his only foreign service in a company under Armistead's command. "I reported to dear old Lewis, a kinsman of mine," Heth remembered, "and I found several officers I knew well in the Sixth Infantry."[90] One of those was Hancock, who served in the same company and with whom he became particularly close.[91] Armistead, Hancock, and Heth became regular messmates in Mexico City and throughout the rest of the campaign.

"Never was a mess happier than ours," Heth wrote:[92]

Armistead was a good-natured man, and I am afraid we teased him too much. Hancock had a joke on him which he often related to the officers. Armistead was the carver. Hancock said, "When we had a turkey, chicken or duck for dinner, Lewis would give us a very small piece and then say, 'Boys, I will take the carcass.'"[93]

In the absence of any serious fighting during the occupation period, the men took time to tour the countryside. While near Toluca in early

1848, Armistead, Hancock, and a group of others, including Buckner and Ralph Kirkham of the Sixth, climbed the highest peak overlooking the vast valley. "The height is about 2,000 feet above the city," Kirkham wrote in his diary on February 12, "and the view is very extensive and it is really magnificent. We propose forming a party and going up to the snow mountain which lies some fifteen or twenty miles off." The snow mountain described here, Nevado de Toluca, rises 14,900 feet above sea level, but there is no record of whether they ever made it before the army moved on to Tacubaya.[94]

In the meantime, negotiators for the two neighboring countries had worked out a preliminary settlement to end the war. For the tidy sum of $15 million (plus the assumption of some Mexican debts), the United States would acquire the vast territories of New Mexico and California, a massive expansion of 529,000 acres that extended the national boundary from the former Republic of Texas to the Pacific Ocean. Mexico also had grudgingly agreed to the long-disputed Rio Grande boundary line. The Treaty of Guadalupe Hidalgo, which included all those terms, was signed on February 2, 1848, and forwarded to both governments for formal ratification.[95]

It took time. After much emotional debate—some loud voices in the United States questioned the morality of seizing another country's territory by war and fretted about the impact of slavery on the new territories—the treaty was ratified by Congress on March 10 and by Mexico on May 30. The last U.S. troops on Mexican soil were from Worth's division and the Sixth Infantry Regiment,[96] among them Armistead and Hancock.

Lieutenant Kirkham described the moment of departure from Mexico City, capturing in his diary a solemn early juncture of American history:

> Today [June 12, 1848] the last of our army left the city of the Aztecs. Our division was formed in the grand plaza at 5 o'clock in the morning. At six, our flag flying on the national palace was saluted by thirty guns from [a U.S.] battery and twenty-one from a Mexican battery. As our colors were lowered, the bands of the different regiments played "The Star-Spangled Banner."[97]

The war was over. Ulysses S. Grant would forever consider it "one of the most unjust ever waged by a stronger against a weaker nation."[98] Another veteran thought he had taken part in "the great event—the epoch—of the 19th century."[99] Little did any of them realize that an even greater epoch would break out thirteen years later, sowing sectional conflict over slavery, pitting members of this grandly victorious U.S. Army against one another in a fight for the country's soul.

CHAPTER SIX

Unimaginable Sadness

THE BRIEF PEACETIME ERA THAT FOLLOWED THE MEXICAN WAR WAS supposed to be a time of rest and revitalization, especially for a soldier who had fought back-to-back wars for six years and distinguished himself on numerous foreign battlefields. But it wasn't to be for Lewis Armistead.

He entered a period of almost unimaginable grief between 1850 and 1855, losing two wives and two children to disease on the frontier and learning that his widowed mother's estate back in Upperville had been destroyed by fire. Armistead took extended leaves of absence to deal with the tragedies, settle his affairs, and try to piece his life back together before it fell apart again. There can be little doubt why a man already hardened by war became even more sullen and bitter, existing in a state where "pain and suffering seemed almost a permanent condition."[1]

The postwar ordeal began with a personal medical challenge after returning from Mexico in the fall of 1848. Assigned to a seemingly stress-free desk job as a recruiter in Louisville, Kentucky,[2] Armistead was diagnosed in November with erysipelas, a fearful-looking bacterial infection that affects the upper layers of skin. The degenerative disease was considered far more serious in the mid-nineteenth century than it is today, when it can be treated with penicillin, and Armistead's physician, Dr. Llewellyn Powell, called in a surgeon "to remove the diseased flesh" from the patient's left arm.[3] Powell reported to army headquarters that the condition "endangered his life and affected extensive destruction of the cellular tissue of the limb."[4] Armistead's commander with the recruiting service, Brevet Colonel C. A. Waite, wrote in April 1849 that "I believe the probabilities are he will never recover the entire use of his left arm."[5]

Armistead was confined to bed for "almost four months,"[6] dealing with high fever, chills, malaise, and debilitating pain after surgery.[7] "My case was an extreme one," he wrote, "resulting no doubt from exposure in Mexico."[8] Regular citizens could contract the bacteria through simple cuts or abrasions, and soldiers were at even more risk because of wounds suffered in battle. Armistead recovered slowly and was still not back to full strength when Powell released him in April, prompting army officials to advise an extended leave of absence. "I have reason to believe that many months must elapse before his health will be re-established," Waite wrote."[9]

Armistead was granted a six-month leave and returned to Upperville that summer, reuniting at long last with his wife, Cecilia, and two young children, Keith and Flora. The time on the home front was a welcome respite, though he found himself battling with headquarters over the reimbursement of medical expenses. Writing in October 1849 to Adjutant General Roger Jones in Washington, Armistead complained that "I have always, as the records in your office will show, exposed myself cheerfully, & fearlessly, to dangers of all kinds, looking to the Government, if not for reward, at least for my Doctor's bill."[10] There is no record, however, that any of his other expenses were repaid.

The army was at least more understanding of his need for time to recover, and Armistead did not return to active duty until February 1850, when he reported with his family to Jefferson Barracks in Missouri.[11] Amazingly, despite earlier concerns to the contrary, there was no apparent long-term impact on the use or appearance of his left arm. Dr. Powell had done his job well.

Less than a month after arriving in the St. Louis area and settling his family into living quarters, Brevet Major Armistead was sent away on detached service to check on hostile Indians in neighboring Iowa.[12] He was once again separated from Cecilia and the children. Other than his recent stint at home on a medical leave of absence while recuperating from erysipelas, they had spent precious little time together since Lewis left for the Mexican War in September 1846.

He barely even knew his daughter, born only months before the war and now almost four years old. Imagine his shock and horror, then, when he returned to Jefferson Barracks in early May and learned that little Flora had contracted an illness and died suddenly on April 29. No cause of death was ever recorded, but it was probably from the vicious cholera epidemic that tore through the post and nearby St. Louis in 1849 and 1850.[13] Flora Love Armistead was buried with other victims at Jefferson Barracks National Cemetery, where her tiny tombstone remains legible today.

Given the cold, random nature of army reassignments, Lewis had less than two weeks to mourn his daughter's death before he was transferred to Fort Snelling in the Minnesota Territory near modern-day Minneapolis.[14] Cecilia's mother made the long trek from Alabama to join the grieving family on the frontier and was listed as an Armistead dependent in the 1850 Fort Snelling census, filed in late September.[15] Her arrival was fortuitous, not only to help Cecilia care for young Keith at an emotional time but also because Lewis was sent away on detached service, dispatched in September to Fort Clarke in Iowa, a distance of roughly two hundred miles.[16] His wife, son, and mother-in-law remained behind at Snelling.

Lewis had not yet completed his assignment or returned to the post when tragedy struck again, as Cecilia fell gravely ill in December 1850—most likely contracting a case of cholera, which was now the scourge of outpost army life. Although her official cause of death was never identified, Cecilia passed away on December 12, the same day as Keith's sixth birthday, leaving the young family in shambles. Suddenly a widower at age thirty-three, Lewis hurried back to Snelling and helped Cecilia's mother send the body home to Alabama, where she was buried in Magnolia Cemetery in Mobile. Her tombstone was carved in the shape of a cross, with a simple inscription reading

CECILIA L. ARMISTEAD
Died December 12, 1850
Aged 27 years & 10 months
Even so Father, for so it seemed good in thy sight[17]

Unfathomably, Lewis was forced to leave Keith in the care of others while resuming his regular army duties, including a stint "in pursuit of Indians" in March, until returning to Fort Clarke on April 13, 1851.[18] It was on that day that he wrote to General Jones to request a four-month leave of absence "in consequence of a severe domestic affliction," wishing to "make some provision for an only child."[19] The leave was granted, but not until June 30.[20] Only then could Lewis head home to Virginia, traversing roughly a thousand miles with a six-year-old in tow, to place Keith in the custody of his grandmother at Upperville.

He reported back to Fort Dodge on November 15, rejoining his company for winter on the Great Plains and taking temporary command of the post in early 1852.[21] By this time, however, he had become a changed man, demonstrably more angry and bitter. A soldier who served with him in Iowa wrote that "the Officers, all with the exception of one Majr. Armistead were very gentlemanly and good officers. Majr. Armistead was very rough and tyrannical with the men [and] he was very severe and unreasonable, which rendered him very unpopular with both officers and men."[22] Such criticism was likely made without the knowledge of Armistead's personal hardships, which were about to become even worse—if that were possible.

In June 1852, word arrived that the Ben Lomond property had been ravaged by fire, destroying the main house and many of the family's belongings.[23] His widowed mother had made it out unharmed, along with Keith and Lewis's younger siblings—there were no reported injuries to anyone involved—but the psychological damage was immense. Lewis had no choice but to request another leave to attend to the problems at home, and on August 1, he wrote to headquarters asking for a minimum of sixty days, with a chance to extend it to four months:

My father's estate was left in an unsettled condition and from mismanagement is still in a very unsatisfactory state—to add to this the family residence has lately been burnt with all the furniture, etc. I think I could be of some service to my mother & to the younger children of the family if at home. My own affairs require attention, and as I will be absent during that season of

the year when it is not practicable to perform in this climate much, if any,
military service, I hope the above application will be fairly considered.[24]

The army reviewed Lewis's situation and granted him leave on October 18, 1852, but it would be much longer than expected—almost nine full months—before he returned to active duty in mid-July 1853.[25]

The only good news during this calamitous period for the family came when Lewis's younger brother, Franck, received an at-large appointment to the U.S. Military Academy at West Point in the spring of 1852.[26]

Elizabeth Armistead had made it a priority since the death of her husband seven years earlier to have another son attend West Point. She thought it would honor the legacy of Walker Sr., one of the school's earliest graduates in 1803—especially after Lewis had been forced to resign in disgrace—but the goal was not easily achieved.

The family's first nominee was Walker Jr., a young man of great promise, who was seventeen years old when he applied in 1848.[27] He had followed the same path as Lewis to that point in his life, attending the preparatory school at Georgetown for two years to hone his academic skills and improve his study habits.[28] Walker's bid for an appointment included recommendations from state and local dignitaries, one of whom wrote that he "invariably conducted himself in a gentlemanly manner" and all of whom mentioned in some form that he was the "son of the late Genl. Armistead."[29]

This was part of a strategic effort by Elizabeth to broaden Walker's appeal. The president of Georgetown College reported that "his application to his studies is laudable and his standing in his respective classes is good." A local legislator tugged at heartstrings by noting that Walker's father spent his "entire life in the military service of the country . . . but, though an officer and gentlemen of merit & distinction, died poor."[30] Elizabeth herself wrote to the army's chief engineer, General Joseph Totten, one of Walker Sr.'s contemporaries, passing on a letter signed by eleven Virginia politicians but worrying that it still might not be enough. "Do you think it justified that I should obtain the names of the other members of the

Virginia Delegation?" she inquired of Totten, all the while reminding him that her daughter, Lucinda, "sends her love to her Father's old friend."[31]

More letters came rolling in—all glowing in their praise, most invoking the memory of "Genl. A."—but it seemed to matter little. Despite the impressive backing, Walker Jr. was rejected.

The family's hope then fell to Franck, the third-oldest son, born in 1835.[32] His first application came in 1850, when he was just fifteen years old, and included a remarkable letter from his mother to the president of the United States, Zachary Taylor—another contemporary of Walker Sr.—who was also well acquainted with Lewis from the Mexican War. She addressed it "To his Excellency, Genl. Taylor":

> *I am the widow of Brvt. Brigr. General Walker K. Armistead, U.S. Army, and I am impelled by various motives to request you to appoint my third son, Franck S. Armistead, a Cadet at West Point. I see from the papers that a vacancy has occurred, and as my son is in his sixteenth year, and as I am informed by his teacher, well qualified to enter West Point, I am desirous that he should be appointed now.*
>
> *The Genl. left his small Estate much embarrassed. I have been compelled to keep a boarding school in order to give my children an education somewhat suitable to their birth. Without your assistance, Franck must in a short time cease [his education], as it is impossible for me to send him to College.*
>
> *I forebear mentioning the services of the Genl. in garrison & in the field, to one who was his companion in arms—preferring to make my application to the President's generosity, because I perceive from other of his appointments to West Point that his sense of justice is already to my plea.*[33]

The letter was written on May 2, 1850. President Taylor died in office two months later, replaced by his vice president, Millard Fillmore, and no action was taken at the time on Mrs. Armistead's request. But she was back at it again in 1851, compiling letters and recommendations in support of Franck's appointment and coercing her brother, U.S. Congressman Edward Stanly of North Carolina, to write to President Fillmore on their behalf.[34] Another group of Virginia congressmen sent a letter describing Franck as a "youth of promise and good habits" who was "the orphan son of a distinguished and gallant officer" and clearly in need of assistance.[35] But the effort failed for the second straight year.

It was not until early 1852 that Congressman Stanly finally uncovered the reason for the repeated West Point rejections. Army regulations at the time prevented a second brother from attending the academy if one brother had already graduated, and the widespread assumption—based on Lewis Armistead's success as an officer and heroism in Mexico—was that Lewis had graduated in the 1830s. If true, it would have made Walker Jr. and Franck ineligible.

Stanly untangled the confusion in a March 11, 1852, letter to Secretary of War Charles M. Conrad (wherein he mistakenly identified Lewis as a captain):

> *Twelve months ago, I applied to the President for a cadet's appointment for Franck S. Armistead, son of the late Genl. Walker K. Armistead, U.S.A. I was informed after the appointments were made that the President would have appointed this young gentleman, but that he could not have done so without violating a rule of the Dept. which forbids appointments to those who had a brother already graduated at West Point, and that Captain Lewis A. Armistead, U.S.A., was a graduate of the West Point academy.*
>
> *I made no complaint & had no right to complain, and heard this by accident. But it is a mistake.*
>
> *Captain Armistead was at the Point a short time, & left, I think, when very young, on account of some boyish frolic. He was appointed to the army from civil life and fought his way through the Mexican War to his present rank—which ought not to operate to the disadvantage of his younger brother Franck, now the son of a widowed mother, who is unable to give him more education . . .*
>
> *I hope young Armistead will be accepted this time.*[36]

Thanks to his uncle's influence and an updated interpretation of the rules, Franck's at-large appointment now seemed almost a certainty. If the young man had any doubts about his future, however, the source may have been another remarkable letter written in early 1852—this one addressed to him from Lewis, who was still on duty at Fort Dodge in Iowa.

The contents reveal a religious side to Lewis that few historians have ever known or assessed. As the older brother by eighteen years, he barely knew Franck on a personal level—he left home to join the army in 1839, when Franck was four years old—but the advice he imparted on February 4, 1852, was equal parts heartfelt and gloomy, poignant, and sorrowful. It was no doubt unsettling to an impressionable younger sibling:

> *The true, the only secret to success, to contentment, to virtue, and to piety even, is in constant employment—all the rest is vain and ideal—as to happiness, you must not expect to find it in this world—but trusting in the mercy of God, and in the atonement of a blessed Savior—look far beyond—feeling confident, that the reward of a well spent life is sure and steadfast as eternal truth—and that the consummation of the Christian's hope is peace and joy forever—without such a hope, how vain are all the sacred ties of earth— without such a hope, how can we ever expect to meet those in heaven whom we have loved so fondly here.*[37]

Lewis rambled on but eventually got around to military matters, having learned from a relative that "Uncle Edward" was working to obtain a cadet's warrant for Franck at West Point. Even then, he could not bring himself to acknowledge the value of military service or endorse a most worthy career opportunity. Hardened by life on the frontier and the recent deaths of his wife and daughter—and perhaps suffering briefly from depression—Lewis counseled Franck to reject the lure of family legacy and pursue another life path:

> *I do not wish to decide for you, but am willing to give you the benefit of my experience, resulting from near thirteen years' service in the army, and my advice, my experience, is that it is a system of favoritism, and of thankless drudgery, and a life in which a man is more tempted to dissipation than in almost any other he may chance to choose. And when he dies, he leave[s] his family poor and dependent, for the pay, except in the highest grades, is not more than sufficient to support him, and keep up the appearance which the world demands. My advice is, therefore, with many thanks to Uncle Edward, to decline it, and to stay where you are. Our dear Father advised me not to enter the army—and for many years past, I have truly, and sorrowfully repented that I did not follow his advice—Now, choose for yourself.*[38]

But Franck's mind was already made up. He had chased the West Point dream and the legacy of his late father for far too long. He signed his conditional warrant on March 27, 1852, officially accepting an appointment to West Point that would begin later that summer.[39] Because he was still only seventeen years old, however, the army required that his mother also sign the same document to grant parental permission for the adventure:

> *I hereby assent to the above acceptance by my son of his conditional appointment as Cadet, and he has my full permission to sign articles by which he will bind himself to serve the United States, eight years unless sooner discharged.*
>   *E. Armistead*[40]

Lewis had not even been granted his leave of absence by the time Franck left for West Point in the summer of 1852. He could not travel east to Virginia until the third week of October, when work had already begun to repair the house and other significant damage at the farm.[41]

The family was still in poor shape financially, but Lewis's arrival was a godsend to his mother and, certainly, to everyone's morale. He anticipated staying six months and ended up staying nine. Part of that was out of necessity, and part was to escape from his recent feelings about army life, laid out in his letter to Franck. But at least some of it was because of a new romantic interest developed through connections in northern Virginia.

Cornelia Taliaferro Jamesson was a twenty-four-year-old widow and single mother whose first husband, U.S. Navy officer William Jamesson, had died in an accident in 1845 after only one year of marriage. Lewis was thirty-five at the time and also a single parent, longing for companionship and in search of a family structure for young Keith. His prospective wife was the daughter of a judge from a distinguished background who also knew the rigors of military life. It seemed to be a perfect match.[42]

The wedding took place on March 17, 1853, in Alexandria, Virginia, where Cornelia lived with her young daughter, Williamina.[43] With his leave of absence about to end, Lewis wrote to the adjutant general four days later to request a two-month extension, citing continuing business issues at Ben Lomond. "This application is made in order to enable me

1852

United States Military Academy
West Point, N.Y. July 1st 1852

I _Franck S Armistead_ of the State
of _Virginia_ aged _Seventeen_ years _Three_ months,
having been selected for an appointment as Cadet in the
Military Academy of the United States, do hereby engage,
with the consent of my _Guardian_
in the event of my receiving such appointment, that
I will serve in the Army of the United States for
eight years unless sooner discharged by competent
authority. And I _Franck S Armistead_
do solemnly swear that I will bear true faith and allegiance to the United States of America, and that I will
serve them honestly and faithfully against all their
enemies or opposers whatsoever, and observe and obey
the orders of the President of the United States, and
the orders of the Officers appointed over me, according
to the Rules and Articles of War.
Sworn and subscribed to, at West Point, New York
this Twenty ____ day of February 1853.
before me _B. F. Dunning_ Franck. S. Armistead
Special County Judge of
Orange County N.Y.

Brother Franck Armistead was accepted to West Point in 1852, sixteen years after Lewis resigned from the academy.

to attend to business connected with my Father's and Grand Father's estates," he explained. "If I can obtain this indulgence I will be able to save a considerable amount to the heirs." He was flaunting the rules once again; his marriage was never mentioned.[44]

But headquarters had grown weary by now of the endless drama and told him no extension was forthcoming. Accordingly, Lewis was marked "absent without leave" on regimental records for April, May, and June and didn't return to duty until July 13, at which point his unit had been sent north from Fort Dodge to the newly established Fort Ridgely in Minnesota. There is no record that he was punished for his tardiness, however, and the army probably was happy just to have him back in the ranks. The Armisteads spent a relatively quiet fourteen months at Ridgely before moving to Jefferson Barracks near St. Louis in late September 1854.[45]

It was here, at a site familiar to Lewis and many other frontier veterans, that the next family tragedy occurred. Genealogical records do not mention the birth of an Armistead child in the previous year, but an infant named Lewis B. Armistead died at the post on December 6, 1854, and is buried in Jefferson Barracks National Cemetery next to Lewis's daughter from his first marriage, Flora.[46] Despite the lack of documentation, it stretches credulity to theorize that little Lewis B. Armistead was *not* the son of Lewis A. Armistead and his second wife, Cornelia. Already haunted by death and misery, he had now lost a second child.

Moving on, their next stop was Fort Riley in the Kansas Territory, where Lewis reported with Cornelia in April 1855.[47] His outlook here seemed brighter than any time since the Mexican War, especially after he was promoted to the regular army rank of captain.[48] The blazing hot summer months involved one perilous expedition against the Sioux Indians and a series of routine garrison assignments, but the highlight was likely the reunion of the entire Armistead clan because both surviving children—Keith, then ten years old, and Williamina, nine—returned from Virginia to join them on the Plains.[49]

A period of general calm and happiness extended into late July when it was brought to a sudden halt by another calamity. Lewis led his company on a mission up the Smoky Hill River on July 30, just as an outbreak of deadly cholera was hitting Fort Riley. It developed so rapidly by the

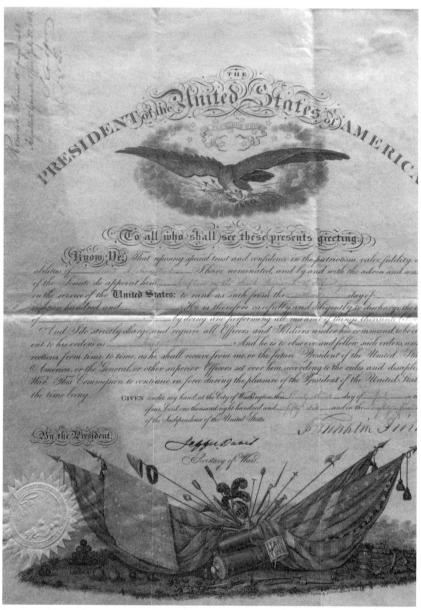

Lewis Armistead's promotion to captain in 1855 was signed by the U.S. secretary of war, Jefferson Davis, future president of the Confederacy.

night of August 1 that, according to one witness, "a burial party and a gang of men to dig graves were organized." The fort's commander and the chief clerk were among those stricken on August 2, as were the wives of several soldiers, including Cornelia Armistead.[50]

Reverend David Clarkson, the post's chaplain, arranged for the care of the sick and dying and was driven to near exhaustion by the task. These were agonizing deaths, with patients suffering muscle cramps, vomiting, diarrhea, and severe dehydration. A local official who was there, Percival Lowe, recalled that Reverend Clarkson and his wife "took Mrs. Armistead's two children home, and did everything that could be done for the others."[51] An ambulance was dispatched to find Lewis and bring him back to the post as quickly as possible, but Cornelia passed away before he could arrive at her bedside. As Lowe described it,

> *Major Armistead's quarters were the second west of the quartermaster's office. Mrs. Clarkson and her niece had prepared the body of Mrs. Armistead for burial, but it was not to be coffined until the major's arrival. . . . From the mantel at the west end of the room a candle shed a dim light over the room and the bed, on which lay Mrs. Armistead, the white bed-clothes covering her as if asleep. Her face was not covered, and to one standing a little way from the bed she seemed to be sleeping peacefully, and no one not cognizant of the fact would have thought her dead—a lovely picture of a lovely woman.*[52]

An unsuspecting Lewis had been located with his unit about thirty miles from the fort.[53] Despondent and panicked, he left immediately, traveling as quickly as possible over difficult terrain, but it was not until about 10:00 p.m. on August 3 that Lowe heard "an ambulance rattling over the stony road." He knew it once that "it was the major, and [I] dreaded to meet him":

> *As the ambulance stopped at the porch, I opened the door and the major sprang out, shook my hand, and inquired: "How about my family?"*
>
> *I hesitated a little, which he interpreted as a bad omen and continued: "Are they all gone—wife, children and all?"*
>
> *"No major," I said, "your children are safe at Mrs. Clarkson's." He said no more then.*

Taking hold of his left arm, we walked to and stepped inside the room. Taking off his hat, he cried out: "Oh, my poor wife! Oh, my poor wife!" The agony of that minute during which he gazed on her was terrible.

I led him gently away. When on the porch, he said, "I will take my children on the plains with me. I will take them away to-morrow." I assured him that I would have his quarters cared for, and he went to Mrs. Clarkson's, where his children, a boy and a girl, were located.[54]

Regaining his composure, however, Lewis chose not to leave Fort Riley immediately, determined to oversee Cornelia's funeral service and burial. On August 4, he hired a stonecutter recently arrived from St. Louis to carve the letters and a figure of the cross on Cornelia's tombstone. But, eerily, with cholera continuing to rip through the post, the stonecutter himself began to feel "not as cheerful as usual," and, as Lowe remembered it, "the next morning this handsome young fellow joined those on the side of the hill [buried] beyond the deep ravine."[55]

Once completed by others, the tombstone carving was Lewis's simple tribute to his life partner of less than three years:

CORNELIA T. ARMISTEAD
AUGUST 2 1855
WIFE OF BVT MAJOR LEWIS A ARMISTEAD US ARMY[56]

Lewis built a wooden trellis over the grave site and planted vines to grow around it, making it stand out from other hastily arranged burial spots, marked mostly with stark wooden headboards. Local workers erected a stone wall around the makeshift cemetery, but it consisted of only loose stones with no mortar, and the haphazard structure soon fell into disrepair. According to the *History of Fort Riley*, "Soldiers hunting rabbits [found them] lodged in the wall, got them out by tearing gaps in it . . . and prairie fires burned many of the head boards and destroyed the trellis and vines over Mrs. Armistead's grave." By the early twentieth century, only a few original tombstones, including Cornelia's, remained.[57]

(As an aside, almost 150 years later in 1998, the Fort Riley Historical and Archeological Society placed a plaque near Cornelia's tombstone at Fort Riley Post Cemetery: "Erected to the memory of Cornelia Taliaferro

Armistead, beloved wife of Brevet Major Lewis A. Armistead, Company F, Sixth United States Infantry Regiment. 'Trust In God And Fear Nothing.' A native of old Virginia. Married in Alexandria, Virginia, March 17, 1853. Devoted mother, military spouse, Kansas pioneer. Died of cholera at Fort Riley, Kansas Territory, August 2, 1855."[58])

At age thirty-eight, Lewis had now lost two wives and two of his three biological children to disease on the frontier. The searing emotional toll of repeated personal tragedies would have been difficult for most to imagine, much less comprehend. Vague reports of Cornelia's death so unnerved Armistead family members back in Virginia that one of his sisters sent a frantic note to the U.S. War Department on August 17, inquiring whether Lewis himself had died.[59] He had not, of course, returning to his duties at Fort Riley later that month, but he asked for and was granted a much-needed leave of absence on September 28.[60]

It was November by the time Lewis arrived home at Ben Lomond with Keith. Williamina, who disappeared from the family record at this point, was probably sent to join her maternal grandparents in Alexandria.[61] Twice over the next few months, Lewis asked the army for significant extensions of his leave "to attend to important matters growing out of a severe affliction."[62] Not until May 13, 1856, did he resume his service at Fort Riley, once again taking command of Company F[63]—albeit as a bitter and brokenhearted middle-aged man.

CHAPTER SEVEN

Hancock the Quartermaster

EVEN AFTER WINFIELD SCOTT HANCOCK GRADUATED FROM THE U.S. Military Academy in 1844, his father clung to a naive hope that he would return to civilian life, perhaps to pursue a career in law with his twin brother.

Much to B. F. Hancock's chagrin, however, any chance of that disappeared in the raw euphoria of victory in Mexico.

"After the stirring scenes in which the young man had been engaged, such a lame and impotent conclusion was in no man's thoughts," a fellow officer wrote. "By nature, Hancock was a soldier, every inch of him. . . . He had had a taste of the sterner parts of war, and he liked them. The smoke of battle had been in his nostrils, and he found it fragrant."[1]

The Sixth Infantry's return trip to the United States in the summer of 1848 offered another window into the young lieutenant's future. He became the regiment's acting quartermaster and commissary, displaying an uncommon knack for detail on the long journey from Vera Cruz through New Orleans to St. Louis.[2] It might seem a contradiction given Hancock's raw skill as a warrior, but a friend said "he loved 'papers,' rejoicing in forms and regulations and requisitions."[3] For the next thirteen years, he served in various staff positions—quartermaster, adjutant, commissary, aide-de-camp—quietly laying the foundation for a career commanding large bodies of troops in the Civil War.

"Looking back upon the period which had elapsed since the close of the war with Mexico . . . the service in which he was engaged was precisely the best-suited to develop the man to his highest capabilities," staff officer Francis Walker wrote. "He was being trained for his high duties by conducting the orders and correspondence of a military department, fitting out expeditions of a company or a squadron, supplying outlying posts or conducting the business of a quartermaster's depot on the plains."[4]

It is a mistake, however, to assume that life after the war was all work and no play for this future hero of the Union army. The base of operations for Hancock and much of his regiment in the immediate aftermath of the war was Jefferson Barracks, just south of St. Louis, a rapidly growing city on the Mississippi River. It was here that Hancock and Henry Heth resumed a friendship that began in the vibrant social scene of Mexico City. During the U.S. occupation in the early part of 1848, the two young bachelors—Hancock, twenty-four, and Heth, twenty-two—had caroused together on an almost nightly basis, cavorting with some of Mexico's most eligible bachelorettes (their messmate Armistead, who was married with two children, apparently declined to take part in the nocturnal escapades).[5]

Hancock at the time was an exceptional physical specimen—a shade over six feet tall, 169 pounds, trim, fit, and strikingly handsome.[6] "He was tall, graceful, a blonde with light hair, the style of all others that at once captivated the Mexican girls," Heth said. Lacking Hancock's good looks and irresistible charm, Heth nonetheless took advantage of their friendship and filled his own datebook by merely tagging along. "Hancock and I were quite often invited to attend entertainments given by Mexican young ladies in the city," he said. "I owed my invitations to Hancock, with whom these senoritas were in love."[7]

After hearing Hancock tell different girls on consecutive dates that he had fallen in love with each of them "like never before," Heth asked how his friend could keep a straight face through the nightly charade. "He replied, 'We are at war with Mexico, peace has not yet been made, and you know all is fair in love and war.'"[8]

Peace came later that summer, but it was only a brief deterrent; their amorous adventures resumed as soon as the two men arrived at Jefferson Barracks with the Sixth Infantry and other units from the war zone. Grateful citizens of Missouri threw celebratory balls in the army's honor, but even on nights when there were no scheduled events, Hancock persuaded Heth that they should "go to St. Louis and make some calls." On one occasion, accompanied by the music of a regimental band, they serenaded several young lovelies at their doorsteps, including a teenage socialite described by a friend as "the most beautiful girl in the west." Properly impressed, she opened her shutters and delicately tossed out a white glove, which Heth picked up and gave to Hancock as a souvenir.[9]

It was only a matter of time, however, before business took precedence and troops were scattered to distant frontier posts around the country. Hancock found himself stationed at remote Fort Crawford in Prairie du Chien, Wisconsin, but he soon had the good fortune to be transferred back to St. Louis in the fall of 1849, assigned on October 1 as regimental adjutant and aide-de-camp.[10] Not long after his return, a mutual friend introduced him to the lady with the white glove—the comely Almira Russell, daughter of a prominent local merchant. The two began a torrid courtship that soon became the talk of the town and led in remarkably short order to marriage and a family.

The Hancock–Russell wedding was held on January 24, 1850, at the home of Almira's father, Samuel. There was such commotion over this rare union of wealth and military prestige (and rumors, proven false, of a glass-spun wedding dress) that a large, boisterous crowd formed outside.[11] "The mob, as it were, impeded every approach to the house," Almira said, "necessitating the assistance of a police force." Adding to the tension, the lights went out three times before and after the ceremony,

Almira Russell Hancock
TAKEN FROM *REMINISCENCES OF WINFIELD SCOTT HANCOCK* BY ALMIRA HANCOCK

causing what she called "a sensation of impending evil in the minds of the superstitious."[12] But the wedding itself went off without a hitch, the new couple settled in at the local barracks, and in October 1850, Almira gave birth to their first child, a son named Russell in honor of her family.

In 1852, when Heth finally returned to St. Louis to visit the Hancocks, he found his old his old partner in shenanigans to be "a changed man . . . happily married and thoroughly domesticated, a one-woman man for the rest of his days."[13]

The army formed three new regiments in 1854, and Hancock sought a promotion to captain by writing to President Franklin Pierce, his old commander in Mexico. The request went nowhere.[14]

There were also openings in the subsistence department and on the staff of the adjutant general, but he was passed over repeatedly by the U.S. secretary of war, Jefferson Davis.[15]

These snubs were demoralizing to a ten-year veteran officer described as "profoundly ambitious of distinction."[16] It did not help Hancock's outlook when men who were younger and of lesser rank, including his friend Heth, were promoted to captain ahead of him.[17] "He was slow in recovering," Almira said, and "I knew how severe was the wound to his professional pride."[18] But he kept up a strict devotion to duty, complaining only mildly, and his reward finally came in November 1855 when he was commissioned a captain in the quartermaster department.[19]

If it was not precisely the role Hancock wanted—at this point in his career, he "very much disliked quartermaster duties," Almira said—it still helped him climb another rung of the army's cluttered hierarchy. "He could not afford to decline promotion," she said, "having been a lieutenant for nearly twelve years."[20]

Three months later, in February 1856, Hancock was reassigned to the swamps of Florida, where hostilities with the Seminole Indians were breaking out again.[21] The prospect of supplying soldiers for guerilla warfare in these onerous conditions was a challenge that may have daunted others, but the new captain, despite his desire for other work, handled the task with skill and determination.[22] Wagons, food, clothing, and ammunition all arrived for the army on time. Lieutenant Thomas M. Vincent, a fellow West Pointer who was adjutant general of the troops in Florida when Hancock arrived, recalled his friend's immediate calming influence:

> *I can attest the pleasant recollections of Hancock, who was Chief Quarter-master of the District of the Caloosahatchee, and the Depot Quartermaster at Fort Myers. . . . Anxiety and concern on the part of the commander of forces disappeared when he knew that Hancock was to have charge of the base.*[23]

Hancock was so attached to his family that Almira and young Russell joined him on the fifteen-month mission to Florida. "Allie" was one of the few army wives to risk the swampland danger, and her presence and generosity at temporary homes in Tampa and Fort Myers were long remembered by the troops. "Their little quarters were a perfect oasis in the desert to the rest of us," said Orlando Willcox, who attended West Point with Hancock and later led a brigade at Antietam. "The liberal hospitality and genial cordiality of Captain and Mrs. Hancock shed a glow of sunshine over our precious visits at Tampa."[24]

Almira had surprisingly fond memories of their time in Florida, the searing heat and hostility notwithstanding. She recognized the value of her husband's work and enjoyed her own interactions with appreciative soldiers who visited often for the pleasure of a home-cooked meal. This period in their lives was especially memorable because she gave birth to the couple's second child, a daughter, in Fort Myers on February 24, 1857. "In this forsaken country, prodigal only in the number and variety of venomous snakes and insects of every kind," Almira wrote, "our sweet child Ada was born."[25]

But Hancock was on the move again that summer, reassigned to Fort Leavenworth in "Bleeding Kansas," where pro- and anti-slavery forces were locked in a deadly struggle for control. It was a precursor to the Civil War, with armed militias brawling to determine the social and economic future of a proposed state.[26] Almira and the children traveled with him once more and, while happy to escape the Florida swamps, were exposed to military peril on an almost daily basis. "Partisan feeling ran high," she said, "and those not in sympathy with armed Federal interference were bitter against us, placing everyone upon the defensive for self-protection."[27]

The spring of 1858 brought yet another new challenge for the army as restive Mormons in Utah conspired to resist federal authority. Colonel Albert Sidney Johnston had been sent with a small force to confront them, but, after a slow slog during the winter months, he needed reinforcements.[28] Hancock was quartermaster of the last detachment from Leavenworth, charged with transporting 128 wagons, 5 ambulances, and 1,000 mules in addition to supplies for the troops.[29] He was saddened to leave Almira behind for the first time in their married life, and yet she noted a curious gleam in his eye at the prospect of undertaking such a mission. She asked why he preferred this risky way of life with the infantry as opposed to seemingly safer roles with other branches.

"Because I am only a soldier," Hancock said. "This resting fancifully upon my guns, or making guns for others to shoot with, though somebody *must* do it, or being a professor at West Point, as you desired, is all well enough, and there must be capable officers to perform such duty, but it does not belong to me."[30]

Peace had been settled by the time Hancock's unit reached Salt Lake City in June 1858, but there so many pockets of turmoil in the wild American West that a new assignment came quickly. Disparate elements of the Sixth Infantry were ordered to reunite at Fort Bridger in what is now Wyoming, marking the first time the full regiment had been together in sixteen years, since before the Mexican War. The next course of action would be a treacherous thousand-mile march to the Pacific coast to protect new settlers from hostile Indians and other impending frontier threats.[31]

It was during this time at Fort Bridger that Hancock had a chance to reacquaint himself with an "old and valued friend."

Still reeling from a devastating sequence of personal loss, Lewis Armistead returned to his post at Fort Riley, Kansas, in the spring of 1856. The drab routine of frontier army life was all he had now, his only constant, even if it sometimes repulsed him. Armistead resumed his regular duties and occasionally filled in as post commander, starting an uninterrupted three-year stint of service that saw his unit become "one of the better drilled companies" in the U.S. military. He was a stickler for discipline and detail, relentlessly conducting "field maneuvers and battalion drills" over the complaints of reticent soldiers, including one who deserted because he "didn't like the way things were going there." Hardened by years of tragedy, he wasn't out to win popularity contests.[32]

Armistead's men probably welcomed the change of scenery that came in May 1858, when Company F was one of the units ordered west to Utah to reinforce Colonel Johnston against the Mormons. But as with Hancock and the others, they saw no action because peace was reached before they arrived,[33] and Johnston took several weeks to ponder his next move while sending the Sixth Infantry to the depot at Fort Bridger. The men lingered there into early August ("allowed only a short period of rest," one complained) before receiving new orders to head farther west to Benicia, California, into more territory acquired by the United States in the Mexican War.[34]

They thus embarked on one of the more remarkable sustained marches in U.S. Army history, covering 1,017 miles in less than three months,[35] leaving Fort Bridger on August 21, traipsing over treacherous mountain trails—at one point encountering snow "two or three feet deep"—and arriving at Benicia on November 15. A soldier remembered two oppressive nights when they were "obliged to camp in the snow without tents, blankets and food, since our wagons were unable to reach us."[36] It was only because of Major Armistead's manic devotion to drill and discipline that his men were able to endure the challenge so well.

Hancock also drew praise for his performance as regimental quartermaster under seemingly impossible conditions. "He had to deal with half-starved animals, broken-down wagons and limited supplies . . . directed upon the formidable and then little-known Sierras," a colleague wrote, but "the troops and trains were finally brought into Benicia in even better condition than when they started. This result was considered at headquarters as reflecting the highest honor upon Captain Hancock."[37] The condition of the troops and trains was, in reality, probably far worse than described—one account said some wagons arrived as "unusable hulks"[38]— but the ability to herd the men and equipment on such an arduous journey testified to Hancock's organizational skill, tenacity, and patience.

The original intent was to have the Sixth move north from Benicia to Walla Walla in the Washington Territory, but army plans, as they often do, changed abruptly that fall.[39] A regimental history notes that "from Benicia Barracks, the Sixth was distributed among different posts and stations in the Department of the Pacific" to deal with new threats from hostile Indians.[40] After spending much of the winter at the Presidio in San Francisco, Armistead's company was part of a small entourage that took a steamship south to San Diego and then traversed east toward the Colorado River into modern-day Arizona, where the Mojave tribe was harassing frontier settlers.[41] Just above Beale's Crossing on the east bank of the Colorado, the major established a new army camp in April 1859, defiantly dubbing it Fort Mojave.[42]

His friend Hancock, meanwhile, headed east on a much-deserved leave of absence.[43]

No longer burdened by wagons or mules, Hancock wasted little time crossing the Isthmus of Tehuantepec in southern Mexico and traveling by boat to Washington, D.C., where, after a lengthy journey, he reunited with Almira and the children.[44] In later years, Almira recalled "a short sojourn of two months delightfully spent in Washington City . . . so rich in memories and reminiscences of men and women who at that time occupied the most honorable and distinguished positions in the Government, and who were destined to play so important a part in the great drama that soon followed."[45] Notably, this was Hancock's final period of rest and relaxation before the start of the Civil War.

It is fascinating to learn how many individuals with southern leanings came into Allie's circle of friends during their brief time in the capital. In addition to Harriet Lane, niece of the bachelor President Buchanan—"the sweetheart of all Washington"—there were Mrs. Jefferson Davis, wife of the future Confederate president, and Mrs. Joseph E. Johnston, wife of the future Rebel general. This couldn't have been coincidence. All three ladies, she said, left "the most agreeable impressions,"[46] and yet none had more impact on the next phase of her life than U.S. Army officer Robert E. Lee, who learned of her plan to remain in the East while Hancock returned to California and advised ardently against it.

"How well I remember General Robert E. Lee, then a major, who was stationed there at the time," Almira wrote:

> *He was the beau ideal of a solider and a gentleman. When bidding us "good-bye" and "godspeed," upon the eve of our departure, he said to me, "I understand that you contemplate deserting your post, which is by your husband's side, and that you are not going to California with him. If you will pardon me, I should like to give you a little advice. You must not think of doing this. As one considerably older than Hancock, and having greater experience, I consider it fatal to the future happiness of young married people, upon small provocation, to live apart, either for a short or long time. The result is invariably that they cease to be essential to each other. Now promise me that you will not permit him to sail without you."[47]*

The Hancocks left Washington on April 27, 1859, on a steamer named, fittingly, *St. Louis*, headed for Havana and the Isthmus of Panama. The ship was overcrowded, bulging with more than 1,100 passengers, and the conditions they faced were miserable throughout. Allie recalled temperatures of "90 to 100 degrees in the shade" when they were detained for fourteen hours on a bridge over the Chagres River and were "warned not to drink the water with dilution," but her quartermaster husband had them "well supplied with ice, claret and lemons." Once on the Pacific side, they boarded another steamer, the *Golden Gate*, with 1,700 on board, and after much more consternation, including a brawl on the ship's upper deck, they reached what they assumed to be their destination, San Francisco, on May 23.[48]

Stunning news greeted Hancock as soon as he set foot on dry land. Sometime during his months-long leave of absence, the army had reassigned him as assistant quartermaster of the southern district of California, with headquarters in the small settlement of Los Angeles, some four hundred miles to the south.[49] Unexpected transfers such as these were the inherent pitfalls of military life, made all the more difficult when a family was involved. Resigned to their fate, the Hancocks left San Francisco the same afternoon, marshaling Russell and Ada onto an even smaller ship for a raucous thirty-six-hour voyage down the coast. That was followed by what Allie described as a "wild ride of eighteen miles behind untamed

California ponies, two of which had never before been in harness," until they reached their new home.[50]

Little Los Angeles would be the Hancock residence for the next two years. Far from its future as a bustling metropolis, it was barely a speck on the map in 1859, a backwater of maybe four thousand inhabitants, with adobe houses lining both sides of the main street and, according to Almira, not much in the way of entertainment. Most of the locals spoke Spanish, which made it difficult to communicate, and

This story from the July 30, 1859, edition of the *Los Angeles Star* describes Hancock and Armistead communicating with one another.

CALIFORNIA DIGITAL NEWSPAPER COLLECTION, CDNC.UCR.EDU, UNIVERSITY OF CALIFORNIA, RIVERSIDE

Los Angeles Star.

Saturday, July 30, 1859.

EXTRA!

Important from the Colorado!!

OUTBREAK OF THE MOJAVE INDIANS!

An express arrived last night from Major Armistead, at Beale's crossing of the Colorado, to Captain Hancock, Q.M. U.S.A., at present residing here, conveying intelligence that the Mojave Indians in the vicinity of his camp had become troublesome.

It appears that Major Armistead had orders from Gen. Clarke to demand the hostages who had lately escaped from Fort Yuma; that he had had a talk with the Indians on the subject, and was determined to arrest the runaways, or chastise the whole tribe.

In the meantime, an agent of the mail company (Stockton and Kansas city) was collecting his animals, and had them near the military post; the Indians, fearing the execution of the punishment justly their due, run off these animals, sixteen in number, and made their escape. At first it was supposed the mules had strayed away, but on searching for them they could not be found; three of them, anti-Union sentiment was prevalent and growing. Some factions carried "Bear" flags promoting California's independence. Uncomfortable as he may have been as the only army officer in town at that time, Hancock nonetheless decided to make the best of it. Allie and the children loved the gorgeous climate and spectacular scenery—and weekly visits to the beach to gather shells—while he settled into the daily routine of his quartermaster duties, overseeing all government property in southern California and the Arizona Territory.[51]

The idea for a quartermaster's depot in Los Angeles had come about when Lieutenant Colonel William Hoffman of the Sixth Infantry conducted a reconnaissance of Mojave positions in Arizona. It was determined that supplies had to be stored nearby to support troops sent to counter the Indian threat.[52] Hoffman's orders in the aftermath of his reconnaissance were to bring the Mojaves "and all others who may assume a hostile attitude . . . to submission."[53]

This task soon fell to Hancock's friend, Armistead, whose men arrived in April and built a fort near the Colorado River. Unsurprisingly, the Mojaves soon challenged the army's presence in their native land. Between July 20 and 31, they conducted a series of hit-and-run attacks on mail wagons and army patrols, confiscating sixteen mules, firing on soldiers, and at times cutting off the key transportation route. Nervous U.S. authorities reminded Armistead that "the post had been established at that point by direction of the Secretary of War for the protection of the road, and this duty must be thoroughly performed."[54] It was a clarion call to action.

The July 30 edition of the *Los Angeles Star* made readers aware of the danger with a large, blaring headline: "OUTBREAK OF THE MOJAVE INDIANS!" The paper reported on page 1 that "an express arrived last night from Major Armistead, at Beale's crossing of the Colorado, to Captain Hancock, Q.M.U.S.A., at present residing here, conveying intelligence that the Mojave Indians in the vicinity of his camp had become troublesome. It appears that Major Armistead had orders from Gen. Clarke to demand the [return of the] hostages who had lately escaped from Fort Yuma; that he had had a talk with the Indians on the subject, and was determined to arrest the runaways, or chastise the whole tribe."[55] The major used the next five days to prepare, organizing two detachments of twenty-five handpicked men to counter the Mojave threat.

Friday, August 5, 1859, marked the only time in his twenty-two years in the U.S. Army that Lewis Armistead commanded a battlefield. Stealthily leading one of the units twelve miles south of the post, "my object being to surprise the Indians," he crawled through brush to fire the first three shots at Mojaves planting beans, killing one of them. The assault touched off two extended firefights—one of thirty minutes, the next of fifteen—during which the soldiers' new muskets gave them a clear advantage over opponents with bows and arrows. Armistead would later praise the "accuracy and coolness of our fire," but he made an error in assuming that the battle had come to an end.[56]

A roving band of Mojaves fell on U.S. troops as they returned to the fort, advancing "more boldly than ever" and using the cover of chaparral and small sand hillocks. The major conceded that "they stood our firing very well, coming up to within twenty and thirty paces," but the training and superior weaponry of Armistead's men eventually won the day. The Indians' four-to-one numerical advantage never became a significant factor. "This time," he said, "they were apparently so well satisfied as to omit their whoop of defiance, which had accompanied their other retreats."[57]

News traveled slowly in that part of the country, and on August 13, the *Star* could only report that "Capt. Hancock, U.S.A., received intelligence from Fort Mojave, that the Indians continued their hostility, and that the troops, under Major Armistead, were engaged in pursuing them." But by August 27, the *Star*'s readers were informed that "the Indians have been driven down the river and are now collected at suitable lurking places."[58]

Army officials soon learned that it was one of the most pitched battles fought by any portion of the Sixth in two decades of service on the frontier. Armistead's performance as commander had been impressive, and on August 31, he reported to headquarters that "I have, at their earnest solicitation, made peace this day with the Mojaves."[59] The major's immediate reward was a two-month leave of absence, set to begin on September 3—

a benefit both well deserved and long overdue.[60] He packed his few belongings and headed back toward Virginia, excited to see his son and extended family for the first time in more than three years.

Having learned over time to master the "leave of absence" system, Armistead did not return to active duty for more than a year, until December 1860. He cleverly obtained three separate extensions and stitched them into a virtually unprecedented fifteen-month vacation from the army.[61] Even after deducting for travel time to and from the West Coast, he spent almost a full year back in Virginia, reuniting with fifteen-year-old Keith and some of his younger siblings and doting on his aging mother.

Armistead knew precisely how to strike the proper tone in his periodic written appeals to headquarters. In March, he focused on family issues, addressing a need to "attend to business connected with my Father's Estate, and to try and make some provision for my mother, who is an old Lady requiring my assistance, and I am the only one of her sons able to help her."[62] One of his early July missives begged for indulgence because otherwise "I will be obliged to travel in the extreme heat of summer." Nor did he hesitate to mention a stellar record of service, adding in July that neither "heat, cold, wet nor dry has ever stopped me in the performance of my duty."[63] In the end, all of the extensions were processed and granted, one official noting that "the services of Bvt. Major Armistead have been of such character that I don't hesitate to approve this application."[64]

It is possible that his brother, Walker Jr., who had been living in California since 1853, joined him on the long trip home.[65] But even if they traveled separately and arrived at different times, it is noteworthy that twenty-nine-year-old Walker and forty-three-year-old Lewis were both present in Upperville for the 1860 U.S. census, taken at Ben Lomond on June 13.[66] This was a unique reconnection for two brothers who didn't know each other very well. Walker was just two years old when Lewis made his first trip to West Point and only eight when he joined the U.S. Army in 1839, but his failure to follow Lewis's path had done nothing to diminish Walker's admiration for his older brother's military achievements.

Young Keith was not there at the time of the census, most likely attending school out of town in the hope of being accepted at West Point; his father *did* write to academy officials to inquire about a cadet's warrant, which, much to his disappointment, was not forthcoming that summer.[67]

Whatever else he did on the home front in Fauquier County, Lewis paid several visits to his neighbor and "warm friend" Turner Ashby, a militia leader and future Confederate cavalry officer.[68] Ashby commanded a local horse unit called the Fauquier Mountain Rangers and had taken part in suppressing John Brown's raid at Harpers Ferry in October 1859. Brown, the radical abolitionist, led a band of twenty-one men into the Ferry with the goal of inciting a slave insurrection that would forever end the shame of human bondage. Militia units from across northern Virginia rushed forward to protect the town and its wealthy inhabitants, and a detachment of ninety U.S. marines (ironically, under Robert E. Lee) arrived from Washington to subdue Brown and take him into custody. Ashby and his men were assigned to picket duty shortly after the arrest and stood guard at Brown's public hanging two months later at Charles Town.[69]

The gruesome experience gave Ashby grave doubts about the future of the country; he believed Brown's raid was a sign of sectional discord that would go down in history as the first unofficial battle of a civil war.[70] But he had trouble convincing Armistead of this view in the summer of 1860. The major had spent so much time away from Virginia that he could not accept or even begin to comprehend the size of the rift that had developed between North and South.

Their differing perspectives were captured years later by Ashby's biographer, who related a conversation between the two men in advance of the 1860 presidential election:

Just before the several conventions met in the Summer of 1860, to bring out their respective candidates for the Presidency, Capt. Ashby was enjoying the society of an old and cherished friend, General L. Armistead, under the hospitable roof of [Ashby's home]. The conversation turned upon the situation of the country.

Capt. Ashby spoke of the danger of a disruption of the Union, and consequent war. General Armistead, then Major Armistead of U.S.A., listened for some time in silence; then, suddenly starting up, exclaimed, "Turner, do not talk so; I know but one country and one flag. Let me sing you a song and drive away your gloom."

And then he sang the "Star-Spangled Banner," Capt. Ashby joining in heartily.[71]

Although he rarely, if ever, discussed it, Armistead would have been well aware of his family's impact on U.S. history, especially his Uncle George, who had defended Fort McHenry in 1814 when Francis Scott Key wrote the song that would one day be the national anthem. He may even have known that his late uncle kept the famous flag after the battle and that it was currently in the possession of his Aunt Louisa at her home in Baltimore.[72] But he could not have imagined how his views on the nation itself, on sectional unity, and on the banner he had pledged to "so proudly hail" would change so completely in the year ahead.

CHAPTER EIGHT

California

WINFIELD HANCOCK WAS THE LONE U.S. ARMY OFFICER STATIONED IN Los Angeles in 1859 when he and his family settled into their temporary living quarters, a one-story red brick cottage on lower Main Street near Third.[1] Despite the uncommonly warm temperatures, sun-splashed landscape, and proximity to the Pacific Ocean—which few easterners had ever seen—it was not always a comfortable existence. They felt isolated at first, almost forgotten.

"The little town of Los Angeles presented nothing of interest in itself, being too small to attract or sustain public amusement of any kind," Almira wrote glumly. "The absence of a daily mail was a source of regret, and we often wished it otherwise, as the distance seemed to be lengthened, in consequence, between us and our loved ones at home."[2]

The Hancocks were essentially strangers in a strange land—a starkly unfamiliar territory that was part of Mexico until the peace settlement of 1848 and where English-speaking Americans remained the minority. Many of the new settlers came from southern states at a time when tension between the regions over slavery was on the rise.[3] The captain could do little more than focus on his supply work, acquiring and then stocking a large quartermaster's warehouse, where he directed the distribution of food, clothing, weapons, and livestock to troops at Fort Mojave.[4] Even at this early date, however, noting a growing scent of independence in the air, he kept a wary eye on guns and ammunition lest they fall into the hands of an especially pernicious militia.[5]

A contemporary biographer wrote that "the duties of this position demanded from the officer in charge wisdom, energy, business tact, and administrative ability," while "the peculiarities of climate, the diversity of production, the formation of the country and the roads and modes of transportation [made] that task of supplying troops in that section a vastly different one from a similar duty in more highly improved parts of the country."[6] Adding to the challenge, it was the first time Hancock had lived in a predominantly civilian environment since leaving Norristown for West Point nineteen years earlier. With no U.S. soldiers under his command, he had to rely on unfamiliar local residents who were recruited by others and paid with federal funds—"clerks, storekeepers, teamsters, a blacksmith, herders, wheelwrights, carpenters," and, eventually, "wagon masters."[7] The captain and his wife found some personal comfort in helping to establish the first Protestant church in the staunchly Catholic region, with Almira volunteering to "preside over the organ."[8]

As weeks and months passed, however, he began to feel more at ease in his new home, developing local friendships, making personal business deals on the side, and hosting military officers who occasionally passed through Los Angeles on the way to other parts.[9] James S. Merryman of the U.S. Revenue Marine recalled "his chivalric nature" and "the impression made upon my mind by his handsome appearance and engaging manner."[10] Hancock's reunion with General Albert Sidney Johnston on March 29, 1860, even found its way into the papers, with the *Los Angeles Star* reporting that Johnston "arrived in this city from Camp Floyd [Utah]" and was "met by Capt. Hancock USA." The *Star* noted that Johnston turned his escort over to Hancock and stayed briefly at the Los Angeles home of his brother-in-law, Dr. J. S. Griffin, before catching a steamer headed for Washington, D.C.[11] Johnston would return in less than a year to take command of the army's Department of the Pacific in San Francisco.

The last half of 1860 brought an intense focus on the U.S. presidential election, especially because the controversial Republican nominee, Abraham Lincoln, had spoken out firmly against the expansion of slavery to new territories. Although not yet a proponent of immediate abolition—it was not deemed politically feasible at the time—Lincoln believed that a policy of containment would eventually lead to slavery's demise. As a result, many southerners and those with southern leanings in California began to whisper among themselves about disunion and rebellion if he won the election.

"Excitement ran high," Almira said of this period. "In Mr. Hancock's opinion, the situation was pregnant with danger in the event of Mr. Lincoln's success. This conviction caused him much uneasiness, which he did not hesitate to express, but few believed it possible that the South had the intention of actually seceding from the Union.

"The suspense in the interval can well be imagined."[12]

Lewis Armistead returned to the West Coast from his yearlong leave of absence in the final months of 1860, reaching San Francisco in mid-December with a detachment of other troops from the East, much to the pleasure of the public. The *Visalia Weekly Delta* reported that "among those who have arrived is Major L.A. Armistead, whose return will be gladly welcomed in this State, as well as those of his brother officers who have before resided among us."[13] Armistead reported to his new post at the New San Diego Barracks on December 26 and resumed command of his company the next day, only to find the army—and the country—in the throes of seismic change.[14]

Much had happened since the day he left Virginia. Lincoln rode his antislavery sentiment to victory over three other candidates, although he received less than 40 percent of the vote, drawing all his support from the North and Far West and not even appearing on the ballot in most southern states.[15] Barely six weeks after the election, fearing that slavery would be abolished by the new administration, South Carolina became the first state to secede from the United States. "A geographical line has been drawn across the Union," the South Carolina secession document said, "and all the States north of that line have united in election of a man to the high office of President of the United States whose opinions and purposes are hostile to slavery." It went on to claim that the federal government had "denounced as sinful the institution of slavery."[16]

"UNION is DISSOLVED!" screamed a headline in the *Charleston (S.C.) Mercury Extra* on December 20,[17] setting in motion a series of legislative chain reactions that threatened to destroy the founding fathers' dream of U.S. nationhood.

Secessionist fever rampaged through the South. In early February 1861, six southern states—South Carolina, Alabama, Mississippi, Florida, Georgia, and Louisiana—met in Montgomery, Alabama, to create an independent government, the Confederate States of America. They were soon joined by five others. Jefferson Davis of Mississippi, a West Point graduate and U.S. secretary of war as recently as 1857 (and a sitting U.S. senator until January 21, 1861), was elected the new country's first president.[18] The sheer speed of change and disruption unsettled career army officers everywhere, especially those on the far reaches of the West Coast.

Given the primitive technology of the time, word of a fledgling southern government traveled slowly across the Plains and did not reach California until February 28. On that day, an angry and flustered Hancock wrote a letter to his father, assessing the dire situation and forecasting that the Pacific states would also declare independence:

> We have to-day heard, by Poney, that a Southern Confederacy has been formed, and that Jefferson Davis is the President and Mr. Stevens the Vice President. That looks to me that they do not intend to come back under any circumstances. . . .
>
> If there is a separation between the whole North and South, the States on the Pacific will secede from both, you may rely on it. There is a strong Union feeling yet, but the Southern element, desire for novelty and self interest to avoid taxation, will inevitably bring about the result I predict.
>
> I can but stand waiting for the future. I have Government property to protect and if there is any unlawful raid upon it, I intend to do my best to defend it. I am not free to go home now; I would not be permitted to do so if I desired. If something is not done soon to sustain the Federal Union its defenders will become demoralized and the people too.
>
> If Lincoln thinks more of his country than his party he may yet do something. He will have to offer the olive branch in one hand and hold the sword in the other. I think it most likely that the Southern Confederacy will be recognized by European Governments, if something is not done to put down the Revolution. We can expect nothing less.
>
> We are all pretty well. Allie, Russell and Ada send much love to you all.[19]

The stunningly emotional letter reflected Hancock's state of mind less than two months before war broke out (even if it ended with a mundane note about his family). He had agonized over the future of the Union for much of the past year and knew that many of his brethren from the army, including Armistead, would likely secede with their native South. A number of them had stopped by the Hancock home to debate the matter over the past six months whenever duty brought them to Los Angeles, but Hancock's stance on secession was blunt and inalterable: Union first, Union always. Beyond that, he told them to follow their own paths.

"Many conferences were held in our home in Los Angeles, between my husband and the Southern officers who were urged by their relatives and friends to resign their commissions and offer their services to their own States," Almira said. "They sought the advice of my husband, hoping to receive from him some comfort or encouragement, but he could give none, and would say to those dear friends, Armistead, Garnett, Pickett, and a host of others whom he loved," that

I can give you no advice, as I shall not fight upon the principle of State-rights, but for the Union whole and undivided, as I do not and will not belong to a country formed of principalities. I cannot sympathize with you: you must be guided by your own convictions, and I hope you will make no mistakes.[20]

Among the first southerners to act was Albert Sidney Johnston, who had returned to California in January as commander of the U.S. Army's Department of the Pacific.[21] A native of Kentucky who later lived in Texas and fought in the Texas War of Independence, Johnston kept his own counsel on secession but decided to resign from the army once Texas left the Union.[22] On April 4, barely a week before the Confederates fired on Fort Sumter, he submitted "the resignation of my commission from the army of the United States" and asked to be relieved "as soon as practicable." He had not yet committed to fight for the Confederacy, but the army, knowing Johnston's background and sensing disloyalty, had already sent a replacement under a cloak of secrecy—perhaps hoping to catch him in a treasonous act.[23]

Johnston was relieved without incident, however, by General E. V. "Bull" Sumner in late April. He left his post in San Francisco and headed south to Los Angeles, where he moved in with his brother-in-law, Dr. Griffin, and rekindled his connection with the Hancocks. Johnston and his family remained in the city for six more harrowing weeks. According to Almira, he thought "it might be within the power of his brother-in-law, who was a prominent physician of that lower country, to assist him in some practical way in the support of his family, which consisted of his wife and five children but he found it impossible to succeed."[24] Hancock may have fretted about rowdy militias prowling the region during this period, but he felt no threat from Johnston or other professional soldiers who were about to resign; their old army friendships, forged from years in Mexico and on the frontier, would remain intact until they all headed east to the war zone.

The militias, however, were more problematic and posed immediate risks. Hancock feared that these amateur bands of ruffians might charge his army depot at any moment in an attempt to seize weapons and supplies. "There are people here anxious for difficulty, and there may be . . . organizations to that end," he wrote to headquarters on May 4. "There is quite a number of reckless people who have nothing to lose, who are ready for any change, and who are active in encouraging acts tending to hostilities."[25] In addition to rabid pro-southern factions, there were advocates of an independent western state, flaunting their "bear" flags and talking of open rebellion. Hancock hastily buried guns and ammunition under massive bags of grain and built a makeshift barricade with wagons and boxes to protect the warehouse, all the while keeping his personal stash of pistols nearby. He even armed Almira.[26] "I believe if there is trouble here I will be able to defend the public property with the supporters of the Federal Government . . . from among the citizens of Los Angeles," he said.[27]

The army took no chances and headed off any threat by sending troops to reinforce Hancock from Fort Mojave and another nearby post, Fort Tejon. Within days of their arrival, they set up a new encampment on the southern outskirts of town called Camp Fitzgerald (named for a late veteran of the Mexican War, Major E. H. Fitzgerald, who, ironically, like Hancock, hailed from Montgomery County, Pennsylvania).[28] Thankfully, rumors that a group of insurgents would stage a protest on May 12 by parading the "bear flag" through the streets proved to be unfounded.[29] Hancock informed his superiors that pro-Union militias would continue to help the army "control matters," at least until "there is a great change in political matters on the Atlantic side."[30]

It was at about the same time that Lewis Armistead traveled north from San Diego and spent several days in Los Angeles in early May. In its May 11 edition, the pro-southern *Star* reported that "this gentleman, lately in command of the post at San Diego, arrived here this week, just in time to go to San Francisco on the steamer. We understand he resigned his command on the seceding of his native State, not feeling disposed to take part in the civil war now raging on the other side of the continent."[31]

Armistead wanted to take part in the war in the East—just not on behalf of the Union.

Legislators in his home state of Virginia passed an ordinance of secession on April 17, five days after Fort Sumter, and word of that action became well known in the West, even though a public vote to approve would not be held until later in May.[32] Armistead did his best to respect army tradition by personally delivering his resignation letter to the Department of the Pacific headquarters in San Francisco on May 13, but, in doing so, he violated protocol.

General Sumner, the new department commander, was apoplectic— not only because Armistead chose to resign and betray the United States but also because he had left his post in San Diego without permission. The letter was rejected, and Armistead was ordered back to southern California, where he would have to compose and copy it again (biographer Wayne Motts thinks he may have been the only Confederate officer to actually resign twice). He passed through Los Angeles a second time that month from May 18 to 21.[33] Armistead's next letter, dated May 26 from "New San Diego, Cal.," said, in the oddly formal language of the time, "I also have the honor to apply for leave of absence of sixty days, with the intention of going to the Eastern States, there to await the acceptance of my resignation."[34]

Satisfied that this second letter complied with regulations, Sumner recommended in a June 4 note to army headquarters that "the resignation be accepted."[35] By one account, it was approved on June 12.[36] Armistead's daily whereabouts during this period are unrecorded, and his San Diego post records are unclear and, at times, contradictory,[37] but he certainly had a window to travel to Los Angeles for the third time in five weeks, and we know from another report that he met with General Johnston's wife in that city sometime around June 25.[38]

It is likely, then, that he was able to see and confer with his old friend Hancock and his former commander Johnston during at least one of his trips to Los Angeles. Mrs. Hancock's account of their emotional farewell does not give a date or provide a full guest list, but there can be little doubt that the conditions existed for such a meeting to take place.

We know for certain that by mid-June, Johnston and a group of other newly pledged rebels, including Armistead, were planning to leave Los Angeles and head east.[39] According to Almira, "A never-to-be-forgotten evening was the one spent at our home by the officers who were to start upon the overland trip to the South at 12 o'clock that night."[40] Johnston's son said in a separate account that the men left the city on June 16.[41]

"Before leaving," Almira wrote, "General Johnston said to his wife, 'Come, sing me one or two of the old songs you used to sing, "Mary of Argyle" and "Kathleen Mavourneen."' She complied reluctantly in the presence of such an audience. . . . Those songs will ever be remembered by the survivors of that mournful gathering":[42]

> Kathleen Mavourneen what slumbering still.
> Oh have you forgotten how soon we must sever?
> Oh have you forgotten this day we must part?
> It may be for years and it may be forever
> Oh why are you silent thou voice of my heart?[43]

The fact that Almira never identified other Confederates at the farewell has frustrated historians for more than a century and a half. She wrote that both Garnett and Pickett visited their home in the prewar era but didn't place either man by name at the famous gathering—revealing merely that "three out of six from whom we departed on that evening in Los Angeles were killed in front of General Hancock's troops [at Gettysburg]."[44] Her only other reference to the group at her home was that "all were endeavoring to conceal, under smiling exteriors, hearts that were filled with sadness over the sundering of life-long ties, and doubts as to the result of the sacrifice."[45]

But one soldier, in particular, sobbing and crying, stood out:

> *The most crushed of the party was Major Armistead, who, with tears which were contagious, streaming down his face, and hands upon Mr. Hancock's shoulders, while looking him steadily in the eye, said, "Hancock, good-by, you can never know what this has cost me, and I hope God will strike me dead if I am ever induced to leave my native soil, should worse come to worst."*[46]

Modern fans of *The Killer Angels* and *Gettysburg* are no doubt confounded by the last sentence—*native soil?*—because both the novelist and the moviemakers rewrote Armistead's quote to make it deeply personal. The movie version, which has impacted so many battlefield visitors since 1993, quotes him as saying, "Win, so help me, *if I ever raise my hand against you*, may God strike me dead."[47] This is an understandable distortion in the name of entertainment, but it is simply not factual. No one other than Almira ever described the conversation, and the most reasonable interpretation of her account is that Armistead committed to defend Virginia and North Carolina ("my native soil") from Union invasion.[48]

She made two other assertions about Armistead from that night:

- that he presented Hancock with his U.S. Army major's uniform, saying the captain "might sometime need it."

- that he placed "a small satchel" in her hand, "requesting that it should not be opened except in the event of his death, in which case the souvenirs it contained, with the exception of a little prayer-book, intended for me, and which I still possess, should be sent to his family. On the fly-leaf of this book is the following: Lewis A. Armistead. Trust in God and fear nothing."[49]

Although some still doubt Almira's account, a nineteenth-century biography by Hancock's friend, D. X. Junkin, confirms a prewar meeting with Armistead in California and includes brief anecdotes about the major's uniform and the prayer book.[50] Skeptics should note that

Junkin and Norton's *The Life of Winfield Scott Hancock* was published in 1880, seven years before Almira's book—and while Hancock was still alive and running for president. The Reverend Junkin, former chaplain of the U.S. Navy, was known to be a guest in the Hancock home, worked at one point from Hancock's own desk, and identified the general as a source of his material.[51]

According to Junkin and Norton,

> *An interesting incident in connection with General Armistead's defection from the United States Army, at the outbreak of the Rebellion, is related by General Hancock. . . . It occurred in Los Angeles early in 1861. Armistead was there with Hancock, a captain and brevet major. Virginia, his native State, called upon him to support her cause, and, under the influence of this demand, he sided with the Confederates. On leaving Los Angeles, he presented General Hancock with his major's uniform, saying that the latter "might sometime need it." He also placed in his hands for safe-keeping, and to be given to his family if he should fall in battle, certain valuable papers. Armistead also presented to Hancock a little prayer-book, which is still in the latter's possession. On a fly-leaf of the book is the following inscription: "Lewis A. Armistead. Trust in God and fear nothing."*

Mrs. Hancock wrote her book in 1887, twenty-six years after the family left California, and it is possible that the "evening" she described was actually a composite of several meetings that took place in May and June 1861. We can never know all the details, but there are enough facts to confirm that Armistead, Hancock, and Johnston all interacted in the spring of that year, just before Armistead and Johnston headed east.

General Johnston and a small band of resigned U.S. Army officers left Los Angeles in the wee hours of Sunday, June 16, skipping out of town before they could be captured by pro-Union forces who were not as benevolent as Hancock.[52] They were aware by now that the army had issued an order for Johnston's arrest.[53]

The caravan numbered about thirty men, including a local militia unit, the Los Angeles Mounted Rifles, and several stouthearted citizens,[54] but, at least for the time being, Armistead was not among them.

He remained behind for more than a week, perhaps for family reasons more than anything else. His brother, Walker Jr., who had returned with him to California in late 1860, now wanted to enlist in the Confederate army and may have needed time to tie up loose ends and gather his belongings. It also is possible that Lewis waited to be officially relieved from command in San Diego (June 19).[55] Despite the delay, both Armistead brothers were among those listed on a document titled "Crossed the Plains with Johnston" that was written by the wife of one of the participants and published that summer in the *Mesilla Times*. (Walker may have been a member or associate of the Los Angeles Mounted Rifles—he would serve with the Sixth Virginia Cavalry during the Civil War—but he was not listed on the unit's original roster compiled in March 1861.[56])

The brothers caught up to Johnston's group in late June at Vallecito in southern California, about 130 miles from Yuma and the Arizona border, the first major junction on their trip. It was here that Lewis delivered a message from Mrs. Johnston to the general. "I received your letter of June 25th by Major Armistead, who arrived here this morning," Johnston wrote to his wife on June 30. "Our party is now as large as need be desired for safety or convenience in traveling. They are good men and well-armed. Late of the army we have Major Armistead, Lieutenants Hardcastle, Brewer, Riley, Shaaf, Mallory and Wickliffe." Still hoping to calm her fears about his well-being, the general added that "by observing a good, compact order of march, and vigilance in camp, we will be free from any danger of attack from Indians."[57]

Moving east, they arrived near the U.S. Army garrison at Fort Yuma at nightfall on the Fourth of July, just as "The Star-Spangled Banner" was being played, an irony not lost on Johnston. "They were firing the Federal salute . . . in honor of the day, thirteen guns," he wrote on July 5. "We were near enough at 12 o'clock to hear the national salute."[58] They didn't seem worried that U.S. troops who were now their mortal enemies were stationed within easy striking distance. On the contrary, when Major Armistead was posted that night as a sentry, he was "approached by a soldier from the garrison, who was one of the major's old regiment . . . with a proposition from some of the soldiers to desert over to us, and then to seize the place and plunder it." Hearing this, Johnston promptly declined the offer, noting that it would be "the equivalent of piracy at sea."[59]

The next part of their journey took them across some of the "hottest and driest regions of the continent,"[60] testing the endurance of every man, horse, and mule and causing a number to drop out along the way. Passing just below the modern-day city of Phoenix, the men angled south toward Tucson and then on to Apache Pass, where, in late July, they saw the results of an attack by the Apache chief Cochise—two burned stagecoaches and fourteen dead bodies strewn along the trail—a grim reminder that danger was ever present.[61] By the time they reached the town of Mesilla (then Arizona, now New Mexico) on July 28, they learned that Texas Confederate militia Colonel John Baylor, a distant cousin of the Armisteads, had captured eleven companies of U.S. troops that were lying in wait at Fort Fillmore. "The audacity of the Mesilla people in keeping up a secession flag" had enraged the U.S. commander, Johnston wrote to his wife.[62]

Some of the group, including Johnston and the Armistead brothers, took a stagecoach to El Paso, where they briefly assisted in commanding Baylor's militia troops.[63] With them was Alonzo Ridley, captain of the Los Angeles Mounted Rifles and a future Confederate cavalry officer. Years later, Ridley recalled a spirited chat involving Johnston, Armistead, and several less experienced militia members before they departed western Texas for Virginia.

"At El Paso, a small party were collected, among whom were the general and Major Armistead," Ridley said. "The usual topic was being discussed—the Yankees and the war. Someone made the remark, 'But they won't stand steel.'"

Johnston and Armistead, both of whom had served for many years as U.S. soldiers, were taken aback.

"The general, who had been a quiet listener, said, 'Gentlemen, I think you are mistaken. We are a proud people. Manners and customs in the different sections make about the only differences that really exists. If we are to be successful, what we have to do must be done quickly. The longer we have them to fight, the more difficult they will be to defeat.'"[64]

Aware by now that battles had been fought in Virginia, the men caught another stagecoach to San Antonio in mid-August, then moved on "by land to New Orleans"[65] and from there northeast to Richmond. Details of the final leg do not exist, but it is known that Johnston reached the rebel capital by September 10, when he was commissioned a full general by President Davis and given command of the western theater (he would die at the Battle of Shiloh in April 1862, the highest-ranking officer to be killed in the Civil War).[66] The two Armisteads took a few days longer but signed their enlistment papers in mid-September, following the lead of their younger brothers, Franck and Bowles, who had already joined the Confederate war effort.[67]

Winfield Hancock remained in California that summer, straining at the leash, anxious to be assigned to the war zone. He pleaded his case in frantic letters to General Scott and Montgomery Blair, postmaster general under Lincoln, a personal friend. He dashed off a note to Andrew Curtin, governor of Pennsylvania, offering his services to the state's new recruits, calling in favors wherever he could. It all was to no avail.[68]

The Fourth of July arrived without incident in hotly divided Los Angeles, but Hancock, as the ranking U.S. officer in the city, was asked to give a speech about patriotism in the face of rebellion. His wife described it as "a strong and impressive, if not eloquent, appeal to his countrymen."[69] Hancock was well regarded as an unrepentant Unionist, and he advised against severing ties and sullying memories that bound the people together under one national flag. Invoking the spirit of 1776, he also warned against actions that would "see the day approach when that occasion would cease to be commemorated."[70]

Following is a portion of the speech, obtained by Reverend Junkin:

And what flag is that we now look to as the banner the carried us through the great contest and was honored by the gallant deeds of its defenders? The Star-Spangled Banner of America, then embracing thirteen pale stars, representing the number of oppressed colonies; now thirty-four bright planets, representing that number of great States. To be sure, clouds intervene between us and eleven of that number; but we will trust that those clouds will soon be dispelled, and that those great stars in the Southern constellation may shine forth again with even greater splendor than before. Let them return to us! We will welcome them as brothers who have been estranged, and love them the more that they were angered and then returned to us . . .

To those who, regardless of these sacred memories, insist on sundering this Union of States, let us, who only wish our birthrights preserved to us, and whose desire it is to still be citizens of the great country that gave us birth, and to live under that flag . . . say, this day: "Your rights we will respect; your wrongs we will assist you to redress; but the Union is a precious heritage that we intend to preserve and defend to the last extremity."[71]

It was almost a month later, on August 3, that Hancock's request for a transfer to the eastern army was finally approved. General Sumner ordered that he "be relieved without delay from duty at Los Angeles" and travel immediately to Washington, D.C., "in connection with the movement of volunteers on the Overland Mail Route."[72] The specifics of the assignment still irked him—it was a quartermaster's role again, not a frontline battle command—but he knew he could address that issue when he reported to the commanding general, who, by the time he arrived, would be his old West Point and Mexican War friend, George McClellan.[73] He also pulled strings and arranged to travel with his family by boat rather than overland.

The steamer left San Francisco in late August, taking the normal route south to Panama, where, at the isthmus, Hancock coerced several sailors to row him briefly ashore. Desperate for word from the front, he obtained the most recent eastern papers, then two weeks old, which told of a Confederate victory at Wilson's Creek in Missouri. Hancock was urged to read the news aloud to fellow passengers, who, remarkably, included future officers of both armies. One historian wrote that "among the strange features of this extraordinary war was the fact that the same vessel was transporting old companions who still fraternized on the best of terms, but who immediately upon their arrival would become relentless enemies on bloody battlefields."[74] Their Atlantic-side ship headed up the East Coast toward New York Harbor but, just before arrival, dropped off the southern soldiers on the Jersey shore.[75]

Hancock wasted precious little time in New York City, catching the first train to Washington, D.C., before Almira even had time to unpack. Their trip was uneventful, she said, "the entire route as calm as a southern sea,"[76] but on the way, they picked up reports of the Union defeat at Bull Run and other such signs of despair. The sole piece of positive news was that McClellan was now in command. "Little Mac" knew Hancock's character from their days at West Point, knew his combat record from Mexico, and, most important, recognized a true leader when he saw one. In the process of reorganizing the army, it was no surprise that he sent for Hancock on the same day the captain arrived.[77]

Recommended by McClellan and approved by Lincoln, Hancock's promotion to brigadier general was dated September 23, 1861. He was freed at last from quartermaster duty and, having skipped several grades in rank, would no longer need Armistead's major's uniform. Assigned to a brigade in William "Baldy" Smith's division, he now commanded four regiments—the Fifth Wisconsin, the Forty-Third New Jersey, the Sixth Maine, and the Forty-Ninth Pennsylvania.[78] It was "merely by chance" that Company F of the Forty-Ninth included a second lieutenant from Norristown named John Hancock, who soon became assistant adjutant general on his older brother's staff.[79]

Winfield would go on to etch his name in history at some of the war's most famous battles, including Gettysburg, but he was never prouder than on the long-forgotten day in September 1861 when he was promoted to general and given a command in the Union army.

According to his staff officer and friend, Francis Walker,

To the very center of his being he was loyal to the Constitution and to the laws; and he never valued his commission in the army so highly as when it gave him a right to be in the front rank of defenders. He knew too many who, like his friend Armistead, had reluctantly and painfully broken the main ties of their lives in taking the other side, to indulge in puerile talk about "traitors and sour apple trees." He knew too much of the Southern temper to make light of the task before the nation, or to predict a holiday parade for the Union armies; but with all his soul he stood by the Government, and never did his faith in the ultimate triumph of the cause waver.[80]

CHAPTER NINE

War Breaks Out

THE ARRIVAL OF FORMER U.S. ARMY OFFICER LEWIS ARMISTEAD AT
Richmond in mid-September 1861 did not go unnoticed by the Confederate high command. He enlisted as a major on September 14 and
was immediately whisked up the ranks, commissioned colonel of the
Fifty-Seventh Virginia regiment, and charged with bringing discipline
to a fervent but untrained hodgepodge of farmers and blacksmiths from
Pittsylvania and nearby counties.[1]

Inexperience was so glaring that one of his junior officers enrolled
in a two-month crash course to learn tactics at the Virginia Military
Institute. A company called the "Franklin Sharpshooters" found its name
absurdly inaccurate because "the majority of the men lacked such essential equipment as muskets."[2] Turning these disparate parts into a smooth,
well-functioning unit was a painstaking process, even with a twenty-two-
year U.S. Army veteran at the helm. "Armistead immediately instituted
a rigorous training schedule," the regimental historian wrote. "At first
many men bitterly complained about the strict discipline, but they soon
felt only love and admiration for the commander."[3] His duties may have
made it impossible for Lewis to attend his mother's funeral when she
died following a long illness on September 30 at Upperville.[4]

Given his family history and command roles in three American wars,
it is mystifying that no contemporary description of Armistead's physical
appearance has ever been found—not even his height or an estimate of
his weight. Two of his younger brothers, Walker and Bowles, are listed in
Confederate military documents as standing five foot eight, so it can be
assumed that Lewis was that height or perhaps a few inches taller (his

son, W. Keith, was five foot nine).[5] A rarely published prewar photograph hints that Lewis was of medium build, although his clothing is rather loose and, therefore, deceptive,[6] and his uncle once wrote that he was "rather athletic" in his youth, but that is the extent of the public record.[7] The more commonly seen portrait photo from the Civil War era shows him to be balding with sad, piercing eyes, a full beard and mustache, and a prominent, gnarled nose. No one compared him to the handsome Hancock. He was forty-four years old when the war began.

Armistead's regiment spent part of its early existence in the Suffolk, Virginia, region, not far from Norfolk and Craney Island, where his father had built defenses for the U.S. Army during the War of 1812. Lewis's tenure there was far less exciting and involved mundane assignments, such as guarding the Blackwater River in North Carolina.[8] Despite the lack of combat action, however—he never led the Fifty-Seventh in battle as its colonel—his previous U.S. Army experience earned him a second Civil War promotion, this time to brigadier general, on April 1, 1862.[9] Within a few months, General Armistead's brigade came to include the Ninth, Fourteenth, Thirty-Eighth, and Fifty-Third Virginia regiments, in addition to the Fifty-Seventh, and began its yearlong march into Confederate military history.[10]

There was perhaps no clearer example of the shifting sands of the national divide than the evolution of young W. Keith Armistead, who had applied to attend the U.S. Military Academy at West Point less than nine months before the start of the Civil War.

In a July 1860 letter to the U.S. secretary of war, Keith's father—then a major in the Sixth Infantry—admitted that he was asking for a favor based solely on his family's long history of distinguished military service:

> *Upperville, Fauquier Co., Va.*
> *July 25, 1860*
>
> *Sir,*
> *I have the honor to apply for the appointment of cadet, to the U.S. Military Academy, for the year 1861, for my son, W. Keith Armistead.*

In a December 1861 letter, Lewis Armistead explained his reasons for leaving the U.S. Army and fighting in the Civil War. It is published here for the first time.
NATIONAL ARCHIVES

W. Keith Armistead will be sixteen years old next December—and, I believe, is fully qualified for the appointment.

Twenty one years of my life have been [spent] in the service, on the frontier; I have therefore had little, if any, opportunity of becoming acquainted with the great or influential men of my country. I do not know, how, if I had the inclination, to request their influence in obtaining the appointment for which I now apply.

If I, or any of my family, have ever done anything deserving of the favor of the War Dept., or of the Executive, it should be on record—it is to that record alone that I can appeal . . .

Very Respectfully,
Your Obedient Servant,
Lewis A. Armistead
Bvt. Maj, 6th Infy.[11]

Lewis was home on leave at the time and likely feeling pangs of guilt for having been such an absentee father; service in the Mexican War and at various frontier outposts had caused him to miss much of the first fifteen years of Keith's life. His own father, Walker Keith Armistead Sr., had dealt with the same situation in much the same way, doting on Lewis from afar and pushing his military career along (albeit with the unparalleled power of a U.S. Army brigadier general).

Finishing his letter with a flourish, the mid-level army officer reminded the secretary of war that he would be "pleased to know, as early as practicable, the result of his application, to the end that my son may pursue such studies as will qualify him for the appointment."[12]

No record exists as to whether the application for an at-large appointment was accepted or rejected, but it became a moot point when Virginia seceded from the Union in May 1861. By September, as the fall semester at West Point was starting, Keith's father and three uncles had all enlisted in the Confederate army, and the young man was making his way back to Richmond from an unidentified preparatory school north of the Mason-Dixon Line.[13]

On December 2, 1861, just ten days before Keith's seventeenth birthday, Lewis wrote another letter applying for a cadetship "for my son," this time in a prospective *Confederate* training program, perhaps at the Virginia Military Institute. The letter, addressed to General Samuel Cooper—a fellow veteran of the Seminole and Mexican wars, who was now adjutant general of the Rebel army—is the most valuable of all existing Armistead family documents from the Civil War era. It reveals Lewis's precise reasons for joining the Confederacy and underscored his deep concern for Keith's education and military future:

Camp Belcher, near Richmond, Va.
Dec. 2, 1861

Sir,

I have the honor to apply for the appointment of cadet for my son, W. Keith Armistead.

I have been a soldier all my life. I was an officer in the Army of the U.S., which service I left to fight for my own country, and for, and with, my own people—and because they were right, and oppressed. My resignation was forwarded in the month of May last, but I was unable to leave California until late in June, which I did with Genl. A.S. Johnson [sic], and other resigned officers of the U.S. Army, and arrived in the City of Richmond, Va. about the 15th of September last.

I never was a man of any wealth, and the little I had was all sacrificed when I left the U.S. Army. I wish it had been more. I am not able to continue my son's education. He is willing to take a musket, but I think he has capacity to do better, and that he is of the right age to begin a military education. He will be seventeen on the 12th inst.

Altho' my services were rendered under a different flag from that which I now acknowledge, I can recall them with pleasure and pride, and I believe they are still remembered by some, perhaps none better than the Adjt. Genl. Of the C.S. Army.

Hoping the foregoing may meet your favorable consideration.

I have the honor to be,
Your (Obedient Servant)
Lewis A. Armistead
Col. 57th Va. Vol.[14]

Especially with the perspective of 20/20 hindsight, the Armistead family turnabout was stunning. In a matter of seventeen months, Keith had gone from applying for a cadet's warrant at the U.S. Military Academy to seeking the same position at a school teaching officers to fight against West Point grads. Lewis even recalled the "pleasure and pride" he once felt while fighting "under a different flag"—the same U.S. flag that his father and uncles, especially his Uncle George, had long defended.

But Keith had been born into a different era. He had never rendered service to the Star-Spangled Banner and carried no such emotional baggage. Anxious to bolster his chances for training as a Confederate officer, he wrote his own letter in late March 1862, inquiring about additional support for his cadet's application. That it was addressed to General Robert E. Lee was clear evidence that the young man brimmed with confidence; he directly sought the endorsement of the rising star of the South, himself a West Point grad and former academy superintendent.[15]

Remarkably, Lee responded within three days. On April 2, he wrote to the Confederate secretary of war to endorse young Armistead for the appointment, even though they had met only recently. Much of Lee's support was based on his familiarity with Lewis Armistead, but another Rebel official added a note to Lee's letter that "Mr. [W. Keith] Armistead has been, in this office, since arrival, most assiduous in the performance of duty, correct in habits, and eager" to prove his worth.

In full, Lee wrote,

> *My personal acquaintance with W. K. Armistead is but of recent date; but the impressions formed of him in this short period are of favorable character; and I hear good accounts of him.*
>
> *The independence and manliness displayed by him in supporting himself, for a time, by manual labor while at school in the North, when cut off by reason of the war, from communication with his friends at the South, and his successful efforts in making his way through the enemy's lines to Virginia, are praiseworthy.*
>
> *I know him to be the son of a brave solider and worthy man, Brig. Genl. Armistead, in the service of the Confederate States.*
>
> *R.E. Lee*[16]

These were high-level endorsements, indeed, but war had erupted, and there was little time for a newfangled army and government to rely on a formal program for military education. The Confederates were outnumbered and outgunned as it was—deficient in all possible metrics but commitment to their cause—and needed every available man in the field. Rather than spending time at focused military schools like the Virginia Military Institute or The Citadel, Keith bypassed such education and entered the Rebel ranks by enlisting in Company A of the Sixth Virginia Cavalry on May 1, 1862. In doing so, he followed the lead of his uncles,

Bowles and Walker Jr.[17] All three Armisteads were present for duty with the Sixth Virginia in late spring and early summer, but Keith was soon assigned to detached service with General J. E. B. Stuart on August 18, and he continued in that capacity for the next eight months.

Stuart, the Confederacy's most famous cavalier, thought so much of Keith that he was still promoting him for the dream of Confederate officer training that September. Keith's military file at the National Archives notes that "Gen. J.E.B. Stuart recommends W. Keith Armistead for cadetship" on September 22.[18]

In early April 1862, still less than a year after Fort Sumter, Union General George McClellan determined to invade the Virginia Peninsula and seize the Confederate capital at Richmond. The result was the massive Peninsula campaign, drawing a quarter of a million men over the next three months into some of the most savage fighting of the war.[19]

With that, Winfield Hancock's pulse quickened. He had spent a lifetime dreaming of the chance to command troops in battle, and now, at long last, the moment was here. As a ten-year-old back in Norristown, marching his "junior militia" through the streets in search of a make-believe "enemy," Hancock had shown innate leadership traits. As a second lieutenant in Mexico, fresh out of West Point and ready for action, he displayed a zest for combat. "The real bent of his character . . . had become manifest beyond the possibility of mistake," a friend said. "By nature, Hancock was a soldier, every inch of him, and he now felt it in every fiber of his being."[20]

Since taking command of a brigade in September, the new general used drill and discipline to train his recruits but earned their devotion with a dynamic personal style. Francis Walker described him as "singularly imposing. Now at the prime of life, in his thirty-eighth year, a perfect blond, standing six feet high, powerfully formed yet easy and graceful in his movements . . . authority was stamped upon him as upon few sons of men."[21] Hancock was always fond of volunteer soldiers, proud of their commitment to the cause, refusing to sneer at them (as other veterans from the old army had) and "unremitting" in his attention to their welfare.[22] Admirable as this approach may have been, however, he still hurled invectives frequently and with vigor. Word passed through the ranks of Baldy Smith's division that Hancock was multilingual, fluent in both English and profanity.

As far back as 1776, General George Washington had issued an order against "that foolish and wicked practice of profane cursing"— there could be little hope, Washington said, "of the blessing of Heaven on our arms if we insult it by our impiety and folly"—but crude language of the sort had become a fact of army life.[23] Francis Walker, who otherwise revered his chief, found it unnecessary and demoralizing. "Only one habit marred Hancock's otherwise invariable dignity, and impressiveness," he said, and "this was an extravagant indulgence, at times, in harsh and profane speech."[24] Nonetheless, the troops of his brigade were loyal, attentive, eager, confident, and thoroughly prepared for battle. If a little intimidation was part of the mix, Hancock deemed it a worthwhile trade-off.

In early May, as the Confederates retreated by design toward Richmond, they set up a temporary defensive line at the old capital city of Williamsburg, centered on a substantial earthwork called Fort Magruder. The Battle of Williamsburg opened on May 5, when a Union division under Joseph Hooker attacked the fort in the driving rain. Hooker fought bravely throughout the morning, but the army's planning was haphazard, reinforcements were slow in coming, and the senior officer on-site, sixty-five-year-old E. V. Sumner—former commander in California—was overwhelmed by the tactical challenge.[25] Fortunes changed only after a group of runaway slaves reported that the Rebels had abandoned a redoubt on their extreme left flank.[26]

Hancock was sent to exploit it. He took five regiments and a battalion of artillery, as well as a young staff officer from Smith's division named George Armstrong Custer. They scrambled over a dam at Cub Dam Creek, passed the redoubt, and, fortuitously, found a second empty redoubt where they set up on a low rise about a mile from the fort. It was early afternoon. "From my position here," Hancock said in his report, "Fort Magruder with all its surroundings could be distinctly seen and all portions of the enemy on the plain between us."[27] Sensing the chance to achieve a great victory in his first battle of the Civil War, he sent his brother, Assistant Adjutant General John Hancock, to ask for reinforcements.[28]

John found General Smith, who approved the request and told him more troops were on the way, but that was before old Bull Sumner got cold feet and recalled them. Still commanding the field because McClellan had not yet arrived, Sumner ordered Hancock to pull back to the first redoubt and await further instructions.[29] Hancock was furious. Perched on the flank of the enemy, he knew he could turn the position and win the day if supported by others and given the chance to attack. "Never at a loss for expletives," Custer said, "Hancock was not at all loathe to express his condemnation."[30] He dispatched another staffer to Sumner to make his case.[31]

Back-and-forth messages continued for the next few hours. At about 3:30, Hancock sent Lieutenant F. U. Farquhar of the engineers "back to represent to General Sumner my position, with a view of showing the disadvantage of falling back at that time and giving up the advantages we had already secured, for which we might have to fight again the next day in order to recover, besides the bad impression it would make on my troops, and the inspiring effect it would have on the enemy." These were valid points, but he knew he was bordering on insubordination. At 4:20, having heard nothing from Farquhar, he wrote to Smith that he would "wait a reasonable time to get an answer from General Sumner before falling back."[32]

By 5:10, with no word from anyone on anything, Hancock resigned himself to pulling out when the Rebels intervened and settled the matter. They attacked.[33]

Confederate Generals Jubal Early and D. H. Hill led a rash advance, but they were outnumbered and outgunned by determined Union troops under a rising star commander. Hancock seized the moment, blunted the assault, and boldly ordered a counterattack. Newspapers reported that the order was "Charge, gentlemen, charge," but a scoffing Maine soldier said Hancock was "more emphatic than that . . . the air was blue all around him."[34] Properly inspired, Union troops inflicted severe casualties, more than five hundred in all, "annihilating" the Fifth North Carolina and capturing their first battle flag. Rebel forces retreated toward Richmond anyway, as planned, but Hancock—though he came very close to disobeying orders—had battered them on the flank.[35]

McClellan arrived near the end of the fighting and took great pleasure in his friend's success. "This was one of the most brilliant engagements of the war," he said in his report, "and General Hancock merits the highest praise for the soldierly qualities displayed, and his perfect appreciation of the vital importance of his position."[36] McClellan was already well known for hyperbole, but the next day, May 6, in a letter wired to his wife, he wrote, simply, "Hancock was superb yesterday." The phrase was meant for private consumption, but once it became known to reporters, it spread like wildfire, and the description stuck: "Hancock the Superb."[37]

Two weeks later, during a lull in the campaign, McClellan placed Hancock and Smith's division in the new Sixth Corps, although they would see only limited action in the upcoming Seven Days Battles.[38] Summing up his mind-set after Williamsburg, the newly dubbed "Superb" wrote home to his mother in Norristown:

> *I am well, and so also is brother John. We are not in Richmond yet; but trust we shall be there, in all good time. I hope that God in his good mercy will permit both your sons to reach that city in safety and honor.*
>
> *Your devoted son,*
> *Winfield S. Hancock*[39]

Armistead's new command went into action twice during the Peninsula campaign, facing a baptism of fire at Seven Pines on June 1 and charging uphill into the mouths of enemy guns at Malvern Hill on July 1, but, as might be expected for untested troops in such circumstances, their results bordered on disastrous.

Most of the men had never even *seen* combat (much less been involved) when the Battle of Seven Pines broke out along the Chickahominy River near Richmond on May 31. Held in reserve all day as part of Benjamin Huger's division, the brigade looked on in horror as disjointed Rebel attacks led to massive casualties with no discernable progress. The most noteworthy occurrence came near sundown when the senior Confederate commander, Joseph E. Johnston, was seriously wounded in the chest and shoulder, knocked unconscious, and carried from the field on a stretcher. His eventual replacement would be Robert E. Lee, the president's top military adviser—a profound change for the southern army—but command in the short term devolved to Gustavus W. Smith, Johnston's top subordinate, who chose illogically to fight again the next day.[40]

Armistead's brigade was one of six units ordered forward on the morning of June 1 in what one man described as a "half-hearted attack on the resilient Federal lines."[41] Moving pensively through thick woods and muddy fields, stepping over dead and gruesomely wounded bodies from the day before, they drifted away from George Pickett's brigade on their right and soon lost their nerve in a hail of Union bullets. "Total confusion resulted," wrote the historian of the Ninth Virginia. The battle-hardened Armistead, fighting for the first time against the Star-Spangled Banner—a jarring thought in itself—did his best to halt a panicked retreat but managed to hold only a few dozen men in place amid the chaos. As John Lewis of the Ninth put it, "Some of the boys just at that time seemed to have urgent business in Richmond."[42]

According to Pickett,

Armistead's brigade had broken and were leaving the field pell-mell. . . . I could scarcely credit my own eyes in witnessing this misfortune on my left. I immediately rode to that part of [the] field; found nothing between me and [the] railroad except the gallant Armistead himself, with a regimental color and some 30 persons, mostly officers, with him.[43]

There were similar reports from other witnesses about the general's bravery, even if troops under his command fared poorly in their first contest. "Armistead's men fled early in the action," wrote D. H. Hill, commanding a nearby division, "with the exception of a few heroic companies, with which that gallant officer maintained his ground against an entire brigade."[44] Leading from the front, Armistead was so exposed to enemy fire that his horse, a favored black mount, was shot out from under him, forcing him to slog ahead on foot.[45] But neither side did enough to claim victory before Smith called off the attack at 11:30 that morning, leaving the result undecided after two hard days of combat.[46]

Armistead's unit suffered relatively few of the Confederates' 1,300 casualties on the second day at Seven Pines,[47] but the condition of one injured soldier was especially troubling to the new brigadier. His younger brother, Franck, had joined his staff as a captain two weeks earlier and suffered a minor (although unidentified) wound in the fighting on June 1. Franck was an 1856 graduate of West Point and former U.S. Army lieutenant who served for five years on the frontier before resigning to enlist in the Confederacy. He returned to action shortly after Seven Pines and remained with Lewis's staff through the end of July, when he was reassigned again, this time to the western theater, never achieving his goal of commanding a regiment in his brother's brigade.[48]

The pace and tone of the campaign and, by extension, the history of the war changed irrevocably when Lee rose to Confederate command on the afternoon of June 1, 1862.

Incensed at the invasion of his native state and anxious to repel McClellan, Lee undertook a series of aggressive actions to defend Richmond and chase Union troops from the Peninsula, culminating in the Seven Days Battles in late June.[49]

The first of these was a minor clash at Oak Grove on June 25, when Armistead's brigade drew picket duty and fired sporadically in inconclusive action, losing one man killed. For the next five days, as battles roared from Beaver Dam Creek to Savage's Station, "there was constant skirmishing along the line," but the brigade was not fully engaged until the seventh day at Malvern Hill, where McClellan's force halted during a steady retreat from Richmond.[50] The Union commander, always melodramatic at times like these, informed headquarters that "we are hard pressed by superior numbers," adding, "if none of us escape, we shall at least have done honor to the country. I shall do my best to save the Army."[51]

Lee's weeklong offensive had been so effective and McClellan's reaction so skittish that Union troops were now only about a mile from their designated fallback point at Harrison's Landing on the James River. It was morning on June 30 when lead Union elements reached the former Malvern Hills Manor and took defensive positions for a last-ditch stand. Located about fifteen miles from the Rebel capital, Malvern Hill (which had long since lost is plural designation) was "not so much a hill" as a gently sloping rise leading to an open, narrow plateau. It was a commanding space for artillery, overlooking a vast, lush valley dotted by four farmhouses and bisected by two creeks. General Fitz John Porter arranged the troops as they clambered in throughout the day and posted more than thirty guns, many of them rifled, a decidedly fearsome arsenal, from Henry J. Hunt's artillery reserve.[52]

Lee was nonplussed and ready for a fight. Armistead's brigade was one of the first to reach the field on July 1, sent there on an early morning march through swamps and woods by division commander Huger and reporting directly to Lee at 10:00 a.m.[53] In the absence of Huger, who trailed well behind and would not catch up until mid-afternoon, Lee placed Armistead opposite the center of the Union line and told him to wait for further orders. In the meantime, Lee and James Longstreet devised a plan calling for grand batteries on the right and left to hammer McClellan's gunners with converging fire, clearing the way for an infantry attack.[54]

It was at that point, however, that Lee, through his aide, Robert H. Chilton, sent one of the most questionable missives of the war, shirking responsibility for ordering the attack and inexplicably turning it over to a junior brigadier:

> *Batteries have been established to rake the enemy's lines. If it is broken, as is probable, Armistead, who can witness the effect of the fire, has been ordered to charge with a yell. Do the same. By order of General Lee.*
>
> *R.H. Chilton*
> *Assistant Adjutant-General*[55]

(Eerily, the same thing would happen one year later at Gettysburg when Lee ordered an artillery barrage to precede Pickett's Charge and Longstreet passed responsibility for signaling the infantry attack to another subordinate officer, E. P. Alexander.)

Armistead never mentioned the order in his report, acknowledging only that he "threw out the necessary pickets and skirmishers in front and took a position with the right of my brigade in a ravine near the edge of the woods," but it became a moot point once the artillery duel began at 1:00 p.m.[56] The Rebels were hopelessly outmatched, failing to coordinate their sixteen cannons in a lopsided contest with thirty-seven well-placed Union guns on the Malvern plateau. The few batteries available to Lee were soon blasted out of action, gun carriages wrecked, limbers ruined, men and animals strewn across the field. One officer said the performance of the Confederate artillery was "most farcical." Union skirmishers then crept forward under cover of shot and shell to inflict more damage and perhaps incite a panicked rout.[57]

It was about 3:30 when Armistead, sensing defeat and possible disaster, *did* in fact act on his own, albeit without the requested "yell." Hoping to check the Union advance, he sent forward parts of three regiments—the Fourteenth, Thirty-Eighth, and Fifty-Third—to establish a new Confederate line. They did so "in handsome style," he bragged later, but "in their ardor they went too far." Caught in no-man's-land, unable to advance or retreat, they at least "gained some protection by a wave of the ground" and remained there, pinned down by Union fire for several more hours.[58]

Eventually, Lee and his staff cobbled together an attack, but it was poorly organized and pointlessly jumbled and never had a chance of success. Brigades went in piecemeal only to be chewed up by Union artillery fire. The lieutenant colonel of Armistead's original regiment, the Fifty-Seventh, led a desperate charge that made some tangible progress, "and, seeing the Stars and Stripes floating defiantly before, we poured in a well-directed fire and had the extreme gratification of seeing the colors totter and fall to the ground."[59] But McClellan's troops rallied in force, stalling the advance and claiming victory on the seventh day after more than five hours of combat, avenging the Star-Spangled Banner on Malvern Hill.[60]

Losses on both sides were ghastly. In the wee hours of the next morning, Armistead's old West Point classmate and mess hall combatant, Jubal Early, was searching for scattered elements of the Rebel army when he approached slowly on horseback:

> *I moved a little further to my right for the purpose of seeing better and discovered a cluster of Confederates, not more than ten or twelve in number. . . . On riding up to this party, I found it to consist of General Armistead of Huger's division with a few men of his brigade. In answer to my question as to where his brigade was, General Armistead replied, "Here are all that I know anything about except those lying out there in front." He had spent the night in a small cluster of trees around some old graves.[61]*

The final tally for Armistead's brigade at Malvern Hill was 49 killed, 272 wounded, and 67 missing, presumed dead or captured—a total of 388 casualties.[62] The sting of loss was softened, however, when McClellan gave up the field on July 2, retreating to the safety of the James River and forsaking his drive on Richmond. Lee had lost the epic battle but won the campaign and saved the Rebel capital.[63]

As it turned out, Armistead was one of a small group of Confederate officers whose reputations were sullied at Malvern Hill. A man in a nearby regiment claimed to have seen him drinking brandy behind a poplar tree during the battle and referred to him ever after as the "Poplar General."[64] Worse, William H. Cocke of the Ninth Virginia accused him of cowardice, writing that "he is full of saying, 'go on boys' but has never said 'come on' when we are going into a fight."[65] Cocke was likely despondent over casualties at Malvern Hill and blamed the often joyless Armistead in a letter to his parents, but no other person—soldier or commander—made a similar charge. General John Bankhead Magruder wrote that Armistead had brought on "the action in the most gallant manner by repulsing an attack of a heavy body of the enemy's skirmishers" and then "skillfully lent support to the contending troops."[66] Cocke's comments are noted as an indelible part of Armistead's Civil War record, but the preponderance of the evidence is that Lewis, for all his many flaws in life, was as brave as any soldier in either army.

Many Armistead men served in "horse militia" units in Virginia over the years, dating back as far as the 1600s, so it was only fitting that Walker Jr. and his youngest brother, Bowles, enlisted in the Sixth Virginia Cavalry in 1861.

Both were natural horsemen, having grown up on expansive farmland in Fauquier County, and Walker may have honed those skills with the Los Angeles Mounted Rifles during his final few months in California in the spring of that year.

Bowles, age twenty-three, attended a local military academy in Upperville and was the first Armistead brother to join the Rebel cause on July 24. Walker Jr., thirty, the only brother without formal military training, enlisted on September 15, one day after arriving from the West Coast. Both became low-ranking members of Company A.[67]

But Walker Jr. had bigger ambitions and sought a transfer and a promotion in less than a week. In a September 20 letter to headquarters, he asked about obtaining "a commission as 1st Lieutenant of Infantry in the Confederate States Army,"[68] hoping to attach himself to his older brother's command. Much as Lewis had done in earlier years, Walker name-dropped unabashedly, invoking his father's legacy and the family's military history—and the recent cross-country journey—to make his case more compelling:

> I am a son of the late Genl. W.K. Armistead, U.S. Army, & a brother of Major L.A. Armistead & Lieut. Franck S. Armistead, formerly of the U.S. Army, now of C.S. Army.
>   I am a native of Virginia & reached here from California a few days ago. I am now a private in R.H. Dulany's company from Loudoun, Va.[69]

Receiving no response by late November, and growing more impatient by the day, he asked his commander to intervene on his behalf. Captain Richard H. Dulany wrote a letter confirming that Walker had been in California when "he heard our state had seceded . . . and although absent from the state for [some] months . . . he came directly to join my company without taking time to visit his home." The new private, he said, "was so cool a man and so good a soldier" that Dulany could not "resist the temptation of trying to forward his wishes."[70] But despite those efforts and his family's reputation, the internal campaign went nowhere.

Walker remained in the cavalry for the duration of the war, advancing to second sergeant in 1862 and first sergeant in 1863 before moving to the brigade's ordnance department.[71] The regimental history notes that during a raid on Union General John Pope's headquarters near Catlett's Station in August 1862, Walker made off with one of Pope's dress uniform coats and helped another man steal the general's boots.[72] Beyond that, however, his four-year service record was unremarkable.

Bowles made a more rapid ascent up the ranks after enlisting as a corporal in Dulany's original unit, the Loudoun Dragoons. Promoted three times in the first year and commissioned a first lieutenant by November 1862—much to the envy of Walker, no doubt—he signed the muster roll that month as "commanding the company" and drew several special assignments from headquarters. A risk taker who often tempted fate, Bowles was wounded three times—at Cold Harbor, Fisher's Hill, and Five Forks—and suffered a fractured clavicle during a fall from his horse.[73] His greatest moment came when he was named acting captain by General William Henry Fitzhugh Payne in 1864, "knighted on the field of battle . . . for especially gallant conduct."[74]

The youngest Armistead soldier of this era, W. Keith, joined his uncles in the Sixth Virginia Cavalry as a seventeen-year-old in May 1862 but spent much of his career on detached service and "seems rarely to have been with the company." He was assigned to his father's staff early in 1863.[75]

CHAPTER TEN

Proclamation

THE RELATIVE SUCCESS OF THE SEVEN DAYS AND A VICTORY AT SECOND Bull Run on August 28–30 convinced Robert E. Lee that his best chance to defeat the Union army and win southern independence would be to take the fight to northern soil in the late summer of 1862.

"The present seems to be the most propitious time since the commencement of the war for the Confederate Army to enter Maryland," he wrote to President Jefferson Davis on September 3, the idea being to "afford her an opportunity of throwing off the oppression to which she is now subject."[1] Doing so, however, might create a moral dilemma for Lewis Armistead and others in the ranks.

It was less than two years earlier, at a final meeting with Hancock before the war, that Armistead said he hoped God would strike him dead "if I am ever induced to leave my native soil."[2] In theory, he envisioned only a defensive war to protect the southern states, never conceiving—and certainly never endorsing—the kind of blatant northern invasion Lee had now proposed. But a full month of hard campaigning and two pitched battles near Richmond conspired to change his mind.

There was some irony in that Lee gave Armistead additional duties for the move across the border in the Maryland campaign. "Brig. Gen. L.A. Armistead is appointed provost-marshal," Lee wrote on September 6, "and will be obeyed accordingly, having authority to call for guards, take all proper measures to correct irregularities against good order and military discipline, and prevent depredations upon the community."[3] This new task—collecting stragglers and preventing desertions—was a thankless job in any army at any time, but never more so than for the

Confederates in September 1862. The decision to drive north drew loud protests from some in the ranks. Soldiers in the Twenty-Fifth North Carolina "said they volunteered to resist invasion and not to invade; some did not believe it right to invade Northern territory."[4] Even in the Ninth Virginia in Armistead's own brigade, "the offensive into 'foreign' territory" was controversial; it was one of many factors that caused some to "fall away in a steady trickle and depleted the tattered army's strength."[5] Such a feeling was not common, of course, but it *did* exist.

Armistead turned out to be an abject failure as provost marshal, though it is doubtful that anyone could have succeeded under the circumstances. Lee admitted as much in his report, blaming many factors for the army's poor condition but seeming to confirm, in his own cleverly worded way, that some men had simply refused to invade the United States. "The arduous service in which our troops had been engaged, their great privations of rest and food, and the long marches without shoes over mountain roads, had greatly reduced our ranks before the action began," Lee wrote. "These causes had compelled thousands of brave men to absent themselves, *and many more had done so from unworthy motives*" (emphasis added).[6]

In addition to provost duties, Armistead remained in command of his brigade during the Battle of Antietam on September 17. It was the bloodiest single day in the Civil War, with more than twenty-two thousand casualties on both sides, and even though his unit was posted in reserve, just north of the Dunker Church, he received a slight wound when a cannonball rolled by and clipped his foot, "knocking him out of action."[7] Another account had "Armistead blown over by a passing shell that narrowly missed him, and feeling grumpy about it."[8] The senior regimental officer, Colonel James G. Hodges of the Fourteenth Virginia, took temporary command of the brigade at that point, although it played virtually no role in the battle.[9]

The pace of action was much different for Winfield Hancock on the Union side of the field. Commanding a brigade in William B. Franklin's Sixth Corps, Hancock arrived at 9:00 a.m. after a ten-mile march from Brownsville and set up on the road to Sharpsburg, "ready to support the attack on the right or left, as might be required." After a brief diversion, he was assigned to a point in the East Woods, where a Second Corps battery was under attack and unsupported by infantry. Hancock brought six regiments and two additional batteries and immediately sent out skirmishers to counter the Confederate fire.[10]

His troops "met those of the enemy advancing through the corn-field separating us," Hancock said. The Rebels unlimbered two new batteries in the West Woods to pound away with "a heavy fire of shell, round shot shrapnel and grape," doing enough damage that Hancock asked for another regiment to bolster his line. General Oliver Otis Howard, commanding a brigade in the Second Corps, personally led the Twentieth Massachusetts to a position on the far right, and "after a severe cannonading, our skirmishers doing good execution at the same time, the enemy's batteries were silenced by our artillery, and withdrawn from the field." Hancock said the loss to his infantry was slight.[11]

As an aside, he mentioned that staff officer John Hancock, his brother, "behaved with gallantry, and rendered very efficient service in carrying orders under the first of the enemy."[12]

By mid-morning, the din of the battle had shifted south over rolling terrain to a sunken farm lane near the Henry Piper Farm. Confederate troops under D. H. Hill took cover behind a dirt embankment gouged out by years of wagon traffic, several feet below the surface, lying in wait for their Union pursuers. They vowed to stay "till the sun went down or victory was won"[13] but were attacked in consecutive waves by two divisions of the Second Corps. This relentless surge by William French and Israel Richardson began to overwhelm the Rebels, who, even after being reinforced, were compelled to fall back.[14]

Over the course of several hours, the toll here was fearsome. Bodies piled up in the "Bloody Lane," often stacked one on another. In Richardson's division, the famous Irish Brigade under Thomas Meagher led the second wave, and fighting eventually spilled onto the Piper farm, where the Confederates rallied.[15] Sometime around noon, with artillery pounding away from both sides, a shell fragment struck Richardson and inflicted a debilitating wound. The hard-charging general was placed on a stretcher and carried out of action, leaving a gaping hole in leadership at the Union center.[16]

No one knew it at the time, but this would be a defining moment in Winfield Hancock's career.

Hancock was still back in the East Woods, dealing with matters on his own front, but McClellan moved quickly to fill the leadership void. The commanding general held Hancock in such high esteem that he didn't hesitate to reach across corps lines and tap him as Richardson's replacement.[17] Doing this in the midst of battle only magnified the risk—a mere brigadier now leading an unfamiliar division—but McClellan knew it was his best option. Hancock made a dramatic entrance to his new command, riding along the line in full view of the troops, and one man, properly inspired by the sight, called him a "fine, soldierly-looking officer."[18] Another said, "No one could have told he had not commanded a division for years."[19]

Francis Walker described the unique scene this way:

It was not amid the pomp of the review, with bands playing and officers saluting, but on the trampled battlefield strewn with bloody stretchers and wreck of caissons and ambulances, the dead and dying thick around, the wounded still limping and crawling to the rear, with shells shrieking through the air, that Hancock first met and greeted the good regiments he was to lead in a score of battles. The lines were ragged from shot and shell; the uniforms were rent and soiled from hedge and ditch; the bands were engaged in carrying off the wounded or assisting the surgeons at their improvised hospitals.[20]

He took charge immediately, shouting, "Now, men, stay there until you are ordered away . . . this place must be held at all hazards."[21]

It was fortunate for Hancock that, while commanding an unfamiliar division for the first time, he had little to do other than holding his line near the lane. There would be no more sustained fighting on this part of the field, even if periodic firing from artillery and sharpshooters continued through the afternoon. At one point, Hancock said, "a command of the enemy was seen in line of battle, preceded by skirmishers, advancing in a direction parallel to our front, and toward a command of ours." But he somehow finagled a battery from his old Sixth Corps, and "the enemy, after a short cannonading, was forced to retire."[22] The focus of the fighting then switched away from the lane to a bridge over Antietam Creek, where Union troops made headway before being halted by a late-arriving Confederate force under A. P. Hill.

The Battle of Antietam was a tactical stalemate, the advantage edging back and forth during the day, but it became a strategic victory for the Union when Lee pulled his bedraggled force back across the Potomac River the next night, September 18. Seizing the moment in the wake of the Rebel retreat, President Lincoln issued the preliminary Emancipation Proclamation on September 22, declaring that by January 1, 1863, "all persons held as slaves within any State, or designated part of a State" that was currently in rebellion against the United States "shall be then, thenceforward, and forever, free."[23] This was Antietam's lasting legacy. Although not outright abolition, as some had hoped, the proclamation was nonetheless the beginning of the end for slavery in the southern states; the purpose of the war in the North now became something grander and far more compelling than mere restoration of the Union.

A chastened Lee headed south to Winchester, Virginia, and used much of the next two months to refit and reorganize his army, filling holes and shuffling assignments.[24] He placed Armistead's brigade in a new division under General George Pickett, enabling Lewis to reconnect with another former U.S. Army comrade, Richard Garnett, one of several new brigadiers. Delighted to be relieved of provost marshal duty, Armistead went about conducting drills with the same kind of "draconian military procedure" that many of his men had come to "detest."[25] Once again, however, they saw little action at the next major battle, being held deep in reserve at Fredericksburg in December 1862.[26]

Lincoln's reaction in the immediate aftermath of Antietam was one of frustration and anger. Putting the proclamation aside for the moment, he was livid at McClellan for failing to capitalize on his numerical advantage and appalled that he hadn't pursued Lee into Virginia. Accordingly, the president traveled to the battlefield in early October to meet with the general in person, urging immediate action with an eye toward ending the war.[27] But after a few halfhearted maneuvers—such as sending Hancock on a probing mission to Harpers Ferry and Charles Town on October 16[28]—McClellan reverted to his natural caution and moved the army at a snail's pace, refusing to engage or even chase Lee. A simmering Lincoln waited until November 5, the day of the midterm elections, before writing the order removing McClellan from army command and replacing him with the decidedly mediocre Ambrose Burnside. It was delivered in a driving snowstorm at Rectortown, Virginia, on November 7.[29]

Burnside, though wary of his ability to command such a large force, wasted little time reorganizing the army into three "grand divisions" of two corps each and vowed to set out after Lee toward Richmond.[30] Hancock was promoted to major general of volunteers on November 29[31] and given formal command of the First Division of the Second Corps, which he had led since Antietam, but more dark days and the Battle of Fredericksburg lay ahead.

Hancock was jolted by the demotion of his friend McClellan. They had known each other since West Point, served together in Mexico, and, as fellow Democrats, shared many of the same political views. But, as had been proven many times since the prewar days of 1860, Hancock was foremost a believer in the cause of the Union, and when rumors of an insurrection on behalf of McClellan spread through the army, he would have none of it.

"The Army are not satisfied with the change, and consider the treatment of McClellan most ungracious and inopportune," he admitted in a letter to Almira. "Yet I do not sympathize in the movement going on to resist the order. 'It is useless,' I tell the gentlemen around me. 'We are serving no one man; we are serving our country.'" The rebellion could not be resisted with fissures in the Union ranks.

McClellan calmed the army's nerves with a final message that was printed and distributed as he prepared to exit: "The battles you have fought under my command will proudly live in the Nation's history. The glory you have achieved, our mutual perils and fatigues, the graves of our comrades fallen in battle and by disease . . . unite us still by an indissoluble tie. We shall ever be Comrades in supporting the Constitution of our country and the nationality of its people."[32] At Burnside's request, he remained on-site for three days to assist in the transition of command.[33]

Burnside's intention was to concentrate the Army of the Potomac at Warrenton and then "make a rapid move of the whole force to Fredericksburg" before heading on to Richmond.[34] Hancock and the rest of the

Second Corps were placed in a grand division under Bull Sumner and directed to a spot across the Rappahannock River from Fredericksburg on November 17. There were so few Rebels on the other side that corps commander Darius N. Couch believed they could have crossed the river at once if the floating pontoon bridges had been there, enabling them to seize the heights above the town.[35] But "a combination of miscommunication, inefficient army bureaucracy and poor weather" delayed the arrival of the pontoons until November 25, by which point Lee's army had taken a strong position in Fredericksburg and entrenched, creating an imposing front.[36] Burnside's plan to use the town as a base had been foiled.

His next idea was to take Fredericksburg by frontal assault, crossing on the pontoons and then charging across seemingly open terrain toward dug-in Confederates at the foot of Marye's Heights. That idea seemed reckless to Hancock and Couch, who voiced their objections to Sumner at an in-person meeting on December 9. An irritated Burnside heard about it and confronted them the following night. "He said he understood, in a way, that we were opposed to his plans," Couch said, but "he seemed rather severe on Hancock," stating that "all he wanted was the devotion of his men." Hancock denied any professional or personal discourtesy, allowing only that he "knew there was a line of fortified heights on the opposite side, and that it would pretty difficult for us to go over there and take them."[37] Burnside was unmoved.

The army commander ordered a multipronged attack by the entire Union force on December 13. Couch's Second Corps was tasked to drive straight forward into an open plain, as Hancock had feared, "for the purpose of seizing the heights in rear of the town." William French's division would lead the way, followed immediately by Hancock's, with O. O. Howard's division held back in support. They were arranged in three lines of brigades, with intervals of about two hundred yards, covered by "heavy" lines of skirmishers in front and on the flanks.[38]

The skirmishers were in position by 11:00 a.m., and French's main force stopped off shortly after noon, coming under intense artillery fire as soon as they were spotted. A canal impeded their approach and broke up formations, as did scattered houses and garden fences. "The difficulty of the movement," Hancock said, "consisted in the fact that we had to march a considerable distance by the flank through the streets of the town, all the time under a heavy fire, before we enabled to deploy; and then, owing to obstacles—among them a mill-race [canal]—it was impossible to deploy, except by marching the whole length of each brigade by the flank, in a line parallel to the enemy's works."[39] He neglected to say, "I told you so."

French's men advanced toward a sunken road at the foot of the heights and were pulverized by a sheet of musketry from Confederates behind a stone wall. The deepest penetration of these first Union troops was to within forty yards of the wall before they were forced back to the cover of a slight rise of ground. French estimated that a fourth of his division had fallen merely by crossing the plain, and bodies strewn across the field were testament to the sacrifice. "My command held its ground but could advance no further," he wrote in his report.

On came Hancock into the melee. Samuel Zook's brigade was in the vanguard, followed by the Irish brigade under a hobbled Thomas Meagher. "It seemed a terrible long distance," said a man in Zook's command, "as with bated breath and heads bowed, we hurried forward, the rebel guns plowing great furrows in our ranks at every step." When they were about three hundred yards from the wall, Zook's survivors let out a yell and plunged forward into the murderous storm of fire. Some of them, probably from Colonel John Brooke's regiment, made it to within thirty yards of the Confederate position, believed to be the farthest Union advance of the day.[40]

Meagher's brigade and another under John C. Caldwell covered the same path with the same alacrity and met the same fate. Meagher's Irishmen wore "sprigs of green in their caps" and charged, ironically, toward Confederate Irish in Thomas Cobb's Georgia brigade, posted safely behind the wall.[41] Having already suffered grievous losses at Antietam, Meagher observed the carnage here and "feared the Irish Brigade was no more."[42] Caldwell's men, coming next and stepping over the bodies of fallen comrades, "behaved with great gallantry and fought with steadiness" but could advance no farther than their predecessors.[43]

The extent of the damage was evident in a comment made by Colonel Joshua Owen of Howard's division, the next unit in line. "I was sent out there to support General Hancock's division," Owen told Howard dolefully, "but there is not much left of it to support."[44]

Burnside kept up the attack, but it resulted in only more senseless slaughter for the Union side. The Confederates held. Couch noted afterward that "the desperate, stubborn fighting was done by Hancock's division and most of French's," but that praise was little consolation to Hancock, who, in his first full battle as division commander, reported a staggering 2,013 losses out of 5,006 engaged, just over 40 percent. The total Union loss was more than twelve thousand.[45]

A historian wrote that "the full depth of the tragedy only gradually came to be realized in the North. Christmas that year was bleak in Northern homes."[46] Lincoln was melancholy, even though the Emancipation Proclamation became effective on New Year's Day. Hancock obtained a leave of absence and went home to St. Louis to visit Almira and the children, thereby avoiding Burnside's futile "mud march," but much changed in his absence. Lincoln replaced Burnside with Joseph Hooker on January 25, Sumner retired, the grand divisions were abolished, and the war soon entered a different phase.[47]

It was in February 1863 that Lewis Armistead's continued impatience with volunteer citizen-soldiers spilled over into a dispute with Colonel John Grammar of the Fifty-Third Virginia. Grammar submitted his resignation and complained to Confederate headquarters that "on every occasion Brig. General Armistead's manner & tone are so offensive & insulting that I can but believe he . . . wishes to force me to resign." Armistead did not, in fact, think Grammar was "competent for the position he holds" but allowed that part of his own behavior stemmed from frustration with non-professionals in the ranks. (In this way, he was much different from Hancock, who, while a disciplinarian, still respected volunteers.) Accustomed to a much more rigid structure during more than two decades in the U.S. Army, Armistead said, "I have felt obliged to speak to him as one military man would to another and as I have passed nearly all my life in camps, my manner may not be understood or appreciated by one who was been all his life a civilian."[48] Grammar was replaced in March by William Aylett, a great-grandson of the Revolutionary patriot Patrick Henry.[49]

Armistead's brigade joined corps commander James Longstreet on a spring deployment to Suffolk, Virginia, where they gathered supplies and kept a constant watch on Union troops in the region with the goal of protecting Richmond. As a result, they were absent from the field (again) as Lee scored perhaps his greatest victory in the Chancellorsville campaign from April 30 to May 6, offsetting superior Union numbers with daring and tactical genius.

Lee had hunkered down at Fredericksburg since the December battle and was momentarily paralyzed when Hooker began a turning movement in late April, trying to lure him out of position. Longstreet's absence meant the Rebel commander was at a greater disadvantage than normal, leading only sixty thousand troops against a Union force that topped one hundred thousand.[50] By April 30, when Hooker's army had arrived at a crossing called Chancellorsville along the Orange Turnpike, Hooker was so pleased that he declared that "the operations of the last three days have determined that the enemy must ingloriously fly, or come out from behind his defense and give us battle on our ground, where certain destruction awaits him."[51] Darius Couch of the Second Corps was somewhat less grandiose but still called it "a brilliantly conceived and executed movement."[52]

The problem for Hooker was that no one relished a challenge more than Lee, and the southern commander tried within hours to reclaim the initiative. He left ten thousand troops to hold Fredericksburg and hurried the rest of his men on the turnpike toward Chancellorsville. Lafayette McLaws was on the march by midnight of April 30, and Stonewall Jackson caught up to him by 8:00 a.m. on May 1.[53] The joint gray force clashed with a Fifth Corps division under George Sykes sometime around noon, but Hooker was so shaken by the sudden presence of Rebel troops that he ordered Sykes to break off the engagement and pull back.

The extent of Union confusion was evident when Hancock's division, which had been sent to support Sykes, received a command to "withdraw all the troops" as soon as they arrived.[54] "I have no doubt that we should have held our advanced positions," a frustrated Hancock said later, but the once-overconfident Hooker had clearly been spooked by Lee and was already losing his nerve.[55]

The next day, May 2, 1863, would become one of the most consequential days in American military history—and one of the most embarrassing ever for the U.S. Army. Sensing an opening because of Hooker's reticence, the always-daring Lee made another bold move, splitting his force in the face of the enemy, directing Jackson with almost thirty thousand men to march under cover and unhinge the right flank. Posted there, virtually unprepared, was the Union Eleventh Corps, now under the command of O. O. Howard, who had been moved up from the division ranks after Fredericksburg. It was a disaster waiting to happen.

Jackson pounced at 5:00 p.m., urging his shock troops forward with the chilling shrieks of the Rebel yell. One of the most devastating flank attacks in the history of modern warfare exploded from the trees, startling Howard, embarrassing Hooker, touching off a fierce firefight, and sending a blizzard of blue uniforms tumbling toward the rear. Some of the Eleventh Corps men fought gamely but were outgunned, outmatched, and overwhelmed in the swirling pandemonium. It is likely that Jackson would have done more damage and possibly rolled up the entire line had not falling darkness and the inevitable mixing of lines caused him to call off the attack sometime after 7:00 p.m.[56]

Lee suffered a severe blow of his own that night when Jackson was mortally wounded, shot inadvertently by his own men while on a reconnaissance, but not even that tragic event could reenergize Hooker or stem the Rebel tide.

The Second Corps was never deployed on a unified front during the seven-day campaign, and Hancock's division was often on the fringe of the action. According to one account, he was stationed along the road to Fredericksburg during the Union retreat from Jackson's attack when a panicked Eleventh Corps soldier approached him, asking for directions to the pontoon bridges. "The answer he received has been handed down by tradition," Francis Walker wrote, "but it is best not to put it in cold and unsympathetic type."[57] Hancock then fought a determined rearguard action as the army pulled back over several days, at one point facing his men in opposite directions to counter Confederate threats, and was praised by General Couch for "gallantry, energy and his example of marked personal bravery."[58] His division suffered one thousand casualties.[59]

"We have had tremendous fighting at Chancellorsville," Hancock wrote to Almira in Missouri:

The losses on both sides are very heavy, more so than any battle of the war. . . . I am unhurt, though I was struck several times with small fragments of shells, and had my horse killed under me. [Brother] John is unhurt. . . . My division did well. . . . Kiss my dear children for me.[60]

It had mattered little to Rebel fortunes that Longstreet was detached and unavailable during the Chancellorsville campaign. Lee's boldness and brilliance as a tactical commander were more evident here than in any other battle, and demoralized Union troops were once again compelled to abandon the field. Still, with Jackson dead and his own casualties mounting, Lee was now acutely aware that the South had no chance of winning a war of attrition and could not dawdle for long. Seeking a decisive victory—one that might embolden the northern peace movement and convince Lincoln to give up the fight—he consolidated his army for a second invasion of the United States, driving north across Maryland into Pennsylvania and heading toward an eventual showdown at Gettysburg, a few miles above the Mason-Dixon Line.[61]

CHAPTER ELEVEN

To Gettysburg

IT WAS A WATERSHED MOMENT IN THE BRIEF AND VIOLENT HISTORY OF the Confederate States of America when Lee's seventy-five-thousand-man army began the move north toward Pennsylvania on June 3, 1863, only a month after the Battle of Chancellorsville.[1]

The commanding general did not divulge his plans at this early stage, but even the lowliest foot soldier knew he hoped to strike a death blow on northern soil in the very state that had hatched the Declaration of Independence—perhaps even by Independence Day.

Pickett's division, with Lewis Armistead and his son, Keith, rejoined the main force for the great invasion following their spring mission with Longstreet at Suffolk. Pickett's division was one of the largest in the army on paper, almost nine thousand strong, but recent edicts from Rebel headquarters had cut away at its vaunted strength. In May and early June, brigades under Micah Jenkins and Montgomery Corse were detached to guard the approaches to Richmond, reducing the division's manpower by about four thousand men.[2] As a result, Pickett moved forward from Culpeper, Virginia, with only three of his five brigades—those under Armistead, Garnett, and the fighting politician, James L. Kemper, former Speaker of the Virginia House of Delegates. They brought just over five thousand fresh troops to the Pennsylvania border, crossing into the small town of Greencastle on June 26.[3]

The march to reach the state line was an ordeal in itself for the largely untested division.[4] Under oppressive summer heat and choking dust, a "great many" of the troops "fainted from exhaustion." Soldiers in Armistead's Thirty-Eighth Virginia had to ford the swollen Shenandoah River, marching "four deep and holding to each other . . . to prevent being washed down."[5] Men were constantly on the lookout for Union cavalry and, on occasion, hometown militiamen (who, in a flush of patriotism, might take random potshots). By the time they reached the prosperous Pennsylvania town of Chambersburg on June 27, however, the troops could take a much-needed break and marvel at the lush northern countryside.

"We are now in the very midst of Yankeedom and have had quite a fine time of it so far," a private in the Fourteenth Virginia wrote home to his parents:

> Pennsylvania is the finest country I ever traveled through in my life. Everything is done up to order after the true Yankee style. We have come this far without any fighting. How much further we will go through Yankee land I don't know.[6]

Another man in the Fifty-Seventh Virginia observed that "the streets & windows were filled with men and women, the latter very common looking, not to be compared to our southern female."[7]

While most of the army kept moving east, headed toward Gettysburg or the state capital at Harrisburg, Pickett's division spent the next four days in the Chambersburg area, "tearing up the tracks, battering down railroad houses, burning railroad cars," and conducting other official mischief.[8] They also seized cattle, horses, pigs, and chickens while gathering cherries, corn, cheese, grain, and other such bounty not available in war-torn Virginia.[9] Given a choice, the troops would have stayed in Chambersburg for many more days, gorging themselves, feasting on the land of plenty, and enjoying the safety of their rearguard post, but Lee was determined to engage the Union army in a decisive clash and needed every man. Benjamin L. Farinholt of the Fifty-Third Virginia had a great sense of foreboding on July 1 when, just before the division moved out, he wrote home to his parents: "I suppose we will necessarily have a big fight before we leave this state, and expect it will be somewhere north of Baltimore probably near Philadelphia or Harrisburg."[10]

The days after Chancellorsville found the defeated Union army in a state of discouragement. Hooker's failure to exploit his manpower advantage and his premature decision to withdraw troops from the field had eroded the confidence of everyone from privates to senior officers. "Hooker's day is over," Hancock predicted to Almira. "I do not know what will be the next turn of the wheel of Fortune, or what Providence has in store for this unhappy army. I have had the blues ever since I returned from the campaign."[11] His corps commander, Darius Couch, took matters a step further and suggested to Lincoln in early May that he remove Hooker from command.[12]

There was little doubt that a change was in the works. Among those Lincoln considered to replace Hooker at the head of the army were John Reynolds, John Sedgwick, George Meade, Couch, and—perhaps only as a long shot—Hancock.[13] "I have been approached again in connection with the command of the Army of the Potomac," Hancock wrote to his wife. "Give yourself no uneasiness—under no conditions would I accept the command. I do not belong to that class of generals whom the Republicans care to bolster up. I should be sacrificed."[14] It is unlikely that he got serious consideration anyway. According to historian Edwin Coddington, "Hancock was a good Democrat and therefore politically undesirable. In view of this fact it is doubtful whether he received a definite offer directly from the War Dept., although somebody might have sounded him out informally."[15]

While Lincoln pondered options, Couch forced his hand at the corps level by requesting a transfer to a new position, saying he could no longer serve under Hooker. "I retired from his presence," Couch said, "with the belief that my commanding general was a whipped man."[16] Couch was reassigned to the Department of the Susquehanna on June 9 and placed in charge of an emergency militia unit that had been called up by Pennsylvania's governor, ensuring that he would not play a direct role in the coming campaign.[17] On the same day, Hancock was promoted to replace him at the head of the Second Corps.[18]

Lee and his army had already been on the march for six days at this point. Seizing the initiative, the Rebel general moved north from his base at Culpeper, trying to lure Hooker out of Virginia and across the Mason-Dixon Line. Lincoln told Hooker on June 10 that "if he comes towards the Upper Potomac, follow on his flank and on his inside track,

This June 25, 1863, letter formally confirmed that President Lincoln had assigned Hancock to command of the Second Corps of the Army of the Potomac. Hancock had already been in charge for several weeks.

shortening your lines, while he lengthens his. Fight him, too, when opportunity offers."[19] But the advice had come too late, and the Union was now playing catch-up. Hancock, on only his fourth day of corps command, put his troops on the road and joined in the desperate pursuit.

The Second Corps formed the rear of the army and pushed its way from Falmouth through Aquia Creek and Dumfries toward Centreville, near Manassas. Facing harsh marching conditions under a blistering summer sun, dozens of Union troops, maybe more, staggered out of the ranks. "Heat caused a great deal of trouble," Hancock reported. "A great many men [were] sun-struck, some of whom died . . . a large amount of sickness has been caused thereby, more than my ambulances can carry."[20] But he gathered up as many stragglers as possible and, after a brief rest at Centreville, crossed Bull Run to Thoroughfare Gap, where he guarded the passes and held until June 24.[21]

The next day brought one of the intriguing but little-known incidents of the war. Arriving at Haymarket, Hancock brushed up against Rebel cavalry under glory-seeking J. E. B. Stuart, who was trying to make a dramatic dash around the Union army before reconnecting with Lee. "We found that Hancock's corps was en route from Hay Market for Gum Springs, his infantry well distributed through his trains," Stuart wrote. "I chose a good position, and opened with artillery on his passing column with effect . . . compelled him to advance in order of battle to compel us to desist." But after inflicting little damage, the Rebel cavalier had to abandon his position and change his route, conceding that Hancock, with a much larger unit, "had the right of way on my road." Stuart stopped to graze his horses and headed farther toward the east, searching for another opening, while the Second Corps drove straight ahead to Gum Springs.[22]

Hancock's three divisions were led by John Gibbon, John Caldwell, and a newcomer to the corps, Alexander Hays, his old West Point class-mate, who was promoted on June 25. Hays had commanded a brigade of New York troops that was absorbed at once into the division and corps. A second key leadership change came in Gibbon's division on the same day when Alexander Webb was tapped to fill a vacancy at the head of the Philadelphia Brigade (Hays and Webb would become central figures a week later in the repulse of Pickett's Charge).[23]

Back in Washington, meanwhile, Lincoln debated Hooker's fate. The prickly army commander did himself no favors by engaging in a petty war of words with General in Chief Henry Halleck over the Union garrison at Harpers Ferry. Constantly in search of reinforcements, Hooker wanted to add these men to his army for the move north; Halleck demurred. Hooker asked again; Halleck said no. Finally, on June 27, an exasperated Hooker wrote directly to army headquarters, saying he could not fulfill his mission "with the means at my disposal" and asking "earnestly . . . that I may at once be relieved from the position I occupy."[24]

Hooker may have been bluffing, perhaps even trying to bully the general in chief, but Halleck sent the resignation note to Lincoln within minutes, and the president accepted it.[25]

On such impulsive sentences do the fates of countries hinge.

Lincoln and Halleck wasted no time appointing George Meade of the Fifth Corps as new commander, scratching out an order the same night, although it would not be delivered until the wee morning hours of June 28. As a final insult to Hooker, they told Meade that "Harper's Ferry and its garrison are under your direct orders."[26] Meade rubbed the sleep from his eyes when a messenger arrived at his tent in Frederick, Maryland, and feared at first that he was being arrested. Even after waking up and coming to his senses, he was less than thrilled with the new assignment but accepted it in the style of a career serviceman. "The order placing me in command of this army is received," Meade wrote at 7:00 a.m. on June 28. "As a soldier, I obey it, and to the utmost of my ability will execute it." He made it clear, however, that he was "in ignorance of the exact condition of the troops and the position of the enemy."[27]

The army was now accustomed to changes at the top—Meade became the fourth commander in eight months, following McClellan, Burnside, and Hooker—but news of Hooker's ouster spread like wildfire through the ranks. "There is not an officer in the army, I think, who does not rejoice at the news," said one man in the Second Corps.[28] Meade had little time to prepare and cobbled together a plan on the fly, telling Halleck within hours of receiving his orders that "I can only now say that it appears to me I must move toward the Susquehanna, keeping Washington and Baltimore well covered, and if the enemy is checked in his attempt to cross the Susquehanna, or if he turns toward Baltimore, to give him battle."[29] He spent every daylight hour on June 28 collecting intelligence, consulting with staff, and issuing orders to bring the disparate parts of his army together, having no idea that he would fight the most pivotal battle of the war in three days. The only vague hint was that Confederates under Jubal Early were already in Pennsylvania and had passed through a town called Gettysburg on the way to Hanover and York.[30]

On June 28, the Second Corps moved up from Banesville, Maryland, to Monocacy Junction, about three miles south of Frederick, giving Hancock and Gibbon a chance to check in directly with Meade on his first day in command.[31] As Gibbon described it,

> *I was delighted, on the road, to hear that Gen. Meade was in command of the army. Hancock and I went up to see him and did not get back until after 10 o'clock. He appears very anxious, but said with a laugh when I first saw him, that he intended to have me shot, I suppose for speaking of him as commander of this army! I now feel confidence restored and believe we shall whip these fellows.*[32]

Hancock's task on June 29 was to march to Uniontown, about thirty miles away, starting at 4:00 a.m.[33] The written order was somehow left on a desk by an orderly, causing a four-hour delay at a crucial time for the army. A mortified Hancock vowed to Meade that "I shall try to make up the most of it by short cuts and rapid marching. Such a mistake can hardly occur again."[34] The men were on the road for fourteen hours that day, stepping off at 8:00 a.m. and finding no rest for their calloused feet until 10:00 p.m., "the longest and most severe march" in corps history.[35] But after accounting for the delay and reaching their destination as expected before midnight, the reward was a one-day layover in Uniontown on June 30.[36]

Looking back, Francis Walker thought, it was the first time since the men left hostile Virginia that they could feel the warmth of "home":

> *At Uniontown the reception of our troops by the patriotic inhabitants had been most friendly and inspiring. Refreshment was freely offered along the*

road at gates and porches, and kind words and good cheer lifted the hearts of
the tired soldiers.

There is some poetry but also much truth in the popular tradition
regarding the spirit of the Army of the Potomac on the route. . . . Once more
in "God's country" as the soldiers termed it . . . moving on good northern
roads, instead of wading ankle-deep in the yellow Virginia mud . . . march-
ing between vine-clad cottages which did not seem to belong to the same
world as the mud-plastered log huts they had left behind . . . they were yet
wonderfully heartened by scene and circumstance, by friendly greeting and
the look of home.[37]

One more day on the calendar changed everything. The morning of July
1, 1863, brought orders for the Second Corps to march six miles north to
Taneytown, where Meade had set up new headquarters within easy reach
of the Pennsylvania border. Following Lincoln's directive in response to
the invasion, they were closing in on their Rebel prey.

Hancock went to Meade's tent at 11:00 a.m. and learned of the commanding general's intent to set up a defensive line along Pipe Creek in
Maryland, which "presented more favorable features than any other position he could see." General John Reynolds, overseeing the left wing of the
army—the First, Third, and Eleventh Corps—had been sent forward to
Gettysburg as a "mask" for this movement but soon would withdraw via
the Taneytown Road to dig in along the creek near Middleburg. Hancock
and the Second Corps were to be held in reserve, waiting to be thrown to
the point of "strongest attack" if and when Lee chose to engage.[38]

"Whether General Reynolds had received this order designating
Pipe Creek as the line of battle which General Meade told me was in
preparation, I do not know," Hancock said.[39]

The point became moot less than two hours later when word reached
Meade that Reynolds was fighting at Gettysburg. Union cavalry general
John Buford had encountered lead elements of Henry Heth's division on
the ridges west of town, and Reynolds rushed in to support, impulsively
committing two brigades to battle.[40] It was ironic that Heth and Hancock
had been good friends since the Mexican War and caroused together on
the streets of St. Louis in less combative times. Heth also knew Reynolds
from their U.S. Army days. But the Civil War had changed things and

disrupted old friendships, causing each man to choose sides; Pennsylvanians such as Meade, Reynolds, and Hancock were incensed that invading Rebel troops had set foot on their own soil.

Concerned now that Reynolds might not be able to cover the road back to Taneytown, which was essential to securing the Pipe Creek line, Meade at 12:30 p.m. issued an order to Hancock "to proceed with your troops out on the direct road to Gettysburg." This was largely a precaution against things getting out of hand. Hancock was told that if he found Reynolds covering the road as ordered, he was to pull the Second Corps back to Frizzellburg, seven miles east of Taneytown, and wait in reserve for further instructions.[41] But things soon *did* get out of hand.

Sometime around 1:00 p.m., Meade received shocking news: Reynolds either had been killed or was so grievously wounded that he could no longer lead troops in battle (he had, in fact, been killed instantly, shot in the head while urging his men forward on McPherson's Ridge). Hurrying over to Hancock's tent, Meade alerted Hancock to the crisis and had his chief of staff issue the following written order at 1:10 p.m.:

> *Major-General Hancock, Commanding Second Corps:*
> *GENERAL: The major-general commanding has just been informed that General Reynolds has been killed or badly wounded. He directs that you turn over the command of your corps to General Gibbon; that you proceed to the front and, by virtue of this order, in case of the truth of General Reynolds' death, you assume command of the corps there assembled, viz, the Eleventh, First and Third [at Emmitsburg]. If you think the ground and position there a better one to fight a battle under existing circumstances, you will so advise the general, and he will order all the troops up.*[42]

There were several irregularities in the order—notably that O. O. Howard of the Eleventh Corps, who was temporarily in charge of the field after Reynolds's death, outranked Hancock and that John Caldwell of the Second Corps outranked Gibbon.[43] But Meade had been given rare power to ignore rank and violate army protocol for the good of the country. Halleck told him in late June, "You are authorized to remove from command, and to send from your army, any officer or other person you may deem proper, and to appoint to command as you may deem expedient . . . you are entrusted with all the power and authority which the President, the Secretary of War and the General-in-Chief can confer."[44] Meade felt he had to remain at Taneytown for the moment to direct the army but wanted someone he trusted at Gettysburg.

He trusted Hancock more than Howard and certainly more than Dan Sickles, commander of the Third Corps, who was still back in Emmitsburg. Meade and Hancock had served together in various capacities from Mexico to Chancellorsville and shared a deep army kinship. There was no greater example of Meade's respect than a scene witnessed by his son and staff officer, George Jr., shortly after the Battle of Fredericksburg in December. The younger Meade saw his father talking in earnest to an officer he didn't recognize. "His bearing was so striking that it would have prompted anyone, ignorant of who he was, to inquire," Meade Jr. said. "And I heartily remember the hearty intonation of voice with which General Meade replied to my question. 'Why, don't you know who that is? Why, *that's Hancock.*'"[45]

Hancock left Taneytown shortly after receiving his orders with a small entourage that included Charles Morgan, his chief of staff. Riding in an ambulance for the first three or four miles, Hancock dutifully studied his orders and pored over maps of the Gettysburg region, but it soon became clear that the speed of the horse-drawn vehicle "could not keep pace with the General's anxiety." They jumped on their horses and rode as fast as they could in the searing heat. "The nature of the ground on either side of the road was continually scanned by the General with a view to the retreat on Pipe Creek, should we deem it advisable," Morgan said. They were about five miles from the battlefield when they met an ambulance headed in the opposite direction, carrying a body wrapped in a blanket. It was sobering. "The General asked whose body it was and was answered, 'General Reynolds, sir,'" Morgan said. "We rode on in silence."[46]

Hancock galloped the last few miles up the Taneytown Road and issued his first order before even reaching Gettysburg, sending wagons and pack animals from the retreating Eleventh Corps "peremptorily" to the rear.[47] This kept the road clear and his options open in the event of a Union withdrawal. But Hancock's first order is a rarely remembered footnote in history, superseded by the moment when he climbed Cemetery

Hill and formally took command of U.S. forces in the field. It began what historian Paul Bretzger called "forty-eight hours of combat leadership that would define his career and alter the battle to an extent that was arguably more substantial than any figure on the Union side."[48]

The precise timing of Hancock's arrival at the hill remains in dispute, but it was likely between 4:00 p.m. and 4:30 p.m., as masses of defeated troops from the First and Eleventh Corps scurried back through the town. He sought out Howard within minutes to inform of the change in leadership. It must have been an awkward meeting. According to Hancock, Howard accepted the news and "acquiesced in my assumption of command," but it defies belief that the senior man so readily complied with an order outside the normal protocol.[49] Howard, in fact, said he was appalled. "It did not strike me then," he wrote, "that Hancock, without troops, was doing more than directing matters as a temporary chief of staff for Meade."[50] There are so many differing accounts from nearby soldiers that an accurate assessment of what was said and exactly how Howard reacted can never be reached.

One frequently mentioned report came from Major E. P. Halstead of the First Corps, who said there was "no person present besides myself when the conversation took place between Howard and Hancock." According to Halstead,

> I returned to where General Howard sat, just as General Hancock approached at a swinging gallop. When near General Howard, who was then alone, he saluted, and with great animation, as though there was no time for ceremony, said General Meade had sent him forward to take command of the three corps. General Howard replied that he was the senior. General Hancock said, "I am aware of that, General, but I have written orders in my pocket from General Meade, which I will show you if you wish to see them." General Howard said, "No, I do not doubt your word, General Hancock, but you can give no orders here while I am here." Hancock replied, "Very well, General Howard, I will second any order that you have to give."[51]

Halstead's account is fascinating and, for the most part, believable, but he stretches credulity in the final sentence. Hancock may have been willing to make certain accommodations to soothe egos and keep the peace, but it is incompatible with his character and comportment to believe he disobeyed orders from Meade and allowed Howard to make key decisions for anything beyond the conduct of his own corps. Nor would he have split the responsibility as Howard suggested, with each man taking one side of the Baltimore Pike. Hancock instead took immediate command. "I lost no time in conversation," he said, "but at once rode away and bent myself to the pressing task of making such dispositions as would prevent the enemy from seizing that vital point."[52] Even Howard admitted that Hancock "said no more and moved off in his peculiar gallant style to gather scattered brigades and put them into position."[53] As often happens with natural leaders in times of crisis, Hancock responded with action, not words.

Howard deserves credit for being the first to note the value of Cemetery Hill—he left a division there in reserve when he passed through earlier in the day[54]—but he did little to reinforce the position when troops fell back in disarray. One man said he "looked the picture of despair."[55] Hancock's most important task, then, was to rally the refugees and bring a sense of calm to the proceedings. He formed the First and Eleventh Corps along the Taneytown Road and Baltimore Pike to hold the Union center, sent a First Corps division under James Wadsworth to occupy Culp's Hill, placed the Fifth Maine Battery on a knoll between Culp's and East Cemetery Hills (turning a "dead angle" into a "most deadly angle"), and directed a newly arrived Twelfth Corps division under John Geary to the vicinity of Little Round Top. In this way, both flanks were covered, and the eventual Union fishhook line was formed. The Twelfth Corps commander, Henry Slocum, had yet to arrive on the field, but once again, it was Hancock who recognized the threat, devised a short-term solution, and stepped in to fill the leadership void.[56]

At 3:20 p.m., before Hancock had reached Gettysburg, Union cavalry officer John Buford wrote to Meade with some alarm that "there seems to be no directing person." But within "a few moments" of Hancock's arrival, Buford said, he had "made a superb disposition to resist any attack that might be made."[57]

Buford was far from the only Union officer to notice the impact of Hancock's presence at this critical time for the army. It was, in fact, that "presence" and soldierly bearing, more than his tactical arrangements, that spurred and stiffened the men. Lieutenant Edward Whittier of the Fifth Maine Battery recalled the "inspiration of his commanding, controlling presence and the fresh courage he imparted" (even noting "his linen, clean and white . . . and his broad wristbands rolled back from his fine, finely moulded hands").[58] General Gouverneur K. Warren, the army's chief of engineers, who had also come forward at Meade's direction, agreed that Hancock's "personal appearance there did a great deal toward restoring order."[59] Even General Carl Schurz of the Eleventh Corps, Howard's most senior subordinate, allowed that his "presence was a reinforcement, and everyone on the field felt stronger for his being there."[60] But the most vivid and poignant description likely came from Sidney Cooke, a second lieutenant in the 147th New York Regiment of the First Corps:

> But if organization was lost, it needed but an organizer to restore it among these veterans. Hancock was there to meet the crisis. I happened to come near enough to note his bearing in that trying moment, and to hear some of his remarks and orders. The enemy was emerging from the streets of the town below, and forming a line as if to drive us from our coveted position. Every man knew how hopeless resistance would be, but Hancock sat his horse, superb and calm as on review; imperturbable, self-reliant, as if the fate of the battle and of the nation were not his to decide. It almost led us to doubt whether there had been cause for retreat at all.[61]

Once the field had been secured, at least temporarily, Hancock went about addressing the second part of his instructions from Meade—to determine whether Gettysburg was a better place to fight a battle than Pipe Creek. Major Halstead claimed to have heard Hancock call Gettysburg "the strongest position by nature on which to fight a battle that I ever saw,"[62] and Hancock sent an aide at once to Meade, telling him they could hold Cemetery Hill until nightfall.[63] But at 5:25 p.m., when Hancock wrote his official dispatch to headquarters, he added a few more details—and qualifiers:

> GENERAL: When I arrived here an hour since, I found that our troops had given up the front of Gettysburg and the town. We have now taken up a

position in the cemetery, and cannot well be taken. It is a position, however, easily turned. Slocum is now coming on the ground, and is taking position on the right, which will protect the right. But we have, as yet, no troops on the left, the Third Corps not having yet reported; but I suppose that it is marching up. If so, its flank march will in a degree protect our left flank. In the meantime, Gibbon [commanding Hancock's Second Corps] had better march on so as to take position on our right or left, to our rear, as may be necessary, in some commanding position. General G. will see this dispatch. The battle is quiet now. I think we will be all right until night. I have sent all the trains back. When night comes, it can be told better what had best be done. I think we can retire; if not, we can fight here, as the ground appears not unfavorable with good troops. I will communicate in a few moments with General Slocum, and transfer the command to him.[64]

Whether Hancock actually "chose" Gettysburg as the place to fight the battle, as his supporters claimed, can never be known. On this topic, Meade gave conflicting accounts. In testimony before the Joint Committee on the Conduct of the War on March 5, 1864, the commanding general said advice from Hancock "caused me at once to determine to fight a battle at that point."[65] But six days later, appearing before the same committee, on the same subject, Meade said it was input from many officers that convinced him to move troops to the front: "I therefore did not wait for the report from General Hancock."[66] (Meade was under pressure in 1864 for not being assertive enough at Gettysburg and may have wanted to change the story to fit his own narrative.[67])

The final decision to stay at Gettysburg was Meade's, of course, but Hancock was far more influential than any other subordinate. Sent forward from Taneytown to assess the situation, he declined to advise a withdrawal to Pipe Creek, rallied the troops on Cemetery Hill, created a broad defensive position from Little Round Top to Culp's Hill, and—by doing so—set the conditions for the army to coalesce. A fight became almost inevitable. In a 6:00 p.m. message to Hancock and Abner Doubleday, temporary commander of the First Corps, Meade said, "It now seems to me we have so concentrated that a battle at Gettysburg is now forced on us, and that, if we get up all our people, and attack with our whole force to-morrow, we ought to defeat the force the enemy has."[68]

At the same time, he also wrote to Halleck in Washington that "I see no other course than to hazard a general battle."[69]

Hancock returned to Taneytown at "about dark" on July 1, riding thirteen miles to report in person to Meade. The two men spoke briefly about the day's events, and Hancock "ascertained that [Meade] had already given orders for the corps in the rear to advance at once to Gettysburg, and was about proceeding there in person."[70] According to Meade's report, he left his headquarters at 10:00 p.m., traveling north in silence and darkness.[71] Hancock, who was understandably "exhausted by the labors of the day," lay down for a few hours of rest at Taneytown before heading back toward Gettysburg and reconnecting with the Second Corps sometime around sunrise on July 2, a few miles south of the town.[72]

CHAPTER TWELVE

Second Day

GENERALS MEADE AND LEE SPENT THE MORNING OF JULY 2 REORGA-
nizing their armies and hustling more troops to the front. Lee had
already deemed it "advisable to renew the attack," which made a larger
battle here "in a measure, unavoidable."[1]

Armistead and the five thousand men of Pickett's division, still
bringing up the Confederate rear, began a twenty-five-mile march from
Chambersburg in the predawn hours but did not approach the Gettysburg area until late afternoon, when they were placed in reserve behind
the lines after an exhausting and sun-blanched trek.

Hancock had no such respite.

He met up with Second Corps just south of the Round Tops and led
it to the battlefield at 6:00 a.m., reporting to Meade at a small house that
soon became army headquarters. Skirmishing could be heard off to the
far right. "When I arrived on the ground in the morning, General Meade
thought there would be a formidable attack by the enemy on the right of
our line," Hancock said. "My corps . . . was formed facing in that direction,
but shortly afterwards was marched over to the position which we held
during the subsequent battle."[2] They settled in finally along Cemetery
Ridge at the center of the Union line, stretching southward from a wood-
lot known as Ziegler's Grove toward the George Weikert farmstead.[3]

Alexander Hays's brigade anchored the right of Hancock's line, with
Gibbon holding the center and Caldwell on the left. Although serious
fighting did not begin until later in the day, Hays's men spent much of
the morning skirmishing with Rebel troops at the William Bliss farm
property, located halfway between the two armies. The most noteworthy

event came when Lieutenant Colonel E. P. Harris of the First Delaware retreated on his own as they came under fire, abandoning the field in advance of his bewildered troops. Hancock was furious. According to a fellow officer, "Upon returning to the main line, I found Lieutenant Col. Harris in the apple orchard, confronted by General Hancock, who, standing erect in his stirrups, was interviewing him in the most choice and forcible language deemed suitable for the occasion." Harris was "then and there 'ordered under arrest for cowardice in the face of the enemy.'"[4]

By midday, the Union Third Corps had been placed on Hancock's left, with orders to extend itself south to Little Round Top, creating one long, formidable line on Cemetery Ridge. But Dan Sickles, the Third's flamboyant commander, didn't like the position and wanted to move. In fairness to Sickles, the Third had been relegated to the lowest portion of the ridge, where it flattened it out before rising precipitously to the Round Tops, and his notion to push his men forward to higher ground on the Emmitsburg Road was understandable. And yet doing so would fly in the face of orders, violate army protocol, disrupt Meade's plan for a coherent defense, and leave a dangerously yawning gap to Hancock's left.[5]

Sickles was undeterred. Forward he went.

Whether this was done as one sweeping movement or in various fits and starts no one knows for sure—there are various accounts—but men back on the ridge watched with astonished bemusement. "We could not conceive what it meant," Gibbon said, "as we had heard of no orders for an advance, and did not understand the meaning of his breaking in our line."[6] Frank Haskell, an aide to Gibbon, remembered that "Generals Hancock and Gibbon, as they saw the move in progress, criticized its propriety sharply."[7] Hancock, observing with several officers on the right of Gibbon's line, said, "Gentlemen, that is a splendid advance," but "those troops will be coming back again very soon."[8]

The battle of the second day began much farther to the south, with Rebel troops under James Longstreet attacking Little Round Top and Devil's Den, but there was no doubt in Hancock's mind that it would quickly push northward up the ridge. He thought the gap left by Sickles's advance made it especially "disadvantageous to us."[9] Indeed, it was not long before Hancock was ordered to transfer a division to his left, beginning a long afternoon of redeploying troops to shore up weaknesses and plug unexpected holes. The first directive was to move John Caldwell's division to the vicinity of the Wheatfield, where the Fifth Corps was frantically trying to prop up Sickles's left.

There were two incidents that made this movement memorable. The first came when thousands of Union soldiers gathered to receive absolution from an army chaplain before stepping off into battle. As Father William Corby of the Irish Brigade climbed a rock to address the troops, a curious Hancock stood nearby, "surrounded by a brilliant throng of officers, who had gathered to witness their very unusual occurrence." It was especially unusual to hear Corby declare that "the Catholic Church refuses Christian burial to the soldier who turns his back upon the foe or deserts his flag."[10] A few minutes later, Hancock approached one of his favorite Second Corps subordinates, the feisty Colonel Edward Cross, and declared, in the manner of a battlefield pep talk, "Colonel Cross, this day will bring you a [general's] star." Cross looked back pensively and shook his head. "No, General," he said. "This is my last battle."[11]

Caldwell's men rushed forward into the Wheatfield, with Cross's brigade joining those under Samuel Zook, Patrick Kelly, and John Brooke. They achieved some early success, pushing back the stunned Rebels— Brooke's men even thundered uphill to a ledge near the Rose farm—but as so often happened in the ebb and flow this day, Rebel counterattacks stopped the momentum. Caldwell's losses were immense, described in one account as 1,200 out of just over three thousand men engaged, including mortal wounds to Zook and Cross.[12] Cross took a bullet in the abdomen, fulfilling his grim premonition of death in battle, and said, in a brief parting message to an aide, "I did hope I should see peace restored to our distressed country. I think the boys will miss me. Say goodbye to all."[13]

A disconsolate Hancock had little time to mourn the death of his dear comrade. Whooping Confederates were swarming through the Wheatfield and Peach Orchard, believing they had victory in sight, and Sickles's frail line along the Emmitsburg Road, where General Andrew A. Humphreys was posted, started to come apart.

Fearful of a breakthrough that could unhinge the army, Hancock commandeered four regiments from Gibbon's division and raced them forward into the fray, hoping to slow the retreat of Humphreys's division. He also snagged Gibbon's First Minnesota, placing it in support of Lieutenant Evan Thomas's artillery battery on Cemetery Ridge.[14] But he knew this was a perilous strategy. The haphazard shuffling of troops, while modestly effective in the short term, threatened to open holes elsewhere in the thinning Union line as the battle moved northward. Eventually, if the Rebels weren't stopped, he would run out of men and pay the price.

Then, just as Hancock was sending another brigade to bolster the left, word arrived from Meade that Sickles had been wounded and carried from the field.[15]

Faced with the loss of a corps commander in the midst of battle, a potentially devastating blow, Meade was fortunate to have Hancock nearby. This was reminiscent of the crisis at Antietam, when George McClellan tapped Hancock to lead Israel Richardson's division after Richardson had fallen at Bloody Lane. "General Meade informed me that General Sickles had been wounded, and directed me to assume command of the Third Corps in addition to my own,"[16] Hancock said. He placed Gibbon in nominal command of the Second Corps and let out a trail of expletives before going off to save the Union again.

As Gibbon recalled, "Hastily turning over the 2nd Corps to me, he started off towards the 3rd and I was not surprised that he should utter some expressions of discontent at being compelled at such a time to give up command of one corps in a sound condition to take command of another which, it was understood, had gone to pieces."[17]

Gibbon's assessment of the Second Corps was not quite accurate, however; it could no longer be called "sound." Caldwell's division had been shot up badly in the Wheatfield and lost two brigade commanders, knocking it out of action for the rest of the day. The equivalent of a full brigade from Gibbon's division had been peeled away in small clusters to rally Union fugitives. Now a brigade from Hays's division, under the command of George Willard, was being hurried to the left by Hancock under duress. These were the "Harpers Ferry Cowards"—made up of the Thirty-Ninth, 111th, 125th, and 126th New York regiments.

The "Cowards" had surrendered to Stonewall Jackson when the great Rebel general rampaged through Harpers Ferry en route to the Battle of Antietam in September 1862. It was not entirely their fault—the whole garrison raised a white flag—but the nickname stuck, the embarrassment lingered, and they had not been afforded a chance to redeem themselves in battle. Hays took them under his wing and found them to be a perfectly suitable brigade; after drilling them for six months, he said that "the Harpers Ferry boys have turned out trumps, and when we do get a chance look out for blood."[18] Suddenly, led by Willard and herded into position by Hancock, the chance they had wanted for so long finally arrived.

The "Cowards" charged headlong into a howling band of Mississippians under William Barksdale, who had crushed Sickles's men along the road and were now making haste toward the ridge. The New Yorkers fixed their bayonets and screamed, "Remember Harpers Ferry! Remember Harpers Ferry!" Dodging obstacles across a bushy swale near Plum Run, one man remembered that "a terrible contest ensued" until the fire of the Mississippi troops "slackened and they began to give back." Barksdale was felled in a torrent of bullets and mortally wounded, and many others surrendered "at the very points of our bayonets."[19] Colonel Willard himself topped the list of Union casualties, killed instantly by a bullet to his head, but the brave men he led in battle here—"Cowards" no more— had regained their honor and thwarted a potential Rebel breakthrough.

Pleased as he was, Hancock had no time to celebrate and barely enough time to think. The battle's next crisis was already looming on his right. Advancing alongside Barksdale was a stout Alabama brigade under Cadmus Wilcox, who had attended West Point with Hancock for two years (Class of 1846) and fought beside him in the Mexican War. Wilcox picked up momentum at the Emmitsburg Road, swept past scattered remnants of the Third Corps near the swale, and drove all before him toward a huge gap in the Union line on Cemetery Ridge. His skirmishers even wounded one of Hancock's aides. The Union commander, perhaps unsettled for the first time that day, glanced to his right and saw only one small regiment, the First Minnesota, assigned there by quirk of fate to support Thomas's Battery C.

"My God!" Hancock exclaimed. "Are these all the men we have here?" They were.

A frothing Hancock raced up to Colonel William Colville and barked orders in a style that the regimental adjutant, William Lochren, would never forget:

> Hancock spurred to where we stood, calling out, as reached us, "What regiment is this?" "First Minnesota," replied Colville. "Charge those lines!" commanded Hancock. Every man realized in an instant what that order meant—death or wounds to us all; the sacrifice of the regiment to gain a few minutes' time and save the position, and probably the battlefield—and every man saw and accepted the necessity for the sacrifice.[20]

The Minnesotans plunged ahead "without waiting to come from column into line," slamming into the Alabamians and halting the advance in the swale.[21] A regimental captain called it "the most stirring spectacle of the war."[22] Civil War casualty figures are often unreliable, but there can no doubt that the toll here was tremendous—by one account, the Minnesotans lost 82 percent (215 out of 262).[23] They had done their duty in "handsome style," Hancock said proudly. "I cannot speak too highly of this regiment and its commander in its attack, as well as in its subsequent advance against the enemy, in which it lost three-fourths of the officers and men engaged."[24]

With that part of the Union line safe for the moment, Hancock again turned to the right. Much to his amazement, *another* mass of Rebel troops, Georgians under the command of Ambrose "Rans" Wright, was churning with vigor toward a stone wall and a small clump of trees. This was much the same ground where Pickett's Charge would be contested the next afternoon. Units under Gibbon and Hays had been hunkered down there for much of the day, but Hancock sent ahead to Meade for reinforcements, and they arrived just in time at another crucial juncture of the battle. Wright's men broke part of the line and got up along the crest, declaring that they were briefly "masters of the field," but Gibbon and the others—including green Vermonters from the First Corps—swung around and stiffened, pushing them back in the falling darkness.

When no more Rebel troops came on in support of Wright, Hancock knew for the first time since mid-afternoon that Cemetery Ridge was secured.

The soldiers of Pickett's division were sound asleep in the wee hours of July 2 when orders reached Chambersburg to head for the battlefield. Stepping off in the pitch-black night at 2:00 a.m., they tramped along the Chambersburg Pike carrying three days' rations and extra ammunition, fully aware of the bloody work up ahead. More than halfway through their twenty-five-mile march, having reached the Cashtown Pass in the South Mountain range, the men encountered their first signs of hostility when "a few random shots" rang out from irate local citizens "secreted in the gorges on the crags of the mountain pass."[25] The heat soon became debilitating as midday approached, and one man complained that "the vertical rays of the sun seeming like real Lances of steel tipped with fire!"[26]

The lead elements halted at 4:00 p.m. about three miles from Gettysburg, setting up camp in the fields along Marsh Creek. The men paused to eat and rub their feet, eager to rest after a fourteen-hour journey, but couldn't avoid the sights and sounds of war all around them.[27] "At this moment," wrote Randolph Shotwell of the Eighth Virginia in Garnett's Brigade, "the solemn forest is quivering under the deep reverberations of heavy cannonading," and a "stream of gory-looking soldiers" was "coming back from the front."[28] For men who had not seen much action for the past year, the scene was both sobering and exhilarating.

They knew that their corps commander, Longstreet, was engaged with his two other divisions in an attack on the Union left flank. Pickett hoped to join in the fray after a brief rest of two hours, sending a staff officer ahead to ask for orders, but Lee chose to hold him in reserve. "Tell Gen. Pickett I shall not want him this evening, to let his men rest, and I will send him word when I want them," Lee said.[29] It was cautious battlefield leadership—saving fresh troops, if necessary, to resume the fight the next day—but every man in the ranks knew the wait would be a brief one. Shotwell heard Garnett tell a staff officer, "Pickett says we must go to Gettysburg tonight, at all risks; the battle is not decided, and if the enemy holds his ground, we must attack him tomorrow ourselves."[30]

A soldier in Armistead's brigade described the esprit de corps as they settled in to wait for their moment of truth approached:

> *The troops had unbounded confidence in themselves and in their leaders. They were full of the fervor of patriots, had abiding faith in their cause and in the favoring will of Heaven. There was an elation from the fact of invading the country of an enemy that had so cruelly invaded theirs. The spirit and elan of our soldiers was beyond description. They could only know it who felt it. They had the courage and dash to accomplish anything.*[31]

Hancock's day wasn't finished even after stabilizing the Union line on Cemetery Ridge. Night fighting was rare in the Civil War, but the deep rumble of artillery and musket fire could be heard distinctly from the eastern slope of Cemetery Hill behind him.

Word soon came that Howard's jittery Eleventh Corps was in trouble again and about to be overrun.

"As darkness approached," Gibbon remembered, "the picket firing heretofore heard in the direction of the Cemetery grew into the roar of a line of battle, so anxious ears were turned in that direction. At last this fire became so heavy and threatening that Hancock, who, in the meantime, had joined me on the hill, said, 'We ought to send some help over there.'" After a brief pause to look around and assess the situation, Hancock shouted the order: "Send a brigade! Send Carroll!"[32]

Colonel Samuel Carroll had a mixed bag of a brigade from Ohio, Indiana, and West Virginia, but the men sprang forward in an instant, careening in the dark through Evergreen Cemetery, picking their way past knee-high stone obstacles until clearing the cemetery gatehouse and crossing the Baltimore Pike. "Attention!—Right face—Double Quick—March!' was instantly obeyed," recalled Private William Kepler of the Fourth Ohio. "We hurried by gravestones struck by the spiteful minie ball—toward the cannons' vivid flash and thundering roar; Baltimore Turnpike was crossed, the position of the rebels determined only by their fire."[33]

Isaac Avery's North Carolina brigade and the "Louisiana Tigers" under Harry T. Hays had by now climbed the east side of Cemetery

Hill and were romping through the artillery near the crest, sensing victory. Union gunners used anything at their disposal—"hand-spikes and rammers," pistols, fence rails, rocks, and bare fists—to fight the manic enemy and save their batteries, but it was only the arrival of Carroll's men, almost ghost-like out of the darkness, that brought the Confederate surge to a halt. "Bayonets and butts of guns at once joined the efforts of the heroic gunners, then infantry and gunner in a general melee, with flanks of regiments overlapping," Kepler said.[34] Several other Eleventh Corps units joined in, and within about thirty minutes, the attack was repulsed, and the Rebels retreated "pell mell."[35]

"The firing continued until about 10:20," Carroll reported, "when they fell back out of range, and skirmishers were advanced in our front."[36]

Late at night, when most of the shooting had died down across the field, Meade took the unusual step of calling together his corps commanders for a council of war. He wanted their views on the condition of the army after two days of brutal fighting and their joint advice for a plan of action for July 3—specifically, whether to renew the contest here or fall back to a safer position. It is easy to forget that he had been in charge for only five days.

All seven corps commanders were present, along with Gibbon and Alpheus Williams, who had briefly led the Second and Twelfth Corps that day. Counting Meade and two of his staffers, there were twelve robust men crammed into a small room of the Lydia Leister house ("no more than 10 or 12 ft. square"), along with a bed, a table, and two chairs. Some stood, some sat, and some lounged on the bed. General G. K. Warren, the chief of engineers, curled up in a corner and fell asleep.[37]

The questions for the group, as written by Meade's chief of staff, Alexander Butterfield, and published later in the *Official Records of the Union and Confederate Armies*, were the following:

1. Under existing circumstances, is it advisable for this army to remain in its present position, or to retire to another nearer its base of supplies?

2. It being determined to remain in present position, shall the army attack or wait attack of the enemy?

3. If we wait attack, how long?[38]

Gibbon was called on first as the junior member. Glancing nervously around the room, he hesitated briefly, took a deep breath—"I had never been in a council of war before"[39]—and said he wanted the army to remain in place but with slight modifications.

The others, with varying degrees of nuance, fell into line:

GIBBON: 1. Correct position of the army, but would not retreat. 2. In no condition to attack, in his opinion. 3. Until he moves.

WILLIAMS: 1. Stay. 2. Wait attack. 3. One day.

BIRNEY: Same as General Williams.

SYKES: Same as General Williams.

NEWTON: 1. Correct position of the army, but would not retreat. 2. By all means not attack. 3. If we wait, it will give them a chance to cut our line.

HOWARD: 1. Remain. 2. Wait attack until 4 p.m. to-morrow. 3. If don't attack, attack them.

HANCOCK: 1. Rectify position without moving so as to give up field. 2. Not attack unless our communications are cut. 3. Can't wait long; can't be idle.

SEDGWICK: 1. Remain, and wait attack at least one day.

SLOCUM: Stay and fight it out.[40]

Hancock, speaking up as always, got in the last word, imploring Meade and the others to "let us have no more retreats. The Army of the Potomac has had too many retreats. Let [us have made] our last retreat."[41]

It was just before midnight, and the room fell eerily silent. Meade tallied the votes in his head and saw that there was no real dissension. "Such, then, is the decision," he said.[42]

With that, Hancock and several others, exhausted by the day's exertions, crawled into an ambulance near Meade's headquarters and, for a few hours at least, went to sleep.[43]

CHAPTER THIRTEEN

The Charge

GEORGE PICKETT'S MEN SPENT A RESTLESS NIGHT BEFORE WAKING AT 3:00 a.m. on the fateful third day of the battle, July 3, 1863, many eating their final breakfast and answering their final roll call.

By a predetermined rotation, James Kemper's brigade took the lead on the march to the battlefield with Richard Garnett in the middle and Armistead bringing up the rear. Robert E. Lee considered several options for the grand attack but settled on a plan calling for three divisions to make a desperate frontal assault against the Union center on the relative high ground of Cemetery Ridge under the overall command of James Longstreet. Pickett's division would form on the right side of the battle line, with Kemper and Garnett in front and Armistead in support.[1]

This plan sat well with everyone but Armistead, who was seething. Frustrated by his lack of action over the past year and eager to match the glory of his forefathers, the forty-six-year-old general dreamed of leading the attack this time or, at the very least, marching on the same line as his fellow brigadiers. He sought out Walter Harrison, an officer on Pickett's staff, to inquire about a change in position, suggesting that he could place his men on Garnett's left to extend the line. Harrison described it this way:

> Brave old Armistead was very tenacious of place to the front. Not seeing Gen. Pickett immediately, and anxious to satisfy Gen. Armistead, I rode up to Gen. Longstreet, whom I saw with Gen. Lee, on top of the ridge in front of us, making a close reconnaissance of the enemy's position, and addressed Gen. Armistead's question to him. [Longstreet] seemed to be in anything but a pleasant humor at the prospect "over the hill"; for he snorted out, rather

sharply, I thought, "Gen. Pickett will attend to that sir." Then, as I was going off—thinking perhaps, in his usual kind-heartedness, that he had unneces-sarily snubbed a poor [subordinate]—he said, "Never mind, colonel, you can tell Gen. Armistead to remain where he is for the present, and he can make up his distance when the advance is made."[2]

It was almost noon now, and a chastened Armistead held his position along a tree line on Seminary Ridge in a depression just north of the Henry Spangler farmstead. The Thirty-Eighth Virginia on the far left had the protection of some trees, but the other four regiments—from left to right, the Fifth-Seventh, Fifty-Third, Ninth, and Fourteenth—were in an open field under the baking sun. Their front covered six hundred yards. A fortuitous rise in the ground sheltered the men from view but also kept them from seeing the Union battle line. Garnett's troops were directly in front, about 150 yards away, and Kemper's men were off to the right front; both, in turn, were behind the artillery. Two other divisions, under J. Johnston Pettigrew and Isaac Trimble, were posted farther to the left.[3]

Lee had decided the attack would be preceded by a massive cannonade of 150 guns, intended to soften (if not destroy) the Union defenses. The barrage began shortly after 1:00 p.m. (1:07 p.m., to be precise, if we believe Michael Jacobs, a professor at Pennsylvania College who kept copious notes) and went on for well over an hour, terrorizing soldiers on both sides of the shallow valley. Up to eighty Union guns soon thundered in response, some finding the range after several rounds and giving as much damage as they got, making the contest a tactical stalemate.[4] Blinding, haunting smoke hung heavy over the field.

"The smoke soon darkened the sun," wrote John Lewis of the Ninth Virginia, on Armistead's right, "and the scene produced was similar to a gigantic thunderstorm, the screeching of shot and shell producing the sound of the whistling blast of winds. Man seldom ever sees or hears the like of this but once in a lifetime; and those that saw and heard the infernal crash and witnessed the havoc made by the shrieking, howling missiles of death as they plowed the earth and tore the trees will never forget it. It seemed that death was in every foot of space."[5]

Hancock had not been convinced there would be a direct attack on his front that day. Skirmishing broke out at 7:00 a.m. on the William Bliss property, but the general thought it a pointless waste of resources and ordered the large barn burned to the ground.[6] Shortly before noon, he sat down with Meade and Gibbon on Cemetery Ridge for an impromptu battlefield feast of stewed rooster, potatoes, and coffee, followed by some leisurely conversation about "the battle and the probable events of the day."[7] But after an "ominous stillness" of almost two hours, a single Rebel shot broke the silence, and "the enemy opened upon our front with the heaviest artillery fire I have ever known."[8]

Projectiles whizzed through the air, and explosions rattled the landscape, terrifying even the veterans. Gibbon called it "pandemonium" and may have been understating things.[9] "All that is hideous in war seemed to have gathered itself together," one man said, "to burst in one fell tornado upon Cemetery Ridge."[10] Expecting a full response from Union artillery but hearing little at the moment, Hancock charged off in a furor to order his Second Corps artillery to fire at the Confederates. He was unaware that the army's chief of artillery, Henry Hunt, had ordered battery commanders to "withhold their fire for fifteen or twenty minutes after the cannonade commenced" in an effort to preserve ammunition—and only then to concentrate their fire with "all possible accuracy" on the "most destructive" Rebel guns.[11]

This decision began a feud between Hancock and Hunt that continued for decades after the battle. Hancock thought an immediate response from Union guns was needed to stiffen the resolve of his infantry, now under siege from a rain of Rebel shells. Hunt disagreed, believing that a tactical delay, followed by deliberate shooting, would increase both accuracy and efficiency.[12] "General Hunt, passing along the line, told me to hold my position and not to return the enemy's fire unless I saw his infantry advancing," one artillerist said.[13] Hancock had effective control over his own Second Corps batteries and overruled Hunt by demanding that that they fire, but he wasn't as successful with the artillery reserve on the left of the Union line, which fell under Hunt's direct command.

One revealing incident came when an incensed Hancock confronted Captain Patrick Hart of the Fifteenth New York in the artillery reserve. As Hart related it,

I did not open fire and some considerable time after the enemy opened fire, General Hancock rode up to me and not in a very mild manner wanted to know why I did not open fire. I informed him that I had received my orders from General Hunt, Chief of arty., and would obey them. [Hancock] ordered me to open fire, that I was in his line. I replied that should he give me a written order that I would open fire under protest.[14]

Hancock had several other expletive-laden discussions, including one with Captain Charles Phillips of the Fifth Massachusetts, who briefly started firing until ordered to stop by Hunt. In time, however, as the requisite delay passed, many more Union guns began to pound the Confederate line, creating a new sense of "pandemonium" on the other side of the field.[15]

Hancock's plan to bolster the morale of his troops during the cannonade took another form when he rode along the Second Corps battle line at great risk to his safety. To many stunned observers, he was little more than a ghostly silhouette against the smoke. "Every soldier's heart stopped beating," one man said, "for this seemed certain death to the general." When a fearful subordinate raced forward amid the carnage, begging him to dismount, Hancock allegedly said, "There are times when a corps commander's life does not count."[16]

Years later, Abner Doubleday of the First Corps wrote,

I can almost fancy I see Hancock again as he rode past the front of his command . . . followed by a single orderly displaying his corps flag, while the missiles from a hundred pieces of artillery tore up the ground around him.[17]

But the artillery duel could not last forever—there was simply not enough ammunition—and commanders on both sides slackened their fire until it stopped almost altogether. Hunt, for his part, claimed this was part of a tactical plan. "I ordered the cessation of our fire," he said, "gradually from left to right, to induce the enemy to believe he had silenced us, and to precipitate his assault." Whether this was Hunt claiming brilliance in hindsight, as it may have been, does not alter the impact of the decision; after more than an hour of mayhem, as a relative silence fell over the field, both sides braced for the next phase of battle.[18]

Running low on ammunition and having failed to achieve Lee's goal of driving off Union gunners, the Confederates had little choice but to ease up on artillery and prepare for the infantry assault. It was the moment Lewis Armistead had waited for all his life. Steadfast, almost glowing in the face of adversity, he used a "stentorian voice" to implore his troops to rise from their prone positions and fall into line. "We had been lying upon our faces in a broiling July sun for several hours, with the artillery playing over us, when the order came from the valiant Armistead," said Robert Tyler Jones, a sergeant in the Fifty-Third Virginia and a grandson of President John Tyler. "I shall never forget the scene. For hours we had watched the hero as he moved with easy step in front of our line, surveying the field and marking the effect of the cannonade."[19] (Jones, a distant cousin of Armistead's, who survived the battle and the war, would name his son Louis Armistead Jones.[20])

Armistead was standing at the center of his brigade line, directly in front of the Fifty-Third, when he spotted the regiment's color sergeant, Leander C. Blackburn, preparing for the charge. Anxious to make a grand display that might inspire (or at least distract) the men, he asked Blackburn, loudly, whether he could "plant those colors on the enemy's works over yonder?" The sergeant, thrilled to be singled out, never hesitated: "Yes, General, if mortal man can do it, I will!" Armistead pulled out a small flask of brandy, and the two men shared a drink.[21]

Acts of inspiration aside, however, Armistead knew the assault would be calamitous for many soldiers. He told the brigade's surgeon, Dr. Arthur R. Barry, "Doctor, all hell is going to turn loose here within fifteen minutes. My brigade must charge those heights, and the slaughter will be terrible. Go and establish your hospital at some convenient point, and be ready, for you will have work to do."[22] To his friend and comrade, Garnett, he added, "The issue is with the Almighty, and we must leave it in his hands."[23]

Image from the early 1900s of the Armistead Brigade marker at Gettysburg
COURTESY OF GETTYSBURG NATIONAL MILITARY PARK

Longstreet's artillery commander, E. P. Alexander, overseeing the cannonade on this part of the field, sent word that the infantry should go in soon to have any chance of success, and Longstreet nodded his grudging assent. Pickett, always dramatic, rode up and down the line, yelling, "Up, men, and to your posts! Don't forget today that you are from old Virginia!"[24] Back in the second line, Armistead invoked memories of firesides, mothers, wives, and sweethearts in comments to his troops, and although most could not hear him because of the din of battle preparation, none would ever forget the example he set.[25] "[Armistead] turned, placed himself about twenty paces in front of his brigade, and took the lead," John Lewis wrote. "After moving, he placed his hat on the point of his sword, and held it above his head, in front of him."[26]

Pickett's Charge (which is inaptly named because Pickett commanded less than half the troops involved) moved forward in grand style, the men seeming to grasp their place in history. The two imposing armies "plumed their banners, reformed their lines and confronted each other on this arena for the greatest battle of modern times," wrote Benjamin Farinholt of the Fifty-Third.[27] Garnett and Kemper were out in front on the right side of the field, marching briskly, the sun reflecting off thousands of bayonets in a stunning spectacle. There was no Union response for the first few hundred yards, an eerie pause, but everyone knew the silence could not last—the calm before a coming storm.

The challenge now for Pickett was to close a roughly four-hundred-yard gap between his left and Pettigrew's right, all while making a deadly charge across an open field under what he knew would be heavy artillery fire. The symbolic focal point was said to be a small copse of trees at the Union center, near the angle of a farmer's stone fence.[28] They still had more than half a mile to cover, and the first devastating shots from U.S. artillery on Little Round Top and Cemetery Ridge would surely start to break up the alignment. It would then be up to the brigade commanders to steady their lines, fill holes in the ranks, and bring as many men as possible into contact with the enemy.

They had not gone far past their own artillery line when the big Union guns opened up. "As soon as we got on top [of the little rise in front of us] and began to advance toward the valley, the enemy's artillery re-opened fire upon us and, oh my!" said J. Wyatt Whitehead of the Fifty-Third. "It seemed to me that the whole of Cemetery Ridge was a blaze of fire."[29] A single U.S. shell knocked down sixteen men in the Fifty-Sixth Virginia in Garnett's brigade. Another killed four and wounded six in the Eighth Virginia. Garnett and Kemper were taking the brunt of the damage at the head of the charge, but Farinholt saw a shot plow into a company in Armistead's brigade, leaving thirteen men "in a perfect mangled mass of flesh and blood indistinguishable one from the other."[30]

Post-and-rail fences along both sides of the Emmitsburg Road—many still standing despite the previous day's battle—were troubling impediments to the advance, forcing men to clamber over them or squeeze through, although rarely with such drama as Lieutenant James Sale of the Fifty-Third, who got his head stuck between two rails. Sale feared that he would die in this embarrassing position before wiggling loose.[31] Others from the Army of Northern Virginia were not so fortunate: "Large numbers were shot down on account of the crowding at the openings where the fences had been thrown down, and on account of the halt in order to climb the fences," said Lieutenant Colonel Rawley Martin of the Fifth-Third, but after bounding over these major obstacles in the midst of musket and canister fire, "the advancing column deliberately rearranged its lines and moved forward."[32]

Somewhere near the road, just a few hundred yards from the Union position, and with the two brigades in front suffering fearful losses, Kemper took matters into his own hands: "Gen. Kemper, on a handsome bay horse, rode up to Gen. Armistead . . . and said to him 'General, I am going to storm those works, and I want you to support me,'" wrote James T. Carter of the Fifty-Third's color guard, who said he was standing only five feet away. "Armistead said that he would, and, calling Gen. Kemper's attention to the perfection of his line, said: 'Did you ever see anything better on parade?' Kemper saluted, and replied, 'I never did.'"[33]

It was at this point, Carter said, that Armistead placed his hat on his sword (eyewitness accounts vary as to when this incident happened during the charge, although many identify the Kemper exchange). Waving the sword over his head, the animated general shouted, "Forward, double quick!" as the hat slid slowly down to the hilt.[34]

Hancock's troops may have marveled at the raw spectacle of Pickett's Charge—"an overwhelming, resistless tide of an ocean of armed men," Haskell called it[35]—but their defensive position along the ridge was not static. Small flanking forces were sent off to the right and left, preparing to inflict as much damage as possible and, if all went well, to clamp the Rebels in a vice at the Union center.

On Hancock's left were Vermonters from the First Corps under the command of General George Stannard, the same green troops who had helped push back Ambrose Wright's Georgians the day before. The Thirteenth and Sixteenth Vermont regiments formed "in the open meadow in front of our lines" and "changed front forward on the first company . . . bringing them in line of battle upon the flank of the charging division of the enemy, and opened a destructive fire at close range."[36] Both Stannard and Hancock claimed credit for ordering this movement, and it is possible that both men reached the conclusion at the same time, but many of the Vermont troops attributed it to Stannard.[37]

About this time, as Union units on the left saw Pickett breaking through, Colonel Arthur Devereux of the Nineteenth Massachusetts in the Second Corps "applied to [Hancock] for permission to move his regiment to the right and to the front." Hancock, whose eyes must have been bulging by now, told him to "go in there pretty God damned quick."[38]

The three brigades of Pickett's division now rushed ahead in one great swarm, regiments and companies intermingled. Formations broke down as Union infantry brought its power to bear over the last few hundred yards between the road and the stone fence. Kemper's men were battered by flank fire from the Vermonters on the far right, and Armistead's troops in the second line pushed forward to bunch up with Garnett's. It was an all-out melee. Armistead noticed that Leander Blackburn and several other color-bearers from the Fifty-Third were wounded and that his distant kinsman, Robert Tyler Jones, had picked up the regimental banner. As Jones described it, "Armistead, who had kept ahead of his line the whole way, said to me: 'Run ahead, Bob, and cheer them up!' I obeyed and passed him and shook the flag over my head. Then the 'wild charge' began."[39]

During this final surge, both Garnett and Kemper went down within a short distance of one another—Garnett killed instantly and Kemper seriously wounded. Armistead was now the senior brigadier on the field. Calling on the same courage that propelled him forward in previous battles, including Chapultepec and Molino del Rey with the U.S. Army, he herded the survivors of his own brigade, mixed with Garnett's, toward an opening at the northwestern angle of the stone wall. Troops from the Seventy-First Pennsylvania Infantry had abandoned their position there as the Rebels approached, and only two guns from Alonzo Cushing's Battery A, Fourth U.S. Artillery—rushed forward by Cushing himself from their line near the crest—stood guard over the crucial fifty-yard gap.[40]

John A. J. Lee of the Twenty-Eighth Virginia in Garnett's brigade may have been the first Confederate to reach the wall here, but Armistead and others were close seconds.[41] There was only a momentary pause to catch their breath and survey the surreal scene. As J. Wyatt Whitehead remembered, "When the brigade reached the stone wall there were very few men left, and General Armistead, turning to Lieutenant Colonel Rawley W. Martin said, 'Colonel, we can't stay here.' To which Colonel Martin replied, 'Then we'll go forward.'"[42]

Armistead and Martin led about one hundred men over the wall, drawn from the remnants of tattered regiments and companies, leaping and stumbling amid the clatter. There were no more formal units, just clumps of individuals and a handful of fluttering battle flags. "Come forward, Virginians!" Armistead shouted. "Come on, Boys, we must give them the cold steel; who will follow me?"[43]

It was a moment of unforgettable despair for Union General Alexander Webb, commanding the Philadelphia Brigade at the "Angle." The deflating retreat of the Seventy-First created a hole for Armistead to exploit, and now the relentless Rebels had gained a toehold on the line. A few stray cannons at the wall weren't enough to prevent the crossing. "When my men fell back, I almost wished to get killed," Webb wrote to his wife three days later. "When [Armistead's men] were over the fence, the Army of the Potomac was nearer being whipped than it was at any other time of the battle."[44]

Sign placed near the site of Armistead's breakthrough at the Angle
AUTHOR PHOTO

Armistead likely would have known by now that his friend Hancock was in command of the Union Second Corps on Cemetery Ridge and probably positioned nearby, but this was no time for sentimentality. The fate of the country—both countries—hung in the balance. Conspicuous to all as the de facto leader of the insurgency, observed by many on both sides of the field, Armistead took a few steps inside the wall, placed his hand on one of Cushing's cannons, and implored the badly outnumbered Rebels to turn the artillery on Hancock's men. "We must use their own guns on them," the general thundered.[45]

It was only when he fell in a hail of U.S. bullets that his troops came to realize their charge was doomed.

Exactly where this incident happened can never be known for certain, the details blurred forever in the fog of war. Various eyewitnesses described it as occurring at different places within the Angle and even

Contrasting images over time of the "Armistead Fell Here" marker at Gettysburg. Note the road in the older photo; it no longer exists.
COURTESY OF GETTYSBURG NATIONAL MILITARY PARK; COLLEEN MCMILLAN PHOTOS

disagreed on the number and location of his wounds. History has done little to sort it out. Today, there is small marker to the site of Armistead's wounding just over one hundred feet from the wall, placed there because the original battlefield historian, John B. Bachelder, concluded that he went down in that area, near "the three guns left at their original position of Cushing's battery."[46] But Professor Earl J. Hess, in *Pickett's Charge—The Last Attack at Gettysburg*, published in 2001, wrote that Armistead "fell within a few feet of the spot where Cushing had been killed only a few minutes earlier, about ten feet inside the angle. The modern monument marking his fall is misplaced."[47] The debate continues more than 150 years after the battle.

Lieutenant George W. Finley of the Fifty-Sixth Virginia was one of those who thought that the wounding happened just inside the wall. His recollection was that "Gen. Armistead, on foot, strode over the stone fence, his hat on his sword and calling upon his men to charge. A few of us followed him until, just as he put his hand upon one of the abandoned guns, he was shot down."[48] Finley's statement was corroborated by U.S. Army Sergeant Frederick Fuger, an officer in Cushing's battery who was posted near the wall when Cushing suffered a fatal wound and fell into his arms. According to Fuger, it was only a few minutes later that "Armistead fell between Cushing and the wall."[49]

But others who seem just as credible and were close enough to the action to observe what happened remembered it differently.

Private Milton Harding of the Ninth Virginia offered a vivid description of Armistead being shot "immediately after crossing the stone wall" and then tottering forward for some distance amid the chaos:

I was within six feet of him to his left, and observed that he staggered painfully, and could barely keep his feet until he reached the enemy's guns (Cushing's, I think), some sixty feet from the wall, although he continued to lead the charge like the hero he was. As he slapped his left hand on the gun he sank to his knees, and then fell full-length to his right. I asked him if I could do anything for him. He requested me to get a small flask of brandy from the satchel he had carried by a strap from his shoulder, and from this he drank a swallow or so. I asked where he was wounded. He replied that he was struck in the breast and arm. In answer to my offer to assist him, he advised me to look out for myself.[50]

Still others recalled an upright and defiant Armistead charging past the wall toward Cushing's original line of guns near the crest, reaching the symbolic high-water mark of the Confederacy before musket fire from Hancock's men finally brought him down.

Sergeant Dennis B. Easley of the Fourteenth Virginia scaled the wall with Armistead and distinctly remembered that "we went up to the second line of artillery." Just before claiming those guns, however, "a squad of from twenty-five to fifty Yankees around a stand of colors to our left fired a volley back at Armistead and he fell forward, his sword and hat almost striking a gun." Trying desperately to save himself at this point, Easley knelt beside his fallen commander and used the cover of one of Cushing's cannons to fight back. "General Armistead did not move, groan or speak while I fired several shots practically over his body," he said, "so I thought he had been killed instantly and did not speak to him."[51]

The most persuasive testimony about Armistead penetrating this far into the Angle, however, came from Union soldiers, who would not have been willing to concede any unearned achievement to the enemy. Private Anthony McDermott of the Sixty-Ninth Pennsylvania, posted along the wall south of the Angle, said that Armistead, after crossing, "continued in a direction towards the clump of trees in our rear" and that two companies of the Sixty-Ninth "moved back to the crest to get between Armistead and Cushing's four pieces." He continued,

> We poured our fire upon him until Armistead received his mortal wound; he swerved from the way in which he winced, as though he was struck in the stomach, after wincing or bending like a person with a cramp, he pressed his left hand on his stomach, his sword and hat (a slouch) fell to the ground. He then made two or three staggering steps, reached out his hands trying to grasp at the muzzle of what was then the 1st piece of Cushing's battery, and fell.[52]

General Webb, commanding the brigade, had a similar recollection, at one point fearing that Armistead had achieved a conclusive breakthrough. He wrote to his wife that "General Armistead, an old army officer, led his men, came over my fence and *passed me with four of his men*" (emphasis added).[53] Webb hustled to the crest in an attempt to rally the Seventy-Second Pennsylvania regiment, pleading with them to advance to the wall, and, according to one soldier, Armistead "was close to where Gen. Webb stood when he was trying to get the 72d to come up to our assistance."[54] Charles S. Banes, the brigade's adjutant, agreed that the Rebel general fell "close to the colors of the Seventy-Second."[55]

Years later, asked whether the stone marking the place where Armistead fell was accurate, Banes said, "It is as near the spot, I suppose, as you could get to it."[56]

Banes was a central figure in another well-publicized story of the general's wounding and capture. Armistead had been for years an active member of the Freemasons, and he is said to have uttered a plea for assistance, a coded Masonic message, that others in the secret fraternal organization would have recognized. "One of the men of that regiment who was near him, asked permission to carry him out of the battle, saying 'He has called for help, as *the son of a widow*,'" Banes wrote.[57] Fellow Masons in the Union army heard the phrase and responded. The order was given, and three men from the Seventy-Second Pennsylvania began to transport the wounded Rebel general toward an ambulance and, eventually, a Union battlefield hospital.[58]

Banes's recollection of that quote was not published until thirteen years later, but the tale of Union Masons tending to a Confederate Mason in the heat of battle became one of the enduring human interest stories of the Civil War, repeated by the influential Bachelder and others. A veteran from the Twentieth Indiana recalled a battlefield tour with Bachelder in 1887 when the historian proclaimed, "I think it is not unbecoming, or improper for me to say here, and thus publicly, that Genl. Armistead was lifted up and borne from the field by virtue of the grand hailing sign of a Mason."[59] Freemasonry had enough of a presence in the ranks of both armies that word spread quickly from North to South and soon became a legend.[60]

Many other members of the fraternity pointed to an even more famous encounter with Armistead in the Angle as validation of the story, although the incident deserves a deeper look.

Union Captain Henry H. Bingham, a member of General Hancock's staff and also a Mason, was riding along the crest when he saw three privates carrying a wounded Confederate officer to the rear. "I ordered them back," Bingham said, but "they replied that they had with them an important prisoner and designated him as General Longstreet." The thought of capturing such a senior commander, second only to Lee in the Confederate hierarchy, was stunning news on what was already one of the greatest days in the history of the Union army.

Describing the scene in a personal letter to General Hancock six years later, Bingham went on at length:

> *By this time I saw from the ornaments on his dress that that he was an officer of rank, and, impressed with the importance of carefully attending to the security of a Commander holding the rank of Longstreet, and observing the great suffering the prisoner was in, I dismounted from my horse and inquired of the prisoner his name; he replied General Armistead of the Confederate Army.*
>
> *Observing that his suffering was very great, I said to him, General, I am Captain Bingham of General Hancock's Staff, and if you have anything valuable in your possession which you desire taken care of, I will take care of it for you. He then asked me if it was General Winfield Scott Hancock and upon my replying in the affirmative, he informed me that you were an old and valued friend of his, and that he desired me to say to you, "Tell Gen. Hancock for me that I have done him and done you all an injury which I shall regret or repent (I forget the exact word) the longest day I live." I then obtained his spurs, watch, chain, seal and pocketbook. I told the men to take him to the rear to one of the Hospitals.*
>
> *. . . I was in the midst of Webb's brigade and on its immediate right during the "pinch of the fight," mounted all the time, save the several minutes that I conversed with Armistead just under the crest, and to the rear of Webb's brigade. I was riding along the line of Webb's troops encouraging and rallying them when I met Armistead.*[61]

The Bingham–Armistead incident is hailed as the most prominent example of Masonic interaction at Gettysburg; their meeting is even depicted by a modern tribute, "The Friend to Friend Memorial," located at the Soldiers' National Cemetery Annex. But it is instructive to note that although Bingham and Hancock were both members of the Masons, Bingham never mentioned a Masonic connection in his encounter with Armistead at the Angle—not even in a private letter to Hancock shortly after the war.

Bingham at first thought the prisoner was Longstreet, who apparently was not a Mason, but acknowledged "the importance of carefully attending to the security of a Commander" of that rank. Indeed, it was common for both armies in the Civil War to treat wounded enemy generals with respect.[62] There may very well have been a Masonic motive in the captain's kindly actions toward Armistead on the third day at Gettysburg, but Bingham did not discuss it in his July 1869 letter to Hancock, a brother Mason, or in any of his other surviving correspondence. Whatever the symbolism, he acted quietly.

There was much more controversy over Armistead's alleged statement, via Bingham, that he regretted or repented his actions. This was interpreted by many northerners as an apology for joining the southern cause, but it is likely that Bingham either got the quote wrong or simply misjudged Armistead's words. The defiant general had left the U.S. Army in 1861 to fight "for my own country and for, and with, my own people,"[63] had been in the thick of bloody fights at Seven Pines and Malvern Hill, and had marched boldly across the field just minutes earlier, urging his troops to give "cold steel" to men under Hancock's command. If he regretted anything, it was fighting directly against his old friend for the first time.

As fate would have it, Hancock was wounded at about the same time as Armistead on July 3, a few hundred yards south of his position on Cemetery Ridge, but neither Bingham nor Armistead would have known that at the time of their encounter. Bingham later said he learned of Hancock's wounding "about 15 minutes after I got Armistead's message and effects."[64]

Rounding out his story, Bingham said, "Shortly after this, I rode back to where you were and gave you the message and effects Armistead entrusted to me."[65]

One final irony is that the personal items collected by Bingham were eventually sent to Armistead's sister, Cornelia, in Philadelphia. Her husband, Major Washington Irving Newton, was a longtime U.S. Army officer.[66] Major Newton served only briefly in the Civil War and had retired from active duty by 1863, but his brother, General John Newton, commanded the Union First Corps on July 3 and would have been nearby when Armistead was wounded and carried off the field.

CHAPTER FOURTEEN

"I Found That He Had Died"

THE UNION ARMY'S ELEVENTH CORPS ESTABLISHED ITS MAKESHIFT Gettysburg field hospital at the George Spangler farm, just over a mile southeast of the Angle, on a "dry, airy knoll" between the Taneytown Road and Baltimore Pike.[1]

By late afternoon on July 3, 1863, it was a distinctly dreadful place. There were more than 1,900 wounded soldiers spread among the large bank barn and outbuildings, some of them placed in the cow stable and horse stalls and many forced to "lie out in the open air."[2] Witnesses said the three operating tables "more resembled a butcher shop than any other institution,"[3] and foul-smelling water from the barnyard "oozed up into [the soldiers'] undressed wounds," making it "harassing in the extreme."[4] A small group of captured Confederates was crammed into the wagon shed in the lower part of the barn—a place of last resort—but one of the wounded Rebels, due to his rank and reputation, was treated in the same caring manner as a Union officer.[5]

General Lewis Armistead was lifted from a small horse-drawn ambulance and placed gently onto a litter. "Edson Ames & me carried him into Geo Spanglers house and lade Him on the bed," wrote John Irvin, a private from the 154th New York. "He had two wounds in the body & one in [the] thigh. I gave Him some liquor."[6] Armistead was seen within the hour by the Eleventh Corps' surgeon in chief, Dr. Daniel G. Brinton, before being transferred to the Spangler summer kitchen and placed on a cot.

"Myself and Dr. Harvey, late of Rochester, N.Y., examined and dressed his wounds," Brinton said. "They were two in number, neither

The refurbished Spangler barn and summer kitchen, at the site of the Union army's Eleventh Corps field hospital where Armistead was treated and died. Today, the area is overseen by the Gettysburg Foundation and is open to public tours.
COLLEEN MCMILLAN PHOTOS

of them of a serious character, apparently." He recalled that the wounds were "in the fleshy part" of the right arm and just below the left knee, both caused by "rifle balls," and that no bone or major artery or nerve had been struck. "His prospects of recovery seemed good," Brinton said.[7]

Another doctor, Henry C. Hendrick of the 157th New York, noted that Armistead "had lost quite a great deal of blood" but said the wounds "were not necessarily fatal" and deemed a recovery likely.[8]

Such optimism from Union surgeons did little to ease the general's pain. He told medical personnel to "please don't step so close to me," fearful that their presence would jostle him and increase his suffering.[9] An observer described him as "irrational, wild, nervous,"[10] and at one point, he deliriously asked to be placed next to his wounded friend, Hancock, who was not even in the same hospital ("Where is General Hancock? Where is General Hancock? Lay me right by the side of General Hancock").[11] Despite this weakened state, however, bandaged and losing blood, Armistead expressed "an intense, all-consuming desire for the Confederates to win the battle."[12] He reached into his pocket, pulled out a handful of raw corn, and said, defiantly, to anyone who would listen, "Men who can subsist on raw corn cannot be whipped."[13]

He lingered through the Fourth of July but began to deteriorate that night and took his last breath at 9:00 a.m. on Sunday, July 5, less than two full days after Pickett's Charge.[14] Dr. Brinton pronounced himself "astonished" to learn of Armistead's death. "It resulted not from his wounds, but from secondary fever and prostration," Brinton said. "The General . . . told me he had suffered much from over-exertion, want of sleep and mental anxiety with the last few days."[15] (Biographer Wayne Motts, however, consulted with modern-day medical experts and theorized that he died of a "pulmonary embolism . . . a blood clot that went from Armistead's leg to his heart."[16])

James Crocker, an adjutant in the Ninth Virginia of Armistead's brigade, was probably the first Confederate outside the Eleventh Corps hospital to learn of the general's demise. Crocker attended Pennsylvania College in Gettysburg for four years in the late 1840s and was well acquainted with the region and its citizens. Accordingly, although he had been taken prisoner while suffering a slight wound in Pickett's Charge, his captors at the Twelfth Corps hospital gave him a pass to enter town—an "honor of personal confidence," Crocker called it. He intended to seek out old college friends, but his first stop was the Spangler farm to check on Armistead.

"I found that he had died," Crocker said:

They showed me his freshly made grave. To my inquiries they gave me full information. They told me that his wound was in the leg; that it ought not to have proved mortal; that his proud spirit chafed under his imprisonment and his restlessness aggravated his wound.[17]

Armistead had, in fact, been buried behind the Spangler barn on the afternoon of July 5, his body wrapped in a blanket and placed in a "rough wooden box," according to Private Alfred J. Rider of the 107th Ohio, who was on cemetery duty.[18] But the story did not end there. Four weeks later, an enterprising but coldhearted army physician, Dr. Cyrus N. Chamberlain, decided to have the general's remains exhumed so he could embalm them, believing that "Armistead's friends (or relatives) would pay a good price for his body."[19]

The intermediary in this scheme was a local physician named John W. C. O'Neal, who had lived in Baltimore for fourteen years until moving to Gettysburg in 1863 and happened to be friends with a distinguished Baltimore businessman, Christopher Hughes Armistead, son of the hero of Fort McHenry.[20] Dr. O'Neal was in the process of charting Confederate grave sites on the battlefield when he began exchanging letters with Lewis's first cousin.

In a message dated October 3, three months to the day after Pickett's Charge, Christopher Armistead asked O'Neal to make "the best arrangement you can with a Dr. Chamberlain, who disinterred the remains of General Armistead, for their delivery to me here, encased so they may be put into a vault." For a total price of $150, Chamberlain also offered the body of another fallen Confederate general, William Barksdale, prompting Christopher to tell him, "Under these circumstances, I want to take charge of both."[21]

Less than two weeks later, however, with the remains still not delivered, Lewis's cousin backed away from the package deal, writing, "I am only particularly interested in those of my relative, and have but little money to spare."[22] Negotiations dragged on until Tuesday, October 27, when a certificate of deposit for the newly agreed-on price of $100 was delivered to O'Neal in Gettysburg. "My thanks for your many kindnesses," Christopher wrote. "I notice particularly your instructions to receive on Thursday evening at Calvert Depot [in Baltimore] the remains of my cousin, the gallant General Armistead."[23]

Lewis Armistead's body was carried to Old St. Paul's Cemetery in Baltimore and quietly placed in the Hughes family vault alongside his uncle, George Armistead, who, almost fifty years earlier, on the edge of the nearby harbor, had defended Fort McHenry for the United States in the War of 1812.[24]

Eighteen-year-old W. Keith Armistead was present on the field at Gettysburg as an aide-de-camp and was seen mounted near his father just before the start of the Pickett's Charge.[25]

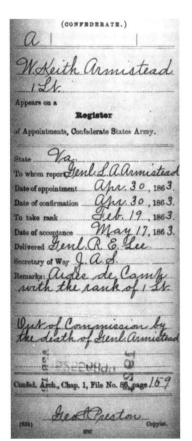

W. Keith Armistead's service record, confirming his promotion to aide-de-camp and first lieutenant on his father's staff in the spring of 1863. Note that later that summer, he was "Out of Commission by the death of Genl. Armistead."
NATIONAL ARCHIVES

We cannot be certain of Keith's actions that day, including whether he actually took part in the attack. It is possible that he did, although no soldier in the brigade mentioned it in voluminous postwar writings, and he suffered no wounds. It is also possible that he peered anxiously through a field glass, watching the bloody carnage from a distance with other staff officers, perhaps even seeing his father cross the stone wall with his hat on his sword—and realizing before long that something was amiss. Whatever the experience, it was dramatic and profound.

Pickett's division suffered close to 50 percent casualties in the cannonade and charge, and Lewis was one of the thousands of wounded victims who never made it back across the field.[26] "Generals Garnett and Armistead are missing," Robert E. Lee wrote in his report on July 4, "and it is feared that the former is killed and the latter wounded and a prisoner."[27] Further information could not be obtained in the immediate aftermath of the battle, and Keith would not learn of his father's death for more than a week, after Lee and the army had returned to the safety of Virginia.

The impact on the ranks and on Keith's career was significant. Commanders were replaced, brigades were reformed, and young Armistead was demoted from first lieutenant on the brigade staff to private in Company A of the Sixth Virginia Cavalry. In the cold language of Confederate military service records, he was declared "Out of Commission by the death of Genl. Armistead."[28] Lee tried to intervene on Keith's behalf, offering him a plum staff role in the ordnance department, but the teenager opted to return to the regular ranks in the Sixth Cavalry with his uncles and friends from Upperville.

Lee wrote about it later to Keith's maternal grandmother, Eliza Matilda Lee Love, a distant relative:

> *I received yesterday your letter . . . in reference to your grd. son, W. Keith Armistead. I have taken much interest in him from the beginning of his career; his amiable disposition, setting aside other considerations, having attracted me towards him.*
>
> *After the death of his gallant father, a position with the Chief of Ordnance of the army was offered him which it was hoped he would accept, but he preferred to remain with his associates in the ranks . . .*
>
> *With great respect, I am your kinsman & obt. Servant,*
>
> *R.E. Lee*[29]

As fate would have it, Keith suffered a slight wound in battle at Stony Creek, Virginia, in June 1864 and was assigned to headquarters duty anyway, having done little to distinguish himself as a combat soldier. He remained in a staff role for the remainder of the war, often acting as courier, and was with the army at Appomattox on April 9, 1865, when the Rebels formally surrendered to Ulysses S. Grant, his father's one-time Mexican War companion.[30]

With no immediate family remaining, Keith headed north after the war and in 1871 married Julia Appleton, granddaughter of Daniel Webster, an influential U.S. senator, congressman, and secretary of state. They lived for a time in both New York and New Jersey but eventually settled in Newport, Rhode Island, where Keith worked as a stenographer and served as president of the Society for the Prevention of Cruelty to Animals. In a salute to family history, two of his sons were named Lewis Addison and Daniel Webster (with Lewis fighting for the U.S. Army in both the Spanish-American War and World War I).[31] The most prominent inscription on Keith's tombstone at Berkeley Memorial Cemetery in Newport ignores his Confederate service but notes that he was the son of "Cecilia Lee Love and Lewis Addison Armistead of Virginia."[32]

Lewis Armistead's three brothers—Bowles, Walker Jr., and Franck—had decidedly different experiences than their nephew on July 3, 1863.

It is possible that Bowles was with the Sixth Virginia Cavalry when it fought a pitched battle at Fairfield, Pennsylvania, about eight miles southwest of Gettysburg, at roughly the same time as Pickett's Charge. He served with the unit for all four years of the war, but his muster roll records for the summer of 1863 are unclear. Walker Jr. was in the same unit but was marked absent in June and July "with paraplegia," a back ailment, and was likely home in Fauquier County.[33] Franck, meanwhile, had been sent to the western theater following the Seven Days Battles and assigned to the Trans-Mississippi Department in April 1863.[34] They would have learned of their brother's death at different times and from different sources as the distressing news from Gettysburg filtered south and west.

The three surviving Armistead siblings continued to serve until the end of the war; all were taken prisoner in the final days before Confederate surrender and signed their oaths of allegiance to the United States in May 1865.[35] Resuming civilian life, none achieved great distinction in the postwar period, although Bowles, the youngest, became a "fine businessman, growing in reputation and fortune."[36] Franck died first, in 1889, in Louisville, Kentucky (possibly, according to one account, in an insane asylum); Walker Jr. died in 1903 at the Lee Camp Soldiers' Home in Richmond; and Bowles died in 1916 in Upperville, where he had been one of the little town's leading citizens. In the family tradition of paying homage to its military past, his tombstone at Ivy Hill Cemetery in Upperville glosses over his own career but identifies him as the son of Brigadier General Walker K. Armistead of the U.S. Army.[37]

It was in the spring of 1887, almost twenty-four years after the Battle of Gettysburg, that surviving Confederate veterans of Pickett's Charge sought to commemorate their place in history with a monument on the battlefield.[38]

Some of their northern counterparts were appalled by this request, noting that the wounds of war had not yet healed, physically or emotionally. "We cannot confound the heroes and martyrs of a noble cause with those whom the twin furies of treason and slavery led forth to battle," one seethed.[39] But others were willing to consider the proposal in tribute to a restored Union. The Philadelphia Brigade Association even invited members of the newly formed Pickett's Division Association to join them for a reunion at Gettysburg that summer, the men having developed a grudging respect for one another over their shared life-and-death battlefield experience at the Angle.[40] (This was a precursor of reunions of all troops, North and South, on various anniversaries at Gettysburg, including the fiftieth in 1913 and the seventy-fifth in 1938.)

Details were discussed at a May 5, 1887, meeting of the Gettysburg Battlefield Memorial Association (GBMA), and the tone remained cordial until Pickett's soldiers brazenly asked that their monument be placed *inside the Union battle line*, near the spot where Armistead fell. When that request was formally rejected, the Rebels threatened to pull out of the event altogether.[41]

GBMA rules called for monuments at Gettysburg to be placed at each unit's original line of battle—which, in this case, was almost a mile away on Seminary Ridge. As an additional impediment, battlefield historian John Bachelder received, by "bushels," angry letters protesting the thought of a Confederate marker inside Union lines. Fearing a backlash, however, and hoping to avoid a southern boycott, John W. Frazier, secretary of the Philadelphia group and a veteran of the Seventy-First Pennsylvania, wrote an open letter to Pickett's men on May 11, urging them to enjoy "the hospitality that we will extend to you" and "the fraternal feelings created by that re-union, the first of the kind held since the war." Perhaps most surprisingly, he promised his brigade's support for "an imperishable monument" honoring "a charge not surpassed in its grandeur and unfaltering courage in the annals of war since time began."[42]

Almost two weeks later, on May 23, Frazier added, in a note to Charles Loehr of Pickett's division,

> *Writing as an individual member of the Brigade Association, I do not hesitate to say that I am sure every member of our Association would gladly and earnestly co-operate with your Association in securing the location of a monument on the spot where the brave General Armistead fell, and I believe that your Association will yet determine to place one there to mark the spot not only where General Armistead laid down his life, but to indicate for all time to come on the historic grounds of Gettysburg the position reached by Pickett's Division in the face of a hail of musket balls, solid shot, and shell, more terrible, perhaps, than was hurled against any body of men on either side during the late war.*[43]

That was enough for the ex-Confederates. About three hundred of them returned to Gettysburg full of hope on July 2 and 3, 1887, and were greeted as honored guests by five hundred Pennsylvanians who had once tried to kill them on the same ground. Attendees included Pickett's widow, LaSalle, and her son, George Jr.[44] A northern band played "Dixie," a southerner waved the Star-Spangled Banner, and U.S. patriotic symbolism abounded on both sides.[45] William Aylett, colonel of the Fifty-Third Virginia in Armistead's brigade at the time of battle and a great-grandson of the Revolutionary patriot Patrick Henry, spoke on behalf of the vanquished visitors:

> *We come as the survivors of a great battle, which illustrated the greatness and glory of the American people. . . . We have come forth from the baptism of*

blood and fire in which we were consumed, as the representatives of a New South, and . . . Above the ashes left by the War and over the tomb of secession and African slavery we have created a new empire, and have built a temple to American liberty, in which you and I can worship, and over it we have run up the Star-Spangled banner.[46]

The reunion's lone controversy arose when a few hardened Confederates demanded that northern soldiers return southern battle flags that had been captured in 1863, but Aylett, in his role as chief peacemaker, diffused the tension. Almost a quarter of a century later, he declared, those battlefield trophies still belonged to the victors. "Southern men don't care who keeps the flags," Aylett said. "The past went down in war, and we recognize now the banner of our fathers." With that, another of Pickett's veterans rushed forward to hoist "the national banner," and, according to one witness, "the audience sprang up and gesticulated wildly."[47]

This new sense of brotherhood among former opponents led the GBMA to make its next magnanimous gesture: the approval of a small marker to Armistead himself, to be placed inside the Angle, at the approximate site near the crest of the ridge where the general went down. It would commemorate the wounding site of an individual officer instead of an entire defeated division. At the GBMA's regular meeting on July 12, 1887, Bachelder and a "Committee on Location" were authorized "to mark with a suitable tablet the spot where General L.A. Armistead of the Confederate army fell mortally wounded July 3d 1863."[48] Designed that autumn and dedicated in February 1888, the "tablet" was a unique four-foot, six-inch stone scroll inscribed "Brigadier General Lewis A. Armistead C.S.A. Fell Here July 3, 1863."[49] Former Union officer Henry Bingham, who assisted Armistead in the Angle shortly after he was cut down, helped his old army comrades identify the location for proper placement.[50]

It had the distinction of being the first acknowledgment of a Confederate soldier on the battlefield—although, as one Gettysburg historian noted with some irony, "it is made of New Hampshire granite and was erected with Yankee money contributed by the members of the 72nd Pennsylvania and the GBMA."[51]

From the perspective of a modern visitor, it also marks a significant line of demarcation in U.S. history, highlighting the great Union victory

Lewis Armistead and his uncle, George, a hero of the War of 1812, are buried in the same cemetery vault in Baltimore.
COLLEEN MCMILLAN PHOTOS

here as much as one soldier's demise. No Rebel general advanced farther into Union territory than Armistead during Pickett's Charge, and Lee's outmanned and defeated army never faced such an opportunity again on northern soil. From that point forward—from that very patch of ground—the war and the country changed forever.

During a two-year period from 1907 to 1909, there were several public initiatives to have Lewis's body disinterred from its resting place in Baltimore and reburied in the Confederate section of Hollywood Cemetery in Richmond on a slope called "Gettysburg Hill."[52] Nothing came of it, but his name continued to remain relevant in the news in the early twentieth century.

He was a focal point of yet another ceremony at the Gettysburg battlefield on September 15, 1906, when survivors of Pickett's division and the Philadelphia Brigade met as organized units for the final time. Forty-three years after the battle, with even the younger veterans now in their sixties, the former Union soldiers had one last piece of business to complete: the return of Armistead's sword, which had been taken by Sergeant Michael Specht of the Seventy-Second Pennsylvania at the height of Pickett's Charge.[53]

According to one account, Specht had "secured the sword, which had fallen from General Armistead's hand, kept it safely until he was promoted to a lieutenancy, and then wore [it] until the close of the war, with honor to himself." Over time, however, and especially after the many Blue–Gray military reunions, Specht began feeling pangs of guilt. "When it has come to pass that the bitterness is all gone," said a spokesman for the Seventy-Second, "it seems right and fitting to Sergeant Specht that he should return this sword to those who followed General Armistead . . . surely no time more fitting than this, which perhaps will be the last time we shall meet as representative bodies."[54]

Specht fell ill during this period and was unable to travel to Gettysburg, but Captain Thomas Longaker of the Seventy-Second took his place at the ceremony, presenting the sword to Captain Thomas D. Jeffress, president of Pickett's Division Association, and, at least symbolically, to General Pickett's widow. Jeffress said the sword would be donated for posterity to a museum of Confederate relics in Richmond, along with Armistead's scabbard and sword belt.[55] In the spirit of reunion, veterans on both sides agreed that Lewis had been "the most conspicuous figure of the frightful melee" at the stone wall.[56]

It was not long before news of the ceremony reached Armistead relatives in Baltimore, who were eager for more details. "We tried again and again to recover the sword of General Armistead after the battle of Gettysburg but could find no trace of it," said another cousin, George Armistead, namesake of his famous grandfather. "We are indeed glad to know of it after all these years." He began a correspondence with John Frazier of the Philadelphia Brigade and, perhaps for the first time in May 1907, mentioned the ancestral connection between George Armistead of Fort McHenry and Lewis Armistead of Pickett's Charge, noting their roles in two of the epic clashes of nineteenth-century military history.[57]

CHAPTER FIFTEEN

"Don't Let Me Bleed to Death"

BACK TO GETTYSBURG ON JULY 3, 1863.

Winfield Scott Hancock was on the left of the Union battle line, positioned near the Vermont troops, and speaking with brigadier George Stannard at about the same time that Armistead and his small band of Rebels reached the stone wall. One historian thought it was the turning point of the Civil War—"the Confederate army was making its great effort to give the Confederacy a permanency among the nations of the earth"[1]—but even for those who judge it less profoundly, there is little doubt that the crisis of the day was at hand. Hancock knew it.

He was about to turn his horse toward the north, in the direction of the "clump of timber" at the Angle, but had not yet ridden off when a bullet thwacked his inner left thigh "about two inches from the groin."[2] Uttering "an exclamation," Hancock reeled in the saddle and was caught by the outstretched arms of two Vermont officers as he began to topple from his horse. Lieutenants George Benedict and George Hooker placed him gingerly on the ground and ripped away part of his pants in an attempt to locate the wound. Benedict, a newspaper editor in Burlington before the war, was mortified by what he saw.

He had watched Hancock approach moments earlier and called him the "most striking man I ever saw on horseback . . . magnificent in the flush and excitement of battle."[3] Wearing a black felt hat with a frock coat opened at the waist and a sword belt under his coat, the thirty-nine-year-old general looked every bit the battlefield hero, barking orders and redeploying troops as bullets zipped all around.[4] Now, however, he was on his back in a possible life-threatening situation, losing copious amounts

199

of blood from his upper leg, wincing in excruciating pain. No doctor was yet on-site to attend to him.

"Hooker and I with a common impulse ran toward him," Benedict wrote:

> General Stannard stood over him as we laid him upon the ground, and opened his clothing where he indicated by a movement of his hand that he was hurt, a ragged hole, an inch or more in diameter, from which the blood was pouring profusely, was disclosed in the upper part and on the right side of his thigh. He was naturally in some alarm for his life.
>
> "Don't let me bleed to death," he said. "Get something around it quick." Stannard had whipped out his handkerchief, and as I helped to pass it around General Hancock's legs I saw that the blood, being of dark color and not coming in jets, could not be from an artery, and I said, to him, "This is not arterial blood, General; you will not bleed to death." From my use of the surgical term he took me for a surgeon and replied, with a sigh of relief: "That's good; thank you for that Doctor." We tightened the ligature by twisting it with the barrel of a pistol, and soon stopped the flow of blood.[5]

Hancock was accompanied only by a color-bearer at the time of his wounding, but one of his staff officers, William Mitchell, soon rode up, aghast, and dashed off to find a physician. Also galloping in to help was the general's brother, John, an adjutant in Caldwell's division.[6] Mitchell returned within minutes, bringing Dr. A. N. Dougherty, medical director of the Second Corps, but Dougherty's treatment options were limited while the battle raged around them.[7] Using his index finger to probe the wound, he found, to his astonishment, only a bent nail and several small pieces of wood. "This is what hit you, General," a relieved Dougherty said, "and you are not hurt as badly as you think."[8]

Hancock, soldierly as ever and emboldened now that the bleeding was under control, refused to be moved from the field until the outcome was decided. He propped himself up on his elbows and "looking through the remains of a very low, disintegrated stone wall . . . could observe the operations of the enemy and give directions."[9] Word soon arrived that Alexander Hays's men were turning back Pettigrew and Trimble on the Union right, inflicting severe casualties, thanks in part to an ambitious flanking force from the Eighth Ohio. As large groups of downtrodden Rebels began to retreat across the entire front of Pickett's Charge, Hancock sent Mitchell off with a note for the commanding general: "Tell General Meade that the troops under my command have repulsed the enemy's assault and we have gained a great victory. The enemy is now flying in all directions on my front."[10]

Mitchell had barely ridden off when Captain Bingham came up to check on his chief and inform him of Armistead's fate. As Hancock described it in an unpublished letter, written five years after the battle in 1868,

> *After the repulse of the enemy, while I was lying on the ground wounded, Bingham brought me a message from General Armistead, who was mortally wounded. . . . Bingham came to me with Armistead's message about the time or after Mitchell returned from carrying my verbal message to General Meade.*[11]

Meade, flushed with victory, sent his own message back with Mitchell: "Say to General Hancock that I regret exceedingly that he is wounded and that I thank him for the Country and for myself for the service he has rendered today."[12]

By this time, a number of Union officers who had seen the increasingly pale-faced Hancock in his wounded state were starting to doubt Dougherty's original assessment that a nail had caused the damage. The general's wound seemed much more severe. Indeed, as later examinations would reveal, a minie ball had "passed through the front of his saddle and carried into the wound with it a large wrought nail from the saddle tree. The bullet and nail entered near the groin, the ball passing back through the thigh, and lodging near the socket of the thigh bone, which is slightly splintered."[13] Dougherty had dug out the nail and a few chips of wood with his primitive probe, but the mangled bullet remained painfully wedged in the thigh socket.

Once Hancock allowed the men to move him, Mitchell commandeered an army "ambulance," and Dougherty took him to a temporary field hospital located beyond the Taneytown Road. Before they reached their destination, however, Hancock said he "dictated a note to General

Meade, by Dr. Dougherty, and sent it to General Meade by Colonel John Hancock, my brother, Assistant Adjt. General, 1st Division, 2nd Corps, who had heard that I was wounded, and came up to see me." The contents of this dispatch showed that Hancock was still thinking clearly in a military sense, focused on annihilating the Confederate army before it could return to Virginia:

> *I have never seen a more formidable attack, and if the Sixth and Fifth Corps have pressed up, the enemy will be destroyed. The enemy must be short of ammunition as I was shot with a tenpenny nail. I did not leave the field till the victory was entirely secured and the enemy no longer in sight. I had to break the line to attack the enemy in flank on my right, where the enemy was most persistent after the front attack was repelled. Not a rebel was in sight upright when I left. The line should be immediately restored and perfected. General Caldwell is in command of the corps, and I have directed him to restore the line.*[14]

Much to his disappointment, there was no counterattack by the Fifth and Sixth Corps, allowing the enemy to escape on a long, sorrowful retreat to Virginia. It is likely that Hancock spent the evening of July 3 at a Second Corps field hospital near the Granite Schoolhouse, somewhere between the Taneytown Road and Baltimore Pike (not far, ironically, from his wounded friend Armistead at the George Spangler farm).[15] The next day, Independence Day, he took a bumpy twenty-three-mile ride to the nearest functioning railroad station at Westminster, Maryland, then traveled by rail on to Baltimore before arriving in Philadelphia on July 6.[16]

Hancock had already sent a dispatch to Almira, visiting her parents in St. Louis, noting that he was "severely wounded, not mortally," and asking her to "join me at once in Philadelphia." An attending physician named Taylor thought he should be more forthcoming about the serious nature of his injury, but, as Almira related later, Hancock refused "to permit the change, in view of the long journey before me, and the unhappiness that would result from knowing the full truth."[17]

Hancock was taken to the La Pierre House in Philadelphia, where he was soon joined by Almira and the children, beginning a convalescence that would take five months—although his wound from Gettysburg would never fully heal.

He was such a dutiful soldier that, on July 22, less than three weeks after being shot, he wrote a formal letter to army headquarters in Washington, D.C., asking whether it would be "deemed permissible" to request a leave of absence for thirty days.[18]

Beyond a line or two in one of the local papers, however, Hancock's presence in Philadelphia was little noted that summer. The "oversight," as Almira called it, was due largely to the fact that this was General Meade's hometown, and residents took great pride in saluting one of their own for defeating the seemingly invincible Robert E. Lee. "Gay bands of music, followed by cheering, exultant crowds, would nightly pass [Hancock's] hotel without a sign of recognition, but heaping upon General Meade's family the entire honor of that victory, which saved Pennsylvania and the Nation," she said. "This oversight, though deeply felt by him, he considered very natural, as General Meade was the commander of the Army of the Potomac, and while the roar of battle still swelled in the air, it was to him the populace wished to express their gratitude."[19] (Nonetheless, if Almira was still writing about it decades later, her husband must have been *fuming* inside.)

Beyond the lack of recognition, there were other factors that made Hancock's time in the city the most miserable period of his life. The thigh wound was not healing "as readily as it ought," the pain he felt had "increased rather than diminished," and doctors believed the oppressive midsummer heat was at least partly responsible for "his slow, weary convalescence."[20] Adding to his agony, a gunshot wound specialist, Dr. D. H. Agnew, kept probing the seeping wound in clumsy, vain attempts to find the bullet.[21] It was not until Hancock decided to leave the city on July 27, headed for his father's home in Norristown, that his spirits brightened and he received the kind of acclaim worthy of a Civil War hero.

As Almira recalled it,

When it became known that it was General Hancock's intention to leave the city, the firemen volunteered to transport him from the hotel La Pierre to the car that had been provided for this purpose without injury to the invalid.

Well did they perform this service. They presented themselves in full regalia at the time appointed for the journey, and in tender, impressive manner, conveyed him, worn and shattered, but without fatigue, to the Philadelphia depot. When he arrived at Norristown, a detachment of the Invalid Guards were in waiting, beside a large concourse of people, to receive him. The Guards carefully bore him along the street to his father's home.[22]

Norristown officials who planned a major celebration were forced to cancel it because the general was in such a weakened state, with the bullet still lodged somewhere in his body. A paper reported incorrectly that he was "getting along very well," but local doctors knew better and beat a path to the Hancock home in repeated attempts to retrieve the offending object.[23] Hancock's only respite came on August 5, when he received a warm note from Secretary of War Edwin Stanton, saying that "of the many gallant officers wounded on the great field of Gettysburg, no one has more sincerely my sympathy, confidence and respect than yourself . . . the blow that struck you down was a heavy and disastrous one to the country."[24] But his condition continued to deteriorate until he was visited in late August by Dr. Louis W. Read, an army surgeon from the McKim United States Hospital in Baltimore, who, by quirk of fate, was a longtime Norristown resident; he received a leave absence from General Meade to return home and examine Hancock.

Read, who knew Hancock by reputation and had served in the Union army medical corps since the outbreak of the war, was distressed at what he saw. "I found him much disheartened," the doctor wrote. "He had grown thin, and looked pale and emaciated. He said he felt as if he was going to die, and that he had been probed and tortured to such an extent that death would be a relief." Read had no thought of inflicting more pain with a similar probe and was about to turn and leave when Hancock blurted out, "See here, Doctor, why don't you try to get this ball out? I have had all the reputation[s] in the country at it; now let's have some of the practical."[25]

Read then came up with an ingenious idea. Every previous probe had taken place when Hancock was flat on his back; why not, Read thought, have him sit upright, "in a position similar to that when he was seated in the saddle when hit?" It would change the body geometry and make the depth of the groin area more accessible, perhaps making it possible to finally find the bullet.[26]

Read and a physician he identified only as "Dr. Cooper" (likely Dr. George E. Cooper, who had cared for Hancock in Philadelphia) helped the general into a chair "on top of the dining room table." Strange as it may have seemed to have the hero of Gettysburg propped up in this manner, Read thought the extra elevation would open a clear path to the bottom of the wound. "I inserted the probe and dropped fully eight inches into the channel and struck the ball, which was imbedded in the sharp bone which you sit upon." Startled a bit by his own success, he returned the next day with different instruments to surgically remove the bullet, describing it only as a "big Minie ball" that was "located posterior to the femur."[27] A Hancock staffer later wrote that it "bore upon it the marks of the nail, which Dr. Dougherty had extracted from the wound upon the field. Its weight was 1 ounce and 90 grains."[28] It was out.

No longer burdened by a foreign object in his body, Hancock's outlook and physical condition improved immediately. He was soon out of bed, walking around on crutches and able to attend a local Masonic meeting.[29] In mid-September, anxious to resume a normal pace of life but still not able to return to active duty, he took the train north through New York City to West Point, where he was greeted as a conquering hero. The visit was a source of great pride and reflection for the No. 18 graduate from the Class of 1844, who had outperformed all his academy classmates. "The scenes of other days came freshly back upon him," a biographer wrote, "and he lived again in the haunts and studies of the past."[30]

From West Point, he traveled to the St. Louis area, joining Almira and the children at her parents' estate, called Longwood. Hancock spent six weeks there, into early November, filling his time by trimming trees and planting brushes when his recovery allowed. On October 12, he wrote home to his father with an update:

I threw aside my crutches a few days after my arrival, and now walk with a cane. I am improving but do not yet walk without a little "roll." My wound is still unhealed, though the doctors say it is closing rapidly. I find some uneasiness in sitting long on a chair, and cannot yet ride [a horse]. The bone appears to be injured, and may give me trouble for a long time. I hope, however, I may be well enough in two weeks to join the Corps. Allie and the children send their best love to you and mother.[31]

Hancock had, indeed, made progress but, despite his optimism, was not yet ready to return to the field. Walking stiffly and still unable to ride a horse, his physical activity was limited, and friends could not overlook a stark turn in his appearance. "After his Gettysburg wound, Hancock underwent a marked change physiologically," staffer Francis Walker wrote, "gaining weight rapidly during his enforced idleness and suffering a permanent loss of some portion of his former activity and elasticity." Despite this development, Walker thought, the newly added bulk actually enhanced his commanding presence: "The change in no degree diminished the impressiveness of his carriage and bearing. He was, if anything, statelier, with an appearance of greater power and more composure."[32]

And yet the general was still no closer to returning to the war. On November 2, while he was at Jefferson Barracks in St. Louis, Dr. John F. Randolph wrote two notes in three weeks declaring Hancock unfit for duty—the "gunshot wound in the left thigh" remained "unhealed"—and predicted he would not be ready for at least another twenty days.[33] Nonetheless, after learning that the Second Corps had fought several small battles under temporary commanders, Hancock was pressing authorities to get back into the field. Meade also was anxious for his return and dashed off a note on November 6, writing, as only Meade could, "Dear Hancock . . . I am glad to hear you are getting along as well as you are. You will have to be patient and resigned, & give your wound time to heal, consoling yourself with reflection that matters might be much worse."[34]

Hancock made what seemed like a triumphant return to command of the Second Corps on December 27, 1863, rejoining his troops near Culpeper, greeting them for the first time since Gettysburg, but it turned out to be a false start—the first of many that would plague him for the rest of his career.[35]

He had charmed his doctors just before Christmas to get official clearance but still was in no condition to lead men in drills or battle, with the wound still tender and draining. Within a few weeks, he was reassigned to recruiting duty and given the outrageous goal of increasing "said Corps to a strength of 50,000 men."[36] It was a daunting task at this late stage of the war, after so much death and bloodshed, but Hancock did his best, setting up an office in Harrisburg, Pennsylvania, about forty miles north of Gettysburg, and playing on the patriotic fervor of his native state. "Let it not be said that Pennsylvania, which has already given so many of her sons to this righteous cause, shall now, at the eleventh hour, be behind her sister States in furnishing her quota of the men deemed necessary to end this rebellion," the general said.[37] When the Second Corps returned to action later that year, however, it did so, through no fault of Hancock's, with fewer than thirty thousand men fit for duty.[38]

It was during this period in the early winter of 1864 that Hancock began to receive formal plaudits for his exemplary work at Gettysburg. The citizens of Philadelphia, who had virtually ignored him when he arrived as an invalid just three days after the battle, now joined together to salute his role in the landmark Union victory. He was afforded the rare honor of a reception at Independence Hall, and the date selected, by no coincidence, was February 22, George Washington's birthday. The official city decree declared that "the THANKS of the Citizens of Philadelphia are eminently due and hereby tended to MAJOR GENERAL HANCOCK for his brilliant services in the cause of the UNION, during the present unholy Rebellion against the authority of the GOVERNMENT AND PEOPLE OF THE UNITED STATES."[39] Local newspapers described the scene as "one of the most imposing that ever occurred within the walls of the sacred old Temple of American Liberty."[40]

There was similar praise when he made recruiting stops in cities through the Northeast, including New York, Albany, and Boston, although Hancock may have been happiest when the people of Norristown, led by his old neighbors and schoolmates, presented him with an ornate silver set, inscribed "To Maj. General Winfield Scott Hancock from Citizens of his Birth place, Norristown, Montgomery County, Pa." All nine pieces were etched with the trefoil badge of the Second Corps. "The value to the recipient cannot be computed in silver or gold," a biographer wrote. "It is a pleasant reminder of the days spent as a boy in Norristown. . . . He had always been a leader among them, and this appropriate memorial was a new assurance that they held him worthy to be a commander of a great army of patriots."[41]

Hancock communicated on several occasions that winter with Meade, who had come under fire from Lincoln for not pursuing the Rebels aggressively enough after Gettysburg. Meade expected to be fired or reassigned, writing to his friend that "I am prepared, at any moment . . . and accordingly keep my sabre packed . . . and shall feel no regret whenever the order relieving me arrives."[42] If there was a hint of awkwardness to their exchanges, it was because Hancock was rumored as the replacement, but Meade's fears were never realized (and Hancock's condition wouldn't have allowed it anyway). Lincoln brought Ulysses S. Grant east from his great victories at Vicksburg and Chattanooga to be lieutenant general of all Union armies, but Meade retained command of the Army of the Potomac, and Hancock, by late March, returned to his place with the Second Corps.[43]

Hancock rejoined the army on March 23 at Stevensburg, Virginia, eliciting rare bursts of excitement from the normally dour Meade. "I'm glad to see you again, Hancock," the commanding general said, clasping an outstretched hand.[44] A blanket of snow was still on the ground, dampening body and spirit, but it was good to have such a determined fighter back in the fold with the fourth year of the war about to begin.

What Meade and the others could not have known was that Hancock would never be the same again after his Gettysburg wound. Staying on his feet and walking long distances remained a challenge, and he could not mount a horse for any length of time without pain, depriving him of the chance to inspire his troops as he had by riding the line during the bombardment of Cemetery Ridge. Excess weight and decreased fitness conspired against him. Hancock still very much looked the part—"a tall, soldierly man . . . with massive features and the heavy folds round the eye that often mark a man of ability"[45]—but he could no longer rely on physical prowess to ensure his success.

The plan Grant had in mind was a relentless drive toward Richmond to grind down the Rebels and end the war in a bloody battle of attrition.

Unlike previous Union commanders in the East, he was committed to always moving forward, even in the face of horrendous personnel losses. Grant's 1864 "Overland Campaign" began near Chancellorsville on May 5–6 in a tangled mess of trees, shrubs, and underbrush known as the Wilderness. A historian called it "perhaps the most confused and disorganized of any in the war," and Hancock's role reflected that confusion; his corps pushed back troops under A. P. Hill, "driving them beautifully," causing Meade to exclaim "bully for Hancock," only to see Hill's men rally on the counterattack and force a stalemate.[46] Grant then chose to disengage and, in a hint of things to come, head thirteen miles southeast to the site of their next encounter, Spotsylvania Court House.

It was at Spotsylvania on May 12 that Hancock and his corps had their greatest day since Gettysburg, breaking through at the Mule Shoe salient and swarming over Confederate breastworks, taking almost four thousand prisoners, including a major general, Edward Johnson.[47] But the Rebel response was fierce once again, leading to what Walker described as a "desperate and protracted contest" for control of the works:

> *The contest had become beyond all comparison the closest and fiercest of the war. For the distance of a mile, in a cold, drenching rain, the combatants were literally struggling across the breastworks. They fired directly into each other's faces . . . men even grappled their antagonists over the piles of logs. . . . Never since the discovery of gunpowder had such a mass of lead been hurled into a space so narrow as that which now embraced the scene of combat.*
>
> *Hancock presided strong, stern and masterful . . . [until] the Confederates, relinquishing their purpose to retake the captured works, began in the darkness to construct a new line to cut off the Salient.*[48]

The new Rebel line was virtually impregnable, leading to another stalemate, until Grant began a series of maneuvers designed to draw Lee into the open and force a decisive outcome farther to the south. Hancock and his corps were involved in a series of bloody actions at North Anna and Cold Harbor, but they made no significant headway before settling in at the start of a long siege of Petersburg. It was here that Hancock's wound started to get the best of him. After the Battle of Cold Harbor, he had resorted to pouring water from his canteen on the affected area—"a doubtful remedy"[49]—but now, as the army sat and waited for Lee to move, he requested a leave of absence on June 17.

Staffer Henry Bingham had been aware of Hancock's physical struggles throughout the spring campaign. "Although he continued with his command," Bingham said, "he was obliged to travel in an ambulance a great portion of the time. His habit on the march was to remain in his ambulance at the head of his column until in the vicinity of the enemy, when he mounted his horse, and so remained until the fighting was over." During these several months, he was "daily attended by a Surgeon on account of his wound, which at that time was much irritated and discharging more or less all the time, small portions of the bone at times passing from it."

But the move to Petersburg and the accompanying siege duties had finally been too much. Hancock was forced to be mounted "nearly all the time, both day and night," Bingham said, and the wound was "so inflamed and dangerous that he was compelled to relinquish command of the corps for a few days." The general remained with the troops and got some much-needed rest while lying down in his tent, doing so well in the short term that he was cleared to return to action after on June 27. Bingham reported that he found "himself much relieved by the discharge of quite a large piece of bone from the wound."[50]

One of Hancock's next significant assignments came in late August, when his corps was sent to tear up the tracks of the Weldon Railroad, cutting a vital Rebel supply route. The enemy soon learned of their presence, and Confederate General A. P. Hill sent out a contending force that included Henry Heth, Hancock's old comrade from the Mexican War. They collided at Reams Station on August 25, with Hill and Heth getting the upper hand, inflicting almost three thousand casualties on the Second Corps—Hancock's greatest defeat as a corps commander.[51] The *New York Times* reported that Hancock was seen "cheering and urging the men forward," a noble tribute to his gallantry, but the Union disaster here turned out to be his last major action of the war.[52]

The stigma of Reams Station remained with him for many years. As his aide, William Mitchell, described it,

It is not surprising that General Hancock was deeply stirred by the situation, for it was the first time he had felt the bitterness of defeat during the war. He had seen his troops fail in their attempts to carry the intrenched positions of the enemy, but he had never before had the mortification of seeing them driven and his lines and guns taken, as on this occasion . . .

Riding up to one of his staff . . . covered with dust and begrimed with powder and smoke, he placed his hand upon the staff officer's shoulder and said, "Colonel, I do not care to die, but I pray God I may never leave this field." The agony of that day never passed away from the proud soldier.[53]

His friend Heth, writing about it years later, after the two had been reunited, said, "I have read that if Hancock's heart could be examined there would have been written on it 'REAMS,' as plainly as the deep scars received at Gettysburg and other fields were visible."[54]

In the fall of 1864, with his battlefield service dwindling, Hancock paid as much attention to the presidential election as any soldier in the army. It pitted his friend and fellow Democrat George McClellan against Lincoln. From the start of the war, Hancock's main focus had been preserving the Union, and he still believed that Lincoln's policies were the best chance to achieve that end. Setting friendship aside for the good of the country, he voted for the president.[55]

"My politics," he wrote to a friend, "are of the practical kind—the integrity of the country, the supremacy of the Federal Government, an honorable peace or none at all."[56]

By the end of November, still bothered by his Gettysburg wound, Hancock asked for another leave of absence from the Second Corps. He had the full intention of returning in the spring but still sent the troops a parting message, saying, "I feel I am severing the strongest ties of my military life."[57] In the interim, Grant sought to capitalize on Hancock's reputation by assigning him to a new kind of recruiting duty: approaching veteran soldiers whose terms had expired and convincing them to reenlist in the army. This unique "Veterans Corps" would require little training and could theoretically help to contain Lee if he broke away from Petersburg and Richmond.[58]

It was one of those ideas that seemed better on paper than in action. The vast majority of veterans felt they had already done their duty to the country, and, even with the great Hancock's prodding, only about four thousand rejoined the cause. In February 1865, he was reassigned to command of the Department of West Virginia and the Middle Military Division, and it was there that he was serving when Lee surrendered to Grant on April 9 at Appomattox.[59] Hancock's last wartime act was to collect Rebel stragglers near Winchester in mid-April, telling one of them, "Let us once more kneel down at the same altar, and be like brothers of the same household."[60]

He left the war as one of the Union's most famous and successful generals, destined, some thought, for many more great things.

CHAPTER SIXTEEN

Almost Mr. President

SOME ACCOUNTS OF HANCOCK'S REMARKABLE LIFE STORY JUMP DIRECTLY from the end of the Civil War in 1865 to the U.S. presidential election of 1880, glossing over the fifteen years in between.

But Hancock filled multiple high-profile roles for the army during this period, serving as both a general and a civil administrator and encountering more than his share of controversy and criticism.

Consider the following:

- In the summer of 1865, as commander of the Middle Military Division in Washington, D.C., he was assigned to oversee the execution of the Lincoln conspirators, including, most contentiously, the lone woman, Mary Surratt.[1]

- Two years later, sent west to fight Indians in Kansas—but with no knowledge of Indian ways—he clumsily touched off a series of battles that became known as "Hancock's War."[2]

- Also in 1867, President Andrew Johnson named him military governor of Louisiana and Texas, where, during his brief four-month reign, he controversially restored civilian rule and sparked a personal feud with Ulysses S. Grant.[3]

Grant, the singular northern hero, aligned himself with the Radical Republicans and was an ardent supporter of reconstructing the South after the war.[4] Hancock, a lifelong Democrat, held opposing views on how the country should be reunited. There is no doubt that the two generals had worked well together on the battlefield and shared a deep respect regarding military matters, dating back to their days at West Point. Grant once wrote that "Hancock stands the most conspicuous figure of all general officers who did not exercise [command of an entire army]" and that "his personal courage and his presence with his command in the thickest of the fight won for him the confidence of troops serving under him."[5] But the immediate postwar period drove a wedge between them.

Grant was furious that President Johnson, a Southern Democrat picked to balance Lincoln's ticket in the 1864 election, wanted to remove General Phil Sheridan as military commander in Louisiana. Of the men who commanded the five military districts in the South, Sheridan had most "briskly" enforced the First Reconstruction Act, which Grant believed was "a fitting end to all our controversy." It included granting full citizenship rights to former slaves. As U.S. general in chief, Grant thought temporary military governments were needed to enforce these new policies and oversee "rebel states until they were fully restored" in relations to the federal government.[6]

The public's views on this were split—not unusual for a country still reeling from a costly civil war. "It was inevitable," wrote Hancock's staffer, Francis Walker, "that widely different views should be held by equally intelligent and patriotic men as to the proper method of treating communities composed of those who had lately been in rebellion. The two policies of generosity and trustfulness on the one hand, of distrust and repression on the other, were certain to find adherents, in great numbers, among those who had been perfectly united and agreed so long as a single soldier of the Confederacy remained in arms."[7]

Johnson's original choice, George Thomas, was unable to serve because of a liver ailment, so the president turned to Hancock as his replacement. In fairness, it was not an assignment that Hancock sought, and he vowed that he would not hold office for long. His views were incompatible with those who expected harsh treatment of the conquered southerners, some of whom had been his dear friends before the war. He did not accept that military rule over a defeated people was the best way to restore the Union. As he said to Almira,

I am expected to exercise extreme military authority over those people. I shall disappoint them. I have not been educated to overthrow the civil authorities in time of peace. I intend to recognize the fact that the Civil War is at an end, and shall issue my order or proclamation accordingly. I tell you this, because I may lose my commission, and I shall do so willingly, rather than retain it at the sacrifice of these lifelong principles.[8]

The order of which he spoke was General Orders No. 40, issued on November 29, 1867, his first day of command. A historian said it "stirred a storm throughout the nation."[9] The order read, in part,

In war it is indispensable to repel force by force, to overthrow and destroy opposition to lawful authority, but when insurrectionary force has been over-thrown and peace established, and the civil authorities are ready and willing to perform their duties, the military power should cease to lead, and the civil administration resume its natural and rightful dominion. Solemnly impressed with these views, the General announces that the great principles of American liberty are still the inheritance of this people, and ever should be.[10]

Stunned southerners responded to this with gratification. Former Confederate General John Gordon, a veteran of Antietam and Gettysburg, later a U.S. senator from Georgia, said that Hancock achieved "undying civil fame by the abnegation of his military power over his defeated countrymen, as he laid his sheathed and untarnished sword—a fitting sacrifice—on the altar of the civil law."[11] Praise also came from some in the North, including General William "Baldy" Smith, Hancock's longtime comrade, whom he had known since West Point. "At a time when military men thirsted for power," Smith wrote, "when one part of our country was demoralized by poverty and defeat, and when even the people of the North were getting accustomed to the despotism of long-continued military authority, General Hancock clearly proclaimed the fundamental principle of the subordination of the military power, which is always abnormal, to the civil."[12]

But the order flew in the face of Reconstruction policies passed by Congress, and it was not long before Hancock and Grant clashed over a decision to oust Sheridan's political appointees. Republicans who shared

Grant's views were said to be "sorely discomfited by Hancock's adminis-tration, and they made the fact known, both on the scene and in commu-nications to Washington."[13] After only four months on the job, Hancock submitted his resignation and asked to be removed.[14]

He traveled from New Orleans to Washington in late March 1868 and took command of the army's Division of the Atlantic, although it was clear to all that his relationship had cooled. He signed the register at Grant's headquarters, as required, but declined to wait for a personal interview.[15] Grant later told William Tecumseh Sherman that Hancock "personally assumed to [me] an unfriendly attitude."[16] As a result of this schism, it was perhaps not surprising that when Grant became president of the United States in 1869, Hancock—one of the highest-ranking generals in the army—was reassigned to the obscurity of the Department of Dakota.[17]

There was a chance that Hancock could have become the Democratic presidential nominee as early as 1868, putting him in a direct showdown with Grant, the Republican standard-bearer. Hancock's Union army war record made him popular in the North, and the defiant nature of General Orders No. 40 drew wide support across the South. Beyond that, he was a native of Pennsylvania, a large and important state, and perhaps the only candidate who could hope to challenge Grant for the soldier vote.

President Johnson, though his reputation had been sullied by impeachment proceedings, was a contender at the start, as were former congressman George Pendleton of Ohio, Senator Thomas Hendricks of Indiana, and former governor Horatio Seymour of New York. A potential dark horse was Salmon P. Chase, chief justice of the Supreme Court.[18] With no clear front-runner, others would certainly enter the fray.

The Democratic convention was held at New York's Tammany Hall from July 4 to July 9, and the party was so fractured that it took twenty-three ballots to select a candidate. Hancock led on several of them but never with enough support to clinch the nomination. His bid lost momentum when the convention was adjourned after the eighteenth ballot on July 8, and the delegates returned to choose Seymour the next day, after several hasty backroom deals.[19] It was nonetheless a strong per-formance for someone with no electoral experience and no organization behind him, and this "accidental candidate" (as Hancock described himself) had earned a spot on the national political stage.[20]

Shortly after Grant's election, Hancock was dispatched to St. Paul, Minnesota, and the Department of Dakota—a military backwater if there ever was one. He dutifully served three years in the beautiful but secluded region, taking advantage of free time to plan the next phase of his life. He wrote frequently to Peter Rothermel, an artist from Philadelphia who was working on a massive painting of the Battle of Gettysburg, anxious to recount his role in detail. He briefly considered running for president again in 1872 and began to lay the groundwork before deciding against it. But it was a tragedy within the army family in November 1872 that caused the biggest change: the death of George Meade left Hancock as the senior major general of the army, and Sherman, with some prodding, convinced Grant to bring him back to the Division of the Atlantic. Hancock took command at new headquarters in New York City on December 16, 1872, finally freed from life on the Plains.[21]

Peacetimes duties for an administrative officer of his rank were frustratingly mundane. There had been plenty of excitement in his life to this point—three wars and a presidential bid—but Hancock kept hoping for a new challenge. He was recruited to run for governor of his native Pennsylvania in 1875, but the timing wasn't right, and he expressed no interest even before the death of his eighteen-year-old daughter, Ada, of typhoid fever on March 28. Her sudden loss numbed the family. Almira wrote of the "seclusion, gloom and depression" that overcame them that spring and summer.[22] Ada was temporarily buried in the tomb of a family friend in Norristown, but within a few years Hancock had his own distinctive mausoleum built for her at a corner of nearby Montgomery Cemetery.[23]

The 1876 presidential election came along just as he was getting over his grief. Grant had been convinced that he shouldn't run for reelection to a third term, leaving wide-open fields on both sides of the political spectrum. Hancock wasn't an "accidental" candidate, as he had been in 1868, and his experience from that campaign gave him an insider's perspective, but he never gained enough traction to lead the six-man Democratic field. The most viable candidates were two sitting governors, Samuel Tilden of New York and Hendricks of Indiana, and their experience running state governments gave them an edge.[24]

The convention was held from July 27 to July 29 in a city that Hancock knew well—St. Louis. It marked the first time the Democrats had convened for such an event west of the Mississippi River, and Almira couldn't have been more pleased. There appeared to be a growing pro-Hancock movement as delegates arrived in Missouri, and Fitzhugh Lee of Virginia pronounced that "only with Hancock can we carry this country against the Radical candidate."[25] But Tilden flexed his political muscles on the first ballot with four hundred votes, well ahead of Hendricks and Hancock, and so impressed the rest of the assembly that he wrapped up the nomination on the second ballot. Hendricks became the vice presidential candidate. Hancock finished a solid but distant third.[26]

The election, pitting Tilden against Civil War veteran Rutherford B. Hayes, the Republican nominee, was one of the most controversial and contentious in American history. Tilden won the popular vote by more than two hundred thousand but fell short in the Electoral College, with results in three southern states—all controlled by Republicans—still in dispute. A commission was formed by Congress to sort out the mess and, with votes cast strictly along party lines, declared Hayes the tainted winner.[27] But because Hayes had announced in advance that he would serve only one term in the White House, both parties would nominate new candidates again in 1880.[28]

The Democratic Party had not won a presidential election since before the Civil War, but it felt renewed vigor amid a changing political landscape in 1880. Democrats controlled both houses of Congress for the first time in twenty years. Reconstruction had weakened, faded, and finally collapsed under the pro-southern policies of the Hayes administration. Moreover, Tilden's win in the popular vote, though hollow, showed that the public was ready to put a Democrat back in the White House for the first time since James Buchanan in 1856.[29]

And yet the specter of Ulysses S. Grant loomed large over the 1880 campaign. Although his two-term administration had been corrupt, he remained the embodiment of Union Civil War power and conqueror of the Confederacy, and he had deftly revamped his reputation with a well-publicized postpresidential world tour. There was no doubt that Grant wanted a third term. While many deemed that idea distasteful—even the great Washington had stepped down after two terms, ensuring there would be no American monarch—there was enough legitimate support to make Grant a leading contender for the Republican nomination as the party's convention approached in early June.[30]

Grant was concerned that a Democratic victory would chip away at the gains he and the Republicans had made since the end of the Civil War. In 1878, perhaps sensing a disturbing trend in the congressional elections, he wrote, "It looks to me that unless the North rallies in 1880, the Government will be in the hands of those who tried so hard fourteen—seventeen—years ago to destroy it."[31] According to his most recent biographer, Ron Chernow, the former president therefore "felt a direct personal stake in the 1880 election," almost that it was his duty to run again "to save the results of the war."[32] But the Republicans were split into three feuding factions at this point, warring over issues such as trade and civil service reform, and there was significant opposition to an un-Washington-like third term.[33]

There was no shortage of candidates when the Republicans gathered for their convention on June 2 in Chicago. Grant, still probably the most famous man in the country and the hands-down early favorite, was joined by Maine Senator James G. Blaine, U.S. Treasury Secretary John Sherman, Vermont Senator George Edmunds, and a slew of lesser-known politicos. Barely mentioned at the time was James A. Garfield, another former Union general and nine-term congressman from Ohio, who was at least symbolically in Sherman's camp but working feverishly for himself behind the scenes. The competition was such that a verdict took thirty-six ballots.[34]

The winning candidate needed 370 votes. Grant led on the first ballot with 304 for a slight edge over Blaine, but he could not add substantially to that total. On the third ballot, Garfield's name was placed in nomination, along with Benjamin Harrison of Indiana, further diluting the field.[35] On and on it went until the thirty-fourth ballot, when the Wisconsin delegation broke the logjam by throwing its support behind Garfield. Delegates from Indiana followed the lead, then Ohio, and by the time they reached the thirty-sixth ballot, Garfield had swept to an unlikely victory, besting Grant, 399–306.[36] His running mate as vice president would be Chester Arthur, another Union veteran of the Civil War.

Almost since the end of the 1876 election, Winfield Scott Hancock had his eye set on 1880 and a third presidential bid in twelve years.

His wide range of credentials, rare among Democrats—Union war veteran, hero of Gettysburg, benevolent military governor—seemed to set him apart from the rest of the field, especially after Samuel Tilden, the most recent nominee, chose not to run again, citing health and other issues.

Hancock tried not to seem too eager. He once told an interviewer that he would not enter into "any contest or fight to secure the nomination," but it was clear that he and his friends were working to garner support.[37] The competition was impressive but not overwhelming: Senator Thomas F. Bayard of Delaware, descended from a staunch military family; Thomas Hendricks, the 1876 vice presidential nominee; Henry B. Payne, a filthy-rich oil man from Ohio; and Allen G. Thurman, a former senator from Ohio.[38]

The fifty-six-year-old Hancock, an imposing figure now weighing 240 pounds, would base his candidacy largely on personality and a lifetime of leadership performance. A biographer noted dryly that he was "not encumbered by complex political views" and had once suggested a platform of "an honest man and the restoration of the Government." He believed foremost in limited government. There would be no sweeping policy initiatives.[39] Setting aside his fame and marketability, he lacked any real political experience, even after nomination bids in 1868 and 1876.

Garfield had been the Republican nominee for three weeks when the Democrats finally met for their convention on June 23 in Cincinnati. Hancock chose not to attend, remaining at his home on Governor's Island, New York, focusing on his military duties and appearing to stay above the fray. Party leaders were aware that their opponents had taken thirty-six ballots over two raucous days to settle on a candidate and hoped to avoid the same kind of drawn-out fiasco. After whisking through a series of nominating speeches to start the event, they wanted to get down to business quickly.

The speech for Hancock, though, set the convention ablaze.

It was delivered by a Philadelphia lawyer named Dan Dougherty, noted for his dynamic oratory, who had been recruited specifically for the occasion. Dougherty was not a delegate but took the place of another attendee who conveniently gave up his seat. "I present to the thoughtful consideration to the convention," Dougherty said, "the name of one who, on the field of battle, was styled 'The Superb.'" That opening sent a buzz through the audience and elicited some early cheers, but anyone who had met the speaker knew he was just warming up:

> *I name one who, if nominated, will suppress every faction, and be alike acceptable to the North and the South, whose nomination will thrill the land from end to end, crush the last embers of sectional strife, and be hailed as the dawn of the long-for day of perpetual brotherhood.*
>
> *. . . We can appeal to the supreme tribunal of the American people against the corruptions of the Republican party and its untold violations of Constitutional liberty. Oh, my countrymen! In this supreme moment—the destinies of the Republic—the imperiled liberties of the people, hang breathlessly on your deliberations. Pause! Reflect! Beware! Make no misstep! I nominate . . . the soldier-statesman, with a record as stainless as his sword.*[40]

The delegates stood and cheered for five minutes. If there was any doubt that this was Hancock's hall, Dougherty's speech demolished it. The first ballot was still relatively close, with 171 votes for Hancock, 153½ for Bayard, 81 for Payne, and 68½ for Thurman—all far short of the 470 needed to nominate—but momentum was clearly in favor of the general. Entire state delegations switched their votes on the second ballot, and Hancock ran up a staggering 705–30 lead over Hendricks to profoundly clinch the nomination. The party then tapped former congressman William F. English of Indiana as its vice presidential candidate, gambling that English could deliver his home state to the Democratic column.[41]

The 1880 election marked the only time in American history that both major parties nominated former Union generals to duel it out for the nation's highest office.[42]

It was not Hancock versus Grant, of course, as some had hoped—and had once seemed possible—but it was still an alluring matchup.

Garfield had entered the war as a lieutenant colonel of volunteers and rose to brigadier general, leading a brigade at the Battle of Shiloh and serving as chief of staff to William Rosecrans at Chickamauga. But he was not a professional soldier and left the army for the House of Representatives in December 1863, beginning a seventeen-year congressional career that forged his political persona.[43] Hancock, by contrast, had known only the army. He marched off to West Point when he was sixteen years old and never looked back, serving on the frontier and in Mexico, becoming "the Superb" at Williamsburg, and stopping the rising Rebel tide on Cemetery Ridge.

Presidential campaigns in the nineteenth century were often homespun affairs, with candidates rarely straying from the comfort of their front porches and supporters arriving in droves to pay homage. Garfield's farm near Mentor, Ohio, became a magnet for "Union veterans, businessmen, women suffragists, politicians," and many other fawning Republican partisans.[44] Well schooled in political style and manners, Garfield handled it superbly, patting heads and shaking hands while being careful not to discuss specific issues. Hancock's reaction was quite the opposite. He was agitated by the steady stream of visitors who found their way to Governor's Island. Even worse, in mid-July, just a few weeks after the nomination, he was mired in personal grief and sadness: his four-month-old grandson and namesake, Winfield Scott Hancock, passed away in his home on July 13.[45] As he had with the death of his daughter five years earlier, however, the general had to endure it and move on.

Garfield's staunch credentials as a soldier-politician should have given him a large edge in the race, but Hancock's rare blend of charm and charisma made it surprisingly competitive. For at least part of the campaign, the Republicans were hesitant to attack him because of his status as a war hero; it gave him a shield that was unavailable to previous Democratic nominees. Only when Hancock clumsily muffed a reporter's question about protective tariffs in early October did the strategy change. The general's uncomplicated answer—"the tariff question is a local question"—brought derision from opponents, who mocked him as a "simple soldier totally unschooled in the ways of government."[46] Sensing that Hancock was reeling, the Republicans pounced, mounting similar attacks and printing a satirical pamphlet titled "A Record of the Statements and Political Achievements of General Winfield Scott Hancock." Inside, the pages were blank.[47]

But the Democrats did not sit idly by as their candidate was pummeled in print. Garfield's seventeen-year record in Congress provided plenty of fodder for criticism, and they launched accusations of rampant corruption. Both sides grew increasingly vicious as election day approached.

Hancock promotional material during the 1880 presidential campaign
LIBRARY OF CONGRESS

It turned out to be the closest popular vote in U.S. presidential history. Garfield was named on 4,453,611 ballots, Hancock 4,445,256—a razor-thin difference of nine thousand votes out of a total of nine million.[48] Garfield had a more significant edge in the Electoral College, 214–155, and yet Hancock would have become president if New York, his state of residence, with its thirty-five electoral votes, had gone his way. The most stunning revelation was the list of states that fell into each man's camp. Hancock, the hero of the Union army at the Battle of Gettysburg, swept the South but lost his native Pennsylvania, lost New York, lost all of New England, and won New Jersey by just two thousand votes.[49]

Hancock went to bed early that night on Governor's Island, long before the results were known. It was daylight when he rolled over and asked Almira for the electoral verdict. "It was been a complete Waterloo for you," she told him. The military reference was wildly overstated, but Hancock didn't bother to inquire about more details. Nonplussed about being a runner-up once again, he puffed up his pillow and went back to sleep.[50]

Hancock was asked to attend Garfield's inauguration in Washington, D.C., on March 4, 1881. He didn't hesitate before accepting.

It began a final phase of reaching out to enemies and salving old wounds, which included leading the procession for Grant's funeral in 1885.

Attending the Garfield ceremony was never an issue for Hancock. From the start of the Civil War, he had been an advocate for restoring the Union, and this would be another step toward bringing the country together, honoring the peaceful transfer of power. "I have no right to any personal feeling in the matter," Hancock wrote to a friend. "A Democratic Congress has formally announced that the people have duly elected a [Republican] President, and that is James A. Garfield. It certainly seems that a Democratic candidate should be there to support the assertion. . . . The will of the majority rules, you know."[51]

That was followed by a series of ceremonial assignments, most notably the centennial celebration of the Continental Army's 1781 victory over Lord Cornwallis at Yorktown. Embracing the moment, Hancock and his staff produced a display of American grandeur unlike any other seen in the nineteenth century. "This Centennial will never be forgotten by those who were privileged to take part in or witness the grand military observances," Almira said.[52] A French diplomat wrote that "the naval review was one of the grandest and most imposing spectacles that we saw while in the United States."[53] The general, indeed, had flair.

It was not long before his Governor's Island headquarters became a popular destination for men who had served with him in Mexico and the Civil War, looking to relive their glories of the past. There were times when guest list also included politicians and bureaucrats—Almira called those meetings "irksome and exacting"—but Hancock understood his obligations and genuinely enjoyed reconnecting with comrades. Walker wrote that his "blond locks had turned gray, his youthful beauty faded under labors, griefs and wounds," but he somehow seemed "more majestic than even in his palmy days." With hundreds of Union veterans making visits, "there was such pleasure to a truly generous soul like his in dispensing the hospitality of headquarters."[54]

These seemingly joyful times were interrupted by a series of personal calamities over a two-year period, beginning with the death of Almira's mother in April 1883. Hancock's long-serving staff officer, William Mitchell, with whom he was exceedingly close, died a month later while still on duty at Governor's Island. But the most crushing news came in December 1884, when the Hancocks' son, Russell, their only remaining child, passed away after a brief illness at age thirty-three, leaving a wife and three young children.[55] "This last and final blow produced a fatal impress upon my husband's mind," Almira said. "Surely, there are as many and as hard-fought battles in life requiring steadfast faith and endurance, as there are on a military field."[56]

A less personal but nonetheless dramatic tragedy occurred when General Grant died of throat cancer on July 23, 1885. The Civil War hero and two-time U.S. president was a transcendent figure of the nineteenth century, superseded only by Lincoln, and the country went into deep mourning at news of his demise. The Grant family held a private funeral service on August 4 and then sent his casket on a two-day procession from Albany to New York City, where it lay in state at City Hall. The public funeral, planned for August 8, was expected to draw 1.5 million people, including some of the Union army's greatest generals, from Phil Sheridan to William Tecumseh Sherman, and a contingent of black Union veterans. At the request of Grant's wife, however, the guest list also featured several Confederate officers and troops from the famed Stonewall Brigade, a tribute to national unity, which one man wrote was "quite a sight."[57]

Hancock, as commander of the Atlantic Division, oversaw the planning and execution and, despite his long-term differences with Grant, vowed that "it should be as imposing as the Government desires and as public sentiment demands."[58] Mounted on a black steed, he rode at the front head of the eight-mile march route, leading a group of twenty generals in a lavish military display. Mourners gasped at the traditional riderless horse with boots faced backward in the stirrups.[59] Grant's friends, some of whom had been wary of Hancock, pronounced themselves pleased with the spectacle. One of them said, "The majestic character of those rites that attracted the attention of the world was greatly due to the tender care and chivalrous punctilio of him who thought the dead chieftain had wounded him."[60]

Perhaps feeling his own mortality in light of recent events, the sixty-one-year-old Hancock traveled to Gettysburg in November 1885 to walk the hallowed ground with historian John Bachelder and several of his staff officers. The general had made a brief visit in 1866, but this would be a more detailed and purposeful trip—not only to reminisce but also to better acquaint Bachelder with troop movements and battle action from Hancock's perspective. His arrival caused the biggest commotion at Gettysburg in years. Local Union veterans fired a seventeen-gun salute, "a vast assembly of citizens" poured into the streets to cheer him, and members of the Gettysburg Grand Army of the Republic (G.A.R.) post band "serenaded" the general with stirring patriotic tunes.[61]

When it came to the battlefield tour with Bachelder and his entourage, the *Gettysburg Compiler* reported that "General Hancock showed very great interest, graphically describing and elucidating many important events which transpired along the line of the left-centre, where he commanded." It continued,

> *He pointed out where Willard's brigade met Barksdale on the second day, the latter being killed; where the First Minnesota charged on Wilcox of Alabama; where Wright's Georgians charged across the Emmitsburg Road and nearly to the Union line on Cemetery Ridge . . . detailed the action of Webb's brigade on the third day, and explained the nature of Pickett's charge; and standing on the very ground, he showed how Stannard's brigade moved out and attacked Pickett's division in flank.*[62]

Hancock quibbled with the location of his wounding site (to be covered in chapter 17) but, according to the *Compiler*, remained in town a second day "to examine other parts of the field and more fully fix his recollections" of the battle. He left Gettysburg "highly pleased with his visit," although he would never have a chance to return again.

It was two months later, during a business trip to Washington on January 27, 1886, that Hancock complained of a painful boil on the back of his neck. He consulted several doctors about his condition, but it worsened rapidly, and it was soon discovered that he suffered from diabetes in addition to a skin ailment. He was, in fact, gravely ill. Hancock rallied slightly on February 6, but doctors were pessimistic about his long-term prognosis, and he slipped into a final state of delirium on February 9, calling out for his wife—"O, Allie, Allie! Myra!"—before losing consciousness. He died at mid-afternoon, five days shy of his sixty-second birthday.[63]

It was sad and jolting news to the public, which had not been aware of the general's illness. A distraught Almira gathered herself to arrange the funeral procession from Trinity Church in New York to the family mausoleum at Montgomery Cemetery, where the vault was opened for the first time since daughter Ada was laid to rest. Veterans from the Norristown G.A.R. post formed the honor guard and kept a crush of mourners back to allow the horse-drawn casket to finish its route. Four loud field guns fired a sad salute to punctuate the moment.[64]

Tributes rolled in from across the country. General Sherman called Hancock "one of the greatest soldiers in history," and former staffer

Hancock's burial site at Montgomery Cemetery in Norristown, Pennsylvania. The general and his daughter, Ada, are buried here.
AUTHOR PHOTO

Henry Bingham declared that "one felt safe when near him," but the most profound summation may have come from former president Rutherford B. Hayes, a fellow war veteran and political adversary:

> *If, when we make up our estimate of a public man, conspicuous as a soldier and in civil life, we are to think first and chiefly of his manhood, his integrity, his purity, his singleness of purpose, and his unselfish devotion, we can say truthfully of Hancock that he was through and through pure gold.*[65]

Chapter Seventeen

Legacy

Winfield Scott Hancock and Lewis Armistead came to symbol-ize the divisive emotional trauma of the American Civil War—longtime friends torn apart, fighting to the death over the country's future—but the connection between the two men was not well known in the nine-teenth century. The legend grew slowly over time.

The first published mention of Hancock and Armistead together did not come until 1880, when the Reverend D. X. Junkin and Frank Norton wrote *The Life of Winfield Scott Hancock*. Junkin was the first to break the news of their prewar encounter in Los Angeles in 1861, but it was over-shadowed by other topics, such as Hancock running for president, and made little impact at the time.[1]

Almira Hancock wrote *Reminiscences* in 1887, the year after her hus-band died, and described the meeting in more detail, including quotes from Armistead. Staffer Francis Walker compiled a Hancock biography in 1895 and referred specifically to "his friend Armistead."[2] Henry Heth, who served with both men in the Mexican War, wrote in his memoirs in 1897 that "Armistead, Hancock and I were messmates, and never was a mess happier than ours."[3] That was the extent of the early record in book form.

Tidbits of their relationship were recorded in other ways, including personal correspondence between Hancock and his staff officer, Henry Bingham, in 1882. The Hancock–Bingham letters were exchanged only after another Union general, Abner Doubleday, published a secondhand version of Armistead's statement to Bingham at the Angle at Gettysburg. "Now, dying," Doubleday wrote, "[Armistead] saw with a clearer vision that he had been engaged in an unholy cause, and said to one of our officers who leaned over him: 'Tell Hancock I have wronged him, and wronged my country.'" Beyond that, Doubleday made the absurd claim that Armistead had fought for the *Union* at the Battle of First Bull Run before switching sides to "join the rebellion."[4]

Armistead's former soldiers and family members were furious at both assertions. After establishing that Lewis was traveling through Arizona at the same time as First Bull Run and certainly never fought for the Union, they doubled down on Doubleday's account of the statement to Bingham. "None of his comrades ever heard the slightest intimation that he had doubted the justice of the cause for which he fought," one wrote. "It would take proof of the very strongest character to convince those who knew him" that Armistead had recanted after suffering his mortal wound.[5]

To bolster their case, members of the Southern Historical Society wrote to Hancock in July 1882 to ask for his opinion. They were under the impression that he had seen Armistead on Cemetery Ridge and had spoken to him directly before his death:

> *In reference to the alleged message to you, I beg to ask if you ever received such a message, and, if so, had you any reason to doubt General Armistead's being himself at the time? To be frank, General Armistead's relatives and friends are very indignant at this statement, and look upon it as leaving a stain upon the memory of that gallant soldier, which they are anxious to wipe out, and they are fully satisfied that either there is some mistake about the terms of the message, or else that he was delirious when he sent it.*[6]

Hancock, of course, never encountered Armistead at Gettysburg and hadn't even seen him since before the war. He dutifully forwarded the note to Bingham in Philadelphia, explaining that "he is the officer to whom the message was delivered, and is the best witness in the case."[7]

Bingham wrote back four days later. It was only the second time he ever addressed the meeting with Armistead in the Angle in writing:

> *Of course, I cannot not recall all the details in the matter of General Armistead's condition and words at the time of his capture, July 3, 1863; but my report, made to you immediately following the battle, is correct in every particular. Armistead, after I informed him that I was an officer upon your*

staff, and would deliver any personal effects that he might desire forwarded to his family, he made use of the words, as I now recall them, "Say to General Hancock for me that I have done him, and you all, a grievous (or serious) injury, which I shall always regret."

His condition at the time was that of a man seriously wounded, completely exhausted and seemingly broken-spirited. I had him carried immediately to the hospital.[8]

The southerners were satisfied with Bingham's account of the exchange, but they wouldn't back off quietly. They mounted a "burning protest against having that fair name and fame tarnished by the flippant reckless pen of General Doubleday" and claimed the book would "be of little value to the future historian if this is a fair specimen of his historic accuracy."[9]

It was a microcosm of how southern historians sought to shape their own story of the war in the late nineteenth century, part of the pervasive "Lost Cause" mentality that downplayed slavery as the cause and replaced it with a focus on southern gallantry.

A modern view of the Hancock wounding site at Gettysburg. During a visit to the battlefield late in his life, the general disputed the location.
COLLEEN MCMILLAN PHOTO

The twenty-five-year anniversary of the battle in 1888 brought with it the first small monument to Hancock at Gettysburg—marking the site of his wounding, several hundred yards south of the Angle on Cemetery Ridge, near two boulders at the end of the Union battle line.[10]

Had the general been alive at the time, he would not have approved the location. This alleged "wounding spot" had been identified to him on his final visit to the battlefield in November 1885, and he did all he could to complain that it was inaccurate. He was angry enough to write two letters within a month of returning home.

In a December 12, 1885, letter to Francis Walker, he claimed,

> I was shot from my horse while leaving the Vermont position by its right, along the high ground, proceeding directly towards the clump of timber. The place where I was shot, as at present marked, is not very accurately indicated. I saw no great boulder in the neighborhood. Lying on my back and looking through the remains of a very low, disintegrated stone wall, I could observe the operations of the enemy and give directions accordingly. . . . In lying down my head was to the south and my feet to the north. From where my horse fell I was carried a few yards to the spot upon which I lay down.[11]

Eight days later, in a December 20 letter to historian John Bachelder, he told much the same story and asked for a correction. He was particularly incensed because Bachelder had met with him on the battlefield as far back as 1866, when Hancock and several others identified the spot where he fell:

> I saw no great boulder in front of the Vermont brigade or about it, and therefore I am satisfied that the position indicating where I was shot is incorrect. It was established in 1866 in your presence, and in that of General Michell, General Stannard, Colonel B. Benedict and others (probably), but is not placed as indicated on that field, on my last visit by a sign-board. You were present, and in due time, I would be pleased if you would work with a stake or small boulder (in such a way that they cannot be moved again) the spot indicated by General Stannard and to which General Mitchell assented as sufficiently near the true place.[12]

Hancock insisted that he was not on the left flank of the Vermont troops when he was shot. His narrative was that he was valiantly head-

Hancock's statue on East Cemetery Hill was dedicated in 1896. It depicts a scene from the first day of the battle, when the general, with his hand outstretched, tried to calm the troops as they reformed nearby.
AUTHOR PHOTO

ing toward the copse of trees at the Angle (although, to be fair, other accounts differ). Unfortunately for Hancock, the notoriously stubborn Bachelder was unmoved by his argument and never seriously considered the requested change. The small monument was placed at the spot they identified in 1885, a bit farther south than Hancock would have liked.[13]

A much more magnificent and far less controversial tribute to Hancock was dedicated on June 5, 1896, on East Cemetery Hill. It was a massive equestrian statue, showing the general calming his frantic troops with an outstretched hand, as he had here on July 1, 1863. Authorities considered several options for the location of the monument, given Hancock's role on all three days at Gettysburg, and many of his supporters thought it should have been on Cemetery Ridge, near the climax of Pickett's Charge. But that plum position went to General George Meade, overall commander of the army, whose equestrian statue was also dedicated on June 5. If it were any consolation, the Gettysburg *Compiler* reported that Hancock's ceremony was attended "by an even greater throng of people than at the Meade statue in the morning."[14]

Longtime staffer Bingham spoke at the dedication and captured the essence of Hancock's impact on Gettysburg and the war. Here was a soldier, Bingham said, who was "devoted to his career, absolute in his faith and fidelity to his government, and knowing no duty other than the upholding of the honor and integrity of his country's flag. . . . And when [war] came in all of the terrible force of civil strife and secession, it found a soldier capable of great deeds, great commands and great victories." After finishing his address, Bingham turned toward the statue, saluted his old chief, and declared, "Well done!"[15]

In the early 1900s, to assist future students of the battle, the War Department placed iron tablets on the Gettysburg battlefield to mark troop positions for every corps, division, and brigade in both armies—including Hancock's corps on Cemetery Ridge and Armistead's brigade on Seminary Ridge. In 1913, figures of several Union generals, including Hancock, were added to Gettysburg's Pennsylvania Memorial.

Renewed interest in the Armistead–Hancock story began with the book *Glory Road*, part of the Army of Potomac trilogy by another Pulitzer Prize–winning author, Bruce Catton, in 1952. It was almost ninety years after the battle.

Catton devoted only a few pages to the two men, but he is believed to be the first historian to use Almira Hancock's book as a source and to retell the story of the California farewell gathering. For readers seeking a fresh human interest angle about the war, it was riveting popular history.

"Then the guests left," Catton wrote,

> *and next morning, Armistead and the others started east, and a little later Hancock himself came east to fight on the Northern side, and he and Armistead had not seen each other since. Now Hancock was on his horse on Cemetery Ridge, waiting with all the guns around him, and Armistead was coming up the slope with his black felt hat on the end of his sword and the strange roads of war the two old friends had followed were coming together at last.*[16]

Catton wrote of Armistead being shot at the height of Pickett's Charge, but it was only a brief passage and left much to the imagination.

It was not until describing Hancock's wounding three pages later that he completed the story, tugging at heartstrings:

> *An aide came up to [Hancock] and handed him a watch, a pair of spurs, and other trinkets. They came from Lewis Armistead, whom the aide had found dying there beside Cushing's last gun. Armistead had asked that these mementos of an old friendship be sent to Hancock, and he had gasped out some sort of farewell message, "Tell Hancock I have done him and my country a great injustice, which I shall never cease to regret," was the way the aide had it; he may have dressed it up a good deal, or, for that matter, he may have dreamed it all, and it does not matter much either way. Armistead had died, going beyond regrets forever, and as if he had been waiting for this last message. Hancock had the stretcher-bearer carry him off to the field hospital.*[17]

There were minor inaccuracies to Catton's story, but the content was clear and compelling, adding a new layer to the friend-versus-friend ethos of the Civil War. It was the first time that most of the public heard about the long-time friendship between the two men. Although other authors referenced the same material over the next twenty years—including the influential Shelby Foote in 1963[18]—there can be little doubt that Catton's work had a huge impact on Michael Shaara, who wrote at length about Armistead and Hancock in the novel *The Killer Angels* in 1974.

Shaara's book won a Pulitzer Prize for fiction and gave the two men a greater heroic status in the final years of the twentieth century. This was especially true after *The Killer Angels* was adapted to the big screen for the movie *Gettysburg* in 1993, with the Armistead and Hancock characters in primary roles. As brilliant as Shaara's writing had been, it could not compete with the intensely personal images that the movie created and sustained for the public: Hancock as the firm but compassionate defender, Armistead as the emotional invader, both men seemingly "pining" for each other as the battle of the third day drew near.[19]

The story was told so deftly that most readers and viewers had no idea it had been enhanced to fit the narrative of the novel.

As discussed previously in chapter 8, the most notable change came in a quote that Almira Hancock attributed to Armistead at the California farewell. Almira, who was the only person at the event to record what was said, wrote that Armistead told her husband, "I hope God will strike me dead if I am ever induced to leave my native soil, should worse come to worst." But the novel altered the quote to significantly heighten the drama: "Win, so help me, if I ever lift a hand *against you*, may God strike me dead." It created one of the most stirring and memorable scenes on the big screen.

Just as gripping were two passages from *The Killer Angels* that had Armistead speaking emotionally about Hancock with his corps commander, James Longstreet, as battle approached. There is no evidence that these discussions ever took place—no source, no written account—but the images left an indelible impression of Armistead's mind-set for readers and viewers:

> *Armistead said, "I hear you have some word of the Union Army."*
> *"Right." Longstreet thought: Hancock.*
> *"Have you heard anything of old Win?"*
> *"Yep. He's got the Second Corps, headed this way. We should be running into him one of these days." Longstreet felt a small jealousy. Armistead and Hancock. He could see them together—graceful Lo, dashing and confident Hancock. They had been closer than brothers before the war. A rare friendship. And now Hancock was coming this way with an enemy corps.*
> *. . . "I sure would like just to talk to him again," Armistead said. He leaned back, closing his eyes. "Last time was in California. When the war was beginning."*[20]

Another scene had Armistead sharing details of the California meeting, even telling Longstreet about the mournful song "Kathleen Mavourneen":

> *Armistead said slowly, "Last time I saw old Win, we played that, round the piano." He glanced at Longstreet, grinned vaguely, glanced away. "We went over there for the last dinner together, night before we all broke up. Spring of sixty-one." He paused, looked into the past, nodded to himself.*
> *"Mira Hancock had us over. One more evening together. You remember Mira. Beautiful woman. Sweet woman. They were a beautiful couple, you know that? Most beautiful couple I ever saw. He sure looks like a soldier now, and that's a fact."*[21]

It was fascinating reading, spellbinding theater, but there is simply no record that Armistead said any of this.

In the end, the everlasting value of *The Killer Angels* and *Gettysburg* is that the novel and the movie brought the story of the long-ago Civil War battle into the libraries and living rooms of a vast new audience in the late twentieth century, creating an enormous spike of interest in one of the defining moments of U.S. history. Combined with Ken Burns's PBS series *The Civil War*, released in 1990, they sparked a massive surge of visitation to Gettysburg and other battlefields and a slew of new Civil War titles on bookshelves, up through the 150th anniversary of the battle in 2013. It is important, however, for readers and viewers to understand that Shaara never intended to write a scholarly history and that the *Gettysburg* moviemakers weren't creating a documentary. They chose instead to tell the story of the battle by dramatizing a handful of key figures from both sides— Joshua Chamberlain and John Buford of the Union army and Longstreet and Lee of the Confederate army in addition to Armistead and Hancock.

In this style, they became two of most impactful pieces ever produced about the war's most famous clash. Historians Wayne Motts and James Hessler wrote that although the novel and film are, indeed, "heavily fictionalized," they have "successfully reached larger audiences than any other Gettysburg works."[22]

In 1993, the same year the movie was released, the next acknowledgment of the Armistead–Hancock legend was dedicated at the Annex to the Soldiers' National Cemetery at Gettysburg. The timing was coincidental.

For three years, a businessman and history buff named Sheldon Munn had been pushing his idea for a Masonic memorial at Gettysburg, honoring "the bonds of friendship which existed between Masons" in the Civil War. Munn was well aware that Masons had laid and dedicated the cornerstone of Gettysburg's Soldiers' National Monument on July 4, 1865, but he wanted a more personal tribute that would resonate with a modern audience. The best example, he thought, was the tale of Armistead and Hancock: two Masonic friends who chose different sides and clashed at the climax of the war's greatest battle. Indeed, the initial proposal for the "Friend to Friend Masonic Memorial" was a sculpture featuring life-size bronze versions of Armistead and Hancock shaking hands, but it was rejected out of hand by the National Park Service because "the incident was not authentic."[23]

Munn and his Masonic cohorts, including John Schwartz, a Gettysburg optometrist, then went looking for other ideas. The best one came from a historian at Gettysburg National Military Park who thought an image of the prone and wounded Armistead being assisted by Hancock staffer Henry Bingham was most appropriate. Both men were Masons, they fought for opposing armies, and, most important, the incident at the Angle "was documented," lending accuracy and relevance. Even for those who weren't Masons, it would symbolize the spirit of national reunion after the war. But the process of gaining approvals from the Grand Lodge of Pennsylvania and the local, regional, and national offices of the Park Service was going to be long and arduous.[24]

Munn and the ten-man Committee to Erect a Masonic Monument at Gettysburg began their work in 1991, undertaking "an incredibly complex and varying array of tasks requiring many thousands of hours of commitment," including significant lobbying efforts in Washington, D.C. Their first suggestion for a location—somewhere near the Peace Light Memorial on Oak Hill—was also rejected by the Park Service, but Jose Cisneros, then the superintendent of Gettysburg National Military Park, offered a reasonable alternative: the "Annex" to the soldiers' cemetery on Cemetery Hill.[25]

The Annex had been created in 1968 because of an influx of requests for additional burials from families of World War II, Korean War, and Vietnam War veterans; the original cemetery, created for Union soldiers from the Civil War, simply ran out of room. As a result, the Park Service had acquired five acres of adjacent land from a private owner and created a design for 1,666 new grave sites in a semicircular layout similar to the Civil War section.[26] At Cisneros's suggestion, the new monument could be placed at the front-center section of the Annex, near the flagpole. The committee had arranged for a backup site at nearby Evergreen Cemetery in the event of further delay, but all agreed the Annex was the preferred location.[27]

Continuing to move the project forward, the Masons hired sculptor Ron Tunison to create a twelve-inch clay model of the Armistead–

Bingham meeting, giving the Park Service and others a sense of the look and scale of what they had in mind.[28]

The most significant breakthrough, however, came when the committee learned that the Park Service lacked funds to improve and refurbish the Annex, which was well over twenty years old in the early 1990s. "It appeared," Munn wrote, "that the proposed Masonic monument . . . may have a chance for approval by the National Park Service in Washington if the Grand Lodge would agree to participate in the restoration and enhancement of the Annex area." The Masons seized on this opportunity. In August 1992, they presented plans for a new granite plaza that could surround their memorial. "The entire Annex perimeter of 1,600 feet would be surrounded by a six-foot high privacy fence with gates opening into an entry plaza along Steinwehr Avenue," Munn wrote. The entrance area would "include an informative wayside exhibit with colored illustrations and a lighted flagpole, enabling the American flag to be flown at night behind the gates."[29]

The plan worked. The Park Service today acknowledges that the Annex "was improved by a generous donation from the Freemasons in

The "Friend to Friend Masonic Memorial" replicates the moment on July 3, 1863, when Captain Henry Bingham of Hancock's staff attended to a wounded Armistead in the aftermath of Pickett's Charge.
COLLEEN MCMILLAN PHOTO

1993," including a "plaza that honors the dead of all American wars" and the Friend to Friend memorial.[30]

The richly detailed, life-size sculpture of Bingham assisting the fallen Armistead won approval from all parties involved. A groundbreaking ceremony was held on February 16, 1993, and the monument was dedicated six months later on August 21. The plaque on the granite base, titled "Friend to Friend," is a straightforward account and does not attempt to embellish the Bingham–Armistead meeting for the modern visitor. Acknowledging that "Union General Winfield Scott Hancock and Confederate General Lewis Addison Armistead were personal friends and members of the Masonic fraternity," it goes on to say, in part,

> *Depicted in this sculpture is Union Captain Henry Bingham, a Mason and staff assistant to General Hancock, himself wounded, rendering aid to the fallen Confederate General. Armistead is shown handing his watch and personal effects to be taken to his friend, Union General Hancock.*[31]

In 2000, a small stone marker was placed at the entrance to the George Spangler Farm lane, site of a large Union field hospital, detailing that the two friends received medical treatment within a short distance of one another. The inscription reads, "Here at the Union Army 11th Corps Field Hospital . . . Armistead died of his wounds on July 5, 1863. Northwest of this marker is the site of the Granite School House, another Union hospital, where Hancock was initially treated for his wounds."[32] Several years earlier, a small plaque was placed on an outside wall of the Spangler summer kitchen, marking the site where Armistead is believed to have died, although it has since been removed and mounted on the ground nearby.[33]

The Gettysburg Foundation, a nonprofit philanthropic, educational organization that supports the national park, acquired the historic Spangler farm property in 2008, spent years working on a meticulous rehabilitation program, and now offers guided tours to the public on summer weekends. The eighty-acre farm is promoted by the foundation as one of the best representations "of a Civil War field hospital site on the battlefield today, where upwards of 1,900 men, including Confederate Brig. Gen. Lewis A Armistead, were treated for wounds both minor and

This marker to the Armistead–Hancock friendship is found at the entrance to the George Spangler farm property.
AUTHOR PHOTO

fatal."[34] Historians Motts and Hessler note that although the Spangler property "had served in a broader perspective as a large Union field hospital, it will undoubtedly be Armistead's memory that will attract many of the site's visitors."[35] It is yet one more example of how the story of two friends who fought against each other here remains fascinating to battlefield visitors today, more than a century and a half later.

Winfield and Almira Hancock may have been the first to grasp the long-term impact of that friendship for the public—the history between the two men, their final conflict at Gettysburg, and the dramatic circumstances of Armistead being wounded by Hancock's troops. In a rarely cited passage from *Reminiscences*, Almira wrote, "Armistead died in the way that he prayed for. I, as well as my husband, believed that he courted the death that finally came to him at Gettysburg, for I have often heard it related how bravely he came to the front of his brigade, waving his sword, and how he was shot through the body, and fell within our lines, asking to be taken to Hancock's tent."[36] She gave no further details, but it is clear that she and Hancock had discussed this incident in later years, looking back at California, musing over what might have been for the two old friends before fate and the war intervened.

Appendix

"Lo" and Behold

EVER SINCE *THE KILLER ANGELS* WAS PUBLISHED 1974, AN ENTIRE GENeration of Gettysburg battlefield visitors has come to know Lewis Armistead by a one-word nickname: "Lo."

Armistead was identified as "Lo" early in the novel, with author Michael Shaara explaining to curious readers that it was "short for Lothario"—a notorious seducer of woman. "A bit of a joke, as you can see," George Pickett is said to have said.[1]

Twenty years later, the movie *Gettysburg* came along and reinforced the nickname to the point that five generals in the script—Pickett, James Longstreet, Richard Garnett, James Kemper, and even Winfield Scott Hancock from the Union side—referred to Armistead as "Lo." It caught on and became so wildly popular among Civil War buffs and amateur historians that a quick Google search of "Lo Armistead" now produces four hundred thousand results in half a second.

And yet few have asked a key follow-up question: Is the nickname accurate?

Many of the esteemed historians who have written at length about Armistead, led by his sole biographer, Wayne Motts, do not identify him as "Lo" in print. Others on that list include noted Gettysburg authors Edwin Coddington (*The Gettysburg Campaign*), Stephen Sears (*Gettysburg*), Dr. Allen C. Guelzo (*Gettysburg: The Final Invasion*), and Earl J. Hess (*Pickett's Charge: The Last Attack at Gettysburg*). Sears, on two occasions, even identifies the general as "Lew."[2] Similarly, Robert J. Krick, longtime chief historian at Fredericksburg and Spotsylvania National Military Park, wrote a detailed essay about Armistead for *The Third Day at Gettysburg & Beyond* and did not reference the nickname, and it does not appear in the most widely acclaimed battlefield tour guide, *A Field Guide to Gettysburg*, by Dr. Carol Reardon and Colonel Tom Vossler.

So what gives?

The foundation for the name is flimsy at best. The *only* contemporary reference to "Lo" from a Civil War soldier came in a much-criticized book of letters that Pickett's wife, LaSalle, published in 1913, fifty years after the battle. Mrs. Pickett claimed that her husband wrote the following flowery passage in a letter to her on July 3, 1863, just before the start of Pickett's Charge:

> *At early dawn, darkened by the threatening rain, Armistead, Garnett, Kemper and Your Soldier held a heart-to-heart powwow.*
>
> *All three sent regards to you, and old Lewis pulled a ring from his little finger and making me take it, said, "Give this little token, George, please, to her of the sunset eyes, with my love, and tell her the 'old man' says since he could not be the lucky dog, he's mighty glad that you are."*
>
> *Dear old Lewis—dear old "Lo," as Magruder always called him, being short for Lothario. Well, my Sally, I'll keep the ring for you, and some day I'll take it to John Tyler and have it made into a breastpin and set around with rubies and diamonds and emeralds. You will be the pearl, the other jewel. Dear old Lewis!*[3]

Historians over the past century have roundly denounced Mrs. Pickett's book, doubting the authenticity of its forty-four letters, including the dubious July 3 composition that mentioned Armistead. Among other flaws, it had baffling references to Little Round Top, Cemetery Ridge, and Seminary Ridge—names that were unknown to the invading Confederates at the time. A skeptical Dr. Reardon wrote that "the effusive missives in *The Heart of a Soldier as Revealed in the Letters of General George E. Pickett, C.S.A.*, contain facts that Pickett could not have known when he allegedly wrote the letters. Indeed, modern scholars have proved conclusively that Sallie herself rather than the general authored them."[4]

Fellow professor Gary Gallagher conducted a blistering study of Pickett's letters in an essay titled "A Widow and Her Soldier: LaSalle Corbell Pickett as the Author of George E. Pickett's Civil War Letters." According to Gallagher, "A careful review of the evidence leads to the conclusion the correspondence published in *The Heart of a Soldier . . .* is worthless as a source on the general's Confederate career. LaSalle Pickett concocted the letters, relying on plagiarism and her own romantic imagination."[5]

An original copy of the July 3 letter was never found, Gallagher said. Only typescripts were available for some of the others. Historian George R. Stewart, author of *Pickett's Charge: A Microhistory of the Final Attack at Gettysburg, July 3, 1863*, determined after lengthy research that the letters "dealing with Gettysburg . . . cannot be considered original historical sources."[6] Douglas Southall Freeman, one of Robert E. Lee's most prominent biographers, declared that no one should ever "believe anything that LaSalle Corbell Pickett had written about her husband."[7]

The peculiar timing of the July 3 letter also raises questions about its validity. Pickett tells LaSalle in the final paragraph that "it is almost three o'clock," leading Reardon to marvel that "somehow Pickett found time to write Sallie a six-page letter just before his great charge."[8] Gallagher speculates that an original copy of the letter has not surfaced "probably because Major General Pickett had his hands full preparing his division for the assault."[9]

With regard to the man named "Magruder" who is mentioned in the July 3 letter, there were, in fact, two Confederate officers named John B. Magruder who would have known Armistead during the war. General John Bankhead Magruder was with the army in the Peninsula campaign, and Colonel John Bowie Magruder commanded the Fifty-Seventh Virginia regiment in Armistead's brigade (and was killed in Pickett's Charge). But historians have found no letters from either man addressing Armistead as "Lo." There also are questions as to whether a twenty-three-year-old subordinate officer such as John Bowie Magruder would have had the temerity to apply a sarcastic nickname to a brigadier general twice his age.

Just as odd was a scene from the movie *Gettysburg* that had Hancock reminiscing about "Lo" in a meeting with Union generals. Even if one accepts the Pickett letter as factual, it makes clear that the name was conceived by *Confederates* during the war. Hancock would not have been aware of it in 1863.

Of course, none of this is definitive proof that "Lo" was *not* Armistead's nickname. It is possible that the name was, indeed, accurate; that Pickett mentioned it in conversations with his wife after the war; and that she added it years later to the embellished or fabricated letters.

But there is simply no other evidence to support the claim—and nothing about it from any of the numerous Confederate soldiers who wrote in detail about Armistead's actions on July 3. He was never referenced by any other contemporary as "Lo." Beyond that, the Pickett "letters" have been so discredited over the years that serious questions exist about the accuracy of *any* of their content, especially the July 3 letter.

Readers will have to draw their own conclusions.

Notes

Chapter 1. Friendship Torn

1. Kathy Georg Harrison and John W. Busey, *Nothing but Glory: Pickett's Division at Gettysburg*, 15, 30–32.
2. Armistead likely knew of Hancock's presence because other Confederate troops had battled Hancock's Second Corps over the same ground the previous day. Reports from prisoners and skirmishers, the sighting of various battle flags, and basic army intelligence gathering would have contributed to the assessment of the Second Corps' presence—although we can never be certain what Armistead knew. The quote about the friendship is attributed to Armistead by Henry H. Bingham in a letter he wrote to Hancock on January 5, 1869, published in John Bachelder, *The Bachelder Papers: Gettysburg in Their Own Words*, Vol. 1, 352 (and also cited in greater detail later in this chapter).
3. Returns from U.S. Military Posts, 1806–1916, for Lewis A. Armistead and Winfield S. Hancock, Fort Towson, OK, October 1844, National Archives. Hancock arrived at Fort Towson on October 13, 1844. It was then considered to be in the Indian Territory of the Choctaw Nation.
4. Wayne E. Motts, *"Trust in God and Fear Nothing": Gen. Lewis A. Armistead, CSA*, 21; Glenn Tucker, *Hancock the Superb*, 39–41; Henry Heth, *The Memoirs of Henry Heth*, 56, 66.
5. Returns from U.S. Military Posts, 1806–1916, for Winfield S. Hancock, Los Angeles, CA, January–June 1861 and Lewis A. Armistead, New San Diego, CA, January–June 1861, National Archives.
6. Almira Hancock, *Reminiscences of Winfield Scott Hancock*, 69.
7. 1830 United States Federal Census for Fauquier County, Va, for Walker K. Armistead; Fauquier County (Va.) Will Book 20, 73, 77, for Lewis's purchase of a slave from his late father's estate. His ownership of a second slave is referenced at www .youtube.com, Wayne E. Motts, "Pickett's Charge at Gettysburg," Gettysburg Foundation Sacred Trust Talks, July 3, 2016. Motts also talks in depth about Armistead's struggles with his decision to resign.
8. Virginia Armistead Garber, *The Armistead Family 1635–1910*, 62–69.
9. Lewis A. Armistead to Samuel Cooper, December 2, 1861, Letters Received by the Adjutant and Inspector General's Office, National Archives. Found in the Compiled Service Records of W. Keith Armistead. Regarding "treason," it is defined this way in Article III, Section 3, of the U.S. Constitution: "Treason against the United States

shall consist only in levying War against them, or in adhering to their Enemies, giving them Aid and Comfort."

10. "The Declaration of Causes of the Seceding States," www.battlefields.org.
11. David M. Jordan, *Winfield Scott Hancock: A Soldier's Life*, 31. According to Jordan, Hancock "believed the federal government had no right to interfere in a domestic institution such as slavery."
12. Hancock, *Reminiscences of Winfield Scott Hancock*, 66.
13. Francis Amasa Walker, *General Hancock*, 9–10. Walker served on Hancock's staff and also wrote a history of the Second Corps.
14. A. M. Gambone, *Hancock at Gettysburg and Beyond*, xiii; Jordan, *Winfield Scott Hancock*, 44–45, 75–76.
15. Motts, *"Trust in God and Fear Nothing,"* 13, 30–31, 38–39.
16. "Gettysburg Script—Dialogue Transcript," www.script-o-rama.com.
17. James A. Hessler and Wayne E. Motts, *Pickett's Charge at Gettysburg: A Guide to the Most Famous Attack in American History*, 121–22.
18. D. Scott Hartwig, *A Killer Angels Companion*, 1.
19. John Deppen, "Old and Valued Friends: Generals Lewis Armistead and Winfield Scott Hancock," *Gettysburg Magazine*, Issue 34 (2006), 40–44. Although there are numerous examples of historians questioning the friendship and, in particular, the 1861 meeting, Deppen deftly gathers them all in one story and essentially debunks them. Deppen ends his piece by describing Hancock as Armistead's "old and valued friend."
20. Reports from U.S. Military Posts, 1806–1916, for Lewis A. Armistead and Winfield S. Hancock, Fort Towson, OK, October 1844 and Fort Washita, OK, November 1845, National Archives; www.youtube.com, Motts, "Pickett's Charge at Gettysburg" (including a visual of the letter from Lewis A. Armistead of Abraham Robinson Johnson, December 16, 1845).
21. Reports of Colonel Newman Clarke, Major Benjamin Bonneville, and Captain William Hoffman, Library of Congress, House Exec. Doc No. 8, "Appendix to the Report of the Secretary of War, Additional Reports from the Army in Mexico," 55, 64, 148. All three commanders mention both Armistead and Hancock; Jordan, *Winfield Scott Hancock*, 16–17; Tucker, *Hancock the Superb*, 41.
22. Henry Heth, *The Memoirs of Henry Heth*, 56, 66.
23. Ibid., 56, 66.
24. Ralph W. Kirkham, *The Mexican War Journal & Letters of Ralph W. Kirkham*, 100.
25. Returns from U.S. Military Posts, 1806–1916, for Lewis A. Armistead and Winfield Scott Hancock, Jefferson Barracks, MO, various dates, National Archives; www.find-a-grave.com for Flora Love Armistead and Lewis B. Armistead; Motts, *"Trust in God and Fear Nothing,"* 31, 33–34.
26. *Los Angeles Star*, July 30, 1859, and August 13, 1859, found in the California Digital Newspaper Collection, https://cdnc.ucr.edu/site/index.html.
27. Hancock was posted at Los Angeles and lived in the city. Johnston moved to Los Angeles from San Francisco after resigning from the U.S. Army in April 1861 and

lived at the home of his brother-in-law, Dr. John S. Griffin, from May 2 to June 16, until departing for the East (William Preston Johnston, *The Life of Gen. Albert Sidney Johnston: Embracing His Services in the Armies of the United States, the Republic of Texas, and the Confederate States*, 274–75). Armistead passed through the city at least twice in May 1861 during trips to and from San Francisco (*Los Angeles Star*, May 11, 1861, "Major Armistead"; www.youtube.com, Motts, "Pickett's Charge at Gettysburg"). A curious addendum to Armistead's military records said he was "transferred to Los Angeles" on May 14 until he was "relieved" on June 19 (Returns from U.S. Military Posts, 1806–1916, for Lewis A. Armistead, New San Diego, CA, June 1861, under "Alterations since last monthly return"). Many published works say that Mrs. Hancock also named Richard Garnett and George Pickett as attending the get-together, but a careful reading of her account shows that she identified only Armistead, Johnston, and her husband as attendees. She mentioned that Garnett and Pickett sought advice from Hancock at their home in the prewar period but never said they attended the event in question.

28. Hancock, *Reminiscences of Winfield Scott Hancock*, 70.
29. D. X. Junkin and Frank Norton, *The Life of Winfield Scott Hancock: Personal, Military and Political*, 118. The Reverend Junkin's book was published in 1880, Mrs. Hancock's in 1887. The significance of this timing is also mentioned in Deppen, "Old and Valued Friends," 44. Motts made the point quite clearly in his "Pickett's Charge at Gettysburg" presentation.
30. Junkin and Norton, *The Life of Winfield Scott Hancock*, 118; Hancock, *Reminiscences of Winfield Scott Hancock*, 70.
31. Letter of Capt. & Judge Advocate Henry H. Bingham to Maj. Gen. Winfield Scott Hancock, January 5, 1869, in Bachelder, *The Bachelder Papers*, Vol. 1, 352.
32. Report of Winfield S. Hancock, *War of the Rebellion: Official Records of the Union and Confederate Armies*, Series 1, Vol. 27, 374.
33. Francis A. Walker, "The Military Character and Services of Major-General Winfield Scott Hancock," from the Papers of the Military Historical Society of Massachusetts, Vol. 10, 55.
34. Heth, *The Memoirs of Henry Heth*, 56.
35. Paul E. Bretzger, *Observing Hancock at Gettysburg: The General's Leadership through Eyewitness Accounts*, 3.
36. John Gibbon, *At Gettysburg and Elsewhere: The Civil War Memoir of John Gibbon*, 114–15.
37. Gambone, *Hancock at Gettysburg and Beyond*, 48; Jordan, *Winfield Scott Hancock*, 45, 99; www.arlingtoncemetery.net/john-hancock.htm.
38. Henry W. Bingham, "Memoirs of Hancock," cited in Bretzger, *Observing Hancock at Gettysburg*, 155.
39. Gibbon, *At Gettysburg and Elsewhere*, 117.
40. Frank Aretas Haskell, *The Battle of Gettysburg*, 63.
41. Compiled Service Records for Franck S. Armistead, Walker K. Armistead (Jr.), Bowles E. Armistead, and W. Keith Armistead, National Archives. Walker Jr. was

also a member of the Sixth Virginia Cavalry and served throughout the war, but his muster roll record for the summer of 1863 said he was "absent, sick" with a "surgeon's certificate," dating from June 1, and suffered from "paraplegia."

42. Walter Harrison, *Pickett's Men: A Fragment of War History*, 80, 86; Harrison and Busey, *Nothing but Glory*, 2–3.

43. B. L. Farinholt, "Battle of Gettysburg—Johnson's Island," *Confederate Veteran*, Vol. V, 467–68; G. Howard Gregory, *53rd Virginia Infantry and 5th Battalion Virginia Infantry*, 49–51; Harrison, *Pickett's Men*, 87.

44. James F. Crocker, *Gettysburg—Pickett's Charge and Other War Addresses*, 41.

45. Harrison and Busey, *Nothing but Glory*, 32.

46. John H. Lewis, *A Rebel in Pickett's Charge at Gettysburg*, 50. Armistead and Tyler were from the same family tree. See Garber, *The Armistead Family 1635–1910*, 29.

47. Robert Tyler Jones, "Gen. L.A. Armistead and R. Tyler Jones," *Confederate Veteran*, Vol. II, 271.

48. Ibid.; Gregory, *53rd Virginia Infantry and 5th Virginia Battalion*, 53–54. Numerous Confederate soldiers made references to Armistead's inspiring comments in their postwar writings, although they had different recollections of his precise words.

49. "Letter of Dr. Rawley Martin," from *War Recollections of The Confederate Veterans of Pittsylvania County, Virginia, 1861–1865*, 40.

Chapter 2. Armistead at the "Point"

1. Virginia Armistead Garber, *The Armistead Family 1635–1910*, 66, 240–41; "Captain William Armistead, Biography and Genealogy," www.alabamapioneers.com. William Armistead first served as a drummer boy in the Revolutionary War and was at Valley Forge. His brother, Westwood, was killed at Brandywine. They are part of the extensive family tree that began when the "original" William Armistead arrived in the New World from England in 1635.

2. Robert Hall, ed., *Register of Cadets Admitted into the United Sates Military Academy, West Point, NY, from Its Establishment till 1880*, 194; West Point Association of Graduates, *Register of Graduates and Former Cadets of the United States Military Academy (2008 edition)*, www.westpointaog.org, 2–5; Arthur P. Wade, *Artillerists and Engineers*, 83.

3. Francis B. Heitman, *Historical Register and Dictionary of the U.S. Army, from Its Organization, September 29, 1789 to March 2, 1903*, Vol. 1, 169; George Washington Cullum, *Biographical Register of the Officers and Graduates of the U.S. Military Academy at West Point, N.Y., 1802–1840, Vol. 1*, 91.

4. Gertrude S. Carraway, *The Stanly Family*, p. 28; Garber, *The Armistead Family 1635–1910*, 66; Wayne E. Motts, *"Trust in God and Fear Nothing": Gen. Lewis A. Armistead, CSA*, 10. John Stanly was furious that his daughter had chosen a career military man as her husband.

5. "New Bernian Led Famed Pickett's Charge at Gettysburg; Gen. Lewis Armistead Died There," *New Bern (N.C.) Sun Journal*, March 13, 1962.

6. Returns from U.S. Military Posts, 1806–1916, for Walker K. Armistead (various dates), National Archives, also available at ancestry.com; Fauquier County, Va., Deed

Book 23, 350. On September 1, 1818, Walker purchased "a certain track or parcel of land in Fauquier" amounting to "323 acres and 27 ½ perches."

7. Motts, *"Trust in God and Fear Nothing,"* 52. It should be noted that the family traveled on occasion to be with Walker at his post, and some of the children were not born at Ben Lomond. Walker Jr., for instance, was born in Maryland, and Franck was born at Fort Monroe, Virginia.

8. 1830 United States Federal Census for Fauquier County, Va., for Walker K. Armistead.

9. Cullum, *Biographical Register of the Officers and Graduates of the U.S. Military Academy at West Point, N.Y., 1802–1840, Vol. 1,* 91.

10. Ibid. The promotion came on November 12, 1828, which was ten years to the day after he was promoted to colonel (and chief engineer).

11. Robert Emmett Curran, *The Bicentennial History of Georgetown University: From Academy to University, 1789–1889,* Vol. 1, 166. Lewis's younger brother, Walker Jr., would also attend Georgetown for one year in the 1840s.

12. "Baptismal Record for Lewis Armistead, March 31, 1831, Entry 2 in Ledger of Baptisms and Confirmations at Georgetown College, 1830–1920," Georgetown University Library, "Shades of Blue and Gray: Georgetown and the Civil War," www.library.georgetown.edu, 18. Armistead, who had just turned fourteen years old, was baptized on campus by Fr. George Fenwick, S.J., a member of the college faculty.

13. Walker K. Armistead to Lewis Cass, January 24, 1833, U.S. Military Academy Application Papers, 1805–1866, National Archives.

14. Robert K. Krick, "Armistead and Garnett: The Parallel Lives of Two Virginia Soldiers," in *The Third Day at Gettysburg & Beyond,* 101.

15. Lewis A. Armistead to Lewis Cass, March 21, 1833, U.S. Military Academy Application Papers, 1805–1866, National Archives.

16. James L. Morrison, *"The Best School," West Point, 1833–1866,* 3–4; Clyde W. Cocke, *Pass in Review: An Illustrated History of West Point Cadets, 1794–Present,* 27–28; Cullum, *Biographical Register of the Officers and Graduates of the U.S. Military Academy at West Point, N.Y., 1802–1840, Vol. 1,* 39, 129.

17. Motts, *"Trust in God and Fear Nothing,"* 11.

18. Morrison, *"The Best School," West Point, 1833–1866,* 101.

19. Ibid., 91–92, 160; Cocke, *Pass in Review,* 29–30.

20. Register of Merit No. 1, 1817–1835, U.S. Military Academy Library, West Point, NY.

21. List of Orders Relating to Cadet Lewis A. Armistead, Extracted from "Post Orders/ No. 6, 1832–1837, U.S. Military Academy," USMA Library, West Point, NY.

22. Walker K. Armistead to Lewis Cass, October 29, 1833, U.S. Military Academy Application Papers, National Archives (also available at USMA Library).

23. Lewis A. Armistead to Lewis Cass, October 30, 1833, U.S. Military Academy Application Papers, National Archives.

24. Rene De Russy to Charles Gratiot, October 29, 1833, Engineering Department Letters Received Relating to USMA, 1819–1866, M2047, Roll 7, National Archives.

25. List of Orders Relating to Cadet Lewis A. Armistead, Extracted from "Post Orders/No. 6, 1832–1837, U.S. Military Academy," USMA Library; Register of Cadet Applicants, 1819–1867, "At Large" applicants for the year 1834, USMA Library, with note regarding General W. K. Armistead.
26. List of Orders Relating to Cadet Lewis A. Armistead, Extracted from "Post Orders/No. 6, 1832–1837, U.S. Military Academy," USMA Library.
27. Cocke, *Pass in Review*, 37–39; Morris, *"The Best School," West Point, 1833–1866*, 73–74.
28. Register of Merit No. 1, 1817–1835, U.S. Military Academy Library, West Point, NY.
29. Ibid.
30. Krick, "Armistead and Garnett," 100.
31. Register of Merit No. 1, 1817–1835, U.S. Military Academy Library, West Point.
32. Ibid.; Motts, *"Trust in God and Fear Nothing,"* 12; Krick, "Armistead and Garnett," 99; Register of Merit No. 1, 1817–1835, U.S. Military Academy Library, West Point, NY.
33. Krick, "Armistead and Garnett," 99.
34. Register of Merit No. 1, 1817–1835, U.S. Military Academy Library, West Point, NY.
35. List of Orders Relating to Cadet Lewis A. Armistead, Extracted from "Post Orders/No. 6, 1832–1837, U.S. Military Academy," USMA Library.
36. Motts, *"Trust in God and Fear Nothing,"* 12–13; Krick, "Armistead and Garnett," 99–100.
37. Harrison, *Pickett's Men: A Fragment of War History*, 33. With quite a turn of phrase, Harrison wrote that Armistead was "retired from that Institution before graduation."
38. Edward Stanly to Charles M. Conrad, March 11, 1852, U.S. Military Academy Application Papers, National Archives. Congressman Stanly wrote to the secretary of war to endorse Lewis's younger brother, Franck, as a candidate for West Point. Had Lewis graduated, Franck would not have been eligible to attend the academy. Stanly wrote to clarify that Lewis had not graduated and, in fact, left the school "when very young, on account of some boyish frolick." Franck was accepted as a cadet and went on to graduate.
39. Cullum, *Biographical Register of the Officers and Graduates of the U.S. Military Academy at West Point, N.Y., 1802–1840, Vol. 1*, 529. Early graduated eighteenth out of fifty in his class.
40. List of Orders Relating to Cadet Lewis A. Armistead, Extracted from "Post Orders/No. 6, 1832–1837, U.S. Military Academy," USMA Library.
41. Motts, *"Trust in God and Fear Nothing,"* 13.
42. List of Orders Relating to Cadet Lewis A. Armistead, Extracted from "Post Orders/No. 6, 1832–1837, U.S. Military Academy," USMA Library. The resignation was to "take effect in the 15th . . . at which time he will be considered as discharged from the service of the U.S."
43. Motts, *"Trust in God and Fear Nothing,"* 52, and various Armistead genealogies.
44. Carraway, *The Stanly Family and the Historic John Wright Stanly House*, 33.
45. Charles L. Coon, *North Carolina Schools and Academies 1790–1840: A Documentary History*, 254, 261–62.

46. "Battalion History," https://rotc.georgetown.edu/about/history. Various sources, including the Georgetown Library, have Armistead attending the Georgetown preparatory school as a thirteen-year-old in 1830–1831. "Shades of Blue and Gray: Georgetown and the Civil War," an online entry of the Georgetown Library, has Armistead attending for only that school year (when he was also baptized). Curran, *The Bicentennial History of Georgetown University*, 166, also lists 1830–1831 as his only academic year there. This information was confirmed further by an e-mail exchange with the Georgetown library.
47. Cullum, *Biographical Register of the Officers and Graduates of the U.S. Military Academy at West Point, N.Y., 1802–1840, Vol. 1*, 91.
48. Motts, *"Trust in God and Fear Nothing,"* 14. Some biographical information is also available in Carraway, *The Stanly Family and the Historic John Wright Stanly House*, 29, and "Edward Stanley," bioguide.congress.gov.
49. Krick, "Armistead and Garnett," 101.
50. USMA Special Collections, Lewis Armistead Commissions.

Chapter 3. Florida and the Frontier

1. Lewis Armistead Commission, Armistead file, Letters Received by the Office of the Adjutant General, 1822–1860, National Archives.
2. Returns from U.S. Military Posts, 1806–1916, for Lewis A. Armistead, Fort Andrews, FL, August 1839.
3. Joe Knetsch, *Florida's Seminole Wars 1817–1858*, 7–8.
4. "The Seminole Wars," Florida Department of State, https://dos.myflorida.com; John K. Mahon, *History of the Second Seminole War 1835–1842*, 138, 140–42, 161; Knetsch, *Florida's Seminole Wars 1817–1858*, 139.
5. Knetsch, *Florida's Seminole Wars 1817–1858*, 23, 41.
6. Thom Hatch, *Osceola and the Great Seminole War: A Struggle for Justice and Freedom*, 74–77.
7. "Treaty with the Seminole 1832 (Payne's Landing)," in ibid., 269–71.
8. Knetsch, *Florida's Seminole Wars 1817–1858*, 69–72.
9. Ibid., 88–89; Mahon, *History of the Second Seminole War 1835–1842*, 157.
10. Knetsch, *Florida's Seminole Wars 1817–1858*, 91.
11. Hatch, *Osceola and the Great Seminole War*, 148; Mahon, *History of the Second Seminole War 1835–1842*, 133; Samuel Watson, "This Thankless . . . Unholy War: Army Officers and Civil-Military Relations in the Second Seminole War," in *The Southern Albatross: Race and Ethnicity in the American South*, ed. Philip L. Dillard and Randal L. Hall, 15.
12. Knetsch, *Florida's Seminole Wars 1817–1858*, 99–100, 102, 104, 106, 111; John C. White, "American Military Strategy during the Second Seminole War," www.global security.org. At the same time he commanded troops in Florida, Jesup was still the army's quartermaster general.
13. Returns from U.S. Military Posts, 1806–1916, for Lewis A. Armistead, Fort Andrews, FL, August 1839.

14. Charles Byrne, "The Sixth Regiment of Infantry," Center of Military History, www .history.army.mil, 485.
15. Knetsch, *Florida's Seminole Wars 1817–1858*, 120.
16. Returns from U.S. Military Posts, 1806–1916, for Lewis A. Armistead, Fort Andrews, FL, September 1839; Walker K. Armistead to Roger Jones, May 5, 1840, Letters Received by the Office of the Adjutant General Main Series 1822–1860, National Archives; Mahon, *History of the Second Seminole War 1835–1842*, 274.
17. Watson, "This Thankless . . . Unholy War," 32.
18. Hatch, *Osceola and the Great Seminole War*, 247. The speaker was Major Ethan Allen Hitchcock. The word means juvenile or childishly silly.
19. Corrina Brown Aldrich to Mannevillette Brown, May 23, 1840, in *Echoes from a Distant Thunder: The Brown Sisters' Correspondence from Antebellum Florida*, ed. James M. Denham and Keith L. Honeycutt, 115.
20. Walker K. Armistead letter, April 19, 1840; Walker K. Armistead to J. R. Poinsett, May 29, 1840; Lewis A. Armistead to Roger Jones, July 8, 1840, Letters Received by the Office of the Adjutant General Main Series 1822–1860, National Archives.
21. Returns from U.S. Military Posts, 1806–1916, for Lewis A. Armistead, Fort Andrews, FL, May 1840; Wayne E. Motts, *"Trust in God and Fear Nothing": Gen. Lewis A. Armistead, CSA*, 15.
22. Returns from U.S. Military Posts, 1806–1916, for Lewis A. Armistead, Fort Columbus, NY, August and September 1840; Robert K. Krick, "Armistead and Garnett: The Parallel Lives of Two Virginia Soldiers," in *Third Day at Gettysburg & Beyond*, 101. Fort Columbus was also known as Fort Jay.
23. Returns from U.S. Military Posts, 1806–1916, for Lewis A. Armistead, Fort Columbus, NY, September and October 1840; Fort Brooke, Tampa, FL, October 1840.
24. Hatch, *Osceola and the Great Seminole War*, 247, 252; Mahon, *History of the Second Seminole War 1835–1842*, 276, 278, 285, 287.
25. Hatch, *Osceola and the Great Seminole War*, 247.
26. Walker K. Armistead to J. R. Poinsett, October 22, 1840, Letters Received by the Office of the Adjutant General Main Series 1822–1860, National Archives.
27. Mahon, *History of the Second Seminole War 1835–1842*, 282.
28. Knetsch, *Florida's Seminole Wars 1817–1858*, 126.
29. Walker K. Armistead to J. R. Poinsett, October 22, 1840, Letters Received by the Office of the Adjutant General Main Series 1822–1860, National Archives.
30. Walker K. Armistead to Roger Jones, December 20, 1840, Letters Received by the Office of the Adjutant General Main Series 1822–1860, National Archives.
31. Mahon, *History of the Second Seminole War 1835–1842*, 285, 287; Knetsch, *Florida's Seminole Wars 1817–1858*, 128.
32. Although there are various estimates of Walker's birth year, the most likely is 1783.
33. Mahon, *History of the Second Seminole War 1835–1842*, 287. Mahon notes that "his record was good."
34. Returns from U.S. Military Posts, 1806–1916, for Lewis A. Armistead, Fort Brooke, Tampa, FL, November and December 1841.

35. Mahon, *History of the Second Seminole War 1835–1842*, 307–8, 318; "The Seminole Wars," https://dos.myflorida.com; Knetsch, *Florida's Seminole Wars 1817–1858*, 150.
36. Byrne, "The Sixth Regiment of Infantry," 4. The Sixth was assigned briefly to Jefferson Barracks in Missouri before heading on to Fort Towson.
37. Robert W. Frazer, *Forts of the West: Military Forts and Presidios and Posts Commonly Called Forts West of the Mississippi River to 1898*, 125.
38. Returns from U.S. Military Posts, 1806–1916, for Lewis A. Armistead, Fort Towson, OK, May–August 1842, National Archives.
39. Frazer, *Forts of the West*, 125; Motts, *"Trust in God and Fear Nothing,"* 17; W. B. Morrison, "Fort Towson," *Chronicles of Oklahoma* 8, no. 2 (June 1930); "The Republic of Texas," www.tsl.texas.gov.
40. Morrison, "Fort Towson"; Motts, *"Trust in God and Fear Nothing,"* 17.
41. Returns from U.S. Military Posts, 1806–1916, for Lewis A. Armistead, Fort Towson, OK, November 1843.
42. Cazenova Gardner Lee Jr., *Lee Chronicle: Studies of the Early Generations of the Lees of Virginia*, 283, 296, 302, 306; www.findagravecom for Cecilia Lee Love Armistead.
43. Motts, *"Trust in God and Fear Nothing,"* 17.
44. Alabama Marriage Indexes, 1814–1935, for Cecilia Lee Love, www.ancestry.com.
45. Walker K. Armistead to Roger Jones, January 12, 1844, Letters Received by the Office of the Adjutant General Main Series 1822–1860, National Archives.
46. Alabama Marriage Indexes, 1814–1935, for Cecilia Lee Love, www.ancestry.com; Lee, *Lee Chronicle*, 296, 299, 302.
47. Motts, *"Trust in God and Fear Nothing,"* 17. Cecilia gave birth to their first son in December, ten months following their wedding day.
48. Lewis Armistead Commissions, USMA Special Collections, West Point, NY. His commission of March 30, 1844, was signed by President John Tyler, a distant relative.
49. Returns from U.S. Military Posts, 1806–1916, for Lewis A. Armistead, Fort Towson, OK, September 1844, National Archives; Returns from Regular Army Regiments, 1821–1916, 6th Infantry, October 1844, National Archives.
50. Returns from Regular Army Regiments, 1821–1916, 6th Infantry, October 1844, National Archives; Motts, *"Trust in God and Fear Nothing,"* 17, 19.
51. The birth date is sometimes recorded as December 11, but Lewis identified it as December 12 in an 1861 letter (Lewis A. Armistead to Samuel Cooper, December 2, 1861, Letters Received by the Adjutant and Inspector General's Office, National Archives). Keith's tombstone also lists the date as December 12 (www.findagrave.com for Walker Keith Armistead); Michael P. Musick, *6th Virginia Cavalry*, 94.
52. Motts, *"Trust in God and Fear Nothing,"* 19. Military documents and letters consistently referred to him as "W. Keith."
53. Returns from U.S. Military Posts, 1806–1916, for Lewis A. Armistead, Fort Towson, OK, May and July 1814.
54. George W. Cullum, *Biographical Register of the Officers and Graduates of the U.S. Military Academy at West Point, N.Y., Vol. 1, 1802–1840*, 91.

55. Walker K. Armistead to Roger Jones, April 1, 1845, Letters Received by the Office of the Adjutant General Main Series 1822–1860, National Archives.
56. George W. Cullum, *Campaigns of the War of 1812–15 against Great Britain . . . with Brief Biographies of the American Engineers*, 302. Stanly adds to the confusion over Walker's age and birth year while writing that "Genl. Armistead was in his 65th year" (this came shortly after he admitted that he did not have enough information to write a proper obituary for this brother-in-law). The "65th year" would have implied a 1781 birth year—to go with previous estimates of 1773, 1785, and the more likely 1783. The author is comfortable with 1783, but we will never know for certain.
57. Edward Stanly to Roger Jones, April 13, 1845, Letters Received by the Office of the Adjutant General Main Series 1822–1860, National Archives.
58. Cullum, *Campaigns of the War of 1812–15 against Great Britain . . . with Brief Biographies of the American Engineers*, 302. It is somehow appropriate that Cullum's chapter about Walker was devoted largely to the career of his brother George.
59. Returns from U.S. Military Posts, 1806–1916, for Lewis A. Armistead, Fort Washita, Choctaw Nation, OK, November 1845 and February 1846; Frazer, *Forts of the West*, 126.
60. Returns from U.S. Military Posts, 1806–1916, for Lewis A. Armistead, Fort Washita, Choctaw Nation, OK, May–August 1846, "extended leave"; Robert W. Johannsen, *To the Halls of the Montezumas: The Mexican War in the American Imagination*, 10.
61. Motts, *"Trust in God and Fear Nothing,"* 31; www.findagrave, for Flora Love Armistead; Lee, *Lee Chronicle*, 280, 293, 296 (for references to Cecilia's sister, Flora).
62. Returns from U.S. Military Posts, 1806–1916, for Lewis A. Armistead, Fort Washita, Choctaw Nation, OK, "On Special Duty with the Army in Mexico . . . Sept. 22, 1846"); Zachary Taylor, *Letters of Zachary Taylor from the Battlefields of the Mexican War*, 64.

Chapter 4. Hancock Comes of Age

1. David M. Jordan, *Winfield Scott Hancock: A Soldier's Life*, 5; Francis H. Casstevens, *Tales from the North and South: Twenty-Four Remarkable People and Events of the Civil War*, 109. The name Hilary Baker does not resonate with present-day Americans, but it was well known in the Philadelphia area at the time the Hancock twins were born.
2. www.arlingtoncemetery.net/john-hancock.htm; www.findagrave.com for John Hancock.
3. Jordan, *Winfield Scott Hancock*, 5.
4. Glenn Tucker, *Hancock the Superb*, 23.
5. Charles Wheeler Denison and George B. Herbert, *Hancock "The Superb": The Early Life and Public Career of Winfield Scott Hancock*, 25.
6. Ibid.; Tucker, *Hancock the Superb*, 20–21, 23.
7. Jordan, *Winfield Scott Hancock*, 7.
8. D. X. Junkin and Frank Norton, *The Life of Winfield Scott Hancock: Personal, Military and Political*, 11.
9. Denison and Herbert, *Hancock "The Superb,"* 40, 47–48; Tucker, *Hancock the Superb*, 18–20, 25.

10. John Fornance to J. R. Poinsett, February 8, 1840, U.S. Military Academy Application Papers, 1805–1866, National Archives (also found at www.fold3.com).

11. Benjamin F. Hancock to J. R. Poinsett, February 14, 1840, U.S. Military Academy Application Papers, 1805–1866, National Archives.

12. Tucker, *Hancock the Superb*, 22, 26.

13. John Fornance to J. R. Poinsett, March 21, 1840, U.S. Military Academy Application Papers, 1805–1866, National Archives.

14. Winfield S. Hancock to J. R. Poinsett, March 31, 1840, U.S. Military Academy Application Papers, 1805–1866, National Archives.

15. Ibid.

16. Tucker, *Hancock the Superb*, 30.

17. Francis Amasa Walker, *General Hancock*, 13.

18. Jordan, *Winfield Scott Hancock*, 9.

19. George W. Cullum, *Biographical Register of the Officers and Graduates of the U.S. Military Academy at West Point, N.Y., Vol. 1, 1802–1840*, 99, 103, 105, 109.

20. Junkin and Norton, *The Life of Winfield Scott Hancock*, 16.

21. Statement of Don Carlos Buell in Military Service Institution, *Letters and Addresses Contributed at a General Meeting of the Military Service Institution Held at Governor's Island, N.Y., February 25, 1886, in Memory of Winfield Scott Hancock* (hereinafter *Letters and Addresses*), 17.

22. Statement of William B. Franklin in ibid., 13.

23. Tucker, *Hancock the Superb*, 34. Tucker says Hancock grew nine inches in height during his time at West Point, but that follows the legend that Hancock eventually stood six foot two. The only specific piece of evidence from his post–West Point days is a letter written by Hancock himself in 1852 in which he states he is "six feet and one-half inch in height" (Winfield S. Hancock to John Earle & Co., February 27, 1852, cited in Jordan, *Winfield Scott Hancock*, 23).

24. Statement of William B. Franklin in *Letters and Addresses*, 13.

25. Cullum, *Biographical Register of the Officers and Graduates of the U.S. Military Academy at West Point, N.Y., Vol. 1, 1802–1840*, 22–192. The graduates are listed by both year and class rank.

26. Tucker, *Hancock the Superb*, 30.

27. Statement of Orlando Willcox in *Letters and Addresses*, 21–22.

28. Cullum, *Biographical Register of the Officers and Graduates of the U.S. Military Academy at West Point, N.Y., Vol. 1, 1802–1840*, 109–10; George T. Fleming, *Life and Letters of Alexander Hays, Brevet Colonel United States Army, Brigadier General and Brevet Major General United States Volunteers*, 5.

29. Fleming, *Life and Letters of Alexander Hays*, 14–15; Jordan, *Winfield Scott Hancock*, 9, 11; Tucker, *Hancock the Superb*, 32–33.

30. Winfield S. Hancock to Annie A. Hays, January 26, 1865, published in Fleming, *Life and Letters of Alexander Hays*, 656–57.

31. Jordan, *Winfield Scott Hancock*, 10; Tucker, *Hancock the Superb*, 36.

32. Walker, *General Hancock*, 13. Walker published a chart of Hancock's class and subject rankings.

33. Junkin and Norton, *The Life of Winfield Scott Hancock*, 16.
34. Jordan, *Winfield Scott Hancock*, 10.
35. Ibid., 11.
36. Junkin and Norton, *The Life of Winfield Scott Hancock*, 18.
37. Ibid., 18.
38. Returns from U.S. Military Posts, 1806–1916, for Lewis A. Armistead and Winfield S. Hancock, Fort Washita, OK, November 1845, National Archives.
39. Returns from U.S. Military Posts, 1806–1916, for Lewis A. Armistead, Fort Washita, OK, February 1846, National Archives.
40. Returns from U.S. Military Posts, 1806–1916, for Winfield S. Hancock, Fort Washita, OK, June 1846, National Archives; Cullum, *Biographical Register of the Officers and Graduates of the U.S. Military Academy at West Point, N.Y., Vol. 1, 1802–1840*, 108.
41. Returns from U.S. Military Posts, 1806–1916, for Winfield S. Hancock, Fort Washita, OK, January 1847, National Archives.
42. Returns for U.S. Military Posts, 1806–1916, for Winfield S. Hancock, Newport Barracks, KY, March and April 1847, National Archives.
43. Winfield S. Hancock to Roger Jones, June 30, 1846, Letters Received by the Office of the Adjutant General Main Series 1822–1860, National Archives.
44. Winfield S. Hancock to Roger Jones, August 17, 1846, Letters Received by the Office of the Adjutant General Main Series 1822–1860, National Archives.
45. Winfield S. Hancock to J. Erving, recruiting service, May 8, 1847, Letters Received by the Office of the Adjutant General Main Series 1822–1860, National Archives.
46. Winfield S. Hancock to Hilary B. Hancock, May 5, 1847, published in Junkin and Norton, *The Life of Winfield Scott Hancock*, 19.
47. Winfield S. Hancock to Roger Jones, May 25, 1847, Letters Received by the Office of the Adjutant General Main Series 1822–1860, National Archives.

Chapter 5. Glory in Mexico

1. John S. D. Eisenhower, *So Far from God: The U.S. War with Mexico, 1846–1848*, xix; Ron Chernow, *Grant*, 40.
2. K. Jack Bauer, *The Mexican War 1846–1848*, 11–12.
3. "Mexican-American War," www.brittanica.com; Eisenhower, *So Far from God*, 46. There were several financial options proposed to purchase land from Mexico.
4. Bauer, *The Mexican War 1846–1848*, 16, 24–26, 33; Eisenhower, *So Far from God*, 49. The diplomat was John Slidell.
5. Bauer, *The Mexican War 1846–1848*, 37; Chernow, *Grant*, 40.
6. U. S. Grant, *The Personal Memoirs of U. S. Grant*, 36.
7. Eisenhower, *So Far from God*, 65; Bauer, *The Mexican War 1846–1848*, 48. Reports of the precise number of casualties varied. The dragoons were under Captain Seth B. Thornton.
8. Robert W. Merry, *A Country of Vast Designs: James K. Polk, the Mexican War and the Conquest of the American Continent*, 242–44.

9. James K. Polk, War Message to Congress, May 11, 1846, "Presidential Transcripts," www.millercenter.org.
10. Ibid.
11. Eisenhower, *So Far from God*, 68; Merry, *A Country of Vast Designs*, 246, 251.
12. Robert W. Johannsen, *To the Halls of the Montezumas: The Mexican War in the American Imagination*, 8.
13. Merry, *A Country of Vast Designs*, 255.
14. Returns from U.S. Military Posts, 1806–1916, for Lewis A. Armistead, Fort Washita, Choctaw Nation, September 1846 and November 1846. Armistead was listed as "absent on recruiting service" and "at Upperville, recruiting" before a notation that he was "on special duty with the army in Mexico, 22 Sept. 1846"; Wayne E. Motts, *"Trust in God and Fear Nothing": Gen. Lewis A. Armistead, CSA*, 20.
15. Fauquier County, Va. Will Book 20, 73, 77, for Lewis's purchase of a slave from his late father's estate. Maria was no longer with the family in the 1850 census. This is also referenced at www.youtube.com, Wayne E. Motts, "Pickett's Charge at Gettysburg," Gettysburg Foundation Sacred Trust Talks, July 3, 2016.
16. Zachary Taylor to Dr. R. C. Wood, October 12, 1846, in Zachary Taylor, *Letters of Zachary Taylor from the Battlefields of the Mexican War*, 64.
17. Ibid., 64–65.
18. Motts, *"Trust in God and Fear Nothing,"* 20, 23.
19. Eisenhower, *So Far from God*, 254, 382.
20. Ibid., 258.
21. Paul C. Clark Jr. and Edward H. Moseley, "D-Day: Veracruz, 1847—A Grand Design," www.dtic.mil, 106.
22. Bauer, *The Mexican War 1846–1848*, 233–35; Eisenhower, *So Far from God*, 172, 257; Donald E. Graves, *First Campaign of an A.D.C.: The War of 1812 Memoir of Lieutenant William Jenkins Worth*, 59.
23. Chernow, *Grant*, 51.
24. Bauer, *The Mexican War 1846–1848*, 244.
25. Grant, *The Personal Memoirs of U. S. Grant*, 62.
26. Bauer, *The Mexican War 1846–1848*, 244.
27. Bauer, *The Mexican War 1846–1848*, 246–47.
28. Ibid., 241, 247–48; Chernow, *Grant*, 51.
29. Cadmus Marcellus Wilcox, *History of the Mexican War*, 250–51, 253.
30. Eisenhower, *So Far from God*, 263; Clark and Moseley, "D-Day: Veracruz, 1847—A Grand Design," www.dtic.mil, 113.
31. Bauer, *The Mexican War 1846–1848*, 251–53.
32. Ibid., 252.
33. Eisenhower, *So Far from God*, 267.
34. Ibid., 269; Chernow, *Grant*, 53.
35. Winfield Scott to William Marcy, April 19, 1847, www.dmwv.org.
36. Ibid., 335–37; Eisenhower, *So Far from God*, 302–4.
37. David M. Jordan, *Winfield Scott Hancock: A Soldier's Life*, 14.

38. Winfield S. Hancock to Hilary B. Hancock, December 6, 1847, in Charles Wheeler Denison and George B. Herbert, *Hancock "The Superb": The Early Life and Public Career of Winfield S. Hancock*, 150.

39. Jordan, *Winfield Scott Hancock*, 15.

40. Wilcox, *History of the Mexican War*, 340.

41. Eisenhower, *So Far from God*, 311; Grant, *The Memoirs of U. S. Grant*, 69; Bauer, *The Mexican War 1846–1848*, 292.

42. Eisenhower, *So Far from God*, 324.

43. Bauer, *The Mexican War 1846–1848*, 296–98.

44. Wilcox, *History of the Mexican War*, 385.

45. Lewis Armistead testimony, Proceedings of a General Court-Martial in the Case of Maj. B. L. E. Bonneville, 6th Infantry, Mexico City, October 1847, "Case EE-565," National Archives, 77–78.

46. Report of Captain William Hoffman, Library of Congress, House Exec. Doc. No. 8, Appendix to the Report of the Secretary of War, Additional Reports from the Army in Mexico, 63. Hoffman filed this report on August 20, 1847.

47. Bauer, *The Mexican War 1846–1848*, 298.

48. Lewis Armistead testimony, Proceedings of a General Court-Martial, October 1847, "Case EE-565," National Archives, 78–79.

49. Ibid., 79.

50. Ibid.

51. Motts, *"Trust in God and Fear Nothing,"* 24.

52. Winfield S. Hancock to Benjamin F. Hancock, August 26, 1847, in Denison and Herbert, *Hancock "The Superb,"* 150; Glenn Tucker, *Hancock the Superb*, 41.

53. Bauer, *The Mexican War 1846–1848*, 300–301.

54. Reports of Colonel Newman Clarke, Major Benjamin Bonneville, and Captain William Hoffman, LC, House Exec. Doc. No. 8, Appendix to the Report of the Secretary of War, Additional Reports from the Army in Mexico, 55, 62, 64.

55. Lewis Armistead Commissions, USMA Special Collections, West Point, NY.

56. Reports of Colonel Newman Clarke and Captain William Hoffman, LC, House Exec. Doc. No. 8, Appendix to the Report of the Secretary of War, Additional Reports from the Army in Mexico, 55, 64; George W. Cullum, *Biographical Register of the Officers and Graduates of the U.S. Military Academy at West Point, N.Y., Vol. 1, 1802–1840*, 108.

57. Eisenhower, *So Far from God*, 330–32.

58. Timothy D. Johnson, *A Gallant Little Army: The Mexico City Campaign*, 202–3.

59. Winfield Scott to William Marcy, September 11, 1847, www.dmwv.org.

60. Ibid.; Eisenhower, *So Far from God*, 334–36.

61. Johnson, *A Gallant Little Army*, 203. Colonel James McIntosh commanded Clarke's brigade on this day because Clarke was ill.

62. Lewis Armistead testimony, Proceedings of a General Court-Martial, October 1847, "Case EE-565," National Archives, 76.

63. Ibid., 76–77.

64. Johnson, *A Gallant Little Army*, 208. Worth entered the battle with 3,450 troops (203).

65. Ralph Kirkham to Catherine Kirkham, September 8, 1847, in Ralph W. Kirkham, *The Mexican War Journal & Letters of Ralph W. Kirkham*, 59.

66. Lewis Armistead Commissions, USMA Special Collections, West Point, NY.

67. Eisenhower, *So Far from God*, 337–38.

68. Wilcox, *History of the Mexican War*, 449.

69. Johnson, *A Gallant Little Army*, 213.

70. Eisenhower, *So Far from God*, 340.

71. Ibid., 338–39; Wilcox, *History of the Mexican War*, 454.

72. Wilcox, *History of the Mexican War*, 460–65; Johnson, *A Gallant Little Army*, 218, 220, 222–23; Bauer, *The Mexican War, 1846–1848*, 316–17; Jordan, *Winfield Scott Hancock*, 16; Grant, *The Personal Memoirs of U. S. Grant*, 30.

73. Motts, *"Trust in God and Fear Nothing,"* 26–28; Wilcox, *History of the Mexican War*, 454; Johnson, *A Gallant Little Army*, 216. While the precise number of soldiers in the storming party varies slightly in officers' reports, both Samuel Mackenzie, who led the attack, and Cadmus Wilcox, who fought at Chapultepec, said it was 260.

74. Report of Captain Samuel Mackenzie, LC, House Exec. Doc. No. 8, Appendix to the Report of the Secretary of War, Additional Reports from the Army in Mexico, 232.

75. Johnson, *A Gallant Little Army*, 218; Eisenhower, *So Far from God*, 340–41. "Voltigeur" was a term taken from the French military, often referring to "foot riflemen."

76. Wilcox, *History of the Mexican War*, 450.

77. Report of Captain Samuel Mackenzie, LC, House Exec. Doc. No. 8, Appendix to the Report of the Secretary of War, Additional Reports from the Army in Mexico, 232.

78. Ibid.

79. Wilcox, *History of the Mexican War*, 462.

80. Ibid. The commanders were Joseph Selden and A. P. Rodgers.

81. P. G. T. Beauregard, *With Beauregard in Mexico*, 81–82; Johnson, *A Gallant Little Army*, 279. In appendix 2, providing details and "remarks" about U.S. officers in the Mexican War, Johnson lists "1st Lt. L.A. Armistead" as "Wounded at Chapultepec, Sep. 13," but Armistead remained in action, and no description of the wound was ever found.

82. Simon B. Buckner testimony, Proceedings of a General Court-Martial in the Case of Maj. B. L. E. Bonneville, 6th Infantry, Mexico City, October 1847, "Case EE-565," National Archives, 40.

83. Ibid. In his testimony, Buckner reported that "Major Bonneville sent the colours of the regiment at the same time to be displayed upon the work by Lieut. Armistead."

84. Ibid., 39–40; Eisenhower, *So Far from God*, 342; Motts, *"Trust in God and Fear Nothing,"* 28.

85. Bauer, *The Mexican War 1846–1848*, 318.

86. Winfield S. Hancock to Hilary B. Hancock, December 6, 1874, in Denison and Wheeler, *Hancock "The Superb,"* 150–51.

87. Johnson, *A Gallant Little Army*, 238.

88. Johannsen, *To the Halls of the Montezumas*, 52–53. Johannsen wrote that "it was not until 1834 that army regulations first specified the flag's design and proclaimed it the official banner of the armed forces. The Mexican War was the first war in which

American soldiers fought under the Stars and Stripes; in earlier engagements the troops had followed their various regimental and unit flags."

89. Henry Heth, *The Memoirs of Henry Heth*, 53.

90. Ibid., 56.

91. Johnson, *A Gallant Little Army*, 255. Johnson notes that "Heth and Hancock, along with Lew Armistead, were fast friends, and in Mexico City, Heth learned to stick close to Hancock."

92. Heth, *The Memoirs of Henry Heth*, 56.

93. Ibid., 66.

94. Kirkham journal entry, February 12, 1848, in Kirkham, *The Mexican War Journal & Letters of Ralph W. Kirkham*, 100 (also 130n3).

95. Johnson, *A Gallant Little Army*, 267–68; Bauer, *The Mexican War 1846–1848*, 384.

96. Eisenhower, *So Far from God*, 366–67, 369–70, 383; Bauer, *The Mexican War 1846–1848*, 388.

97. Kirkham journal entry, June 12, 1848, in Kirkham, *The Mexican War Journal & Letters of Ralph W. Kirkham*, 111.

98. Grant, *The Personal Memoirs of U. S. Grant*, 29.

99. Lieutenant Thomas Williams, quoted in Johnson, *A Gallant Little Army*, 268.

Chapter 6. Unimaginable Sadness

1. Wayne E. Motts, *"Trust in God and Fear Nothing": Gen. Lewis A. Armistead, CSA*, 4.

2. Lewis Armistead to Roger Jones, September 21, 1848; Gustavus Loomis to Roger Jones, October 10, 1848, Letters Received by the Office of the Adjutant General Main Series, 1822–1860, National Archives.

3. Lewis Armistead to Roger Jones, October 1, 1849, Letters Received by the Office of the Adjutant General Main Series, 1822–1860, National Archives. Armistead said he was diagnosed with the disease on November 25, 1848.

4. Llewelyn Powell to C. A. Waite, April 6, 1849, Letters Received by the Office of the Adjutant General Main Series, 1822–1860, National Archives.

5. C. A. Waite to Roger Jones, April 9, 1849, Letters Received by the Office of the Adjutant General Main Series, 1822–1860, National Archives.

6. Lewis Armistead to Roger Jones, October 1, 1849, Letters Received by the Office of the Adjutant General Main Series, 1822–1860, National Archives.

7. www.merckmanuels.com. For additional information on erysipelas, see htttps://rareidseases.org and www.healthline.com.

8. Lewis Armistead to Roger Jones, October 1, 1849, Letters Received by the Office of the Adjutant General Main Series, 1822–1860, National Archives.

9. C. A. Waite to Roger Jones, April 9, 1849; Llewelyn Powell to C. A. Waite, April 6, 1849, Letters Received by the Office of the Adjutant General Main Series, 1822–1860, National Archives.

10. Lewis Armistead to Roger Jones, October 1, 1849, Letters Received by the Office of the Adjutant General Main Series, 1822–1860, National Archives.

11. Returns from U.S. Military Posts, 1806–1916, for Lewis A. Armistead, Jefferson Barracks, MO, February 1850, National Archives, also available at ancestry.com. Armistead "joined by transfer" on February 16.

12. Returns from Regular Army Infantry Regiments, June 1821–December 1916, "Sixth United States Infantry Regiment," April 1850, National Archives.

13. www.findagrave.com for Flora Love Armistead, including a photo of her tombstone from Jefferson Barracks National Cemetery, with the inscription of her death date. For the cholera epidemic of 1849–1850, see David Goodwin, *Ghosts of Jefferson Barracks: History & Hauntings of Old St. Louis*, 105–6. Cholera was a deadly intestinal disease.

14. Returns from U.S. Military Posts, 1806–1916, for Lewis A. Armistead, Jefferson Barracks, MO, May 1850, denotes that he was transferred to Fort Snelling on May 10.

15. 1850 United States Federal Census, Fort Snelling & Vicinity, Minnesota Territory. An "E. M. Love," age sixty, born in Virginia, is listed as living with Lewis and Cecilia Armistead and their young son, "W.K." The census was taken on September 18, 1850. For more information on Eliza Matilda Love, see Cazenove Gardner Lee Jr., *Lee Chronicle: Studies of the Early Generations of the Lees of Virginia*, 295–96, 306. She had moved to Alabama to live with another daughter in 1836.

16. Returns from U.S. Military Posts, 1806–1916, for Lewis A. Armistead, Fort Clarke, IA, September 1850, National Archives. The names "Fort Clarke" and "Fort Dodge" refer to the same outpost in Iowa and are sometimes used interchangeably. However, according to historian Robert W. Frazer, the official name was Fort Clarke until September 25, 1851, at which point it was changed to Fort Dodge. It is more commonly called Fort Dodge. From Robert W. Frazer, *Forts of the West: Military Forts and Presidios and Posts Commonly Called Forts West of the Mississippi River to 1898*, 49.

17. www.findagrave.com for Cecilia Lee Love Armistead, including a photo of her tombstone from Magnolia Cemetery, with the inscription of her death date.

18. Returns from U.S. Military Posts, 1806–1916, for Lewis A. Armistead, Fort Clarke/Fort Dodge, IA, January, February and March 1851, National Archives.

19. Lewis Armistead to Roger Jones, April 13, 1851, Letters Received by the Office of the Adjutant General Main Series, 1822–1860, National Archives.

20. Returns from U.S. Military Posts, 1806–1916, for Lewis A. Armistead, Fort Clarke/Fort Dodge, IA, July 1851, National Archives.

21. Returns from U.S. Military Posts, 1806–1916, for Lewis A. Armistead, Fort Clarke/Fort Dodge, IA, November 1851 and January 1852, National Archives.

22. Motts, *"Trust in God and Fear Nothing,"* 30, 55n53.

23. "Multiple News Items," *Daily National Intelligencer*, Washington, D.C., June 25, 1852, and "Fire in Virginia," *Baltimore Sun*, June 24, 1852. According to the reports, the house "accidentally caught fire . . . and was burned down. All the furniture was consumed."

24. Lewis Armistead to W. W. Bliss, August 1, 1852, Letters Received by the Office of the Adjutant General Main Series, 1822–1860, National Archives.

25. Returns from U.S. Military Posts, 1806–1916, for Lewis A. Armistead, Fort Dodge, IA, October 1852, and Fort Ridgely, MT, July 1853, National Archives.
26. Franck S. Armistead conditional appointment, May 27, 1852, U.S. Military Academy Cadet Application Papers, 1805–1866, National Archives, also found at www .ancestry.com.
27. Register of Cadet Applications 1819–1867, No. 21, 1848–1849, National Archives. Walker K. Armistead is listed as an "At-Large" applicant, with a notation that he is the "son of the late Genl. A."
28. Robert Emmett Curran, *The Bicentennial History of Georgetown University: From Academy to University, 1789–1889*, Vol. 1, 166. Walker Jr. attended for eighteen months from 1846 to 1848.
29. Letters from Thomas F. Mulledy, president of Georgetown College, and a group of Virginia legislators, both dated January 28, 1848, found in Walker K. Armistead's file, U.S. Military Academy Cadet Application Papers, 1805–1866, National Archives.
30. Ibid.
31. Elizabeth Armistead to Joseph Totten, February 17, 1848, U.S. Military Academy Cadet Application Papers, 1805–1866, for Franck S. Armistead, National Archives.
32. Gertrude S. Carraway, *The Stanly Family and the Historic John Wright Stanly House*, 23; 1850 United States Federal Census, Fauquier County, VA. Franck was named for his maternal grandmother, Elizabeth Franck—hence the unique spelling.
33. Elizabeth Armistead to Zachary Taylor, May 2, 1850, U.S. Military Academy Cadet Application Papers, 1805–1866, for Franck S. Armistead, National Archives.
34. Edward Stanly to Millard Fillmore, February 2, 1851, U.S. Military Academy Cadet Application Papers, 1805–1866, for Franck S. Armistead, National Archives.
35. Virginia delegation to Millard Fillmore, January 28, 1851, U.S. Military Academy Cadet Application Papers, 1805–1866, for Franck S. Armistead, National Archives.
36. Edward Stanly to C. M. Conrad, March 11, 1852, U.S. Military Academy Cadet Application Papers, 1805–1866, for Franck S. Armistead, National Archives.
37. Lewis Armistead to Franck Armistead, February 4, 1852, from Flavius Burfoot Walker Jr., "Lewis Addison Armistead," University of Richmond Honors Theses, 1939, 8–9, available at http://scholarship.richmond.edu/honors-theses. The author quoted from an original copy of the letter provided by a member of the Armistead family during his research in 1939.
38. Ibid., 9.
39. Franck S. Armistead conditional appointment, May 27, 1852, U.S. Military Academy Cadet Application Papers, 1805–1866, National Archives.
40. Ibid.
41. Returns from U.S. Military Posts, 1806–1916, for Lewis A. Armistead, Fort Dodge, IA, October 1852, National Archives; George W. Cullum, *Biographical Register of the Officers and Graduates of the U.S. Military Academy at West Point, N.Y., Vol. 2, 1841–1867*, 439. Franck reported to West Point on July 1, 1852.
42. Nell Watson Sherman, *Taliaferro-Toliver Family Records*, 23; Motts, *"Trust in God and Fear Nothing,"* 30–31.

43. District of Columbia Marriage Records, 1810–1953, for Cornelia Lee Taliaferro, www.ancestry.com; 1850 United States Federal Census, Alexandria, VA.

44. Lewis Armistead to Samuel Cooper, March 21, 1853, Letters Received by the Office of the Adjutant General Main Series, 1822–1860, National Archives.

45. Returns from U.S. Military Posts, 1806–1916, for Lewis A. Armistead, Fort Dodge, IA, April, May, and June 1853; for Fort Ridgely, Minnesota Territory, July 1853 and September 1854, National Archives.

46. www.findagrave.com for Lewis B. Armistead, including a photo of his tombstone from Jefferson Barracks National Cemetery, with the inscription of his death date; Motts, *"Trust in God and Fear Nothing,"* 31–32.

47. Returns from U.S. Military Posts, 1806–1916, for Lewis A. Armistead, Jefferson Barracks, MO, April 1855, and Fort Riley, Kansas Territory, May 1855, National Archives.

48. Francis B. Heitman, *Historical Register and Dictionary of the U.S. Army, from Its Organization, September 29, 1789 to March 2, 1903*, Vol. 1, 169. Heitman records the date as March 3. One of Lewis's regimental returns identifies the date as May 13.

49. Motts, *"Trust in God and Fear Nothing,"* 33.

50. Percival G. Lowe, *Five Years a Dragoon (49 to 54)*, 192–94; Motts, *"Trust in God and Fear Nothing,"* 32.

51. Lowe, *Five Years a Dragoon (49 to 54)*, 194–95.

52. Ibid., 202–3.

53. Motts, *"Trust in God and Fear Nothing,"* 33.

54. Lowe, *Five Years a Dragoon (49 to 54)*, 203–4.

55. Ibid., 208.

56. www.findagrave.com for Cornelia T. Armistead, including a photo of her tombstone from Fort Riley Post Cemetery, with the inscription of her death date; U.S. Burial Registers, Military Posts & National Cemeteries, Fort Riley, Mrs. C. L. T Armistead, www.ancestry.com.

57. W. F. Pride, *The History of Fort Riley*, 93. Pride quoted George Faringhy, the hospital steward.

58. www.findagrave.com for Cornelia T. Armistead, including a photo of the plaque from Fort Riley Post Cemetery. It is located next to her tombstone.

59. Washington & New Orleans Telegraph Line, August 17, 1855, Alexandria, VA, included in Letters Received by the Office of the Adjutant General Main Series, 1822–1860, National Archives. The note said, "Is Major Armistead dead? His sister wishes information."

60. Lewis Armistead to Samuel Cooper, November 27, 1855, Letters Received by the Office of the Adjutant General Main Series, 1822–1860, National Archives; Returns from U.S. Military Posts, 1806–1916, for Lewis A. Armistead, Fort Riley, Kansas Territory, September 1855 and January 1856. One return identifies the date of Armistead's leave as September 25.

61. 1860 United States Federal Census, Alexandria, VA.

62. Lewis Armistead to Samuel Cooper, November 27, 1855, and February 1, 1856, Letters Received by the Office of the Adjutant General Main Series, 1822–1860, National Archives.

63. Returns from U.S. Military Posts, 1806–1916, for Lewis A. Armistead, Fort Riley, Kansas Territory, May 1856, National Archives.

Chapter 7. Hancock the Quartermaster

1. Francis Amasa Walker, *General Hancock*, 20–21.
2. Glenn Tucker, *Hancock the Superb*, 44.
3. Walker, *General Hancock*, 21.
4. Ibid., 28.
5. David M. Jordan, *Winfield Scott Hancock: A Soldier's Life*, 17, 20–21.
6. Ibid., 23. Hancock described himself in a contemporary letter as "six feet and one-half inch in height, weighing 169 pounds."
7. Henry Heth, *The Memoirs of Henry Heth*, 59–60.
8. Ibid., 60.
9. Ibid., 70–72.
10. Jordan, *Winfield Scott Hancock*, 21, 23. Hancock was on the staff of General Newman Clarke of the Sixth Infantry.
11. Tucker, *Hancock the Superb*, 45–46. The soldier who introduced Hancock to Almira was Don Carlos Buell. The two men attended West Point together.
12. Almira Hancock, *Reminiscences of Winfield Scott Hancock*, 1, 3.
13. Jordan, *Winfield Scott Hancock*, 23. Russell was born on October 29, 1850.
14. Hancock, *Reminiscences of Winfield Scott Hancock*, 7.
15. Tucker, *Hancock the Superb*, 47.
16. Walker, *General Hancock*, 21.
17. George W. Cullum, *Biographical Register of the Officers and Graduates of the U.S. Military Academy at West Point, N.Y., Vol. 2, 1841–1867*, 206. Heth was named captain of the Tenth Infantry on March 3, 1855. He had graduated thirty-eighth and last in his class in 1847.
18. Hancock, *Reminiscences of Winfield Scott Hancock*, 7–8. According to Heth in his memoirs, "Hancock was much disappointed at not being promoted, and I thought he deserved promotion much more than I did, for he had a gallant Mexican War record, which should have counted in his favor." Heth, *The Memoirs of Henry Heth*, 123–24.
19. Cullum, *Biographical Register of the Officers and Graduates of the U.S. Military Academy at West Point, N.Y., Vol. 2, 1841–1867*, 108.
20. Hancock, *Reminiscences of Winfield Scott Hancock*, 25.
21. Jordan, *Winfield Scott Hancock*, 24.
22. Hancock, *Reminiscences of Winfield Scott Hancock*, 26.
23. Statement of Thomas M. Vincent, in Military Service Institution, *Letters and Addresses Contributed at a General Meeting of the Military Service Institution Held at Governor's Island, N.Y., February 25, 1886, in Memory of Winfield Scott Hancock* (hereinafter *Letters and Addresses*), 27.
24. Statement of Orlando B. Willcox in *Letters and Addresses*, 22.
25. Hancock, *Reminiscences of Winfield Scott Hancock*, 34.
26. Jordan, *Winfield Scott Hancock*, 24.

27. Hancock, *Reminiscences of Winfield Scott Hancock*, 36.
28. Tucker, *Hancock the Superb*, 53.
29. Hancock, *Reminiscences of Winfield Scott Hancock*, 39.
30. Winfield S. Hancock to Almira Hancock, cited in Hancock, *Reminiscences of Winfield Scott Hancock*, 44.
31. Jordan, *Winfield Scott Hancock*, 26.
32. Returns from U.S. Military Posts, 1806–1916, for Lewis A. Armistead, Fort Riley, Kansas Territory, May 1856, National Archives; Wayne E. Motts, *"Trust in God and Fear Nothing": Gen. Lewis A. Armistead, CSA*, 34; Moses Harris, "The Old Army," October 3, 1894, *War Papers Read before the Commander of Wisconsin, Military Order of the Loyal Legion of the United States*, Vol. II, 335–36.
33. Returns from U.S. Military Posts, 1806–1916, for Lewis A. Armistead, Fort Riley, Kansas Territory, May 1858, National Archives, noting that he "left Fort Riley on May 8 for Utah"; Robert K. Krick, "Armistead and Garnett: The Parallel Lives of Two Virginia Soldiers," in *The Third Day at Gettysburg & Beyond*, 107. Krick writes that it was "popularly, if inaptly, known as the Mormon War."
34. Eugene Bandel, *Frontier Life in the Army, 1854–1861*, 55–56.
35. Charles Byrne, "The Sixth Regiment of Infantry," Center of Military History, www.history.army.mil, 491.
36. Bandel, *Frontier Life in the Army, 1854–1861*, 237–38.
37. Walker, *General Hancock*, 23.
38. George Stammerjohan, "Winfield Scott Hancock in California," from "Bugler, Sound the Charge," by Will Gorenfeld, www.chargeofthedragoons.com, 3.
39. Krick, "Armistead and Garnett," 108.
40. Byrne, "The Sixth Regiment of Infantry," 491.
41. W. W. Mackall to William Hoffman, January 31, 1859, LC, U.S. Senate 1859–60, Exec. Doc., Report of the Secretary of War, Serial 1024, 407–8.
42. Lewis A. Armistead to Samuel Cooper, May 1, 1859, LC, U.S. Senate 1859–60, Exec. Doc., Report of the Secretary of War, Serial 1024, 405. The name of the tribe was alternately spelled "Mojave" and "Mohave" during this period. Armistead and others used both spellings, but, for clarity, it will be "Mojave" throughout the text. See also Krick, "Armistead and Garnett," 109.
43. Hancock, *Reminiscences of Winfield Scott Hancock*, 45; Walker, *General Hancock*, 24.
44. Walker, *General Hancock*, 24; Jordan, *Winfield Scott Hancock*, 26.
45. Hancock, *Reminiscences of Winfield Scott Hancock*, 45.
46. Ibid., 45–46; Tucker, *Hancock the Superb*, 59.
47. Hancock, *Reminiscences of Winfield Scott Hancock*, 46–47. Lee was a colonel at the time, having been promoted at the end of the Mexican War.
48. Ibid., 47–51. Almira tells of a scene where Hancock had to rescue his son, Russell, from an attack by "six villains. . . . He warned them, at their peril, never to approach him, and never again to lay their hands upon his child, or he would kill every man who attempted it. This salutary lesson had the desired effect for the rest of the voyage."
49. Cullum, *Biographical Register of the Officers and Graduates of the U.S. Military Academy at West Point, N.Y., Vol. 2, 1841–1867*, 108. Hancock was officially assigned

on May 5, 1859, while he was still at sea. He served at the same post until August 1861, when he headed east for the Civil War.

50. Hancock, *Reminiscences of Winfield Scott Hancock*, 51–52.

51. Ibid., 54–57; Jordan, *Winfield Scott Hancock*, 28; John W. Robinson, *Los Angeles in Civil War Days 1860–1865*, 47.

52. George Stammerjohan, "The Camel Experiment in California," *Dogtown Territorial Quarterly*, no. 18 (Summer 1994), 46.

53. W. W. Mackall to William Hoffman, January 31, 1859, LC, U.S. Senate 1859–60, Exec. Doc., Report of the Secretary of War, Serial 1024, 408.

54. N. S. Clarke to Lewis A. Armistead, October 3, 1859, LC, U.S. Senate 1859–60, Exec. Doc., Report of the Secretary of War, Serial 1024, 421.

55. *Los Angeles Star*, July 30, 1859, "EXTRA! Important from the Colorado!! OUTBREAK OF THE MOJAVE INDIANS," found in the California Digital Newspaper Collection, https://cdnc.ucr.edu/site/index.html.

56. Lewis A. Armistead to W. W. Mackall, August 6, 1859, LC, U.S. Senate 1859–60, Exec. Doc., Report of the Secretary of War, Serial 1024, 419–20; Krick, "Armistead and Garnett," 110.

57. Lewis A. Armistead to W. W. Mackall, August 6, 1859, LC, U.S. Senate 1859–60, Exec. Doc., Report of the Secretary of War, Serial 1024, 419.

58. *Los Angeles Star*, August 13, 1859, and August 27, 1859, California Digital Newspaper Collection, https://cdnc.ucr.edu/site/index.html.

59. Lewis A. Armistead to W. W. Mackall, August 31, 1859, LC, U.S. Senate 1859–60, Exec. Doc., Report of the Secretary of War, Serial 1024, 421; Krick, "Armistead and Garnett," 110.

60. Returns from U.S. Military Posts, 1806–1916, for Lewis A. Armistead, Fort Mojave, AZ (sometimes listed as NM), September 1859, National Archives.

61. Returns from U.S. Military Post, 1806–1916, for Lewis A. Armistead, Fort Yuma, CA, January, March, and September 1860, and New San Diego, CA, December 1860, National Archives.

62. Lewis A. Armistead to Samuel Cooper, March 6, 1860, Letters Received by the Office of the Adjutant General Main Series, 1822–1860, National Archives.

63. Lewis A. Armistead to Lorenzo Thomas, July 5, 1860, Letters Received by the Office of the Adjutant General Main Series, 1822–1860, National Archives.

64. W. A. Nichols to Samuel Cooper, July 11, 1860, Armistead file, Letters Received by the Office of the Adjutant General Main Series, 1822–1860, National Archives.

65. Walker K. Armistead (Jr.) to Samuel Cooper, September 20, 1861, Compiled Service Records for Walker K. Armistead (Jr.), National Archives.

66. 1860 U.S. Federal Census for Upperville, Fauquier County, VA, www.ancestry.com.

67. Lewis A. Armistead to J. B. Floyd, July 25, 1860, U.S. Military Academy Cadet Records and Applications, 1805–1908, for W. Keith Armistead, www.fold3.com and www.ancestry.com.

68. Clarence Thomas, *General Turner Ashby: The Centaur of the South*, 15.

69. James B. Avirett, *The Memoirs of General Turner Ashby and His Compeers*, 58–64; Tom McMillan, *Gettysburg Rebels: Five Native Sons Who Came Home to Fight as Confederate Soldiers*, 35–37, 42, 44–45; "Turner Ashby," www.encyclopediavirginia.org.

70. Avirett, *The Memoirs of General Turner Ashby and His Compeers*, 51.

71. Ibid., 69–70.

72. The original Star-Spangled Banner remained in the possession of George Armistead's direct descendants for more than ninety years until his grandson, Ethan Appleton, turned it over to the Smithsonian in the early twentieth century. It is now in display in the Smithsonian's National Museum of American History in Washington, D.C.

Chapter 8. California

1. John Crandell, "Grievous Angels from Third and Main to Gettysburg: General Winfield Scott Hancock in Los Angeles," 315–16, 319. Crandell also wrote about this in the spring 1977 edition of the *Quarterly*. Hancock may have established temporary quarters in the Temple Block section at first, but most accounts and biographies cite Third and Main as his predominant Los Angeles residence. He also used it as an office.

2. Almira Hancock, *Reminiscences of Winfield Scott Hancock*, 55.

3. John W. Robinson, *Los Angeles in Civil War Days 1860–1865*, 16–17; Hancock, *Reminiscences of Winfield Scott Hancock*, 57–58.

4. Crandell, "Winfield Hancock and His Grievous Angels—Revisited," 6.

5. Robinson, *Los Angeles in Civil War Days 1860–1865*, 47.

6. D. X. Junkin and Frank Norton, *The Life of Winfield Scott Hancock: Personal, Military and Political*, 40.

7. George Stammerjohan, "Winfield Scott (Hancock) in California," in "Bugler, Sound the Charge," by Will Gorenfeld, 4, www.chargeofthedragoons.com.

8. Hancock, *Reminiscences of Winfield Scott Hancock*, 57; David M. Jordan, *Winfield Scott Hancock: A Soldier's Life*, 28.

9. For a recap of some of Hancock's private business dealings, see Jordan, *Winfield Scott Hancock*, 29–30. Jordan wrote that "had Winfield Scott Hancock chosen to resign from the army while in California, there is little doubt that he could, with the connections he quickly acquired, have made himself wealthy there. . . . But there is no evidence that he ever considered such a step."

10. Statement of James H. Merryman, in Military Service Institution, *Letters and Addresses Contributed at a General Meeting of the Military Service Institution Held at Governor's Island, N.Y., February 25, 1886, in Memory of Winfield Scott Hancock*, 35–36.

11. "Arrival of Gen. Johnston," *Los Angeles Star*, March 31, 1860. The escort was described as "horses, mules, wagons and a harness," turned over to "Capt. Hancock, A.Q.M. residing here."

12. Hancock, *Reminiscences of Winfield Scott Hancock*, 58.

13. "Arrival of Troops," *Visalia Weekly Delta*, December 22, 1860.

14. Returns from U.S. Military Posts, 1806–1916, for Lewis A. Armistead, New San Diego, CA, December 1860, National Archives.
15. "United States Presidential Election of 1860," www.brittanica.com.
16. South Carolina secession document, "The Declaration of Causes of Seceding States," www.battlefields.org.
17. *Charleston Mercury Extra*, December 20, 1860, John G. Nicolay Papers, Manuscript Division, LC. Also available at www.loc.gov, "Civil War in America: Prologue."
18. "States Meet to Form Confederacy," www.history.org; "Acts and Resolutions of the First Session of the Provisional Congress of the Confederate States, Montgomery, Alabama," Barrett, Wimbish & Co., 1861, Rare Book and Special Collections Division, LC.
19. Winfield Scott Hancock to Benjamin Hancock, February 28, 1861, http://suvcw .org/mollus/pcinc/wshancock.htm.
20. Hancock, *Reminiscences of Winfield Scott Hancock*, 66. Richard Garnett's service records show that he was in and around southern California in late 1860 and early 1861. George Pickett was posted farther up the coast in the Washington Territory but possibly could have traveled to Los Angeles—although no such record exists.
21. A. S. Johnston to W. W. Mackall, January 15, 1861, *The War of the Rebellion: Official Records of the Union and Confederate Armies* (hereinafter cited as *OR*), Series 1, Vol. 50, Part 2, 434.
22. William Preston Johnston, *The Life of Gen. Albert Sidney Johnston: Embracing His Services in the Armies of the United States, the Republic of Texas, and the Confederate States*, 1–3, 68–69.
23. A. S. Johnston to Lorenzo Thomas, April 4, 1861, Letters Received by the Office of the Adjutant General Main Series, 1822–1860, National Archives; Johnston, *The Life of Gen. Albert Sidney Johnston*, 275; Glenn Tucker, *Hancock the Superb*, 64.
24. Hancock, *Reminiscences of Winfield Scott Hancock*, 68.
25. Winfield S. Hancock to W. W. Mackall, May 4, 1861, *OR*, Series 1, Vol. 50, 479.
26. Robinson, *Los Angeles in Civil War Days 1860–1865*, 51.
27. Winfield S. Hancock to W. W. Mackall, May 4, 1861, *OR*, Series 1, Vol. 50, 479.
28. W. W. Mackall to Winfield S. Hancock, April 29, 1861, and W. W. Mackall to J. J. Carleton, May 3, 1861, *OR*, Series 1, Vol. 50, 473, 477; Robinson, *Los Angeles in Civil War Days 1860–1865*, 58; "Death of Major E. H. Fitzgerald," *Los Angeles Star*, January 14, 1860.
29. Winfield S. Hancock to W. W. Mackall, May 7 1861, *OR*, Series 1, Vol. 50, 481.
30. Winfield S. Hancock to W. W. Mackall, May 11, 1861, *OR*, Series 1, Vol. 50, 483.
31. "Major Armistead," *Los Angeles Star*, May 11, 1861.
32. "The Virginia Secession Ordinance," *New York Times*, April 28, 1861.
33. www.youtube.com, Wayne E. Motts, "Pickett's Charge at Gettysburg," Gettysburg Foundation Sacred Trust Talks, July 3, 2016. The original resignation letter, cited by Motts and shown on a slide in his presentation, is dated May 13, from Armistead to W. W. Mackall, the assistant adjutant general under Sumner.
34. L. A. Armistead to W. W. Mackall, May 26, 1861, Letters Received by the Office of the Adjutant General, Main Series, 1861–1870, National Archives.

35. Edwin Sumner's note, attached to Armistead's resignation letter, June 4, 1861, Letters Received by the Office of the Adjutant General, Main Series, 1861–1870, National Archives. Sumner wrote, "I would respectfully recommend that the resignation be accepted," and passed it on to the general in chief.

36. Wayne E. Motts, *"Trust in God and Fear Nothing": Gen. Lewis A. Armistead, CSA*, 36.

37. Returns from U.S. Military Posts, 1806–1916, for Lewis A. Armistead, New San Diego, CA, June 1861, "Alterations since last monthly return"; Richard C. Drum, May 14, 1861, Special Orders No. 82, "By command of Brigadier-General Sumner," *OR* Series 1, Vol. 50, 486. The special order, written on May 14, said that "upon the arrival of Major Haller's company, Company F, Sixth Infantry [Brevet Major Armistead's] will proceed as soon as possible to Los Angeles." The addendum to his post return said Armistead was transferred to Los Angeles with his company on May 14 and relieved of command on June 19. Haller's company did not arrive in San Diego until June. But, regarding his personal dispositions, it should be noted again that Armistead's intention to resign was published in a Los Angeles paper as early as May 11, his resignation letters were dated May 13 and May 26, Sumner recommended approval of his resignation on June 4, and one account had the resignation approved on June 12. As with all soldiers of this era, his daily whereabouts were not recorded by the army, which posted only monthly returns.

38. A. S. Johnston to Eliza Johnston, June 30, 1861, in Johnston, *The Life of Gen. Albert Sidney Johnston*, 279–80. In this letter, written from Vallecito, California, Johnston tells his wife, "I received your letter of June 25 from Major Armistead, who arrived here this morning." Armistead did not leave Los Angeles at the same time as Johnston and the others, so it is clear that he met with Eliza Johnston in Los Angeles to pick up the letter sometime before departing.

39. George Gift account, in Johnston, *The Life of Gen. Albert Sidney Johnston*, 278.

40. Hancock, *Reminiscences of Winfield Scott Hancock*, 69.

41. Johnston, *The Life of Gen. Albert Sidney Johnston*, 275, 278. The author was the general's son. William was practicing law in Louisville when his father was in Los Angeles, but he went on to serve in the Confederate army and as an aide to President Jefferson Davis. He later became president of Louisiana State University and Tulane University. Also found at www.find-a-grave.com for William Preston Johnston.

42. Hancock, *Reminiscences of Winfield Scott Hancock*, 69.

43. "Kathleen Mavourneen," www.bellsirishlyrics.com.

44. Hancock, *Reminiscences of Winfield Scott Hancock*, 70.

45. Ibid., 69.

46. Ibid., 69–70.

47. Michael Shaara, *The Killer Angels*, 252; *Gettysburg*, Turner Pictures and New Line Cinema, released 1993. The versions are only slightly different. The book quotes Armistead as saying, "Well, I was crying, and I went up to Win and I took him by the shoulder and I said, 'Win, so help me, if I ever lift a hand against you, may God strike me dead.'"

48. Tucker, *Hancock the Superb*, 65. The author agrees with this assessment.

49. Hancock, *Reminiscences of Winfield Scott Hancock*, 70.

50. Junkin and Norton, *The Life of Winfield Scott Hancock*, 118–19.
51. D. X. Junkin letter to the "Presbyterian," September 1878, ibid., 398. See also the "prefatory" to the book by coauthor Frank Norton. The manuscript was Junkin's, but Norton picked up the project after Junkin passed away in April 1880. For more perspective, see also James Cephas Derby, *Fifty Years among Authors, Books and Publishers*, 715–18.
52. George Gift account, in Johnston, *The Life of Gen. Albert Sidney Johnston*, 278.
53. *OR*, Series 1, Vol. 50, 497. The order was sent from General Winfield Scott to Major S. Williams of the Department of the West in St. Louis and dated June 3. It said, "The Secretary of War directs that you arrest General A.S. Johnston, if he returns from California by overland route."
54. Gene C. Armistead, "California's Confederate Militia: The Los Angeles Mounted Rifles," www.militarymuseum.org, 3; Mary Holman, "Crossed the Plains with Johnston," 333; Johnston, *The Life of Gen. Albert Sidney Johnston*, 279. The three publications have differing totals but all range between thirty-three and thirty-six.
55. Returns from U.S. Military Posts, 1806–1916, for Lewis A. Armistead, New San Diego, CA, June 1861, "Alterations since last monthly return."
56. Holman, "Crossed the Plains with Johnston," 333. Holman's husband, Cyrus K. Holman, was part of the group heading east with Johnston. The story was published in the *Mesilla (N.M.) Times* under the headline "Arrival of Californians." The original handwritten roster of the Los Angeles Mounted Rifles can be found in "Los Angeles Mounted Rifles," www.militarymuseum.org.
57. A. S. Johnston to Eliza Johnston, June 30, 1861, in Johnston, *The Life of Gen. Albert Sidney Johnston*, 279–80.
58. A. S. Johnston to Eliza Johnston, July 5, 1861, in ibid., 280.
59. George Gift account, in ibid., 282.
60. Armistead, "California's Confederate Militia," 3.
61. Ibid., 4–5; Robert K. Krick, "Armistead and Garnett: The Parallel Lives of Two Virginia Soldiers," in *The Third Day at Gettysburg & Beyond*, 113.
62. A. S. Johnston to Eliza Johnston, August 7, 1861, in Johnston, *The Life of Gen. Albert Sidney Johnston*, 287–88. Via Armistead genealogy, the mother of George Armistead and Walker Sr. was a Baylor. Colonel Baylor's brother wrote a letter requesting a "photo of cousin George Armistead."
63. Armistead, "California's Confederate Militia," 5–6; Johnston, *The Life of Gen. Albert Sidney Johnston*, 288–89.
64. Alonzo Ridley account, in Johnston, *The Life of Gen. Albert Sidney Johnston*, 289.
65. Ibid.
66. American Battlefield Trust, "Albert Sidney Johnston," www.battlefield.org.
67. Compiled Service Records for Lewis A. Armistead, Walker K. Armistead (Jr.), Franck Armistead, and Bowles Armistead, National Archives.
68. Tucker, *Hancock the Superb*, 63; Hancock, *Reminiscences of Winfield Scott Hancock*, 65.
69. Hancock, *Reminiscences of Winfield Scott Hancock*, 63. She gives the year as 1860, but it is evident, from other references in this passage of her book, that it was 1861.

70. Hancock speech, July 4, 1861, in Junkin and Norton, *The Life of Winfield Scott Hancock*, 45.
71. Ibid., 45–46. The last line was in italics in the original, as Hancock emphasized the importance of the Union.
72. "By order of Brigadier-General Sumner," *OR*, Series 1, Vol. 50, 555.
73. Jordan, *Winfield Scott Hancock*, 35–36.
74. Tucker, *Hancock the Superb*, 67–68.
75. Hancock, *Reminiscences of Winfield Scott Hancock*, 75–76.
76. Ibid., 77.
77. Tucker, *Hancock the Superb*, 68. According to Almira, she rented a home in the Washington area during this time.
78. Jordan, *Winfield Scott Hancock*, 36–37. The brigade originally included the Forty-Seventh Pennsylvania, but it was replaced almost immediately by the Sixth Maine.
79. Tucker, *Hancock the Superb*, 72.
80. Francis Amasa Walker, *General Hancock*, 25.

Chapter 9. War Breaks Out

1. Compiled Service Records for Lewis A. Armistead, National Archives, www.fold3 .com; Charles W. Sublett, *57th Virginia Infantry*, 1–5.
2. Charles W. Sublett, *57th Virginia Infantry*, 2, 4–5.
3. Ibid., 5.
4. www.findagrave.com for Elizabeth Stanly Armistead; tombstone inscription—author visit to the private Armistead family grave site in Fauquier County, Virginia.
5. Compiled Service Records for Walker K. Armistead, Bowles E. Armistead and W. Keith Armistead, National Archives.
6. Wayne E. Motts, *"Trust in God and Fear Nothing": Gen. Lewis A. Armistead, CSA*, 16. The photo of a dapper-looking Lewis Armistead was from the private collection of Larry Jones and William Turner.
7. Ibid., 14, quoting an 1839 letter from Edward Stanly to Joel Poinsett.
8. Sublett, *57th Virginia Infantry*, 6.
9. Compiled Service Records for Lewis A. Armistead, National Archives.
10. Benjamin H. Trask, *9th Virginia Infantry*, 11; G. Howard Gregory, *38th Virginia Infantry*, 20.
11. Lewis A. Armistead to J. B. Floyd, July 25, 1860, U.S. Military Academy Cadet Records and Applications, 1805–1908, for W. Keith Armistead, www.fold3.com and www.ancestry.com.
12. Ibid.
13. Compiled Service Records for W. Keith Armistead, Letters Received by the Adjutant and Inspector General's Office, from R. E. Lee, April 2, 1862, National Archives. Lee mentioned in his recommendation letter that W. Keith had been "at school in the North." (These records may also be accessed at www.fold3.com.)
14. Compiled Service Records for W. Keith Armistead, Lewis A. Armistead to Samuel Cooper, December 2, 1861. It includes the following notation: "Application for the appointment of cadet for his son, W. Keith Armistead."

15. Compiled Service Records for W. Keith Armistead, W. Keith Armistead to R. E. Lee, March 31, 1862.
16. Compiled Service Records for W. Keith Armistead, from R. E. Lee, April 2, 1862. The letter was originally filed under "Rebel Archives, Records Division, War Department."
17. Compiled Service Records for W. Keith Armistead, Bowles E. Armistead and Walker K. Armistead (Jr.).
18. Compiled Service Records for W. Keith Armistead.
19. Stephen W. Sears, *To the Gates of Richmond: The Peninsula Campaign*, xi, 35–36. McClellan put his army on the march on April 4, 1862.
20. Francis Amasa Walker, *General Hancock*, 21.
21. Ibid., 32.
22. David M. Jordan, *Winfield Scott Hancock: A Soldier's Life*, 37.
23. Glenn Tucker, *Hancock the Superb*, 69.
24. Walker, *General Hancock*, 33.
25. Sears, *To the Gates of Richmond*, 70–75; Jordan, *Winfield Scott Hancock*, 42–43.
26. Glenn David Brashear, "General Hancock's Hour," *New York Times*, May 8, 2012.
27. *The War of the Rebellion: Official Records of the Union and Confederate Armies* (hereinafter cited as *OR*), Series 1, Vol. 11, Part 1, 536–37. Three of the regiments were Hancock's own; two were from another brigade.
28. Ibid., 544–45; John Hancock to W. S. Hancock, May 5, 1862. Hancock's younger brother concluded his report with typical military formality: "I am, sir, very respectfully, your obedient servant." He had been trained well.
29. Sears, *To the Gates of Richmond*, 78.
30. J. M. Carroll, ed., *Custer in the Civil War: His Unfinished Memoirs*, 153, as cited in Jordan, *Winfield Scott Hancock*, 44.
31. Sears, *To the Gates of Richmond*, 78.
32. *OR*, Series 1, Vol. 11, Part 1, 538.
33. Ibid.
34. Sears, *To the Gates of Richmond*, 80.
35. *OR*, Series 1, Vol. 11, Part 1, 540–41; Jordan, *Winfield Scott Hancock*, 44. Hancock suffered about one hundred casualties.
36. *OR*, Series 1, Vol. 11, Part 1, 22–23.
37. George McClellan to Mary Ellen McClellan, May 6, 1862, in George B. McClellan, *The Civil War Papers of George B. McClellan, Selected Correspondence, 1860–1865*, 256–57; Jordan, *Winfield Scott Hancock*, 44. It is often reported that the phrase was included in a message sent to army headquarters, but it was actually used in a private letter to McClellan's wife.
38. During the Seven Days Battles in late June, Hancock's men had a forty-five-minute firefight at Garnett's Farm and were present at White Oak Swamp but otherwise were on the fringe of the action. They were posted on the extreme right at Malvern Hill on July 1 but were not engaged. They also did not arrive in time to fight at Second Bull Run in late August. Summary from Jordan, *Winfield Scott Hancock*, 45–47, 49.

39. Winfield S. Hancock to Elizabeth Hancock, May 23, 1862 ("In Camp Near Richmond"), in Frederick Elizur Goodrich, *The Life and Public Services of Winfield Scott Hancock, Major-General, U.S.A.*, 101.

40. Sears, *To the Gates of Richmond*, 118, 138, 140–45.

41. Trask, *9th Virginia Infantry*, 12.

42. Ibid., 12–13.

43. *OR*, Series 1, Vol. 11, Part 2, 982–83.

44. *OR*, Series 1, Vol. 11, Part 2, 945.

45. Compiled Service Records for Lewis A. Armistead, National Archives: "We hereby certify that Br. General Armistead's black horse died from the effect of a wound received in the battle of Seven Pines."

46. Sears, *To the Gates of Richmond*, 144.

47. Ibid.

48. Compiled Service Records for Franck S. Armistead, National Archives.

49. Clifford Dowdey, *The Seven Days: The Emergence of Robert E. Lee and the Dawn of a Legend*, 131, 153, 159–60.

50. *OR*, Series 1, Vol. 11, Part 2, 817–18; Edward R. Crews and Timothy A. Parrish, *14th Virginia Infantry*, 25.

51. Sears, *To the Gates of Richmond*, 308.

52. Ibid., 309–12. Sears's book is the definitive study of the Peninsula campaign. The four farms referenced here were Crews, West, Carter, and Poindexter.

53. *OR*, Series 1, Vol. 11, Part 2, 790; G. Howard Gregory, *53rd Virginia Infantry and 5th Battalion Virginia Infantry*, 31.

54. Dowdey, *The Seven Days*, 330–31.

55. *OR*, Series 1, Vol. 11, Part 2, 677.

56. Ibid., 818.

57. Daniel Harvey Hill, *McClellan's Change of Base and Malvern Hill*; Sears, *To the Gates of Richmond*, 318–19, 322.

58. *OR*, Series 1, Vol. 11, Part 2, 819.

59. Ibid., 833.

60. Sears, *To the Gates of Richmond*, 334.

61. Jubal Early, *Lieutenant Jubal Anderson Early, C.S.A.: Autobiographical Sketch and Narrative of the War between the States*, 83.

62. *OR*, Series 1, Vol. 11, Part 2, 982.

63. Dowdey, *The Seven Days*, 348, 351–52.

64. Robert K. Krick, "Armistead and Garnett: The Parallel Lives of Two Virginia Soldiers," in *The Third Day at Gettysburg & Beyond*, 117.

65. Motts, *"Trust in God and Fear Nothing,"* 40.

66. *OR*, Series 1, Vol. 11, Part 2, 673.

67. Compiled Service Records for Walker Jr. and Bowles E. Armistead, National Archives; Michael P. Musick, *6th Virginia Cavalry*, 94.

68. Walker K. Armistead Jr. to Samuel Cooper, September 1861, Compiled Service Records for Walker K. Armistead Jr., National Archives.

69. Ibid.

70. R. H. Dulany to Samuel Cooper, November 26, 1861, Compiled Service Records for Walker K. Armistead Jr., National Archives.
71. Compiled Service Records for Walker K. Armistead Jr., National Archives.
72. Musick, *6th Virginia Cavalry*, 18. This also could have been his nephew, W. Keith.
73. Ibid., 2, 94; Compiled Service Records for Bowles E. Armistead, National Archives.
74. Clarence Thomas, *General Turner Ashby: The Centaur of the South*, 101.
75. Compiled Service Records for W. Keith Armistead, National Archives; Musick, *6th Virginia Cavalry*, 94.

Chapter 10. Proclamation

1. Robert E. Lee to Jefferson Davis, September 3, 1861, *The War of the Rebellion: Official Records of the Union and Confederate Armies* (hereinafter cited as *OR*), Series 1, Vol. 19, Part 2, 590.
2. Almira Hancock, *Reminiscences of Winfield Scott Hancock*, 69–70.
3. *OR*, Series 1, Vol. 19, Part 2, 596.
4. Douglas Southall Freeman, *Lee's Lieutenants: A Study in Command—Abridged in One Volume by Stephen W. Sears*, 337–38.
5. Benjamin H. Trask, *9th Virginia Infantry*, 17.
6. *OR*, Series 1, Vol. 19, Part I, 141.
7. "Casualties of Battle at Antietam," www.nps.gov; Wayne E. Motts, *"Trust in God and Fear Nothing": Gen. Lewis A. Armistead, CSA*, 40.
8. Robert K. Krick, "It Appeared as though Mutual Extermination Would Put a Stop to the Awful Carnage: Confederates in Sharpsburg's Bloody Lane," 255n39.
9. Motts, *"Trust in God and Fear Nothing,"* 40.
10. *OR*, Series 1, Vol. 19, Part 1, 402, 406; Marion V. Armstrong Jr., *Unfurl Those Colors! McClellan, Sumner & The Second Army Corps in the Antietam Campaign*, 260–61.
11. *OR*, Series 1, Vol. 19, Part 1, 406–7; Armstrong, *Unfurl Those Colors!*, 261.
12. *OR*, Series 1, Vol. 19, Part 1, 407.
13. John Gordon, *Reminiscences of the Civil War*, 84.
14. Stephen W. Sears, *Landscape Turned Red*, 236, 241–43.
15. Ibid., 243, 251.
16. *OR*, Series 1, Vol. 19, Part 1, 60, 279; Armstrong, *Unfurl Those Colors!*, 246–47. Richardson's wound was mortal, and he would die six weeks later.
17. *OR*, Series 1, Vol. 19, Part 2, 316, "Special Orders—In the Field, September 17, 1862"; Sears, *Landscape Turned Red*, 255, 257.
18. David M. Jordan, *Winfield Scott Hancock: A Soldier's Life*, 54.
19. Glenn Tucker, *Hancock the Superb*, 93.
20. Francis Amasa Walker, *General Hancock*, 51–52.
21. Sears, *Landscape Turned Red*, 257.
22. *OR*, Series 1, Vol. 19, Part 1, 60, 279–80.
23. "Preliminary Emancipation Proclamation, 1862," www.archives.gov.
24. Carol Reardon and Tom Vossler, *A Field Guide to Antietam: Experiencing the Battlefield through Its History, Places and People*, 308.
25. Trask, *9th Virginia Infantry*, 11.

26. Robert K. Krick, "Armistead and Garnett: The Parallel Lives of Two Virginia Soldiers," in *The Third Day at Gettysburg & Beyond*, 118.
27. Sears, *Landscape Turned Red*, 323–25.
28. *OR*, Series 1, Vol. 19, Part 2, 90–93; Jordan, *Winfield Scott Hancock*, 55.
29. *OR*, Series 1, Vol. 19, Part 2, 545, 549, 551; Robert Underwood Johnson and Clarence Clough Buel, eds., *Battles and Leaders of the Civil War*, Vol. 3, 103–4. Lincoln's order was dated November 5 from the Executive Mansion and became General Orders No. 182.
30. *OR*, Series 1, Vol. 19, Part 2, 552–54 (this is Burnside's first report as army commander, dated November 7 and addressed to General G. W. Cullum, chief of staff in Washington, D.C.); Jordan, *Winfield Scott Hancock*, 59.
31. Francis B. Heitman, *Historical Register and Dictionary of the U.S. Army, from Its Organization, September 29, 1789 to March 2, 1903*, Vol. 1, 496–97.
32. *OR*, Series 1, Part 2, 551.
33. Sears, *The Landscape Turned Red*, 341–42.
34. *OR*, Series 1, Part 2, 552.
35. Darius N. Couch, "Sumner's 'Right Grand Division,'" in Johnson and Buel, eds., *Battles and Leaders of the Civil War*, Vol. 3, 107.
36. "Battle of Fredericksburg History," www.nps.gov.
37. Couch, "Sumner's Right Grand Division,'" 107–8.
38. *OR*, Series 1, Vol. 21, 222. These orders came directly from Sumner, and Couch said he received them at 8:15 a.m. on December 13.
39. Couch, "Sumner's 'Right Grand Division,'" 11; *OR*, Series 1 Vol. 21, 227.
40. Jordan, *Winfield Scott Hancock*, 63. Brooke's regiment was the Fifty-Third Pennsylvania.
41. Walker, *General Hancock*, 66; Tucker, *Hancock the Superb*, 109.
42. *OR*, Series 1, Vol. 21, 243.
43. Ibid., 233.
44. Ira Holcombe, *History of the First Regiment Minnesota Volunteer Infantry, 1861–1864*, 255–56.
45. *OR*, Series 1, Vol. 21, 130, 142, 224, 228. The official army figure for Hancock's division was slightly higher at 2,032.
46. Tucker, *Hancock the Superb*, 114.
47. Couch, "Sumner's 'Right Grand Division,'" 118–19; Jordan, *Winfield Scott Hancock*, 65. The "mud march" was Burnside's failed attempt to renew the offensive and save his reputation on January 20–21; it got bogged down in the rain and mud.
48. Compiled Service Records for John Grammer, National Archives, also cited in Krick, "Armistead and Garnett," 119.
49. Edward R. Crews and Timothy A. Parrish, *14th Virginia Infantry*, 47, 143; Kathy Georg Harrison and John W. Busey, *Nothing but Glory: Pickett's Division at Gettysburg*, 6.
50. "Battle of Chancellorsville" summary, www.battlefields.org; "Battle of Chancellorsville," www.nps.gov.
51. *OR*, Series 1, Vol. 25, Part 1, 171. This was General Orders No. 47.

52. Couch, "The Chancellorsville Campaign," *Battles and Leaders of the Civil War*, Vol. 3. 157.

53. *OR*, Series 1, Vol. 25, Part 1, 797.

54. Ibid., 311.

55. Report, Joint Committee on the Conduct of the War, 38th Congress, 2nd session, 66, cited in Jordan, *Winfield Scott Hancock*, 70.

56. "Battle of Chancellorsville," www.nps.gov.

57. Walker, *General Hancock*, 83.

58. *OR*, Series 1, Vol. 25, Part 1, 307–8, 314.

59. Ibid., 316. Including two batteries of artillery that were with him, Hancock reported 77 killed, 444 wounded, and 601 missing, for a total of 1,122.

60. Winfield S. Hancock to Almira Hancock, May 4, 1863, in Hancock, *Reminiscences of Winfield Scott Hancock*, 93–94.

61. Crews and Parrish, *14th Virginia Infantry*, 22–24.

Chapter 11. To Gettysburg

1. *The War of the Rebellion: Official Records of the Union and Confederate Armies* (hereinafter cited as *OR*), Series 1, Vol. 27, Part 2, 273.

2. Wayne E. Motts, *"Trust in God and Fear Nothing": Gen. Lewis A. Armistead, CSA*, 41; Kathy Georg Harrison and John W. Busey, *Nothing but Glory: Pickett's Division at Gettysburg*, 1–2.

3. James A. Hessler and Wayne E. Motts, *Pickett's Charge at Gettysburg: A Guide to the Most Famous Attack in American History*, 46, 51–52; Harrison and Busey, *Nothing but Glory*, 2. Estimates for the strength of Pickett's infantry on July 3 range from 4,481 to 5,820.

4. Pickett's division, which was formed in the fall of 1862 after the Battle of Antietam, was only lightly engaged at Fredericksburg and missed Chancellorsville altogether. Gettysburg would be its first significant battle as a unit.

5. G. Howard Gregory, *38th Virginia Infantry*, 35.

6. Edward R. Crews and Timothy A. Parrish, *14th Virginia Infantry*, 35–36, 136. The writer, Private William Daniel Ross of Company C, was killed in action during Pickett's Charge.

7. Charles W. Sublett, *57th Virginia Infantry*, 24.

8. Harrison and Busey, *Nothing but Glory*, 3.

9. Ibid.; Crews and Parrish, *14th Virginia Infantry*, 35–36; Gregory, *38th Virginia Infantry*, 36.

10. Benjamin Farinholt to Leila Farinholt, July 1, 1863, in G. Howard Gregory, *53rd Virginia Infantry and 5th Battalion Virginia Infantry*, 49–50.

11. Almira Hancock, *Reminiscences of Winfield Scott Hancock*, 94.

12. Edwin B. Coddington, *The Gettysburg Campaign: A Study in Command*, 36; Stephen W. Sears, *Gettysburg*, 19.

13. Coddington, *The Gettysburg Campaign*, 37; Sears, *Gettysburg*, 24–26.

14. Hancock, *Reminiscences of Winfield Scott Hancock*, 95.

15. Coddington, *The Gettysburg Campaign*, 611n39.

16. Walter H. Hebert, *Fighting Joe Hooker*, ix.
17. *OR*, Series 1, Vol. 27, Part 3, 55, 68. In General Orders No. 1 issued by the Department of the Susquehanna on June 11, it was stated, "To prevent serious raids by the enemy, it is deemed necessary to call upon the citizens of Pennsylvania to furnish promptly all the men necessary to organize an army corps of volunteer infantry, artillery and cavalry." Couch did funnel information to army headquarters from Pennsylvania.
18. Ibid., General Orders No. 186, 299. Although he effectively took over the Second Corps on June 10, the official order was not filed until June 24: "Maj. Gen. W.S. Hancock, U.S. Volunteers, is, by direction of the President, assigned to command of the Second Army Corps, in place of Maj. Gen. D.N. Couch, transferred to another command."
19. Abraham Lincoln to Joseph Hooker, June 10, 1863, *OR*, Series 1, Vol. 27, Part 1, 35.
20. *OR*, Series 1, Vol. 27, Part 3, 147.
21. C. H. Morgan, "Narrative of the Operations of the Second Army Corps from the Time General Hancock Assumed Command, June 9, 1863, until the Close of Battle at Gettysburg," appendix A in Almira Hancock, *Reminiscences of Winfield Scott Hancock*, 183; David M. Jordan, *Winfield Scott Hancock: A Soldier's Life*, 77.
22. *OR*, Series 1, Vol. 27, Part 2, 692–93.
23. Jordan, *Winfield Scott Hancock*, 78. Hays replaced William French, who was reassigned. George Willard took over Hays's brigade.
24. *OR*, Series 1, Vol. 27, Part 1, 59–60.
25. Coddington, *The Gettysburg Campaign*, 130–31; Jordan, *Winfield Scott Hancock*, 79.
26. H. W. Halleck to George G. Meade, June 27, 1863, *OR*, Series 1, Vol. 27, Part 1, 61.
27. George G. Meade to H. W. Halleck, June 28, 1863, *OR*, Series 1, Vol. 27, Part 1, 61.
28. Josiah Marshall Favill, *The Diary of a Young Officer*, 242. Favill was in Zook's brigade in the Second Corps.
29. *OR*, Series 1, Vol. 27, Part 1, 61.
30. Coddington, *The Gettysburg Campaign*, 220, 224–25.
31. *OR*, Series 1, Vol. 27, Part 1, 143.
32. John Gibbon, *At Gettysburg and Elsewhere: The Civil War Memoir of John Gibbon*, 100.
33. *OR*, Series 1, Vol. 27, Part 1, 144.
34. *OR*, Series 1, Vol. 27, Part 3, 396. Hancock said the delay was caused "by the order having been left with an irresponsible person at these headquarters, a clerk, who failed to deliver it . . . the man in question has already been brought to punishment" (395–96).
35. Josiah Marshall Favill, *The Diary of a Young Officer, Serving with the Armies of the United States during the War of Rebellion* 241; Jordan, *Winfield Scott Hancock*, 79.
36. Gibbon, *At Gettysburg and Elsewhere*, 101.
37. Francis Amasa Walker, *General Hancock*, 99–100.
38. Hancock testimony, March 22, 1864, *Report on the Joint Committee on the Conduct of the War*, Vol. 1, 403–4; see also 353–54 ("Circular," July 1, 1863, from AAG Seth Williams, "by command of Major General Meade"). Two letters from Meade to Halleck, written on the morning of July 1, are also revealing (485–86), as is Meade's

own testimony before the committee (347–48). The Joint Committee report is hereinafter cited as *JCCW*.

39. Hancock testimony, *JCCW*, 404.

40. These were the brigades under Solomon Meredith (Iron Brigade) and Lysnder Cutler, both from James Wadsworth's division of the First Corps.

41. *OR*, Series 1, Vol. 27, Part 3, 461.

42. Ibid.

43. Hancock testimony, *JCCW*, 404. Hancock stated, "I was not the senior of either General Howard, of the 11th corps, or General Sickles, of the 3rd corps. My commission bore date on the same day with theirs; but my prior commission they both ranked me"; Paul E. Bretzger, *Observing Hancock at Gettysburg: The General's Leadership through Eyewitness Accounts*, 35.

44. *OR*, Series 1, Vol. 27, Part 1, 61.

45. George Meade (Jr.) statement, in Military Service Institution, *Letters and Addresses Contributed at a General Meeting of the Military Service Institution Held at Governor's Island, N.Y., February 25, 1886, in Memory of Winfield Scott Hancock*, 33.

46. C. H. Morgan to John Bachelder, in John Bachelder, *The Bachelder Papers: Gettysburg in Their Own Words*, Vol. 3, 1350.

47. Ibid.

48. Bretzger, *Observing Hancock at Gettysburg*, 37. Bretzger's book is a valuable resource for anyone researching Hancock and his actions at the battle.

49. Winfield Scott Hancock, "Reply to General Howard," *The Galaxy*, Vol. 22, 822.

50. Oliver Otis Howard, "Campaign and Battle of Gettysburg, June and July 1863," *The Atlantic Monthly*, Vol. 38, 59.

51. E. P. Halstead, "Incidents of the First Day at Gettysburg," in Robert Underwood Johnson and Clarence Clough Buel, eds., *Battles and Leaders of the Civil War*, Vol. 3, 285.

52. Hancock, "Reply to General Howard," 822–23.

53. Howard, "Campaign and Battle of Gettysburg, June and July 1863," 58.

54. *OR*, Series 1, Vol. 27, Part 1, 701–2; Coddington, *The Gettysburg Campaign*, 279. Howard placed his Second Division under Adolph von Steinwehr as a reserve on Cemetery Hill—consisting of two brigades under Charles Coster and Orland Smith. But Coster's brigade was sent forward to cover the Eleventh Corps retreat, so only Smith remained to hold the hill.

55. Halstead, "Incidents of the First Day at Gettysburg," 285.

56. *OR*, Series 1, Vol. 27, Part 1, 368; Bretzger, *Observing Hancock at Gettysburg*, 54–55.

57. *OR*, Series 1, Vol. 27, Part 1, 925, 927.

58. Bretzger, *Observing Hancock at Gettysburg*, 40.

59. G. K. Warren testimony, March 9, 1864, *JCCW*, 376.

60. Glenn Tucker, *Hancock the Superb*, 134.

61. Bretzger, *Observing Hancock at Gettysburg*, 39.

62. Halstead, "Incidents of the First Day at Gettysburg," 285. Halstead quoted Hancock as saying, "I select this as the battlefield."

63. Morgan, "Narrative," in Hancock, *Reminiscences of Winfield Scott Hancock*, 191.
64. *OR*, Series 1, Vol. 27, Part 1, 366.
65. George Meade testimony, March 5, 1864, *JCCW*, Vol. 1, 330.
66. George Meade testimony, March 11, 1864, *JCCW*, Vol. 1, 348.
67. Bretzger, *Observing Hancock at Gettysburg*, 61.
68. *OR*, Series 1, Vol. 27, Part 3, 466.
69. *OR*, Series 1, Vol. 27, Part 1, 72.
70. Ibid., 369.
71. Ibid., 115.
72. Morgan, "Narrative," in Hancock, *Reminiscences of Winfield Scott Hancock*, 191, 194.

Chapter 12. Second Day

1. *The War of the Rebellion: Official Records of the Union and Confederate Armies* (herein-after cited as *OR*), Series 1, Vol. 27, Part 2, 308.
2. Hancock testimony, March 22, 1864, *Report on the Joint Committee on the Conduct of the War*, Vol. 1, 406; John Gibbon, *At Gettysburg and Elsewhere: The Civil War Memoir of John Gibbon*, 104. The Weikert House is at the intersection of modern-day Hancock Avenue and United States Avenue.
3. Paul E. Bretzger, *Observing Hancock at Gettysburg: The General's Leadership through Eyewitness Accounts*, 73.
4. John L. Brady to John Bachelder, May 24, 1886, in John Bachelder, *The Bachelder Papers: Gettysburg in Their Own Words*, Vol. 3, 1389.
5. Harry W. Pfanz, *Gettysburg: The Second Day*, 46–47, 91–92, 125; Edwin B. Coddington, *The Gettysburg Campaign: A Study in Command*, 343–51. This incident with Sickles is covered in virtually every book about the battle. Sickles had murdered his wife's lover in Washington, D.C., but was acquitted because it was a crime of passion, often described as "temporary insanity." He thought that heroism in the Civil War would give him a chance to revive his fading career.
6. Gibbon, *At Gettysburg and Elsewhere*, 106.
7. Frank Aretas Haskell, *The Battle of Gettysburg*, 28.
8. Francis Amasa Walker, *General Hancock*, 125. Gibbon, in *At Gettysburg and Elsewhere*, 106, said they were watching from a "hill occupied by the right of my division."
9. Hancock testimony, March 24, 1864, *Report on the Joint Committee on the Conduct of the War*, Vol. 1, 406.
10. Bretzger, *Observing Hancock at Gettysburg*, 94–96. St. Clair A. Mulholland, whom Bretzger quoted, was colonel of the 116th Pennsylvania in the Irish Brigade.
11. Charles A. Hale, "With Colonel Cross," vii, Brooke Papers, cited in Pfanz, *Gettysburg*, 269.
12. Bretzger, *Observing Hancock at Gettysburg*, 96–98; Pfanz, *Gettysburg*, 270–86; Allen C. Guelzo, *Gettysburg: The Last Invasion*, 292–95.
13. Pfanz, *Gettysburg*, 273.
14. *OR*, Series 1, Vol. 27, Part 1, 370. The regiments were the Fifteenth Massachusetts, Eighty-Second New York, Nineteenth Massachusetts, and Forty-Second New York.

15. Ibid., 370. Sickles was hit by an artillery shell near the Trostle farm. He had his leg amputated but survived the wound to return to politics and live a robust, controversial life until 1914.
16. Ibid.
17. Gibbon, *At Gettysburg and Elsewhere*, 107.
18. Guelzo, *Gettysburg*, 323–24.
19. Guelzo, *Gettysburg*, 324; Bretzger, *Observing Hancock at Gettysburg*, 110–12.
20. William Lochren, "Narrative of the First Regiment," *Minnesota in the Civil and Indian Wars, 1861–1865*, 35, cited in Bretzger, *Observing Hancock at Gettysburg*, 114.
21. Walker, *General Hancock*, 128.
22. Bretzger, *Observing Hancock at Gettysburg*, 114.
23. Inscription on the First Minnesota monument at Gettysburg National Military Park.
24. *OR*, Series 1, Vol. 27, Part 1, 371.
25. Walter Harrison, *Pickett's Men: A Fragment of War History*, 87. Harrison served on Pickett's staff.
26. Richard Rollins, ed., *Pickett's Charge: Eyewitness Accounts*, 54. The quote is from the autobiography of Randolph Shotwell of the Eighth Virginia Infantry in Garnett's brigade.
27. Ibid., 54; G. Howard Gregory, *53rd Virginia Infantry and 5th Battalion Virginia Infantry*, 51.
28. Shotwell's account, July 2, 1863, from Rollins, *Pickett's Charge*, 53.
29. Harrison, *Pickett's Men*, 88.
30. Shotwell's account, July 2, 1863, from Rollins, *Pickett's Charge: Eyewitness Accounts*, 54.
31. James F. Crocker, "My Personal Experiences in Taking Up Arms," *Southern Historical Society Papers*, Vol. 33, reprinted in Rollins, *Pickett's Charge*, 3.
32. Gibbon, *At Gettysburg and Elsewhere*, 138; *OR*, Series 1, Vol. 27, Part 1, 457.
33. Bretzger, *Observing Hancock at Gettysburg*, 136.
34. Ibid., 137.
35. Guelzo, *Gettysburg*, 343.
36. *OR*, Series 1, Vol. 27, Part 1, 457.
37. Gibbon, *At Gettysburg and Elsewhere*, 109.
38. "Minutes of Council, July 2, 1863," *OR*, Series 1, Vol. 27, Part 1, 73.
39. Gibbon, *At Gettysburg and Elsewhere*, 110.
40. "Minutes of Council, July 2, 1863," *OR*, Series 1, Vol. 27, Part 1, 73. The officers, in order that their opinions were recorded, were Gibbon, Second Corps; Williams, Twelfth Corps; David Birney, Third Corps; George Sykes, Fifth Corps; John Newton, First Corps; Howard, Eleventh Corps; Hancock, Second Corps; John Sedgwick, Sixth Corps; and Henry Slocum, Twelfth Corps. Others in attendance were Meade, Warren, and Butterfield.
41. Guelzo, *Gettysburg*, 356. In the "Minutes of Council" in the *Official Records*, a memorandum notes that Hancock was "puzzled about the practicability of retiring; thinks by holding on [illegible] to mass forces and attack."
42. David M. Jordan, *Winfield Scott Hancock: A Soldier's Life*, 94.

43. Gibbon, *At Gettysburg and Elsewhere*, 114. The three men sleeping in the ambulance were Hancock, Gibbon, and John Newton.

Chapter 13. The Charge

1. Walter Harrison, *Pickett's Men: A Fragment of War History*, 90–91; Kathy Georg Harrison and John W. Busey, *Nothing but Glory: Pickett's Division at Gettysburg*, 13, 15, 18.
2. Harrison, *Pickett's Men*, 92.
3. James A. Hessler and Wayne E. Motts, *Pickett's Charge at Gettysburg: A Guide to the Most Famous Attack in American History*, 73, 119.
4. Ibid., 12, 117, 169.
5. John H. Lewis, *A Rebel in Pickett's Charge at Gettysburg*, 50.
6. Paul E. Bretzger, *Observing Hancock at Gettysburg: The General's Leadership through Eyewitness Accounts*, 147.
7. John Gibbon, *At Gettysburg and Elsewhere: The Civil War Memoir of John Gibbon*, 114.
8. *The War of the Rebellion: Official Records of the Union and Confederate Armies* (hereinafter cited as *OR*), Series 1, Vol. 27, Part 1, 372.
9. Gibbon, *At Gettysburg and Elsewhere*, 115.
10. Francis Amasa Walker, *History of The Second Army Corps in the Army of the Potomac*, 292.
11. Henry J. Hunt, "The Third Day at Gettysburg," *Battles and Leaders*, Vol. 3, 372.
12. Eric A. Campbell, "A Brief History and Analysis of the Hunt-Hancock Controversy," www.npshistory.com, 251–54; Bretzger, *Observing Hancock at Gettysburg*, 156.
13. *OR*, Series 1, Vol. 27, Part 1, 888.
14. Patrick Hart to John Bachelder, February 23, 1891, in John Bachelder, *The Bachelder Papers: Gettysburg in Their Own Words*, 1798. Hart never said whether Hancock wrote the order. Apparently, he did not.
15. Campbell, "A Brief History and Analysis of the Hunt-Hancock Controversy," www.npshistory.com, 254–55.
16. Glenn Tucker, *Hancock the Superb*, 150–51. In the movie *Gettysburg*, the man playing the subordinate is documentarian Ken Burns.
17. Statement of Abner Doubleday, in Military Service Institution, *Letters and Addresses Contributed at a General Meeting of the Military Service Institution Held at Governor's Island, N.Y., February 25, 1886, in Memory of Winfield Scott Hancock*, 21.
18. Henry J. Hunt to John Bachelder, January 6, 1866, in Bachelder, *The Bachelder Papers*, 229; *OR*, Series 1, Vol. 27, 229. Hunt's claim about slackening his fire to "induce the enemy to believe he had silenced us" does not appear in his official battle report. Written in September 1863, barely two months after the Battle of Gettysburg, his report said the decision was made because "ammunition was running low," a number of caissons and limbers had exploded, and it was deemed "unsafe" to bring up more. The claim about deceiving the enemy appeared in a letter Hunt wrote to John Bachelder in January 1866, almost a year after the end of the war. Several other commanders, including Meade, claimed credit for advising the cease-fire. See Hessler and Motts, *Pickett's Charge*, 170.

19. Robert Tyler Jones, "Gen. L.A. Armistead and R. Tyler Jones," *Confederate Veteran*, Vol. II, 271.

20. "Grandson of President Tyler: His Death in Washington amid Destitution and Want," *The (New Orleans) Daily Picayune*, May 20, 1895. Jones's obituary noted that, at the time, he had been the only male child ever born in the White House. Regarding his son, Jones misspelled the first name as "Louis."

21. James E. Poindexter, "Gen. Lewis Addison Armistead," *Confederate Veteran*, Vol. XXII, 503; James T. Carter, "Flag of the Fifth-Third Va. Regiment," *Confederate Veteran*, Vol. X, 263; Earl J. Hess, *Pickett's Charge—The Final Attack at Gettysburg*, 169.

22. Rhea Kuykendall, "Surgeons of the Confederacy," *Confederate Veteran*, Vol. XXXIV, 209.

23. Jeffrey D. Wert, *Gettysburg: Day Three*, 191.

24. Hessler and Motts, *Pickett's Charge*, 130.

25. Poindexter, "Gen. Lewis Addison Armistead," 503. Poindexter served in the Thirty-Eighth Virginia.

26. Lewis, *A Rebel in Pickett's Charge at Gettysburg*, 51.

27. B. L. Farinholt, "Battle of Gettysburg—Johnson's Island," *Confederate Veteran*, Vol. V, 468.

28. Hess, *Pickett's Charge*, 173–77.

29. J. W. Whitehead, "Company I, 53rd Va. Regiment, Armistead's Brigade, Pickett's Division in the Battle of Gettysburg," in *War Recollections of the Confederate Veterans of Pittsylvania County Virginia, 1861–1865*.

30. Hess, *Pickett's Charge*, 172.

31. Hess, *Pickett's Charge*, 223.

32. Hessler and Motts, *Pickett's Charge*, 137.

33. James T. Carter, "Flag of the Fifty-Third Va. Regiment," *Confederate Veteran*, Vol. X, 263.

34. Ibid.

35. Haskell's account quoted in Richard Rollins, ed., *Pickett's Charge: Eyewitness Accounts*, 329.

36. *OR*, Series 1, Vol. 27, 350.

37. For more details of this relatively minor controversy, see Hess, *Pickett's Charge*, 237–38, and Bretzger, *Observing Hancock at Gettysburg*, 173, 179–81.

38. There are various similar versions of this Deveraux quote. See Arthur F. Devereaux to John Bachelder, in Bachelder, *The Bachelder Papers*, Vol. 3, 1609; Hess, *Pickett's Charge*, 275; and Stephen W. Sears, *Gettysburg*, 437.

39. Jones, "Gen. L.A. Armistead and R. Tyler Jones," 271. Jones and Armstead were distant cousins. For the Tyler–Armistead family lineage, see Virginia Armistead Garber, *The Armistead Family 1635–1910*, 231.

40. Harrison and Busey, *Nothing but Glory*, 65–66, 78–79; Hess, *Pickett's Charge*, 232, 261; Hessler and Motts, *Pickett's Charge*, 216. Some accounts said there were three guns at the wall.

41. T. C. Holland, "What Did We Fight For?" *Confederate Veteran*, Vol. XXXI, 423; Harrison and Busey, *Nothing but Glory*, 313. Both Holland and Lee served in the Twenty-Eighth Virginia in Garnett's brigade.
42. Wyatt Whitehead's account, in Rollins, *Pickett's Charge*, 183.
43. Hess, *Pickett's Charge*, 261.
44. "Letter of Brig. Gen. Alexander S. Webb to His Wife," July 6, 1863, in Bachelder, *The Bachelder Papers*, Vol. 1, 19. The Philadelphia Brigade was made up of the Sixty-Ninth, Seventy-First, Seventy-Second, and 106th Pennsylvania regiments.
45. Harrison and Busey, *Nothing but Glory*, 113.
46. "Bachelder Material," in Bachelder, *The Bachelder Papers*, Vol. 3, Appendix D, 1989; Hessler and Motts, *Pickett's Charge*, 217.
47. Hess, *Pickett's Charge*, 263.
48. Harrison and Busey, *Nothing but Glory*, 107.
49. Frederick Fuger's testimony before the Supreme Court of Pennsylvania, found in Rollins, *Pickett's Charge*, 338.
50. Milton Harding, "With Armistead When He Fell," *Confederate Veteran*, Vol. XIX, 371.
51. D. B. Easley, "With Armistead When He Was Killed," *Confederate Veteran*, Vol. XX, 379.
52. "Letter of Anthony McDermott," June 2, 1886, in Bachelder, *The Bachelder Papers*, Vol. 3, 1411–13. In another letter written three years later, McDermott said Armistead fell "near the crest" (*The Bachelder Papers*, Vol. 3, 1647).
53. "Letter of Brig. Gen. Alexander S. Webb to His Wife," July 6, 1863, in Bachelder, *The Bachelder Papers*, Vol. 1, 18.
54. "Letter of Anthony McDermott," June 2, 1886, in Bachelder, *The Bachelder Papers*, Vol. 3, 1411.
55. Charles H. Banes, *History of the Philadelphia Brigade*, 192.
56. "Testimony of Charles H. Banes," April 24, 1890, in Bachelder, *The Bachelder Papers*, Vol. 3, 1705.
57. Banes, *History of the Philadelphia Brigade*, 192. Banes added that "an order was given to take [Armistead] to an ambulance, and when his revolver was removed from his belt, it was seen that he had obeyed his own command, 'to give the cold steel,' as no shot had been fired from it."
58. "Testimony of Charles H. Banes," April 24, 1890, in Bachelder, *The Bachelder Papers*, Vol. 3, 1705.
59. "Letter of Capt. John C. Brown," July 1, 1887, in Bachelder, *The Bachelder Papers*, Vol. 3, 1495. Brown, who served in the Twentieth Indiana at Gettysburg, said he assisted a wounded Rebel officer who identified himself as a Mason and often wondered whether it was Armistead; that seems unlikely, however.
60. Sheldon A. Munn, *Freemasons at Gettysburg*, 23, 30–102. It is estimated that Masons made up about 11 percent of the Union and Confederate armies. In addition to Armistead, Hancock, and Bingham, other Masons at Gettysburg included Union officers Daniel Butterfield, David Birney, Joshua Chamberlain, Edward

Cross, John Geary, Solomon Meredith, Thomas Smyth, and George Stannard and Confederate officers George "Tige" Anderson, William Barksdale, John Gordon, Henry Heth, Alfred Iverson, James Kemper, Joseph Kershaw, and George Pickett. Drew B. Easley, who crossed the wall with Armistead, said he "refused to bayonet several Yankees who displayed the 'Masonic mark of distress.'"

61. Henry H. Bingham to Winfield S. Hancock, January 5, 1869, in Bachelder, *The Bachelder Papers*, Vol. 1, 351–52. It should be noted that in the movie *Gettysburg*, the character who attends to Armistead is incorrectly portrayed as Joshua Chamberlain's brother (a cinematic tactic to move the story along). The movie also gives the impression that Armistead was informed at once of Hancock's wounding, which is not correct. Bingham was unaware at this time of Hancock's fate.

62. For example, on July 2, Union soldiers had carried wounded Confederate General William Barksdale to a house behind the Union lines.

63. Lewis A. Armistead to Samuel Cooper, December 2, 1861, Compiled Service Records for W. Keith Armistead, Letters Received by the Adjutant and Inspector General's Office, National Archives.

64. Henry H. Bingham to Winfield S. Hancock, January 5, 1869, in Bachelder, *The Bachelder Papers*, Vol. 1, 351.

65. Ibid., 352. Hancock was at a temporary hospital in the woods.

66. Wayne E. Motts, *"Trust in God and Fear Nothing": Gen. Lewis A. Armistead, CSA*, 47; Francis B. Heitman, *Historical Register and Dictionary of the United States Army, from Its Organization, September 29, 1789 to March 2, 1903*, Vol. 1, 746; www.findagrave.com for Cornelia Stanly Armistead Newton and Major Washington Irving Newton. Cornelia and her husband lived in Philadelphia at the time of the battle. Major Newton retired from active duty in October 1861, six months after the start of the Civil War. According to biographer Motts, the items have never been found.

Chapter 14. "I Found That He Had Died"

1. Gregory A. Coco, *A Vast Sea of Misery: A History and Guide to the Union and Confederate Field Hospitals at Gettysburg, July 1–November 20 1863*. The description was from the New York General Agent of the Sanitary Commission.

2. Ibid., 105, taken from an account by Justus Silliman of the Seventeenth Connecticut.

3. Gregory A. Coco, *A Strange and Blighted Land: Gettysburg: The Aftermath of a Battle*, 208.

4. Dr. D. G. Brinton, "From Chancellorsville to Gettysburg: A Doctor's Diary," https://journals.psu.edu, 313.

5. Coco, *A Vast Sea of Misery*, 105; Coco, *A Strange and Blighted Land*, 208.

6. John Irvin bio card, "Stand in Their Footsteps," Gettysburg Foundation, Spangler Farm historic site.

7. "Letter of Daniel G. Brinton," March 22, 1869, in John Bachelder, *The Bachelder Papers*, Vol. I, 358–59.

8. "The Death of General Armistead," *Gettysburg Star and Sentinel*, July 11, 1893, 3.

9. T. C. Holland, "With Armistead at Gettysburg," *Confederate Veteran*, Vol. XXIX, 62.

10. "The Journey of the Wounded from Cemetery Ridge to the Spangler Farm," www .youtube.com, July 3, 2014, with Rangers Chris Gwynn and Dan Welch, Gettysburg National Military Park.

11. "The Death of General Armistead," 3.

12. Wayne E. Motts, *"Trust in God and Fear Nothing": Gen. Lewis A. Armistead, CSA*, 46. The soldier was W. H. Moore of the Ninety-Seventh New York.

13. "The Death of General Armistead," 3.

14. Holland, "With Armistead at Gettysburg," 62.

15. "Letter of Daniel G. Brinton," 358–59.

16. James A. Hessler and Wayne E. Motts, *Pickett's Charge at Gettysburg: A Guide to the Most Famous Attack in American History*, 293n98.

17. James F. Crocker, *Gettysburg—Pickett's Charge and Other War Addresses*, "Prison Reminiscences," 53–54; William A. Frassanito, *Early Photography at Gettysburg*, 377–78; Natalie Sherif, "James Crocker: A Pennsylvania College Graduate Returns to Gettysburg," https://gettysburgcompiler.org. Pennsylvania College later became Gettysburg College.

18. A. J. Rider to John Bachelder, October 2, 1885, Gettysburg National Military Park, Armistead file; Frassanito, *Early Photography at Gettysburg*, 365; Coco, *A Strange and Blighted Land*, 132.

19. Frassanito, *Early Photography at Gettysburg*, 365; Coco, *A Strange and Blighted Land*, 130–32; Robert K. Krick, "Armistead and Garnett: The Parallel Lives of Two Virginia Soldiers," in *The Third Day at Gettysburg & Beyond*, 123.

20. Sheldon A. Munn, *Freemasons at Gettysburg*, 73–74; Coco, *A Strange and Blighted Land*, 99–100.

21. C. Hughes Armistead to J. W. C. O'Neal, October 3, 1863, Gettysburg National Military Park, Armistead file, "Copy of correspondence of C.H. Armistead with J. W. C. O'Neal, referring to removing the remains of General Lewis Armistead, who was killed at Gettysburg." Hughes made it clear that he was skeptical of the need to embalm the remains. "I would have greatly preferred his having done nothing to them, and his embalming process I think is a pretense."

22. C. Hughes Armistead to J. W. C. O'Neal, October 15, 1863, Gettysburg National Military Park, Armistead file.

23. C. Hughes Armistead to J. W. C. O'Neal, October 27, 1863, Gettysburg National Military Park, Armistead file.

24. Scott Sumpter Sheads, *Guardian of the Star-Spangled Banner: Lt. Colonel George Armistead and the Fort McHenry Flag*, 24–29; Frederick N. Rasmussen, "Armistead's Journey to Baltimore," *Baltimore Sun*, July 4, 2013; Motts, *"Trust in God and Fear Nothing,"* 48; Kathy Georg Harrison and John W. Busey, *Nothing but Glory: Pickett's Division at Gettysburg*, 115; Krick, "Armistead and Garnett," 123. The Hughes family connection stems from George Armistead's marriage to Louisa Hughes in Baltimore in 1810. They named their only son after Louisa's brother, Christopher Hughes Jr., who helped negotiate the end of the War of 1812.

25. Keith's exact whereabouts during the charge are unknown, but there is no published account of his moving forward with his father's troops, and Lewis likely would

have wanted his only child to stay back. Hessler and Motts, in *Pickett's Charge at Gettysburg*, tell the story of a fellow Confederate soldier who saw both Armisteads on horseback together before the attack (123). "God bless you, Keith!" the soldier said. But we know that when Lewis moved forward, it was on foot.

26. Hessler and Motts, *Pickett's Charge at Gettysburg*, 255–56. Estimates range from as low as 42.5 percent to more than 50 percent.

27. "Report of General Robert E. Lee, Headquarters Army of Northern Virginia, near Gettysburg, PA, July 4, 1863," www.civil-war.net/searchofficialrecords.

28. Compiled Service Records for W. Keith Armistead, National Archives.

29. R. E. Lee to Mrs. E. M. Love, December 23, 1863, found in Cazenove Gardner Lee Jr., *Lee Chronicle: Studies of the Early Generations of the Lees of Virginia*, 306.

30. Compiled Service Records for W. Keith Armistead, National Archives; Michael P. Musick, *6th Virginia Cavalry*, 94.

31. Ibid.; "I'm a Good Old Rebel: Ocean State Confederates," http://smallstatebighistory.com, 3.

32. www.findagrave.com for W. Keith Armistead (born 1844).

33. Musick, *6th Virginia Cavalry*, 94.

34. Compiled Service Records for Franck S. Armistead, National Archives (a one-page summation of Franck's Civil War career is included in the "Compiled Service Records of Confederate General and Staff Officers"; his final service appears to have been in North Carolina, where he was assigned in 1864 to command the "Junior Reserves").

35. Compiled Service Records for Walker K. Armistead Jr., Franck S. Armistead, and Bowles E. Armistead, National Archives; Musick, *6th Virginia Cavalry*, 94.

36. Louise Pecquet du Bellet, *Some Prominent Virginia Families*, Vol. I, Chapter VII, 251.

37. www.findagrave.com for Franck S. Armistead and Bowles E. Armistead; Musick, *6th Virginia Cavalry*, 94.

38. "Minute Book of the Gettysburg Battlefield Memorial Association, 1874–1895," Gettysburg National Military Park, Armistead file, 151, 159; John Mitchell Vanderslice, *Gettysburg: A History of the Battle-field Memorial Association, with an Account of the Battle, Giving Movements, Positions, and Losses of the Commands Engaged*, 232.

39. Carol Reardon, *Pickett's Charge in History and Memory*, 92. Reardon details the reunion/monument issue (91–98).

40. The original purpose of the event was to place and dedicate monuments to the Sixty-Ninth and Seventy-First Pennsylvania regiments of the Philadelphia Brigade.

41. Vanderslice, *Gettysburg*, 232; Reardon, *Pickett's Charge in History and Memory*, 93–95.

42. John W. Frazier to Charles T. Loehr, May 11, 1887, reprinted in John Tregaskis, *Souvenir of the Re-union of the Blue and the Gray, on the Battlefield of Gettysburg, July 1, 2, 3 and 4, 1888. How to Get There, and What Is to Be Done during the Year*, Chapter 20, 5. Also cited in Reardon, *Pickett's Charge in History and Memory*, 94–95.

43. John W. Frazier to Charles T. Loehr, May 23, 1887, reprinted in Tregaskis, *Souvenir of the Re-union of the Blue and the Gray*, Chapter 20, 6.

44. Tregaskis, *Souvenir of the Re-union of the Blue and the Gray*, Chapter 20, 1, 8. General Pickett died in 1875.

45. Carol Reardon, "Pickett's Charge: The Convergence of History and Myth in the Southern Past," in *The Third Day at Gettysburg & Beyond*, 69.

46. Ibid.; John E. Reilly, *A Brief History of the 69th Regiment Pennsylvania Veteran Volunteers*, 60–61 (the Aylett quote is included in Reilly's story of the reunion). Aylett rose to brigade command later in the war.

47. Peter S. Carmichael, *The Last Generation: Young Virginians in Peace, War and Reunion*, 1.

48. "Minute Book of the Gettysburg Battlefield Memorial Association, 1874–1895," Gettysburg National Military Park, Armistead file, 159; Vanderslice, *Gettysburg*, 234.

49. David G. Martin, *Confederate Monuments at Gettysburg: The Gettysburg Battle Monuments, Volume 1*, 148–49.

50. "General Armistead Was Only Southern Leader to Cross Wall at 'Angle' in Pickett's Charge," *Gettysburg Times*, March 23, 1939, 8. According to a photo cutline, "The place for the tablet was selected by General H.H. Bingham, who was a member of General Hancock's staff."

51. Charles C. Fennell, "A Battle from the Start: The Creation of the Memorial Landscape at the Bloody Angle in Gettysburg National Military Park," www.npshistory.com, 10.

52. "Gen Armistead's Body to Go to Gettysburg: Ex-Confederates Will Reinter Remains of the Gallant Southern Soldier," *Baltimore American*, April 14, 1907; "Wants Armistead's Body: Richmond Would Take Hero's Remains Away from Baltimore," *Baltimore Sun*, March 17, 1909.

53. John W. Frazier, *Reunion of the Blue and Gray, Philadelphia Brigade and Pickett's Division, July 2, 3, 4, 1887 and September 15, 16, 17, 1906*, 6, 10.

54. "Address of Comrade Joseph McCarroll," in ibid., 14.

55. Ibid., 14, 17; American Civil War Museum collection in Richmond, http://moconfederacy.pastperfectonline.com (Lewis Armistead sword, belt, and scabbard).

56. "Address of Sergt. John W. Frazier," in Frazier, *Reunion of the Blue and Gray*, 14, 33.

57. George Armistead (grandson) to John W. Frazier, May 9, 1907, published in the *Baltimore Sun*, May 21, 1907.

Chapter 15. "Don't Let Me Bleed to Death"

1. James Henry Stine, *History of the Army of the Potomac*, 529. Stine published his history in 1893 and used many Union veterans as primary sources.

2. Surgeon's note from George E. Cooper, July 22, 1863, Hancock file, No. 941, Letters Received by Commission Branch, 1863–1870, National Archives (the Hancock documents are filed under the year 1864, but they range from 1863 to 1865). At least four letters and surgeon's certificates in Hancock's file say that he was wounded in the inner part of the left thigh (although many historians identify it as his right thigh). Cooper's letter—written less than three weeks after the battle—said it was in the "inner portion of the left thigh, two inches from the groin." Hancock's description of the "clump of timber" comes from a letter he wrote to Francis Walker in 1885, cited in Jay Wright's "'Don't Let Me Bleed to Death': The Wounding of Maj. Gen. Winfield Scott Hancock," *Gettysburg Magazine*, Issue 6 (January 1992), 87.

3. George G. Benedict, *Army Life in Virginia: Letters from the Twelfth Vermont Regiment and Personal Experiences of Volunteer Service in the War for the Union, 1862–1863*, 183. Benedict said that Hancock "was nearly facing the enemy when hit."

4. Winfield S. Hancock to Peter Rothermel, December 31, 1863, Hancock file, Gettysburg National Military Park library. Hancock provided the self-description of his uniform at the battle. That hat, he said, "was not a 'slouch,' but was stiff enough to keep its shape in the top and brim."

5. Benedict, *Army Life in Virginia*, 183–84.

6. C. H. Morgan, "General Hancock at the Battle of Gettysburg, Prepared at St. Paul, Minn. May 1872," Hancock file, Gettysburg National Military Park library; David M. Jordan, *Winfield Scott Hancock: A Soldier's Life*, 99. The color-bearer was Private James Wells of the Sixth New York Cavalry.

7. William Mitchell to Dr. L. W. Read, September 20, 1880, Hancock file, Gettysburg National Military Park library.

8. Benedict, *Army Life in Virginia*, 183.

9. Winfield Hancock to Francis Walker, December 12, 1855, cited in A. M. Gambone, *Hancock at Gettysburg and Beyond*, 142.

10. William Mitchell to Winfield Hancock, January 10, 1866, in John Bachelder, *The Bachelder Papers*, Vol. 1, 231.

11. Winfield Hancock to Peter Rothermel, December 31, 1868, Hancock file, Gettysburg National Military Park library.

12. William Mitchell to Winfield Hancock, January 10, 1866, in Bachelder, *The Bachelder Papers*, Vol. 1, 231. Mitchell added in a "P.S." at the end of his letter, "The message from General Hancock, and the reply of General Meade above given, are taken from a written memorandum made by me on the evening of the 3d July 1863. This is a true copy."

13. Henry H. Bingham, "Anecdotes concerning Gen. Hancock and other officers at Gettysburg and elsewhere," 797, Hancock file, Gettysburg National Military Park library, used with the permission of the Western Reserve Historical Society, Cleveland, Ohio. The file of Bingham's "Anecdotes" is located in the historical society's William P. Palmer Collection.

14. *The War of the Rebellion: Official Records of the Union and Confederate Armies*, Series 1, Vol. 27, Part 1, 366. Hancock began his note with "I repulsed a tremendous attack" and then briefly delved into criticism of the artillery command.

15. Gregory A. Coco, *A Vast Sea of Misery: A History and Guide to the Union and Confederate Field Hospitals at Gettysburg, July 1–November 20 1863*, 72, 91. The field hospital was located "in an opening of the woods, along the crossroad from the Taneytown Road to the Baltimore Pike, with headquarters at the Granite Schoolhouse."

16. William Mitchell to Dr. L. W. Read, September 20, 1880, Hancock file, Gettysburg National Military Park library; Wright, "'Don't Let Me Bleed to Death,'" 92n21. In Coco's *Vast Sea of Misery*, a Union soldier is quoted as saying that Hancock was treated at the David Wills house in Gettysburg for several weeks (33–34), but that is a case of mistaken identity; Hancock was in Westminster on July 4 and in Philadelphia by July 6.

17. Almira Hancock, *Reminiscences of Winfield Scott Hancock*, 97. William Mitchell identified the physician only as "Surgeon Taylor" in his letter to Dr. Read.

18. Winfield Hancock to General L. Thomas, July 22, 1863, Hancock file, No. 941, Letters Received by Commission Branch, 1863–1870, National Archives. Hancock attached the "surgeon's certificate" that Dr. Cooper had written the same day, referenced above in note 2. It was addressed from "La Pierre House, Phila."

19. Hancock, *Reminiscences of Winfield Scott Hancock*, 98.

20. Ibid., 98–99.

21. Jordan, *Winfield Scott Hancock*, 101.

22. Hancock, *Reminiscences of Winfield Scott Hancock*, 99.

23. *National Defender*, August 4, 1863, cited in Gambone, *Hancock at Gettysburg and Beyond*, 167.

24. Edwin Stanton to Winfield Hancock, August 5, 1863, cited in Gambone, *Hancock at Gettysburg and Beyond*, 167–68.

25. *Philadelphia Times*, undated clipping, cited in Gambone, *Hancock at Gettysburg and Beyond*, 168–69; Joseph T. Reimer, "General Hancock and Dr. Read," *Bulletin of the Historical Society of Montgomery County, Pennsylvania* (Spring 1972), found at http://www.oocities.org/superbhancock/current01.html.

26. Gambone, *Hancock at Gettysburg and Beyond*, 170.

27. Ibid.

28. William Mitchell to Dr. L. W. Read, September 20, 1880, Hancock file, Gettysburg National Military Park library.

29. Gambone, *Hancock at Gettysburg and Beyond*, 170.

30. Charles Wheeler Denison and George B. Herbert, *Hancock "The Superb": The Early Life and Public Career of Winfield S. Hancock*, 214–15. The book notes that he wrote home to Norristown from New York City on September 15, "requesting that certain military documents should be arranged and forwarded, in order that he might hasten his return to the field."

31. Ibid., 215.

32. Francis Amasa Walker, *General Hancock*, 148–49.

33. Surgeon's notes from John F. Randolph, October 12 and November 2, 1863, Hancock file, No. 941, Letters Received by Commission Branch, 1863–1870, National Archives.

34. George Meade to Winfield Hancock, November 6, 1863, Letters to the Commission Branch 1863–1870, from W. S. Hancock Papers, Special Collections Library, Duke University. The temporary commanders of the Second Corps during this period were John Caldwell and G. K. Warren. The actions were at Bristoe Station and Mine Run.

35. General Orders No. 34, December 27, 1863, Hancock file, No. 941, Letters Received by the Commission Branch, 1863–1870, National Archives. "The undersigned resumes command of the Corps." The order was signed by Hancock and endorsed by Bingham; Jordan, *Winfield Scott Hancock*, 104.

36. J. B. Fry (provost marshal) to Winfield Hancock, January 7, 1864, Hancock file, No. 941, Letters Received by the Commission Branch, 1863–1870, National Archives.

37. Hancock address, January 15, 1864, cited in James S. Brisbin, *Winfield Scott Hancock, Major-General, U.S.A.: His Life*, 61.
38. Jordan, *Winfield Scott Hancock*, 105. This number included men from the Third Corps, which was absorbed as the army realigned. Hancock did not add many new recruits.
39. Decree from the Select and Common Councils of the City of Philadelphia, approved February 18, 1864, cited in Denison and Herbert, *Hancock "The Superb,"* 219–20.
40. Denison and Herbert, *Hancock "The Superb,"* 221.
41. Matt Hagans, "Silver for the Superb: Hometown Tribute to a National Hero," *Military Images* 36, no. 3 (Summer 2018), 38–39. The set was inscribed with the date "July 4" but is included here as extension of the honors Hancock received that year.
42. George Meade to Winfield Hancock, November 6, 1863, Letters to the Commission Branch 1863–1870, from W. S. Hancock Papers, Special Collections Library, Duke University.
43. Glenn Tucker, *Hancock the Superb*, 175–76; Jordan, *Winfield Scott Hancock*, 109.
44. Tucker, *Hancock the Superb*, 178.
45. Ibid., 177–78.
46. Ibid., 181–82, 187, 191; Gordon Rhea, "The Battle of the Wilderness" and "The Overland Campaign of 1864," www.battlefields.org.
47. Francis Amasa Walker, *History of the Second Army Corps in the Army of the Potomac*, 470.
48. Walker, *General Hancock*, 200–202.
49. Tucker, *Hancock the Superb*, 234.
50. Bingham, "Anecdotes concerning Gen. Hancock and other officers at Gettysburg and elsewhere," 798.
51. "Reams Station: The Last Hours," www.nps.gov, 2; Christian Andros, "Winfield Scott Hancock," www.essentialcivilwarcurriculum.com.
52. "The Battle at Ream's Station: Interesting Description of the Struggle," *New York Times*, August 31, 1864.
53. Cited in Walker, *General Hancock*, 275.
54. Henry Heth, *The Memoirs of Henry Heth*, 206.
55. Jordan, *Winfield Scott Hancock*, 165. Hancock once said that "a good soldier knows no party but his country" (Tucker, *Hancock the Superb*, 265).
56. D. X. Junkin and Frank Norton, *The Life of Winfield Scott Hancock: Personal, Military and Political*, 48.
57. Walker, *General Hancock*, 291.
58. General Orders No. 287, "Order for raising and organizing a new Volunteer Army Corps, November 28, 1864," Hancock file, No. 941, Letters Received by the Commission Branch, 1863–1870, National Archives.
59. General Orders No. 25, Headquarters, Middle Military Division, February 27, 1865, Hancock file, No. 941, Letters Received by the Commission Branch, 1863–1870, National Archives; Jordan, *Winfield Scott Hancock*, 173–75.
60. Tucker, *Hancock the Superb*, 268.

Chapter 16. Almost Mr. President

1. "End of the Assassins: Execution of Mrs. Surratt, Payne, Herrold and Atzeroth," *New York Times*, July 8, 1865; David M. Jordan, *Winfield Scott Hancock: A Soldier's Life*, 177.
2. "Hancock's War," www.nps.gov, Fort Larned, National Historic Site, Kansas.
3. Ron Chernow, *Grant*, 596; Jordan, *Winfield Scott Hancock*, 201.
4. "Ulysses S. Grant," www.whitehouse.gov.
5. U. S. Grant, *The Personal Memoirs of U. S. Grant*, 582.
6. Chernow, *Grant*, 585–87, 596. Chernow cites two letters from *The Papers of Ulysses S. Grant*: Grant to Elihu B. Washburne, March 4, 1867, and Grant to General Philp H. Sheridan, April 21, 1867. The military districts in the South were (1) Virginia; (2) North Carolina and South Carolina; (3) Alabama, Florida, and Georgia; (4) Mississippi and Arkansas; and (5) Louisiana and Texas.
7. Francis Amasa Walker, *General Hancock*, 298–99.
8. Almira Hancock, *Reminiscences of Winfield Scott Hancock*, 121–22.
9. Jordan, *Winfield Scott Hancock*, 204.
10. General Orders No. 40, Headquarters, Fifth Military District, New Orleans, La., November 29, 1867, cited in Hancock, *Reminiscences of Winfield Scott Hancock*, Appendix B, 223.
11. Statement of John B. Gordon, in Military Service Institution, *Letters and Addresses Contributed at a General Meeting of the Military Service Institution Held at Governor's Island, N.Y., February 25, 1886, in Memory of Winfield Scott Hancock*, 69.
12. Statement of William Farrar Smith, in ibid., 2.
13. Jordan, *Winfield Scott Hancock*, 207, 210–11.
14. Ibid., 211.
15. Ibid., 213.
16. W. T. Sherman to W. S. Hancock, May 21, 1870, from *Correspondence between General W. T. Sherman, U.S. Army, and Major General W. S. Hancock, U.S. Army*, 9–10.
17. Glenn Tucker, *Hancock the Superb*, 290.
18. Jordan, *Winfield Scott Hancock*, 214, 216. Jordan offers a detailed, ballot-by-ballot account of the convention (221–26). Johnson was a Democrat but was chosen to be Lincoln's vice president in 1864 to balance the ticket and win Democratic votes.
19. "1868 Democratic Convention," www.loc.gov, Democratic National Political Conventions, 1832–2008.
20. Jordan, *Winfield Scott Hancock*, 218.
21. Ibid., 229, 234–36.
22. Tucker, *Hancock the Superb*, 295; Jordan, *Winfield Scott Hancock*, 237.
23. A. M. Gambone, *Hancock at Gettysburg and Beyond*, 195. Ada had said she did not want to be buried in the ground. Hancock was aware that Almira wanted to be buried with their family in St. Louis, but he left enough room in the Norristown tomb for his own body. See also Jordan, *Winfield Scott Hancock*, 310–11.
24. "1876 Democratic Convention," www.loc.gov, Democratic National Political Conventions, 1832–2008.

25. Jordan, *Winfield Scott Hancock*, 238.
26. *Official proceedings of the National Democratic convention, held in St. Louis, Mo., June 27th, 28th and 29th, 1876.*
27. "The Disputed Election of 1876," www.rbhayes.org; "How the 1876 Election Effectively Ended Reconstruction," www.history.com.
28. "Rutherford B. Hayes," www.whitehouse.gov.
29. *Harpers Weekly*, Explore History, "1880 Overview," www.elections.harpweek.com, "Introduction; Democratic Candidates and Convention."
30. Ibid.
31. Ulysses S. Grant to Abel R. Corbin, March 29, 1878, *The Papers of Ulysses S. Grant*, cited in Chernow, *Grant*, 890.
32. Cited in ibid.
33. *Harpers Weekly*, Explore History, "1880 Overview," www.elections.harpweek.com, "The Republican Nomination."
34. Ibid.
35. Chernow, *Grant*, 902.
36. *Harpers Weekly*, Explore History, "1880 Overview," www.elections.harpweek.com, "The Republican Nomination."
37. Jordan, *Winfield Scott Hancock*, 256.
38. *Harpers Weekly*, Explore History, "1880 Overview," www.elections.harpweek.com, "Democratic Candidates and Convention."
39. Jordan, *Winfield Scott Hancock*, 255.
40. Ibid., 275–76; *Official proceedings of the National Democratic convention, held in St. Louis, Mo., June 27th, 28th and 29th, 1876*, 85.
41. *Harpers Weekly*, Explore History, "1880 Overview," www.elections.harpweek.com, "Democratic Candidates and Convention"; Jordan, *Winfield Scott Hancock*, 275–80. Once again, Jordan offers the most detailed account of the convention.
42. Todd Arrington, "Two Union Veterans: The Election of 1880, Part 1," 1, www.emergingcivilwar.com.
43. "James Garfield," www.whitehouse.gov; "James A. Garfield," www.brittanica.com.
44. *Harpers Weekly*, Explore History, "1880 Overview," www.elections.harpweek.com, "Republican Campaign."
45. Jordan, *Winfield Scott Hancock*, 287; www.findagrave.com for Winfield Scott Hancock (1880–1880). The child was buried at Montgomery Cemetery in Norristown.
46. Jordan, *Winfield Scott Hancock*, 301. The interview was in the October 8 edition of the *Paterson (N.J.) Daily Guardian*.
47. *Harpers Weekly*, Explore History, "1880 Overview," www.elections.harpweek.com, "Republican Campaign."
48. "Presidential Election of 1880: A Resource Guide," www.loc.gov.
49. www.uselectionatlas.org.
50. Hancock, *Reminiscences of Winfield Scott Hancock*, 172. Of his defeat, Hancock told Almira, "That is all right. I can stand it."
51. Ibid., 175.
52. Ibid., 177.

53. "Yorktown: Centenaire de l'Independance des Etats-Unis d'Amerique, 1781–1881," by Rochambeau, cited and translated in Hancock, *Reminiscences of Winfield Scott Hancock*, 176–77.

54. Walker, *General Hancock*, 308–9.

55. Jordan, *Winfield Scott Hancock*, 311; www.findagrave.com for Adaline D. Russell, William G. Mitchell, and Russell Hancock.

56. Hancock, *Reminiscences of Winfield Scott Hancock*, 177–78.

57. Chernow, *Grant*, 955–56. The former Confederate generals in the procession were Joseph Johnston and Simon Buckner.

58. Jordan, *Winfield Scott Hancock*, 312.

59. Chernow, *Grant*, 955.

60. Jordan, *Winfield Scott Hancock*, 312.

61. "Hancock Again at Gettysburg," *Gettysburg Compiler*, November 24, 1885, copy at Gettysburg National Military Park library. One specific reference to the 1865 visit is found in Tucker's *Hancock the Superb*, 307. It said he "served as escort for his beloved daughter Ada."

62. "Hancock Again at Gettysburg."

63. Paul E. Bretzger, *Observing Hancock at Gettysburg: The General's Leadership through Eyewitness Accounts*, 213; Jordan, *Winfield Scott Hancock*, 313–15.

64. Gambone, *Hancock at Gettysburg and Beyond*, 221–22; Bretzger, *Observing Hancock at Gettysburg*, 213. The local G.A.R. post was named for Samuel Zook, who served under Hancock at Gettysburg.

65. Gambone, *Hancock at Gettysburg and Beyond*, 203–5; Jordan, *Winfield Scott Hancock*, 317, 319. It should also be noted that Hancock's younger brother, John, who served at Gettysburg and rose to the rank of brevet colonel, survived until 1912 and is buried in Arlington National Cemetery. Hancock's twin brother, Hilary, who did not serve in the military, died in 1908 and is buried in Montgomery Cemetery, although not in the Hancock vault (www.find-a-grave.com for Colonel John Hancock and Hilary Baker Hancock). There was a movement to disinter General Hancock's body and move it to Arlington, but nothing ever came of it.

Chapter 17. Legacy

1. D. X. Junkin and Frank Norton, *The Life of Winfield Scott Hancock: Personal, Military and Political*, 118.

2. Francis Amasa Walker, *General Hancock*, 25.

3. Henry Heth, *The Memoirs of Henry Heth*, 56.

4. Abner Doubleday, *Chancellorsville and Gettysburg*, 128. At the time of the Bull Run battle in late July 1861, Armistead was traveling through Arizona with Albert Sydney Johnston to join the Confederacy. He left Los Angeles in late June and arrived in Richmond in mid-September.

5. J. W. Jones, "Notes and Quotes," *Southern Historical Society Papers*, Vol. 10, 425.

6. J. W. Jones to Winfield Scott Hancock, July 10, 1882, *Southern Historical Society Papers*, Vol. 10, 426–27.

7. Winfield S. Hancock to J. W. Jones, July 15, 1882, *Southern Historical Society Papers*, Vol. 10, 427–28.
8. Henry Bingham to Winfield Scott Hancock, July 19, 1882, *Southern Historical Society Papers*, Vol. 10, 428.
9. J. W. Jones, *Southern Historical Society Papers*, Vol. 10, 429.
10. James A. Hessler and Wayne E. Motts, *Pickett's Charge at Gettysburg: A Guide to the Most Famous Attack in American History*, 180.
11. Winfield S. Hancock to Francis A. Walker, December 12, 1885, cited in Wright, "'Don't Let Me Bleed to Death,'" *Gettysburg Magazine*, Issue 6 (January 1992).
12. Winfield S. Hancock to John Bachelder, December 20, 1885, in John Bachelder, *The Bachelder Papers*, Vol. 3, 1949.
13. Although he never publicly identified what he thought was the correct "wounding" position, it is assumed that Hancock would have preferred something closer to the Angle.
14. Hessler and Motts, *Pickett's Charge at Gettysburg*, 249; Deppen, "A Lion in Winter: The Last Years of Maj. Gen. Winfield Scott Hancock, 1880–1886," *Gettysburg Magazine*, Issue 38 (July 2008), 124.
15. Henry H. Bingham, "An Oration at the Unveiling of the Equestrian Statue of Major-General Winfield Scott Hancock on the Battlefield of Gettysburg, June 5, 1856," 5–6, 13.
16. Bruce Catton, *Glory Road*, 315.
17. Ibid., 321.
18. Shelby Foote, *Stars in Their Courses: The Gettysburg Campaign*, 183–84. This small book is an excerpt from Foote's *The Civil War: A Narrative*, Vol. 2.
19. Hessler and Motts, *Pickett's Charge at Gettysburg*, 121–22.
20. Michael Shaara, *The Killer Angels*, 59–60.
21. Ibid., 251.
22. Hessler and Motts, *Pickett's Charge*, 121.
23. Sheldon A. Munn, *Freemasons at Gettysburg*, 1, 4; inscription, wayside marker.
24. Munn, *Freemasons at Gettysburg*, 1, 2, 4. The idea came from the park's longtime historian, Kathy Georg Harrison.
25. Ibid., 2, 3, 5. Chairman of the committee was George Hohenshildt, with Munn, Lee Whitaker, and Dean Vaughn as cochairs. Schwartz was one of six other members. Masonic Grand Master Edward H. Fowler Jr. was also involved in the process.
26. John Heiser, "Our Ever Changing National Cemeteries," www.npshistory.com, 103. Heiser, historian at Gettysburg National Military Park, writes that the private owner was the Bethlehem Steel Company. The land was transferred in 1960, but several debates on proper use led to a delay.
27. Munn, *Freemasons at Gettysburg*, 4.
28. Ibid., 5.
29. Ibid., 5–6.
30. "History of the Soldiers' National Cemetery at Gettysburg," www.nps.gov.
31. Plaque at the base of the "Friend to Friend Masonic Memorial" in Gettysburg.

32. Stone memorial at the entrance to the George Spangler farm lane; Hessler and Motts, *Pickett's Charge*, 222.
33. Hessler and Motts, *Pickett's Charge*, 222; "Gettysburg Hospitals, Part 5, with Licensed Battlefield Guide Phil Lechak," www.gettysburgdaily.com. These were placed by the Armistead Marker Preservation Committee.
34. "George Spangler Farm and Field Hospital," www.gettysburgfoundation.org (also "Spangler Farm Field Hospital Begins Summer Programs").
35. Hessler and Motts, *Pickett's Charge*, 222.
36. Almira Hancock, *Reminiscences of Winfield Scott Hancock*, 70.

Appendix. "Lo" and Behold

1. Michael Shaara, *The Killer Angels*, 55.
2. Stephen W. Sears, *Gettysburg*, 416, 426.
3. LaSalle Pickett, ed., *The Heart of a Soldier: Intimate Wartime Letters from General George E. Pickett, C.S.A., to His Wife*, "Written while He Awaited the Order to Charge at Gettysburg," July 3, 1863, 93.
4. Carol Reardon, "Pickett's Charge: The Convergence of History and Myth in the Southern Past," *The Third Day at Gettysburg & Beyond*, 82.
5. Gary W. Gallagher, *Lee and His Generals in War and Memory*, 233.
6. George R. Stewart, *Pickett's Charge: A Microhistory of the Final Attack at Gettysburg, July 3, 1863*, 297 (appendix B).
7. Gallagher, *Lee and His Generals in War and Memory*, 229.
8. Carol Reardon, *Pickett's Charge in History and Memory*, 186.
9. Gallagher, *Lee and His Generals in War and Memory*, 240.

Bibliography

Primary Sources
Books

Bachelder, John. *The Bachelder Papers: Gettysburg in Their Own Words*. Vols. 1–3. Edited by David L. Ladd and Audrey J. Ladd. Dayton, OH: Morningside House, 1994–1995.

Bandel, Eugene. *Frontier Life in the Army, 1854–1861*. Glendale, CA: Arthur H. Clarke, 1932.

Banes, Charles H. *History of the Philadelphia Brigade*. Philadelphia: Lippincott, 1876.

Beauregard, P. G. T. *With Beauregard in Mexico*. Edited by T. Harry Williams. New York: Da Capo Press, 1969.

Benedict, George G. *Army Life in Virginia: Letters from the Twelfth Vermont Regiment and Personal Services of Volunteer Service in the War for the Union, 1862–63*. Burlington, VT: Free Press Association, 1895.

Crocker, James F. *Gettysburg—Pickett's Charge and Other War Addresses*. Portsmouth, VA: C. W. Fiske, Printer and Bookbinder, 1915.

———. "My Personal Experiences in Taking Up Arms." *Southern Historical Papers* 33 (1905).

Doubleday, Abner. *Chancellorsville and Gettysburg*. New York: Civil War Classic Library, 1882.

Early, Jubal Anderson. *Lieutenant General Jubal Anderson Early, C.S.A.: Autobiographical Sketch and Narrative of the War between the States*. Philadelphia: Lippincott, 1912.

Favill, Josiah Marshall. *Diary of a Young Officer, Serving with the Armies of the United States during the War of Rebellion*. Chicago: R. R. Donnelley & Sons, 1909.

Frazier, John W. *Reunion of the Blue and Gray, Philadelphia Brigade and Pickett's Division, July 2, 3, 4, 1887 and September 15, 16, 17, 1906*. Philadelphia: Ware Bros. Company Printers, 1906. (Reprinted from University of Michigan Library collection.)

Gibbon, John. *At Gettysburg and Elsewhere: The Civil War Memoir of John Gibbon*. (Originally published in 1885, reprinted by Big Byte Books, Middletown, DE, 2016.)

Gordon, John. *Reminiscences of the Civil War*. New York: Charles Scribner's Sons, 1904.

Grant, U. S. *The Personal Memoirs of U. S. Grant*. Vols. 1 and 2. Digireads.com Publishing, 2018.

Hancock, Almira. *Reminiscences of Winfield Scott Hancock*. New York: Charles L. Webster & Company, 1887.

Harrison, Walter. *Pickett's Men: A Fragment of War History*. New York: D. Van Nostrand, 1870.

Haskell, Frank Aretas. *The Battle of Gettysburg*. (Originally published in 1908, reprinted by Big Byte Books, Middletown, DE, 2016.)

Heth, Henry. *The Memoirs of Henry Heth*. Edited by James L. Morrison. Westport, CT: Greenwood Press, 1974. (Heth completed his memoirs in 1897, but they were not published in book form until 1974.)

Johnson, Robert Underwood, and Clarence Clough Buel, eds. *Battles and Leaders of the Civil War*. Vol. 3. New York: Castle Books, 1884.

Kirkham, Ralph W. *The Mexican War Journal & Letters of Ralph W. Kirkham*. Edited by Robert Ryal Miller. College Station: Texas A&M University Press, 1991

Lewis, John H. *A Rebel in Pickett's Charge at Gettysburg*. (Originally published in 1895, reprinted by Big Byte Books, Middletown, DE, 2016.)

Lowe, Percival G. *Five Years a Dragoon (49 to 54)*. Kansas City, MO: Franklin Hudson Publishing Co., 1906.

McLellan, George B. *The Civil War Papers of George B. McClellan, Selected Correspondence, 1860–1865*. Edited by Stephen Sears. New York: Tricknor & Fields, 1989.

Military Service Institution. *Letters and Addresses Contributed at a General Meeting of the Military Service Institution Held at Governor's Island, N.Y., February 25, 1886, in Memory of Winfield Scott Hancock*. New York: G. P. Putnam's Sons, 1886.

Reilly, John F. *An Account of the Reunion of the Survivors of the Philadelphia Brigade and Pickett's Division of Confederate Soldiers*. Philadelphia: D. J. Gallagher & Co., 1889.

Reilly, John F., with Anthony W. McDermott. *A Brief History of the 69th Regiment Pennsylvania Veteran Volunteers*. Philadelphia: D. J. Gallagher & Co., 1889.

Rollins, Richard, ed. *Pickett's Charge: Eyewitness Accounts*. Redondo Beach, CA: Rank and File Publications, 1994.

Taylor, Zachary. *Letters of Zachary Taylor from the Battlefields of the Mexican War*. Edited by William K. Bixby. Rochester, NY: Genesee Press, 1908.

U.S. Congress. *Report of the Joint Committee on the Conduct of the War* (Second Session, Thirty-Eighth Congress). Vol. 1. Washington, DC: Government Printing Office, 1865.

U.S. War Department. *The War of the Rebellion: Official Records of the Union and Confederate Armies*. Various volumes. Washington, DC: Government Printing Office, 1887–1889.

Walker, Francis Amasa. *General Hancock*. New York: D. Appleton and Company, 1895. (Walker served on Hancock's staff.)

———. *History of the Second Army Corps in the Army of the Potomac*. New York: Charles Scribner's Sons, 1886.

Wilcox, Cadmus Marcellus. *History of the Mexican War*. Washington, DC: Church News Publishing Company, 1892.

Essays, Periodicals

Carter, James T. "Flag of the Fifty-Third Va. Regiment." *Confederate Veteran*, Vol. X.

Couch, Darius N. "The Chancellorsville Campaign." *Battles and Leaders*, Vol. 3.

———. "Sumner's 'Right Grand Division.'" *Battles and Leaders*, Vol. 3.

Easley, D. B. "With Armistead When He Was Killed." *Confederate Veteran*, Vol. XX.

Farinholt, B. L. "Battle of Gettysburg—Johnson's Island." *Confederate Veteran*, Vol. V.

Halstead, E. P. "Incidents of the First Day at Gettysburg." *Battles and Leaders*, Vol. 3.

Hancock, Winfield Scott. "Reply to General Howard." *The Galaxy*, Vol. 22.

Harding, Milton. "With Armistead When He Fell." *Confederate Veteran*, Vol. XIX.

Harris, Moses. "The Old Army." October 3, 1894. *War Papers Read before the Commander of Wisconsin, Military Order of the Loyal Legion of the United States, Vol. II.* Milwaukee, WI: Burdick, Armitage & Allen, 1896.

Holland, T. C. "What Did We Fight For?" *Confederate Veteran*, Vol. XXXI.

———. "With Armistead at Gettysburg." *Confederate Veteran*, Vol. XXIX.

Holman, Mary. "Crossed the Plains with Johnston." *Confederate Veteran*, Vol. III.

Howard, O. O. "Campaign and Battle of Gettysburg, June and July, 1863." *Atlantic Monthly*, Vol. 38.

Jones, Robert Tyler. "Gen. L.A. Armistead and R. Tyler Jones." *Confederate Veteran*, Vol. II.

Kuykendall, Rhea. "Surgeons of the Confederacy." *Confederate Veteran*, Vol. XXXIV.

Martin, Rawley. "Letter of Doctor Rawley Martin." In *War Recollections of the Confederate Veterans of Pittsylvania County, Va., 1861–1865.*

Poindexter, James E. "Gen. Lewis Addison Armistead." *Confederate Veteran*, Vol. XXII.

———. "General Armistead's Portrait Presented." *Southern Historical Society Papers*, Vol. 37, from an address delivered in Richmond January 29, 1909.

Whitehead, J. W. "Company I, 53rd Va. Regiment, Armistead's Brigade, Pickett's Division, in the Battle of Gettysburg." In *War Recollections of the Confederate Veterans of Pittsylvania County, Va., 1861–1865.*

Military Service and Pension Records (National Archives and www.fold3.com)

Bowles E. Armistead, Compiled Service Records, CSA.

Franck S. Armistead, Compiled Service Records, CSA.

John Hancock, Compiled Service Records, USA.

Lewis A. Armistead, Compiled Service Records, CSA.

Lewis A. Armistead, General and Staff Officers, CSA.

Walker K. Armistead (Jr.), Compiled Service Records, CSA.

W. Keith Armistead, Compiled Service Records, CSA.

Winfield Scott Hancock, Letters to the Commission Branch, 1863–1870.

Additional National Archives Documents (many copies also available at www.fold3.com and some at www.ancestry.com)

Engineering Department Letters Relating to the USMA, 1812–1867, Military Academy Orders.

Letters Received by the Office of the Adjutant General Main Series, 1822–1860.

Letters Received by the (Confederate) Adjutant and Inspector General's Office.

Proceedings of a General Court-Martial in the Case of Maj. B.L.E. Bonneville, 6th Infantry, Mexico City, October 1847, Case EE-565 (Lewis Armistead testimony).

Registers of Enlistments in the United States Army, 1798–1914.
U.S. Military Academy Cadet Application Papers, 1805–1866.
U.S. Returns from Military Posts, 1806–1916.

United States Military Academy Library Records
Engineering Department Letters Relating to the USMA, January 1833–December 1834.
List of Orders Relating to Cadet Lewis A. Armistead, Extracted from "Post Orders/No.
6, 1832–1837, U.S. Military Academy."
Register of Merit, No. 1, 1817–1835 (academy academic and disciplinary records).
Special Collections, Lewis Armistead Commissions.
U.S. Military Academy Cadet Application Papers, 1805–1866, for Lewis A. Armistead,
Franck S. Armistead, Walker K. Armistead (Jr.), and Winfield S. Hancock.

Library of Congress
Correspondence between General W. T. Sherman, U.S. Army, and Major General W. S. Hancock, U.S. Army, published in pamphlet form, 1871.
Lewis A. Armistead to Major N. S. Clarke, U.S. Senator, 1859–60. Exec. Doc., Report of the Secretary of War, Serial 1024.
Lewis A. Armistead to Major W. W. Mackall, U.S. Senate 1859–60 Exec. Doc., Report of the Secretary of War, Serial 1024.
Report of Captain Samuel McKenzie, House Exec. Doc. No. 8, Appendix to the Report of the Secretary of War, Additional Reports from the Army in Mexico, January 6, 1848.
Report of Captain William Hoffman, House Exec. Doc. No. 8, Appendix to the Report of the Secretary of War, Additional Reports from the Army in Mexico, January 6, 1848.
Report of Colonel Newman Clarke, House Exec. Doc. No. 8, Appendix to the Report of the Secretary of War, Additional Reports from the Army in Mexico, January 6, 1848.
Report of Major Benjamin Bonneville, House Exec. Doc. No. 8, Appendix to the Report of the Secretary of War, Additional Reports from the Army in Mexico, January 6, 1848.

Digital Sources
www.antietam.aotw.org, "Gen. Robert E. Lee's Official Report, Operations in Maryland 1862."
https://journals.psu.edu, Dr. D. G. Brinton, "From Chancellorsville to Gettysburg, A Doctor's Diary."

County Courthouse Documents
Fauquier County, Va. Deed Book 23, Walker K. Armistead.

SECONDARY SOURCES
Books

Armstrong, Marion V., Jr. *Unfurl Those Colors! McClellan, Sumner & The Second Army Corps in the Antietam Campaign.* Tuscaloosa: University of Alabama Press, 2008.

Avirett, James B. *The Memoirs of General Turner Ashby and His Compeers.* Baltimore, MD: Selby and Dulany, 1867.

Bauer, K. Jack. *The Mexican War 1846–1848.* Lincoln: University of Nebraska Press, 1974.

Bretzger, Paul E. *Observing Hancock at Gettysburg: The General's Leadership through Eyewitness Accounts.* Jefferson, NC: McFarland, 2016.

Brisbin, James S. *Winfield Scott Hancock, Major-General, U.S.A.: His Life.* Philadelphia, PA: Smith, 1880.

Carmichael, Peter S. *The Last Generation: Young Virginians in Peace, War and Reunion.* Chapel Hill: University of North Carolina Press, 2005.

Carraway, Gertrude S. *The Stanly Family and the Historic John Wright Stanly House.* High Point, NC: Hall Printing Company, 1969.

Casstevens, Francis H. *Tales from the North and the South: Twenty-Four Remarkable People and Events of the Civil War.* Jefferson, NC: McFarland, 2007.

Cate, Margaret Randolph, and Wirt Armistead Cate. *The Armistead Family and Collaterals,* Nashville, TN: Reed Printing Company, 1971.

Catton, Bruce. *Glory Road.* New York: Anchor Books, Doubleday, 1952.

Chernow, Ron. *Grant.* New York: Penguin Press, 2014.

Cocke, Clyde W. *Pass in Review: An Illustrated History of West Point Cadets, 1794–Present.* Oxford: Osprey, 2012.

Coco, Gregory A. *A Strange and Blighted Land: Gettysburg: The Aftermath of a Battle.* El Dorado Hills, CA: Savas Beatie LLC, 1995.

———. *A Vast Sea of Misery: A History and Guide to the Union and Confederate Field Hospitals at Gettysburg, July 1–November 20, 1863.* Gettysburg, PA: Thomas Publications, 1988.

Coddington, Edwin B. *The Gettysburg Campaign: A Study in Command.* New York: Charles Scribner's Sons, 1968.

Coon, Charles L. *North Carolina Schools and Academies 1790–1840: A Documentary History.* Raleigh, NC: Edwards & Broughton Printing Company, 1915.

Crews, Edward R., and Timothy A. Parrish. *14th Virginia Infantry.* Lynchburg, VA: H. E. Howard, 1995.

Cullum, George W. *Biographical Register of the Officers and Graduates of the U.S. Military Academy at West Point, N.Y., Vol. 1, 1802–1840.* New York: D. Van Nostrand, 1868.

———. *Biographical Register of the Officers and Graduates of the U.S. Military Academy at West Point, N.Y., Vol. 2, 1841–1867.* New York: C. W. Westcott and Company, Printers, 1868. (Reprinted by Forgotten Books.)

———. *Campaigns of the War of 1812–15 Against Britain Sketched and Criticised, with Brief Biographies of the American Engineers.* New York: James Miller, 1879.

Curran, Robert Emmett. *The Bicentennial History of Georgetown University: From Academy to University, 1789–1889*. Vol. 1. Washington, DC: Georgetown University Press, 1993.

Denham, James M., and Keith L. Honeycutt, eds. *Echoes from a Distant Thunder: The Brown Sisters' Correspondence from Antebellum Florida*. Columbia: University of South Carolina Press, 2004.

Denison, Charles Wheeler, and George B. Herbert. *Hancock "The Superb": The Early Life and Public Career of Winfield S. Hancock*. Philadelphia: National Publishing Company, 1880.

Derby, James Cephas. *Fifty Years Among Authors, Books and Publishers*. New York: G. W. Carleton, 1886.

Dougherty, Kevin. *Civil War Leadership and Mexican War Experience*. Jackson: University Press of Mississippi, 2007.

Dowdey, Clifford. *The Seven Days: The Emergence of Robert E. Lee and the Dawn of a Legend*. New York: Skyhorse, 1964.

du Bellet, Louise Pecquet. *Some Prominent Virginia Families*. Vols. 1 and 2. Lynchburg, VA: J. P. Bell Company, 1907.

Eisenhower, John S. D. *So Far from God: The U.S. War with Mexico, 1846–1848*. Norman: University of Oklahoma Press, 1989.

Fleming, George T. *Life and Letters of Alexander Hays, Brevet Colonel United States Army, Brigadier General and Brevet Major General United States Volunteers*. Pittsburgh, PA: 1919. (Reprinted by Andesite Press.)

Foote, Shelby. *The Civil War: A Narrative*. 3 volumes. New York: Vintage Books, 1986.

———. *Stars in Their Courses: The Gettysburg Campaign*. New York: Modern Library, 1994.

Frassanito, William A. *Early Photography at Gettysburg*. Gettysburg, PA: Thomas Publications, 1995.

Frazer, Robert W. *Forts of the West: Military Forts and Presidios and Posts Commonly Called Forts West of the Mississippi River to 1898*. Norman: University of Oklahoma Press, 1965.

Freeman, Douglas Southall. *Lee's Lieutenants: A Study in Command—Abridged in One Volume by Stephen W. Sears*. New York: Simon and Schuster, 1998.

Gallagher, Gary W. *Lee and His Generals in War and Memory*. Baton Rouge: Louisiana State University Press, 1998.

Gambone, A. M. *Hancock at Gettysburg and Beyond*. Baltimore, MD: Butternut and Blue, 2002.

Garber, Virginia Armistead. *The Armistead Family 1635–1910*. Richmond, VA: Whittet and Shepherson Printers, 1910.

Goodrich, Frederick Elizur. *The Life and Public Services of Winfield Scott Hancock, Major-General, U.S.A.* Boston: Lee & Shepard, 1880.

Goodwin, David. *Ghosts of Jefferson Barracks: History and Hauntings of Old St. Louis*. Alton, IL: Whitechapel Productions Press, 2001.

Graves, Donald E. *First Campaign of an A.D.C.: The War of 1812 Memoir of Lieutenant William Jennings Worth, United States Army*. Youngstown, NY: Old Fort Niagara Association, 2012.

Green, Bennett W. *Word-Book of Virginia Folk-Speech*. Richmond, VA: Wm. Ellis Jones' Sons, 1912.

Gregory, G. Howard. *38th Virginia Infantry*. Lynchburg, VA: H. E. Howard, 1988.

———. *53rd Virginia Infantry and 5th Battalion Virginia Infantry*. Appomattox, VA: H. E. Howard, 1999.

Guelzo, Allen C. *Gettysburg: The Last Invasion*. New York: Alfred E. Knopf, 2013.

Hall, Robert. *Register of Cadets Admitted into the United States Military Academy at West Point, N.Y., from Its Establishment till 1880*. Washington, DC: T. H. S. Hamersly, 1880.

Harrison, Kathy Georg, and John W. Busey. *Nothing but Glory: Pickett's Division at Gettysburg*. Gettysburg, PA: Thomas Publications, 1987.

Hartwig, D. Scott. *A Killer Angels Companion*. Gettysburg, PA: Thomas Publications, 1996.

Hatch, Thom. *Osceola and the Great Seminole War: A Struggle for Justice and Freedom*. New York: St. Martin's Press, 2012.

Hebert, Walter H. *Fighting Joe Hooker*. Lincoln: University of Nebraska Press, 1999.

Heitman, Francis B. *Historical Register and Dictionary of the U.S. Army, from Its Organization, September 29, 1789 to March 2, 1903*. Vol. 1. Washington, DC: Government Printing Office, 1903.

Hess, Earl J. *Pickett's Charge—The Last Attack at Gettysburg*. Chapel Hill: University of North Carolina Press, 2001.

Hessler, James A., and Wayne E. Motts. *Pickett's Charge at Gettysburg: A Guide to the Most Famous Attack in American History*. El Dorado Hills, CA: Savas Beatie LLC, 2015.

Hill, Daniel Harvey. *McClellan's Change of Base and Malvern Hill*. eBooksOnDisk.com (Kindle edition), 2011.

Holcombe, Ira. *History of the First Regiment Minnesota Volunteers, 1861–1864*. Stillwater, MN: Easton & Masterman, 1916. (Regimental veterans Jasper Newton and Matthew Taylor also contributed to this book, giving it a primary-source appeal, but they credited Holcombe, a veteran of a Missouri regiment who later lived in Minnesota, with preparing the body of the text.)

Johannsen, Robert W. *To the Halls of the Montezumas: The Mexican War in the American Imagination*. New York: Oxford University Press, 1985.

Johnson, Timothy D. *A Gallant Little Army: The Mexico City Campaign*. Lawrence: University Press of Kansas, 2007.

Johnston, William Preston. *The Life of Gen. Albert Sidney Johnston: Embracing His Services in the Armies of the United States, the Republic of Texas, and the Confederate States*. New York: D. Appleton and Company, 1878.

Jordan, David M. *Winfield Scott Hancock: A Soldier's Life*. Bloomington: Indiana University Press, 1988.

Junkin, D. X., and Frank Norton. *The Life of Winfield Scott Hancock: Personal, Military and Political*. New York: D. Appleton and Company, 1880.

Kennedy, Mary Selden. *Seldens of Virginia and Allied Families*. Vol. 1. New York: Frank Allaben Genealogical Company, 1911.

Knetsch, Joe. *Florida's Seminole Wars 1817–1858*. Charleston, SC: Arcadia, 2003.

Kollbaum, Marc E. *Gateway to the West: The History of Jefferson Barracks from 1826–1894, Volume 1*. St. Louis, MO: Friends of Jefferson Barracks, 2002.

Lee, Cazenove Gardner, Jr. *Lee Chronicle: Studies of the Early Generations of the Lees of Virginia*. New York: Vantage Press, 1957.

Mahon, John K. *History of the Second Seminole War 1835–1842*. Rev. ed. Gainesville: University Press of Florida, 1985.

Martin, David G. *Confederate Monuments at Gettysburg: The Gettysburg Battle Monuments*. Vol. 1. Hightstown, NJ: Longstreet House, 1986.

McMillan, Tom. *Gettysburg Rebels: Five Native Sons Who Came Home to Fight as Confederate Soldiers*. Washington, DC: Regnery History, 2017.

Merry, Robert W. *A Country of Vast Designs: James K. Polk, the Mexican War and the Conquest of the American Continent*. New York: Simon and Shuster Paperbacks, 2009.

Morrison, James L. *"The Best School," West Point, 1833–1866*. Kent, OH: Kent State University Press, 1986.

Motts, Wayne E. *"Trust in God and Fear Nothing": Gen. Lewis A. Armistead, CSA*, Gettysburg, PA: Farnsworth House Military Impressions, 1994.

Munn, Sheldon A. *Freemasons at Gettysburg*. Foreword by Wayne E. Motts. Mechanicsburg, PA: Sunbury Press, 1993.

Musick, Michael P. *6th Virginia Cavalry*. Lynchburg, VA: H. E. Howard, 1990.

Pappas, George S. *To the Point: The United States Military Academy, 1802–1902*. Westport, CT: Praeger, 1993.

Pfanz, Harry W. *Gettysburg: The Second Day*. Chapel Hill: University of North Carolina Press, 1987.

Pickett, LaSalle, ed. *The Heart of a Soldier: Intimate Wartime Letters from General George E. Pickett, C.S.A. to His Wife*. Gettysburg, PA: Stan Clark Military Books, 1913 (reprinted 1995).

Pride, W. F. *The History of Fort Riley*. Fort Riley, KS: U.S. Government, 1926.

Reardon, Carol. *Pickett's Charge in History and Memory*. Chapel Hill: University of North Carolina Press, 1997.

Reardon, Carol, and Tom Vossler. *A Field Guide to Antietam: Experiencing the Battlefield through Its History, Places and People*. Chapel Hill: University of North Carolina Press, 2016.

Robinson, John W. *Los Angeles in Civil War Days 1860–1865*. Norman: University of Oklahoma Press, 1977.

Sears, Stephen W. *Gettysburg*. Boston: Houghton Mifflin, 2003.

———. *Landscape Turned Red: The Battle of Antietam*. New York: Houghton Mifflin, 1983.

———. *To the Gates of Richmond: The Peninsula Campaign*. Boston: Houghton Mifflin, 1992.

Shaara, Michael. *The Killer Angels*. New York: Ballantine Books, 1974.

Sheads, Scott Sumpter. *Guardian of the Star-Spangled Banner: Lt. Colonel George Armistead and the Fort McHenry Flag*. Baltimore, MD: Toomey Press, 1999.

Sherman, Nell Watson. *Taliaferro-Toliver Family Records*. Peoria, IL: Self-published, 1961, available at https://babel.hathitrust.org.

Stewart, George R. *Pickett's Charge: A Microhistory of the Final Attack at Gettysburg, July 3, 1863*. Boston: Houghton Mifflin, 1959.

Stine, James Henry. *History of the Army of the Potomac*. Philadelphia, PA: J.B. Rodgers, 1892.

Sublett, Charles W. *57th Virginia Infantry*. Lynchburg, VA: H. E. Howard, 1985.

Thomas, Clarence. *General Turner Ashby: The Centaur of the South*. Winchester, VA: Eddy Press Corporation, 1907.

Trask, Benjamin H. *9th Virginia Infantry*. Lynchburg, VA: H. E. Howard, 1984.

Tregaskis, John. *Souvenir of the Re-Union of the Blue and the Gray, Battle of Gettysburg*. New York: American Graphic Co., 1888.

Tucker, Glenn. *Hancock the Superb*. Dayton, OH: Morningside Bookshop, 1980.

Vanderslice, John Mitchell. *Gettysburg: A History of the Gettysburg Battle-field Memorial Association, with an Account of the Battle, Giving Movements, Positions, and Losses of the Commands Engaged*. Philadelphia, PA: Gettysburg Battlefield Memorial Association, 1897.

Wade, Arthur P. *Artillerists and Engineers: The Beginnings of American Seacoast Fortifications, 1794–1815*. McLean, VA: CDSG Press, 1977.

Watson, Samuel. "This Thankless . . . Unholy War." In *The Southern Albatross: Race and Ethnicity in the American South*, edited by Philip L. Dillard and Randal L. Hall. Macon, GA: Mercer University Press, 1999.

Wert, Jeffrey D. *Gettysburg: Day Three*. New York: Simon and Shuster, 2001.

West Point Association of Graduates. *The Register of Graduates and Former Cadets of the United States Military Academy, West Point, New York*. West Point, NY: West Point Association of Graduates, 2008.

Young, Maureen. *A Tapestry of Heroes: Appleton, Armistead, Baylor, Donnel, Faris, Hughes, Hunter, Kerr*. Middletown, DE: Create Space, 2011.

Essays, Periodicals

"Armistead Family." *William and Mary Quarterly* 6, no. 3 (January 1898).

Banta, Byron Bertrand, Jr. "A History of Jefferson Barracks, 1826–1860." https://digitalcommons.lsu.edu.

Campbell, Eric A. "A Brief History and Analysis of the Hunt-Hancock Controversy." www.npshistory.com, Gettysburg Seminars.

Clark, Paul C., Jr., and Edward H. Moseley. "D-Day: Veracruz, 1847—A Grand Design." National Defense University, Institute for National Strategic Studies, www.dtic.mil, 1996.

Crandell, John. "Grievous Angels from Third and Main to Gettysburg: General Winfield S. Hancock in Los Angeles." *Southern California Quarterly* 77, no. 4 (Winter 1995).

———. "Winfield Hancock and His Grievous Angels—Revisited." *Southern California Quarterly* 79, no. 1 (Spring 1997).

Deppen, John. "A Lion in Winter: The Last Years of Maj. Gen. Winfield Scott Hancock, 1880–1886." *Gettysburg Magazine*, Issue 38 (July 2008).

———. "Old and Valued Friends: Generals Lewis Armistead and Winfield Scott Hancock." *Gettysburg Magazine*, Issue 34 (July 2006).

Fennell, Charles C. "A Battle from the Start: The Creation of the Memorial Landscape at the Bloody Angle in Gettysburg National Military Park." www.npshistory.com.

Hagans, Matt. "Silver for the Superb: Hometown Tribute to a National Hero." *Military Images* 36, no. 3 (Summer 2018).

Heiser, John. "Our Ever Changing National Cemeteries." www.npshistory.com.

Krick, Robert K. "Armistead and Garnett: The Parallel Lives of Two Virginia Soldiers." In *The Third Day at Gettysburg & Beyond*, edited by Gary Gallagher. Chapel Hill: University of North Carolina Press, 1994.

———. "It Appeared as though Mutual Extermination Would Put a Stop to the Awful Carnage: Confederates in Sharpsburg's Bloody Lane." In *The Antietam Campaign*, edited by Gary Gallagher. Chapel Hill: University of North Carolina Press, 1999.

Morrison, W. B. "Fort Towson." *Chronicles of Oklahoma* 8, no. 2 (June 1930).

Myers, J. Jay. "Who Will Follow Me? The Story of Confederate Brigadier General Lewis Armistead, a Hero of the Battle of Gettysburg." *Civil War Times* (July/August 1993).

Reardon, Carol. "Pickett's Charge: The Convergence of History and Myth in the Southern Past." In *The Third Day at Gettysburg & Beyond*, edited by Gary Gallagher. Chapel Hill: University of North Carolina Press, 1994.

Sherif, Natalie. "James Crocker: A Pennsylvania College Graduate Returns to Gettysburg." https://gettysburgcompiler.org.

Stammerjohan, George. "The Camel Experiment in California." *Dogtown Territorial Quarterly*, no. 18 (Summer 1994).

———. "Winfield Scott (Hancock) in California." In Will Gorenfeld, "Bugler, Sound the Charge," www.chargeofthedragoons.com.

Walker, Flavius Burfoot, Jr. "Lewis Addison Armistead." Honors thesis, University of Richmond, 1939, available at http://scholarship.richmond.edu/honors-theses.

Wright, Jay. "'Don't Let Me Bleed to Death': The Wounding of Maj. Gen. Winfield Scott Hancock." *Gettysburg Magazine*, Issue 6 (January 1992).

Digital Sources

www.ancestry.com, *Colonial Families of the United States, 1607–1775*, Vol. 1, "Armistead."

www.battlefields.org, "Albert Sidney Johnston," American Battlefield Trust.

www.britannica.com, "Mexican-American War."

https://dos.myflorida.com, "The Seminole Wars."

www.emergingcivilwar.com, Todd Arrington, "Two Union Veterans: The Election of 1880, Part 1."

www.famguardian.org, "Thomas Jefferson on Politics & Government."

www.globalsecurity.org, John C. White, "American Military Strategy during the Second Seminole War."

www.history.army.mil, Lieutenant Charles Byrne, Center of Military History, "Sixth Regiment of Infantry."

www.library.georgetown.edu, "Shades of Blue and Gray: Georgetown and the Civil War."

www.militarymuseum.org, George C. Armistead, "California's Confederate Militia: The Los Angeles Mounted Rifles."

www.nps.gov, "Battle of Fredericksburg History."

www.nps.gov, "Casualties of Battle at Antietam."

www.nps.gov, "Hancock's War."

http://smallstatebighistory.com, "I'm a Good Old Rebel: Ocean State Confederates."

www.smithsonianmag.com, "Brainpower and Brawn in the Mexican-American War."

www.youtube.com, Wayne Motts, "Pickett's Charge at Gettysburg," Gettysburg Foundation Sacred Trust Talks, July 3, 2016.

Newspapers

Charleston (S.C.) Mercury Extra
Charleston (S.C.) Post and Courier
Charleston (S.C.) Times
Gettysburg Star and Sentinel
Gettysburg Times
Los Angeles Star
New Bern (N.C.) Sun Journal
New York Herald
New York Times
Raleigh Register and North-Carolina Weekly Advertiser
Richmond Dispatch
Richmond Examiner
Savannah (Ga.) Republican
Virginia Gazette

Index